"This book is unique in many ways. Professor Nilmini Wickramasinghe brings to the fore multi-continent experiences which permeate the chapters and give the book global relevance. The sections and associated chapters span the range of contemporary issues in digital health. The result is a useful compendium for a wide range of healthcare stakeholders."

Professor Doug Vogel, *Association for Information Systems Fellow and Past-President, Australasian Institute of Digital Health Fellow, Professor and eHealth Research Institute Director, Harbin Institute of Technology, P.R. China*

"Digital transformation in healthcare is a megatrand that gets momentum rapidly. Beyond striking impacts on medical aspects there are important contextual factors to consider. This book takes a wander through technologies, processes, people, and more involved in this fascinating future."

Professor Freimut Bodendorf, *Head of the Management Intelligence Systems of the Institute of Information Systems, Friedrich Alexander University Erlangen-Nuremberg, Germany*

"Professor Nilmini Wickramasinghe, an esteemed leader in digital health with national and international acclaim, compiles together her vision, thought leadership, and practical experiences into this very insightful primer that explores the fundamental aspects of digital health. I cannot think of anyone more fitting to present this critical topic, effectively bridging the knowledge gaps in technology, people, and processes within the industry. This book assures all healthcare stakeholders a reliable and comprehensive overview, offering valuable guidance in the digital health domain."

Professor Wenny Rahayu, *Dean of School of Computing, Engineering and Mathematical Sciences, La Trobe University, Australia*

"We are in an era where we need to reimagine how we deliver far-reaching, high quality and connected healthcare – with greater efficiency and value. Digital solutions are key enablers to support data-navigated analytics and insights to enable adaptive change, business intelligence and strategic prioritisation. However this needs to be achieved through co-design partnerships, to truly release the potential of this rapidly and exponentially advancing technological world. 'Primer' recognises the importance of healthcare stakeholders in this relationship and their domain specific knowledge, to navigate context appropriate digital solutions that are fit for purpose and truly transformative."

A/Prof Kate Burbury, *MBBS(Hons) FRACP FRCPA DPhil, Executive Director, Digital and Healthcare Innovations, Consultant Haematologist, The Sir Peter MacCallum Department of Oncology, The University of Melbourne, Australia*

Digital Health

Healthcare systems globally are grappling with how best to implement effective and efficient patient-centred care while simultaneously trying to contain runaway costs and provide high quality. This book explores the essential enabling role of digital health, taking a socio-technical perspective and looking at the key facets of technology, people and process in turn.

This book examines the opportunities of key digital health components, demystifying digital health and demonstrating how to use its key precepts effectively. The book presents evidence and anecdotes from stakeholders around the world, demonstrating the global relevance and the ability of digital health to uplift and upskill care delivery as it is applied commercially. Bridging academic theory and practice, this is a functional and accessible text for all digital health stakeholders.

The text introduces critical issues and is suitable reading for students, practitioners and researchers in digital health and all healthcare-related domains.

Analytics and AI for Healthcare

Artificial Intelligence (AI) and analytics are increasingly being applied to various healthcare settings. AI and analytics are salient to facilitate better understanding and identifying key insights from healthcare data in many areas of practice and enquiry including at the genomic, individual, hospital, community and/or population levels. The Chapman & Hall/CRC Press Analytics and AI in Healthcare Series aims to help professionals upskill and leverage the techniques, tools, technologies and tactics of analytics and AI to achieve better healthcare delivery, access, and outcomes. The series covers all areas of analytics and AI as applied to healthcare. It will look at critical areas including prevention, prediction, diagnosis, treatment, monitoring, rehabilitation and survivorship.

About the Series Editor

Professor Nilmini Wickramasinghe is the inaugural Optus Chair and Professor of Digital Health at La Trobe University. She is also the Professor–Director Health Informatics Management at Epworth HealthCare and holds honorary research professor positions at the Peter MacCallum Cancer Centre and Northern Health. After completing 5 degrees at the University of Melbourne, she was awarded a full scholarship to complete PhD studies at Case Western Reserve University, Cleveland, Ohio, USA and later she was sponsored to complete executive education at Harvard Business School, Harvard University, Cambridge, Massachusetts, USA in Value-based HealthCare. For over 20 years, Professor Wickramasinghe has been actively, researching and teaching within the health informatics/digital health domain in the United States, Germany and Australia with a particular focus on designing, developing and deploying suitable models, strategies and techniques grounded in various management principles to facilitate the implementation and adoption of technology solutions to effect superior, value-based patient centric care delivery. Professor Wickramasinghe collaborates with leading scholars at various premier healthcare organizations and universities throughout Australasia, the United States and Europe and is well published with more than 400 refereed scholarly articles, more than 15 books, numerous book chapters, an encyclopaedia and a well established funded research track record securing over

$25M in funding from grants in the United States, Australia, Germany and China as a chief investigator. She holds a patent around analytics solution for managing healthcare data and is the editor-in-chief of two scholarly journals published by InderScience: *International Journal of Biomedical Engineering and Technology* (www.inderscience.com/ijbet) and *International Journal of Networking and Virtual Organisations* (www.inderscience.com/ijnvo) as well as the editor of the Springer book series Healthcare Delivery in the Information Age. In 2020 she was awarded the prestigious Alexander von Humboldt Award for outstanding contribution to digital health, the first time this honour has been bestowed to someone in the discipline of digital health.

Translational Application of Artificial Intelligence in Healthcare–A Textbook
Edited by Sandeep Reddy

Dimensions of Intelligent Analytics for Smart Digital Health Solutions
Edited by Nilmini Wickramasinghe, Freimut Bodendorf and Mathias Kraus

Digital Health
A Primer
Nilmini Wickramasinghe

For more information about this series please visit: www.routledge.com/analytics-and-ai-for-healthcare/book-series/Aforhealth

Digital Health

A Primer

Nilmini Wickramasinghe

CRC Press
Taylor & Francis Group

A CHAPMAN & HALL BOOK

Designed cover image: ©Shutterstock

First edition published 2024
by CRC Press
2385 NW Executive Center Drive, Suite 320, Boca Raton FL 33431

and by CRC Press
4 Park Square, Milton Park, Abingdon, Oxon, OX14 4RN

CRC Press is an imprint of Taylor & Francis Group, LLC

© 2024 Nilmini Wickramasinghe

ISBN: 978-1-032-33169-0 (hbk)
ISBN: 978-1-032-33168-3 (pbk)
ISBN: 978-1-003-31853-8 (ebk)

DOI: 10.1201/9781003318538

Typeset in Times New Roman
by Newgen Publishing UK

This book is dedicated to the three Gs in my life for their ongoing guidance, my 3Ms – Minnehaha, Minnetonka and Minnewawa – and not forgetting Nokomis, "daughter of the moon".

Contents

Foreword

Not often does one get to see the culmination of a career's worth of work in one comprehensive book. *Digital Health: A Primer* is not only a personal accomplishment of Professor Wickramasinghe, but also comes at a critical time in the rapid evolution of our digital world and its impact on healthcare. Rising costs and quality challenges, the shock of COVID, growing dominance of chronic diseases, environmental and social drivers, and a host of other factors have changed the landscape of healthcare. And data is the key to dealing with them all.

Digital approaches to addressing these complex problems couldn't have come at a more opportune time. The topology provided in the book covers a wide range of the sometimes confusing and prolific but promising uses of digital technology in healthcare. This encyclopaedic review addresses the wide range and types of innovations in computer-assisted prevention, care and recovery. In five sections, it covers the technology, people and process considerations underlying successful implementation. It will be an essential guide to innovators determining areas of greater need, clinicians wanting to improve care, patients engaged in co-producing health services, managers deciding their strategy and next investments and policy makers who shape the decision environment.

The extensive documentation and references included also will allow the reader to go beyond this primer in specific areas of interest to each. As such, this is destined to be a resource for a broad population needing assistance as to their next steps in this digital world. Our thanks to Nilmini Wickramasinghe for her insights and guidance along this winding path.

JB Silvers
Albert J. Weatherhead III Professorship of Management
Interim Co-Dean and Professor, Department of Banking and Finance
Weatherhead School of Management
Case Western Reserve University, Ohio, USA
14 November 2023

Preface

My journey into digital health began at Case Western Reserve University where I did my PhD at the Weatherhead School of Management in Management Information Systems and Healthcare. During this time, I was inspired by the various and world-renowned healthcare facilities such as the Cleveland Clinic. Since receiving my PhD, I have been fortunate to research and teach in many countries and regions of the world including North America, especially in Cleveland and Chicago as well as Europe, especially in Germany and Australasia, most notably China and Australia from where I write this book. I have, thus, had the unique opportunity to observe and experience firsthand different health systems, healthcare organisations and a myriad of health care professionals.

Many of the challenges in delivering high quality care are similar such as escalating costs, navigating a multi-stakeholder environment, treating patients of varying levels of health literacy and severity of illness and trying to do so without doing harm and providing the best possible care. Yet, I have observed differences and nuances with respect to tackling these challenges and as much as I have advised I have also learnt.

During this journey, the rapid advances in technology have been staggering. Computing power has increased exponentially, but so has the volume of data we generate today as well as the complex and dynamic nature of healthcare operations. Therefore, the opportunities for digital health have also grown. Without a doubt, one of the major lessons from the recent COVID-19 pandemic was that we can benefit so much by leveraging technology and embracing digital health. It is now important to ensure we design, develop and deploy superior, successful and sustainable digital health solutions.

In 2020, I was honoured to receive the Alexander von Humbolt award for outstanding contribution to the field of digital health. This did give me an opportunity to have a Janus moment, as I call it, that is, to look back to where we started and how far we have come and then look forward at the journey ahead. Indeed, there is much to do, and I do believe there is a great need to understand the fundamentals of digital health for all stakeholders and from this recognise the critical success factors as well as the necessary yet not sufficient aspects that must be given due consideration if we are to progress the field and realise the full potential of digital health. In so doing, we can deliver to a healthcare value proposition of better access, quality and value for everyone, everywhere, every time.

It is for these reasons that I have compiled this primer on digital health. This primer is designed to assist all healthcare stakeholders so that they can quickly grasp the critical and fundamental aspects of digital health and thereby be able to be more effective in their specific roles as well as better equipped to do their part in realising superior, successful and sustainable digital health solutions.

The book is written in five sections as follows:

Section I: The Fundamentals

This section serves to set the foundations that need to be considered for any digital health initiative or to facilitate the evaluation and assessment of an existing or proposed digital health initiative.

Chapter 1: The Evolution and Rise of Digital Health

Digital health has developed and evolved primarily due to the advancement of digital technologies. This chapter serves to succinctly discuss this evolution including the related and connected domains of health informatics, ehealth and mhealth as well as information communication technologies in healthcare and information systems/information technology in healthcare. The objective is to trace the genesis of digital health over the last 30 years. In so doing, the key enablers, barriers and facilitators of digital health are identified.

Chapter 2: The Technology Side of Digital Health

Without a doubt a key enabler of digital health is the underlying technologies. This chapter serves to highlight these key technologies. Moreover, it presents relevant technology developments including the technologies which make up the Internet of Things, analytics, augmented reality/virtual reality and/or mixed reality, 3D printing, mobile solutions, platforms and sensors. The chapter explores how these technologies can be harnessed to provide, enable and support superior healthcare delivery.

Chapter 3: The People Side of Digital Health

Ultimately healthcare is always about people; patients, clinicians and hospital administrators are some of these key groups. All healthcare stakeholders are agreed that healthcare delivery quintessentially needs to be patient centred. However, this is not so simple to achieve in practice. This chapter addresses some of the key considerations that must be taken on board to ensure that digital health solutions are always in fact patient or human centred and the people perspective does not come second to the technology.

Chapter 4: The Process Side of Digital Health

To be truly beneficial, digital health solutions must support and enable a myriad of healthcare processes. These processes could be at any stage of the patient journey, including prehab, intake and registration, pre-surgery, peri operative, post-surgery and discharge, rehab and/ or hospital in the home. In addition, given the rise in chronic conditions today, prudent digital health solutions should also support better wellness management. Further, as the population ages, digital health solutions that support ageing at home including trying to slow cognitive impairment from conditions such as Dementia are becoming equally essential. This chapter will serve to highlight these key areas and how we might best ensure that our digital health solutions provide the needed support to essential healthcare processes thereby making them more effective, efficient and efficacious.

Section II: Technology Considerations

In this section the key areas of technology are unpacked and more carefully and critically discussed with particular care to identify critical success factors necessary for any minimally viable digital health solution.

Chapter 5: IoT, Analytics, ML and AI

This chapter highlights key emerging trends in IoT, analytics, AI and ML. It will also touch on important developments in robotics and digital twins. Taken together these technological solutions enable more precision and personalisation in the delivery of healthcare care as well as enable better wellness and prevention management to ensue.

Chapter 6: APPs, Platforms, Mobile Solutions and Telehealth

COVID-19 has served to underscore the importance of tele health and mobile digital health solutions to support and facilitate anywhere anytime care. However, this is only one aspect of the role for APPs, Platforms Mobile solutions and telehealth. This chapter shows how these types of technologies can enable superior care delivery in a variety of contexts and what essential considerations are necessary to ensure it is possible to realise the full potential of such solutions.

Chapter 7: AR/VR/MR and 3D Printing

Often less well known and definitely still under-utilised are the benefits of augmented reality, virtual reality or mixed reality as well as 3D printing in healthcare. This chapter explores the potential of these solutions as well as the opportunities for their use in key areas such as dementia, pain management and training for AR/VR and/or MR; and within orthopaedics and training for 3D printing. In addition, new domains such as digital anatomy will be presented as opportunities for leveraging the benefits these technologies can provide.

Chapter 8: Exploring the Potential of ChatGPT, Responsible AI, Explainable AI and Generative AI

Healthcare delivery relies on data to make better decisions. Today, in healthcare as in other contexts, we are drowning in data and it is often difficult to separate critical, relevant data, pertinent information and germane knowledge from noise. Yet this is essential to make timely, prudent and effective healthcare decisions. This chapter thus outlines how AI has advanced to address this challenge. In particular it will highlight the strengths and weaknesses of key advances such as generative AI, explainable AI and emphasise the need for responsible AI.

Section III: The People Considerations

In this section the key people aspects will be unpacked and more carefully and critically discussed with particular care to identify critical success factors necessary for any digital health initiative.

Chapter 9: Behavioural Change, Adherence and Monitoring

This chapter addresses important aspects around behaviour change and adherence as well as self-management and monitoring to ensure and facilitate the attainment of better clinical outcomes. Key strategies such as nudge, persuasion, change management and behaviour change are presented and discussed as well as how to incorporate these into digital health design including gamification to ensure optimal success and sustainment.

Chapter 10: User Adoption and Satisfaction: One Size Does Not Fit All

While it is clear people are different, too often digital health solutions tend to assume homogenous users. This chapter, drawing from key theories around user adoption and satisfaction, serves to outline critical success factors in designing and developing high fidelity, useful and useable digital health solutions. Key aspects include co-design, co-creation and user-centred design principles as well as following a design science methodology. In addition, this chapter serves to stress the importance of designing solution that simultaneously appeal to clinical and patient user groups.

Chapter 11: Agency Theory and Stakeholders: The Power–Knowledge Dichotomy

This chapter focuses on goal alignment, stakeholder alignment as well as power-knowledge differences. In addition, theories such as the theory of reasoned action, relationship equity, technology affordance and structuration are briefly presented to highlight the importance of managing different stakeholder groups, aligning goals, and, thus, ensuring appropriately designed digital health solutions ensue.

Chapter 12: Social Determinants of Health and Digital Health Literacy

Many groups within the population are vulnerable when it comes to healthcare due to either having poor digital, health and/or digital health literacy. This is unpacked in this chapter and strategies to address this problem will be outlined. In addition, the chapter discusses and outlines the social determinants of health and how digital health can serve to ameliorate key disparities.

Section IV: The Process Considerations

In this section, the key health care process considerations are unpacked and more carefully and critically discussed with particular attention given to identify critical success factors necessary for any digital health initiative.

Chapter 13: Value-Based Healthcare and the Business Value of Health IT

In today's challenging healthcare environment, the model of value-based care is gaining traction and appeal. This model and related issues of the business value of IT in health are presented and discussed. In addition, other models such as fee for service, managed care, focused factory as well as the tensions between public and private healthcare models and public private partnership models are also be presented.

Chapter 14: Process Flow, Six Sigma and TQM

Delivering quality care is an essential aspect of any healthcare value proposition. This chapter presents and discusses key techniques in this regard to optimise process aspects including process flow management, six sigma and total quality management. These techniques are discussed with respect to key areas in hospitals such as the emergency department, ICU, intake and registration, peri-operative and operative processes as well as patient discharge.

Chapter 15: Risk Management and Cyber Security

As we become more reliant on digital solutions, we also need to ensure they are safe and protected. Cyber security has thus become a vital consideration in any digital health initiative. This chapter outlines current best practices and how to establish trusted digital health networks and solutions between and within healthcare stakeholders. Related to ensuring secure systems is risk mitigation. Thus, the chapter also examines strategies and techniques to mitigate various types of risk including unplanned readmissions, extended stay and/or clinical risks so as to ensure highest possible clinical outcomes ensue.

Chapter 16: Network-Centric Healthcare

This chapter summarises the doctrine of network-centric healthcare which is essential to fully realise the benefits of any digital health initiative. As distinct from typical platform-centric approaches, a network-centric approach ensures that relevant data, pertinent information and germane knowledge are always shared and accessible as required at the point of care. This ensures timely and high-quality decisions can be made and facilitates the best possible clinical outcomes. While logically this makes sense, to put it into practice is much more difficult and thus the essential barriers, facilitators and enablers are presented to successfully design, develop and deploy network centric healthcare.

Section V: Putting It All Together: Delivering Superior Health and Wellness

This section serves to bring things all together and enables the reader to understand how to design, develop and deploy superior digital health and wellness solutions to facilitate and support high value, high quality care to everyone, everywhere, every time.

Chapter 17: Delivering Superior Digital Health Solutions

This chapter addresses the topic of how to deliver superior digital health solutions by pulling together all the preceding material and outlining four key areas as follows: i) The goals of wellness management and role for digital health; ii) The role for digital health in the acute care sector; iii) The need for digital health in all contexts and iv) The tools, technologies, techniques and tactics of superior digital health for all. In this way, not only is there a clear road map provided to readers there is also a rubric to assess and evaluate current solutions and address current issues to enable them to be more suitable, fully realise desired goals and be fit for purpose.

Epilogue

It is my hope that this primer will be useful to all healthcare stakeholders: regulators, governments, payers, clinicians, healthcare organisation administrators and C-suite and most importantly patients, their families and carers. The primer is designed to provide a high-level summary of the most critical issues that must be considered to design, develop and deploy superior, successful and sustainable digital health solutions. Clearly, these are necessary but not sufficient criteria as each situation brings its own unique aspects and nuances; however, over the years I have found that keeping these criteria in mind certainly is very helpful. I have also found that it is very important at all times to keep a patient-centred or patient-centric focus and never stop thinking! Healthcare is dynamic and complex and we must at all times be prepared and ready.

In closing, I trust this primer will be enjoyable, useful and provide the needed assistance so that we can together advance digital health and support the realisation of a healthcare value proposition of better access, quality, and value for everyone, everywhere, every time.

Nilmini Wickramasinghe
Alexander von Humboldt Awardee
Optus Chair and Professor Digital Health
La Trobe University, Australia
14 November 2023

Acknowledgements

This work would not be possible without the support of many people, too numerous to name individually. Moreover, as we have been coming out of COVID-19 during this time, it has been particularly challenging for us all; and hence, I am doubly indebted to everyone who has, despite their own personal hardships, continued to give their support so that this project could be completed in a timely fashion. I am indebted to my institution for affording me the time to work on this book project and all my colleagues for their help. The corridor discussions, zoom calls and emails with feedback and suggestions have been greatly valued and appreciated. It is indeed through discourse and discussion that we can refine thinking and content – thank you! In addition, I am most grateful to the wonderful assistance provided by the team at CRC Press/Routledge. Further, I acknowledge the Alexander von Humboldt Stiftung for bestowing on me the Alexander von Humboldt Award and funding me to conduct research work at Friedrich Alexander University, Nuremberg, Germany, with Professor Freimut Bodendorf and his group; this book, being one of the outcomes of our research collaboration. Finally, I thank my family for their ongoing encouragement and support in all my endeavours.

Author

Nilmini Wickramasinghe is the Professor and Optus Chair of Digital Health at La Trobe University. In addition, she is the inaugural Professor–Director Health Informatics Management at Epworth HealthCare. She also holds honorary research professor positions at the Peter MacCallum Cancer Centre, Murdoch Research Children's Institute (MCRI) and Northern Health. After completing five degrees at the University of Melbourne, she completed PhD studies at Case Western Reserve University, Cleveland, Ohio, USA, and later completed executive education at Harvard Business School, Harvard University, Cambridge, Massachusetts, USA, in value-based healthcare. For over 25 years, Professor Wickramasinghe has been actively researching and teaching within the health informatics/digital health domain in the United States, Germany and Australia, with a particular focus on designing, developing and deploying suitable models, strategies and techniques grounded in various management principles to facilitate the implementation and adoption of technology solutions to effect superior, value-based patient centric care delivery. Professor Wickramasinghe collaborates with leading scholars at various premier healthcare organisations and universities throughout Australasia, the United States and Europe and is well published with more than 400 refereed scholarly articles, more than 25 books, numerous book chapters, an encyclopaedia and a well-established funded research track record securing over $25M in funding from grants in the United States, Australia, Germany and China as a chief investigator. She holds a patent around analytics solution for managing healthcare data and is the editor-in-chief of *International Journal of Networking and Virtual Organisations* (www.inderscience.com/ijnvo) as well as the editor of the Springer book series Healthcare Delivery in the Information Age and the Routledge/CRC Press series editor for AI and Analytics in Healthcare. In 2020, she was awarded the prestigious Alexander von Humboldt Award for outstanding contribution to digital health, the first time this honour has been bestowed to someone in the discipline of digital health.

Section I

The Fundamentals

This section serves to set the foundations that need to be considered for any digital health initiative or to facilitate the evaluation and assessment of a digital health initiative. It consists of four chapters as follows:

Chapter 1: The Evolution and Rise of Digital Health

Digital health has developed and evolved primarily due to the advancement of digital technologies. This chapter will serve to succinctly discuss this evolution as well as the related and connected domains of health informatics, eHealth and mHealth as well as information communication technologies in healthcare and information systems/information technology in healthcare. The objective is to trace the genesis of digital health over the last 30 years. In so doing, the key enablers, barriers and facilitators of digital health are identified.

Chapter 2: The Technology Side of Digital Health

Without a doubt a key enabler of digital health is the underlying technologies. This chapter will serve to highlight these key technologies. Moreover, it will present relevant technology developments including the technologies which make up the Internet of Things, analytics, augmented reality/virtual reality and/or mixed reality, 3D printing, mobile solutions, platforms and sensors. The chapter will explore how these technologies can be harnessed to provide, enable and support superior healthcare delivery.

Chapter 3: The People Side of Digital Health

Ultimately healthcare is always about people; patients, clinicians and hospital administrators are some of these key groups. All healthcare stakeholders are agreed that healthcare delivery quintessentially needs to be patient-centred. However, this is not so simple to achieve in practice. This chapter addresses some of the key considerations that must be taken on board to ensure that digital health solutions are in fact patient- or human-centred and at all times the people perspective does not come second to the technology.

DOI: 10.1201/9781003318538-1

Chapter 4: The Process Side of Digital Health

To be truly beneficial, digital health solutions must support and enable a myriad of healthcare processes. These processes could be at any stage of the patient journey, including prehab, intake and registration, pre-surgery, peri operative, post-surgery and discharge, rehab and/or hospital in the home. In addition, given the rise in chronic conditions today, prudent digital health solutions should also support better wellness management. Further, as the population ages, digital health solutions that support ageing at home, including trying to slow cognitive impairment from conditions such as Dementia, are becoming equally essential. This chapter will serve to highlight these key areas and how we might best ensure that our digital health solutions provide the needed support to essential healthcare processes; thereby making them more effective, efficient and efficacious.

1 The Evolution and Rise of Digital Health

Objectives

At the conclusion of this chapter, it should be evident:

a) What digital health is and is not.
b) What are the key considerations when designing and developing digital health solutions.
c) Who are the key stakeholders to be included when designing and developing digital health solutions.
d) What are the major enablers, facilitators and challenges regarding digital health.

Definition

To begin it is necessary to try to define digital health and similar terminology such as eHealth, health informatics and health information systems. Simply stated, digital health denotes the utilisation of digital technologies in the provision of healthcare as well as to support prevention and / or wellness management of people (Wickramasinghe & Gibbings, 2023). Further, digital health involves the digital transformation of healthcare delivery (ibid.). Meskó et al (2017) assert that digital health is a new phenomenon that revolves around the cultural transformation of the disruptive technologies that facilitate the provision of care and practicing medicine. Technological innovations in today's contemporary world are increasingly becoming inseparable from healthcare. With healthcare delivery frameworks or systems becoming financially unsustainable, a paradigm shift is imminent (ibid.). Various healthcare organisations across the globe are developing and/or implementing digital health strategies (Wickramaisnghe & Gibbings, 2023). When defining digital health, then, it is essential to assert that it is a scientific discipline that revolves around varying forms of concepts, notions and ideas. An essential aspect is that digital health incorporates both hardware and software components to facilitate varying patient needs. Physicians therefore utilise platforms, sensors and even connectivity software. Nevertheless, the digital health discipline also encompasses applications that are designed to be utilised as medical products or medical technology solutions (at times referred to as MedTech).

DOI: 10.1201/9781003318538-2

According to Park et al. (2022) digital health is an umbrella term for categories like the electronic health records, electronic medical records wearable devices, telehealth, personalised medicine solutions and even telemedicine. For the purposes of this chapter the definition used is that which has been also used initially to describe health informatics by Kidd (1994): namely, that digital health is "an evolving scientific discipline that deals with the collection, storage, retrieval, communication and optimal use of health-related data, information and knowledge. The discipline utilises the methods and technologies of the information sciences for the purposes of problem solving, decision making and assuring highest quality health care in all basic and applied areas of the biomedical sciences." By using this definition, it is also important to note that there are subtle differences between eHealth, health informatics and digital health in essence, and for the purpose of this chapter they are treated essentially to be synonymous.

History of Digital Health

Renowned American poet Maya Angelou famously noted that one cannot fathom where one is going if one does not know where one has come from (McGrath, 2014). The implication of this quote to the context of digital health, then, is that in order to understand where digital health is headed, we must first appreciate and be aware of where it has come from; hence, we must delve into its history.

Since the dawn of the health and medical sector, healthcare professionals have strived to foster informed decisions to treat patient maladies while being aided by the limited set of tools of the day and as per the Hypocritic oath "do no harm". In this regard, digital health dates back approximately to the end of the 19th century through the subfield named telemedicine. Hamilton (2016) asserts that telemedicine revolves around the utilisation of electronic tools of communication in the quest to perform medical diagnosis. The first documented form of telemedicine occurred in 1897 whereby a child was diagnosed through a phone conversation with a doctor (ibid.). However, it was not until late in the 20th century when long distance diagnosis became adopted for space missions, military activities and Antarctica expeditions that interest in this opportunity for healthcare in general grew (ibid.).

The 20th century witnessed numerous developments which physicians utilised in enhancing the wellbeing of individuals (Rampton, Böhmer & Winkler, 2022). For instance, the second half of the 20th century saw the development of technologies like imaging techniques, DNA sequencing and artificial organs. Such inventions formed the basis of digital health and strove to go beyond the boundaries and barriers of telemedicine; for example, the invention of the radio ensured that physicians could attend to patients remotely (Rampton, Böhmer & Winkler, 2022). Further, the sending of radiology images between two townships 24 miles apart are noted as some of the first electronic medical record transfers (Lagunsad, 2022).

The 1950s serve as the starting point of the evolutionary pathway of digital health when information technology (IT) and telecommunications started to become integrated into the health sector. The 1950s are often dubbed the electronic age and it was an era when the first computer was created (Lagunsad, 2022). The computer revolved around large key parts and the code was typically written in assembly and machine languages (Live Science, 2022). Moreover, software and hardware components were extremely expensive (ibid.). Computers would therefore be utilised in automating typically highly standardised yet process-intensive aspects such as pay roll and accounting (ibid.). By the mid-1960s, shared data processing centres strove to offer large hospitals business system processing and some started to implement patient care platforms (ibid.).

In 1965, the United States Congress amended the Social Security Act, including Medicaid and Medicare (Lagunsad, 2022). This had the far-reaching implications that now, in order to qualify for their reimbursements, nurses were obliged to offer data in the quest to document the care they delivered (Lagunsad, 2022). This development gave the impetus for the development of contemporary performance reporting and nursing informatics.

The 1980s and 1990s served as a golden period as different technologies and data analysis tools began to be designed, developed and adopted (Lagunsad, 2022). Moreover, it was a period where numerous professional associations started to appear in America and across the globe with the key aim of enhancing healthcare delivery through digital tools. Examples include the International Medical Informatics Association, the European Health Telematics Association and the American Telemedicine Association (Lagunsad, 2022).

From the 1990s onwards, various stakeholders started to signpost their desire to digitise medicine significantly (Lagunsad, 2022). This awakening or interest coincided with rapid technological advances in innovations like the world wide web. This in turn led to patients starting to gain easier access to medical data and thus their expectations grew. New terms revolving around digital health like eHealth, personalised health and mHealth started to appear. The momentum for technology innovations within healthcare was rapidly enhancing, so much so that in the first decade of the 21st century the invention of digital therapeutics had emerged (ibid.). Digital therapeutics is a treatment option that typically utilises digital/online technologies in the quest to prevent and treat psychological and medical issues (ibid.). An example of this is WellDoc which is a platform that was crafted in 2005. Meanwhile another company, Fitbit, developed a new wireless invention that enabled individuals to monitor themselves; such as calories burnt, heart rate and steps taken per day. Hamilton (2016) notes that Fitbit was instrumental in initiating the wave of commercial wearable devices in digital health. The trend or shift that was developing then (and has since continued) was the role of the individual patient in taking a greater active involvement and being empowered in their health and wellness management which was in distinct contrast to previous times in which the patient was a more passive actor. In addition, many of the technological developments were now being directed directly to the patient to support self-management.

The Enablers of Digital Health

Today digital health is no longer on the fringes of healthcare delivery, experimental or an optional alternative for tech savvy individuals to enjoy as they wish. Rather, it has become a lucrative industry that not only attracts new players and consumers but also investors and is generally accepted as part of main stream healthcare delivery (Lagunsad, 2022). In fact, it is difficult indeed to find healthcare being delivered without some technological solutions being involved at some point. This is analogous to the digital transformation in banking. Hamilton (2016) notes that the last few decades have witnessed a rise in capital investment when it comes to digital healthcare. In this light, companies are striving to design and develop solutions to address key healthcare challenges, including physician shortage, rising healthcare costs and even the need for better prevention and the management of expensive chronic ailments. Technology has evolved within the healthcare sector in such a fashion that it is possible to access telemedicine and virtual consultation platforms from a smartphone. Digital healthcare, therefore, emerges today as a sector that is set to have significant growth. The growth is already occurring, and it is being driven by several enablers or one could categorise them as exogenous changes in the healthcare environment. These are now presented and discussed in turn and summarised in Table 1.1.

The Shift Towards Value-Based Healthcare

In today's contemporary healthcare industry there is an increasing focus on delving into patient outcomes rather than just the procedures that are utilised. Stakeholders within this sector are therefore facing significant pressure to offer higher-quality care at low costs (Wickramasinghe & Schaffer, 2019). Key stakeholders, such as clinicians, payers, hospital organisations and regulators, often noted as the web of players (ibid.), realise that digital health solutions often hold the key to attain this goal. For instance, measuring patient outcomes and sharing data has been simplified by the use of digital tools. Scholars note (Porter & Tiesberg, 2006; Hamilton, 2016; Wickramasinghe & Schaffer, 2019) that value-based care revolves around a health framework where value and the end results are rewarded, while access to and quality of care are of equal importance. Hence a healthcare value proposition

Table 1.1 Summary of Key Enablers

I	The Shift Towards Value-Based Healthcare
II	Mobile Technology
III	Growing Investment
IV	Digital Health Policies
V	Changing Consumer Preferences
VI	eHealth and mHealth
VII	Telemedicine and Telehealth

of access, quality and value becomes significant (Wickramasinghe & Schaffer, 2019). The focus of value-based care is the patient and their needs contrary to previous models such as fee-for-service which tended to focus on physician activities (ibid.); however, without digital health solutions it is not possible to easily adopt a value-based care paradigm.

Specifically, digital health becomes a key enabler in offering value-based care as it can identify unique patient motivators, monitor patient progress and care pathways, support behaviour change and at the same time facilitate the personalisation of approaches when it comes to chronic-care management (ibid.). Monacelli (2022) emphasises that digital health tools foster the thoughtful collection of data, and then its subsequent analysis to develop pertinent information and germane knowledge (Wickramaisnghe & Schaffer, 2019), which in turn gives rise for a high value, more holistic patient experience. Such tools also and simultaneously offer key insights into payers' and providers' perspectives and activities (Monacelli, 2022). Thus, providers become more empowered to make better, more informed decisions with higher-quality objective insights while payers are able to evaluate care outcomes regarding diverse patient populations more easily and accurately. As digital health adoption grows, a unique opportunity to deploy the value-based care paradigm is also realised (Dalton, 2017).

Mobile Technology

In the last three decades, the world has witnessed significant technological progress with respect to portable computing devices, smartphones and tablets. Moreover, the global connection emanating from satellite and broadband technologies has fostered a pool of connected users. Notably, in healthcare, rapid communication is paramount, thus faster and superior communication is highly desirable to provide needed and vital health-related services in any context. Communication is therefore an essential link between the healthcare provider and patients (Dalton, 2017). In conventional contexts, the physical visit has served as the primary means for patients to communicate about their health issues. However, mobile technology has revolutionised this aspect and during the COVID-19 pandemic the ability to support non-face-to-face doctor visits was paramount.

Mobile phones which were once considered a luxury item at the start of the century have now become a necessity and most people have at least one mobile phone. Sharma and Kshetri (2022) note that there are approximately 7 billion wireless subscribers globally and an estimated 3.9 billion can access the internet. Mobile phones have therefore emerged as essential tools of communication as they offer a rapid channel to transmit clinical, demographic and even investigational data to healthcare providers. Smartphones and mobiles are unique in the sense that they save time significantly (Miller & Tucker, 2017). In developed countries, providers utilise smartphones to electronically send data, for instance revolving around prescribed medicines directly to the medical store or the pharmacy. Mobile devices also emerge as a significant enabler of digital health due to the availability of medical software applications. Sharma and Kshetri (2020) state that software programs run on computers and mobiles with the goal of performing certain key tasks. Moreover, mobile technology contributes to the varying community health initiatives including advising, educating, building awareness and providing important warnings and information.

Growing Investment

Investment and funding with respect to digital health technology has been rising steadily. Global funding for digital health tools was around $1.2 billion as of 2010; however by 2017, this figure had risen to around $11.7 billion (Basu et al., 2020). The trend of rising investment in digital health technology continues to rise exponentially without an end in sight (ibid.). A point worth stating is that most of the investment is typically directed towards tools that enhance the empowerment of patients, biometric data acquisition and wellness. The digital health market was valued at $71.4 billion and it is expected to reach $379 billion by 2024 which would translate to a compound annual growth rate of 28% (ibid.). Moreover, nations all over the world are striving to incorporate digital health into their health frameworks, delivery and policy initiatives.

Of significance is that China spent approximately $700 million in venture funding linked to digital health in 2014 (ibid.). Such investments are used to support several digital health platforms including disease management apps, online physician and patient communication service and ecommerce. Moreover, the Chinese government has, over the last decade, invested significantly into new technologies like mHealth, wearable health tech devices and telemedicine. Another emerging nation that has taken huge steps towards the integration of digital health is India. India's digital health market grew from around $100 million in 2011 to around $400 million as of 2017 (Basu et al., 2020). mHealth remains a core sector in India and it has consequently redefined varying aspects of care (ibid.). The United States as well as the United Kingdom and the EU are also key nations that have seen huge investments in digital health. Moreover, private enterprises are also striving to partner with the government with respect to device manufacture and simplifying device data aggregation and hence new public-private partnerships are beginning to emerge in the health sector (ibid.).

Digital Health Policies

It is essential to assert that public health policy tends to play a major role when it comes to the optimisation of the benefits fostered by the digital health initiatives. In this light, Basu et al (2020) underscores that policies which support digital health can encourage its utilisation while those that hamper the new emerging technologies can counteract or mute realisation of key benefits. Conducive policies across the globe with respect to digital health are therefore encouraged and we are witnessing the development of digital solutions accompanies with such policies; such as, in the US; The Affordable Care Act and US Health IT Strategic Plan, in

Australia, the design, development and deployment of the now My Health Record (formerly the Personally Controlled Health Record) or in Germany, the design, development and deployment of the German eHealth card.

Within the last two decades, the World Health Organization has played a significant role in encouraging policies that favour the use of digital health (World Health Organization, 2021). The global health organisation has even rolled out guidelines linked to digital health in its quest to attain universal healthcare coverage. Notably, the WHO asserts that around 90% of all the eHealth approaches and strategies that are crafted by member states tend to reference UHC (universal health coverage) and that it has become clear that the UHC goal cannot be attained without the integration and utilisation of the new technologies (ibid.). The WHO also adopted unanimously a resolution in 2018 to recognise the potential linked to digital health technologies (ibid.). Moreover, the resolution strives to ensure that digital technologies are adopted by the mainstream health sector. WHO also partnered with stakeholders like PATH (a global non-profit health entity) with the aim of delivering the next wave of digital health innovations (ibid.). The partnership will also delve into fostering universal health coverage and sustainable development goals while at the same time preparing for future challenges within the sector (World Health Organization, 2021).

Another aspect regarding favourable policies being a significant driver of digital health adoption is that the European Commission (EC) views digital health in a favourable manner (Basu et al., 2020). The entity believes that digital technologies in healthcare can enhance the wellbeing of numerous global individuals and at the same time evolve how care gets delivered (ibid.). For instance, the European Commission designed and implemented a digital health policy dubbed the eHealth Action Plan from 2012 to 2020 (EPHA, 2022). This policy strives to offer citizens high-quality and safe digital health services (ibid.). Varying global governments have also ensured that they strengthen their digital health contexts through the active implementation of varying supportive policies (ibid.). Some of these nations include Germany, South Africa, Mexico, China, Chile, Brazil, Colombia and France (Basu et al., 2020). The governments moreover aim at crafting more policies that define the liability of the digital health frameworks, encourage public/ private collaborations, foster infrastructural obligations, redefine the ownership of data and even prioritise the telemedicine frameworks.

Changing Consumer Preferences

Consumers within the last three decades have witnessed significant shifts when it comes to the delivery of healthcare let alone the embracement and diffusion of technology in their daily lives, be it banking, travelling, paying bills and grocery shopping. Notably, the digitally inclined population has experienced the most change given that its size has doubled. The implication of the growth is that healthcare entities should strive to invest in digital health frameworks urgently in the quest to facilitate brand loyalty and patient satisfaction. For instance Vayena et al (2018) assert that the digitally inclined segment takes around 34% of the total healthcare consumers. The numbers are rising as consumers across all demographic groups continue to report being digitally fluent and active which translates to the readiness to adopt digital health technologies (ibid.). Moreover, most contemporary consumers stipulate that they have the desire to attain a more connected yet personalised end-to-end experience (ibid.). The digitally inclined consumers tend to value the flexibility of their digital tool frameworks. A case in point is that a consumer can go through reviews or comparisons online from websites like PatientsLikeMe or even just using a search engine like Google to assess and evaluate a healthcare issue and assist them to make an (informed) healthcare decision. A consumer-first mindset is therefore critical for all providers and other stakeholders to be mindful of going forward which in turn necessitates that the significantly digitally inclined cohort is served efficiently (Bhavnani, Narula & Sengupta, 2016). Further, the varying healthcare organisations should be willing to offer stable forms or security and privacy when it comes to patient data. Thus, healthcare entities should also strive to become transparent regarding how the collected data is utilised and the varying steps to protect it. Overall, however, consumer demands continue to foster the urgent need of high-quality care with the incorporation of digital health solutions (ibid.).

eHealth and mHealth

It is useful to note that digital health can be categorised or subdivided into mHealth and eHealth. Consumers and the different stakeholders tend to use these two terms interchangeably in the quest to depict the utilisation of information and communication technologies in healthcare. However, they are different. Moss, Süle and Kohl (2019) assert that electronic health – dubbed eHealth – denotes the healthcare services that get offered through the support of ICT (information and communication technologies), like satellite communication, mobile phones and computers. On the other hand, the utilisation portable or smart tools in the healthcare sector are dubbed mHealth. At times the difference is subtle and essentially means that eHealth encompasses a broader aspect of the health practices that are enhanced by electronic processes. Christian (2020) asserts that some of the technologies that are utilised in enhancing healthcare practices include lab systems, patient administration frameworks, electronic health records and other types of record that cannot be stored in mobile tools. Eysenbach (2001) noted that there are approximately 10 e's that revolve around eHealth (Table 1.2): the first "e" is efficiency. Efficiency revolves around streamlining the relationship between the provider and patient for instance by avoiding unnecessary duplication. The next "e" is enhancing quality. The various providers are obliged to have access to notes which come in handy in the prevention of the duplication of aspects like exams. Another "e" is evidence-based. The evidence-based aspect asserts that scientific evidence regarding the basis of the data offered within the eHealth frameworks is crucial. A further "e" is empowerment. eHealth frameworks, he notes, should be designed in such a manner that they encourage the patients to be part of the health process.

Table 1.2 E's in eHealth (Eysenbach, (2001))

Efficiency
Enhancing quality
Evidence-based
Empowerment
Encouragement
Education
Enabling
Extending
Ethics
Equity

Another "e" is encouragement. These frameworks should also strive to enhance the relationship that exists between the providers and the patients through an active partnership. One "e" revolves around education whereby the healthcare providers and the patients should have enhanced educational resources to learn about varying health aspects. And another "e" is enabling, which means that the eHealth systems should foster easy communication between the patients and the providers. A further aspect of eHealth is extending which means that the digital health frameworks should get fostered across the globe (Chan, 2021). The final two include ethics and equity. On ethics, the eHealth frameworks should strive to sustain values linked to professional practice, privacy and even informed consent. Besides, the tools should ensure that healthcare becomes more equitable to varying users (Christian, 2020).

Focusing on mHealth, which has been defined as an abbreviation for mobile health that utilises portable devices like a tablet and smartphones to enhance healthcare practices is growing in uptake and acceptance (Christian, 2020). The availability of mHealth services ensures that diverse groups of patients varying in health literacy and perhaps language skills are able to monitor their health and at the same time store and log data into their mobile devices. In this light, the different mobile applications available today enable and support boosting the healthcare delivery efficiency, reach, range and access. Given the universality of smartphones today, this means that the mHealth tools can be utilised by patients, practitioners and even researchers. The health tracking tools and wearable devices are also becoming popular. Christian (2020) asserts that there are approximately 318,000 applications on the market that consumers can chose. Moss, Süle and Kohl (2019) assert that mHealth entails the utilisation of mobile devices which according to the specific type may support photography, video, sensors, humidity, magnetometer, temperature, heart rate or even proximity. Moreover, different ancillary tools like bands and watches can be connected to mobile devices which fosters unique yet innovative frameworks and extends the span of care. The advancements within the mHealth sector are significantly facilitated by the support of the operating systems that exist within mobile devices (Rowlands, 2020). Key examples include Apple which released a development kit in 2014 that strove to give a combination of software whose role is to collect different forms of health data. It saw Apple also collaborate with key keyholders in digital health like the Ochsner Health system, Nike and the Mayo Clinic to stream mHealth capabilities. In March 2015, Apple rolled out a research kit whose mandate was to foster application development in medical studies. Notably, the research kit possesses an integrated form regarding informed consent that captures the signature of the participants. These capabilities facilitated the utilisation of remote participants and consequently data for different clinical trial (Moss, Süle & Kohl, 2019). Another point worth stating is that Android platforms have also been vocal when it comes to mHealth. An example of this is through Samsung's health tracking app. While the app was originally available only on Samsung phones, these days it is available on the Google Play Store and is dependent on several sensors. Google has also crafted a tool dubbed the Google Fit SDK whose mandate is to aid developers in sensor data acquisition. According to Moss, Süle and Kohl (2019), the implications linked to mHealth for the varying types of integrated platforms are starting to get realised. However, the technological landscape is also evolving rapidly which means that the successful mHealth engagements can only end up benefitting if they can delve into the traits of mobile devices and comprehending how the varying traits can get integrated into fare (Davis, DiClemente & Prietula, 2016).

The Core mHealth Traits in the 21st Century

Moss, Süle and Kohl (2019) note that the core traits of mHealth revolve around its penetration into diverse populations, the availability of different applications, broadband access to online platforms and the ability to become tethered to individuals. Notably, most of the traits or capabilities exist in layers given that some of the capabilities get fostered onto others. An example is the social networking capability that can get built on the internet access frameworks that are tethered to individuals. The varying traits of mHealth are now briefly discussed in turn below (ibid.):

Population Penetration
The first major trait of mobile health platforms revolves around its penetration into the United States and around the globe which results in affording high levels of connectivity and even connectivity quality. For instance, wireless penetration in the United States is estimated to be around 110 mobile subscriptions in every 100 individuals and the ownership of the devices rests at 80% (Moss, Süle & Kohl, 2019). On the global front, ITU (International Telecommunications Union) stipulates that the mobile penetration rate is around 96.8% when it comes to the global population, 120.6% in the varying developed nations and the developing nations are at 91.8%. Further, evolving expectations and preferences tend to play a significant role in the adoption of mHealth services. An example is that around 88% of American teens between 13 and 17 years old can access a mobile phone, while 73% own a digital device (Moss, Süle & Kohl, 2019). Conversely, this demographic group encompasses unique behavioural risk patterns compared to the older populations,

for instance with respect to the human immunodeficiency virus infection patterns (ibid.). The differences could result in impacting the intervention designs and what the target populations can support. Nevertheless, most American teens utilise the internet as their primary health data source.

On the other hand, connectivity can be an issue in the different developing nations in regions like Africa and Asia (Moss, Süle & Kohl, 2019). However, the rise in fundamental mobile-based accessibility fosters messaging which conse-quently reduces the need for the face-to-face healthcare visits (ibid.). Overall, this means that even with costs linked to owning a digital device are decreasing glo-bally and the ownership of these devices is rising, the adoption and penetration of the mHealth technologies is yet to be uniform.

The Availability of Apps

Another trait linked to mHealth technologies revolves around the availability of the applications that can be installed. In this regard, applications are typically built for the specific operating system. Some of the operating frameworks in the contemporary world revolve around the operating system: Apple and Android. Moreover, applications can be crafted to interact with varying connected tools, either wireless or wired. There are several general applications under the Apple and Android platforms which as of July 2015 were 1.5 million and 1.6 million respectively (Moss, Süle & Kohl, 2019). Many healthcare applications tend to exist within significantly powerful hardware contexts which consequently foster data acquisition, computation of the varying intensive processes and communica-tion (ibid.). These capabilities come with important implications, for instance by bringing essential analytics that support and facilitate better informed treatment decisions. In this way, the availability of applications can foster the critically obliged point of need, analytics or care even in the resource-poor contexts (ibid.). Besides, the ability to gain access to different broadband, connectivity fosters personalisation in the applications, real-time data acquisition and several other possibilities that are linked to monitoring or even assessment of individual health (ibid.).

Broadband Access

A further trait of mHealth technologies is their unique ability to access the world wide web or the internet through mobile broadband. In this regard, it is suffi-cient that most of the mHealth devices are powerful, portable and can run mul-tiple applications. They should also have the capability to communicate through internet pathways. The ITU refers to mobile broadband as download speeds of around 256 Kbit/s through the utilisation of internet protocols and access to higher internet levels (Moss, Süle & Kohl, 2019). Mobile broadband can also be defined with respect to the technological generations where 2G, 2.5 G and 2.75 G were among the earliest generations in the 1990s. 3G technologies are more recent and faster and became the global base standard when it comes to the mobile broad-band. But now we are witnessing 4G and even 5G. Another aspect worth noting is that other niche standards have been crafted like the WiGig which is significantly faster and is uniquely designed for close connectivity (ibid.). Increasing penetration linked to mobile broadband surpassed the fixed type of broadband in 2017. For instance, around 34 member states of the organisation linked to economic development and cooperation assert that they are experiencing 81.3% of the broadband penetration (Moss, Süle & Kohl, 2019). Mobile broadband is critical in ensuring that the healthcare stakeholders access internet resources and that components of communication like video are functional. In recent years, the smartphone has emerged, offering internet connectivity through mobile hotspot. This means that other devices can attach to the internet connectivity in a rapid manner.

Tethered to Individuals

The final mHealth trait of note is that varying devices, including mobile phones, tend to become tethered to individuals. This tethering ability fosters intervention delivery and data monitoring properties. Physicians can therefore attain data rapidly, for instance, due to the activity sensor capabilities in the mHealth tools (Nisha et al., 2016). The tethering capability also ensures that personalised medicine can be practiced across diverse contexts. Moss, Süle and Kohl (2019) support this by underscoring that the individually-tailored messages regarding public health strategies and interventions are bound to be more effective compared to generic ones.

Telemedicine and Telehealth

Telemedicine and Telehealth are being more and more utilised by patients, physicians and allied health providers. However, they are different: By definition, telehealth is a generic term that denotes the utilisation of varying telecommunication and electronic data frameworks in the quest to promote, yet support long distance clinical services while telemedicine revolves around the provision of different healthcare services whereby the conventional face-to-face physician-patient interactions get replaced by remote interactions aided by ICT frameworks (Christian, 2020). While the definitions of telehealth and telemedicine are almost similar, there exists a subtle difference. Notably, telehealth tends to cover the non-clinical aspects such as physical training, continuing medical education and administrative meetings which are not covered by telemedicine. This in turn means that telehealth is not essentially a specific service but revolves around a collection of procedures and approaches that strive to enhance education and patient care delivery (ibid.). Besides, it would mean that telemedicine is a facet of telehealth (Mbunge, Muchemwa & Batani, 2022). Irrespective of definitions, what is germane is that ICT tools are key when it comes to the telemedicine and telehealth models.

Telemedicine

Telemedicine covers wide levels of techniques, procedures, services and products which foster the progressive transformation in the healthcare sector. Telemedicine also depends on the continuous investment in different health information platforms and digital skills (Mbunge, Muchemwa & Batani, 2022). Telemedicine has therefore gained significant attention and visibility among market players and in the government. An example is that the telemedicine infrastructure tends to guide the digital strategy of the European Union. In this light, the technologies oblige both ICT and aspects like leveraging human skills. The market trends and drivers in the recent past linked to telemedicine have evolved significantly, hence fostering debates within the healthcare field (Patrick et al., 2016). As technology continues to develop, the two terms are bound to become indistinguishable from one another. Conversely, telemedicine is not a contemporary practice. The reason is that telemedicine dates back to the 19th century through the quest of hospitals in striving to reach patients in remote locations. According to Giacalone et al. (2022), telemedicine emerged with the inception of the various telecommunications tools like the radio, telephone and telegraph. An example is that injuries and casualties of war got reported through the use of the telegraph and this also facilitated consultations and ordering supplies. In the 20th century, stakeholders in the healthcare industry like Dr Hugo Gernsback strove to innovate by featuring a teledactyl. Hugo predicted that the device would allow physicians to see patients through a screen and even touch them remotely through the use of robotic arms. The 20th century would also see radiologic images sent through the telephone between physicians. In the contemporary world and specifically within the last three decades, numerous individuals have access to fundamental telemedicine tools like computers and mobile phones. Such enhanced accessibility means that individuals in busy urban contexts and even rural areas can engage with physicians easily. Moreover, the home-use devices allow caregivers to monitor different aspects like the glucose levels of patients. Still, physicians can attain critical data and at the same time conduct a diagnosis remotely.

Advantages and Disadvantages of Telemedicine

Telemedicine is able to offer several benefits to patients, providers and even payers. For the providers, most are utilising telemedicine to offer care in a more efficient manner. Giacalone et al (2022) assert that modern telemedicine technologies come integrated with software like medical streaming devices and electronic medical records which assist the providers in aspects like diagnosis and treatment. Moreover, the providers are able to monitor their patients and at the same time adjust interventions when prompted. This helps foster enhanced patient outcomes. The providers also benefit significantly from enhanced levels of revenue. The reason is that they can attend to more patients without necessarily increasing the office space or hiring more staff.

On the other hand, telemedicine benefits patients in the sense that those who previously possessed limited access to care services can engage with providers remotely. An example is that there are older adults who would prefer to age in specific locations. They can effectively do so for instance through the utilisation of the medical streaming devices. The implication is that even contagious ailments are controlled so that patients are not exposed to crowded rooms. Besides, telemedicine benefits patients as they get to save on transportation fees and they do not miss work since they can connect with the providers at any place. Finally, telemedicine also benefits the payers. An example is that patients with substance use disorders can get treated through diverse strategies which leads to cost savings. It then means that the cost savings are bound to increase as the technological platforms improve.

Applications of Telemedicine

Individuals may wonder what are the most valuable applications of telemedicine. In this regard, telemedicine can be utilised in chronic disease management. The reason is that physicians can strive to monitor the patient's health remotely. Moreover, the touchscreen capabilities of telemedicine ensure that providers are able to access significant aspects such as glucose levels, blood glucose and heart rate. In countries like the US, around 75% of healthcare spending is dedicated to handling chronic ailments like diabetes, cancer and heart disease (Giacalone et al., 2022). Besides addressing the chronic disease itself, as patients are able to participate in their care process in real-time, this also consequently fosters positive and enhanced outcomes. Telemedicine can also be utilised in medication management. In this way, it provides support for enhanced medication management that tends to be a significant challenge especially when it comes to the older adults. The reason is that they are bound to forget to take medications and this can negatively affect their health. Telemedicine comes in handy as the varying population groups can be monitored, leading to lower readmissions while at the same time enhancing medication compliance. Another application of telemedicine occurs within the area of sharing medical data. Mbunge, Muchemwa and Batani (2022) assert that the store and forward framework is a form of telemedicine that ensures that providers are able to share data remotely. The implication is that primary care physicians are able to connect with different specialists that may be at separate locations. Healthcare aspects like blood analysis, diagnostic images and even more end up getting shared for efficient patient assessment in real-time. Finally, telemedicine can also be applied in emergency room diversion. The reason is that the emergency room in the contemporary world tends to be an overcrowded, expensive yet stressful context. Telemedicine can come in handy in the emergency rooms for instance by having some patients see a remote provider through video chats. The remote provider can then determine if the individual should get care at the emergency departments and this enhances the efficiency of the emergency room.

Telehealth and Telemedicine During the COVID-19 Pandemic

During the early periods of the COVID-19 pandemic, telehealth surged as providers and consumers strove to get ways to access or deliver care safely. This favourable consumer perception, tangible investments in the digital health space and continued uptake ensured that telehealth and telemedicine grew healthily from 2020 through to 2022 (Giacalone et al., 2022). Telehealth offered a unique bridge to care and currently it offers an ideal chance to re-invent yet foster hybrid in-person healthcare frameworks with the sole aim of enhancing affordability, access and even outcomes of care. In countries like the US, telehealth utilisation during the pandemic surged an estimated 38-fold from 2020. Moreover, Bestsennyy et al. (2022) stipulate that provider and consumer attitudes towards telehealth and telemedicine improved. Consumer research, for instance, asserts that consumers continue to perceive telehealth as essential in meeting their future needs. Moreover, the COVID-19 pandemic has been termed as a significant public health issue in the contemporary world given that it fostered several negative social and economic effects. Increasing pressure therefore saw the global healthcare sector being obliged to adapt to the challenge of delivering services (Shachar, Engel & Elwyn, 2020). Consequently, it necessitated the adoption of telehealth and telemedicine solutions in the quest to ensure that patient care was optimised (Bestsennyy et al., 2022). Moreover, it facilitated the acceptability, utilisation and accelerated development of digital health frameworks. Before the pandemic, the utilisation of telehealth was limited for instance to the care of patients with chronic ailments like diabetes. However, the pandemic endured that eHealth was widely adopted in varying healthcare contexts.

Mental health issues also increased especially during the earlier periods of the COVID-19 pandemic probably due to measures such as the fear of social interactions and social isolation. Telehealth and telemedicine therefore came in handy with data illustrating that around 41% of the mental health issues and services were fostered by telehealth interventions during the peri-pandemic (Giacalone et al., 2022). Moreover, the implementation of tele mental health frameworks as an appropriate yet viable strategy to support patients, providers and even families was recommended. The periods of confinement also saw numerous people changing their eating habits and the consequent reduction in the exercise levels. An example of this is patients with the non-alcoholic fatty liver disease whose rise in body weight facilitated disease progression. Further, weight gain in patients with HIV is also linked to the start of cardiovascular disease. Telehealth and telemedicine came in handy in monitoring the dietary habits of such patients which limited aspects like weight gain (McCool et al., 2020).

Another study depicts that telemedicine and its significant level of cost effectiveness enhanced access to varying specialty services. This came in handy in mitigating the issue of physician shortage across different contexts. An example is that over 4,548 physical therapy sessions were conducted via telemedicine frameworks from March to May of 2020 (Giacalone et al., 2022). In this regard, surveys completed by patients indicate that around 94% of the participants were satisfied with the outcomes of the telehealth interventions while around 92% stated that they would gladly attend another telehealth initiative. The pandemic also saw telehealth-based frameworks of care being developed and implemented in the healthcare context. It is therefore evident that scaling telehealth and telemedicine adoption alleviated provider and patient concerns especially before the COVID-19 vaccines were developed. Bestsennyy et al. (2022) assert that telehealth platforms enhanced access to critical care particularly in areas with shortages like behavioural health. The technologies also played a crucial role in enhancing patient experiences and enhancing healthcare outcomes. The integration of these solutions ensures that care is brought closer to home contexts. This has the dual purpose of a) enhancing the convenience for patients to access care on demand and b) increasing the probability that the varying stakeholders will adopt the right steps towards the management of care. Overall, the real opportunity exists in the varying stakeholders striving to embed telehealth and telemedicine into the traditional care frameworks.

In the quest to ensure that the varying healthcare stakeholders take action to shape the opportunity presented by digital health, they should strive to define a value-based virtual roadmap for instance that takes into account data to prioritise interventions. The stakeholders can also engage in optimising provider frameworks and consequently accelerate value-linked contracting which would incentivise telehealth (Bestsennyy et al., 2022). An example of this would be defining the various approaches that revolve around optimising networks, embedding these in contracts and varying services that are reimbursed. The current pandemic has illustrated that telehealth and telemedicine are relevant and modernisation through embedding digital health in the care context on a significant scale could be achieved.

Facilitators of Digital Health

Palacholla et al. (2019) assert that digital health initiatives possess the potential to foster active self-management of chronic ailments through monitoring, support, education, timely feedback and remote access to physicians. In this vein, the successful design and implementation of digital health intervention provides a unique opportunity to enhance healthcare: by reducing costs, enhancing physician satisfaction and the patient's experience and bolstering various health outcomes. There are specific facilitators that have fostered the success of digital health in the healthcare sector which include (Palacholla et al., 2019):

- Easy integration with physician tasks-integration of the varying digital health platforms and technologies into the present workflow of providers facilitates its adoption. In this regard, the physicists and other stakeholders stipulate that they are able to adopt digital health successfully in instances when the data offered by the frameworks was actionable. Moreover, the practitioners assert that integration with the contemporary frameworks allowed them to foster timeline interventions which consequently enhanced the outcomes (Palacholla et al., 2019). The providers also posit that the digital health tools and platforms are attractive and efficient when it comes to the provision of automatic notifications. It allows the provider to be on time when changing medications or doses. It therefore means easy integration of digital health, hence making routine tasks a core facilitator of adoption especially in the last few years.
- Enhanced patient outcomes: the adoption of digital health is facilitated by the fact that it leads to enhanced patient outcomes. Providers also assert the enhanced outcomes are linked to positive aspects such as patients being prompted to become active and at the same time engaged in their health. For example, in the context of BP checking, the enhanced outcomes are facilitated by the ability of the digital health tools and platforms to assist physicians in addressing the issues of adverse outcomes and addressing this in a timely fashion and prompting the patient to make timely corrective steps (Palacholla et al., 2019).

- Technical support and usability: another facilitator is the technical usability and support of the digital health tools. The providers therefore strive to work with systems that are simple to use, require minimal training and come with significant technical support. In the modern healthcare context, the availability of applications, wearable devices and even software like the electronic health register ensures that the practitioners are able facilitate effective yet timely care to patients (Palacholla et al., 2019). In the recent pandemic, the usability and technical support aspects came in handy as patients strove to schedule meetings with physicians due to the social distancing regulations.
- Financial aspects: several financial aspects facilitate the adoption of digital health. For instance, physician reimbursements and other types of incentives ensure that the providers implement the digital health frameworks. Moreover, significant investments from different stakeholders continue to foster the adoption of digital health technologies. The reason is that the practitioners end up acquiring tools that facilitate the integration of the varying platforms and contemporary practice (Palacholla et al., 2019).
- Organisational and leadership support: a healthcare culture that revolves around innovation from the physicians may foster the adoption of the digital tools. It may be difficult to implement digital health without the support of the organisation or stable leadership, for instance due to the personnel and budget.

There are also patient factors that serve as facilitators in the adoption of digital health within modern healthcare delivery including (ibid.):

- Technical support and usability: digital health platforms that patients termed as easy to use include timely technical support and significant patient engagement. In this light, most of the older clients stipulated that technical support is a critical facilitator of the adoption. Moreover, patients value solutions that are easy to integrate into daily activities. The implication is that digital health interventions are bound to be easily adopted by patients if they are culturally unique (Palacholla et al., 2019).
- Enhanced provider-patient communication: enhanced communication between patients and providers is a core facilitator in the adoption of digital health. For instance, some patients may state that the digital health tools allowed them to have direct contact with their physicians hence being able to share varying types of health data. The technologies also allow the patient to comprehend their care plans and consequently engage in informed health decision making (Palacholla et al., 2019). Further, digital health frameworks are facilitated by the fact that they promote visit preparation and accuracy of patient-linked data.
- Patient experience and enhanced self-management: digital health adoption in patients is eased by their increased motivation to engage in their care plans. Most patients report that they feel encouraged to be more proactive in their health as they get to view their statistics on personal devices. Others assert that the utilisation of digital health platforms in monitoring conditions like blood pressure led to alleviation of health-linked anxieties.

Challenges with Digital Health

While digital health offers and promises numerous benefits to contemporary healthcare delivery, there are challenges that need to be considered. The challenges include societal factors, technology regulations, technological capacities, medical regulations and medical capacities. These challenges are covered below:

Societal Factors

Even with technology existing at the heart of digital health frameworks, the associated transformations cannot be viewed only through a technological perspective. The reason is that the digital health frameworks are obliged to deliver easy-to-use yet affordable solutions to an ageing population that tends to be slow in adopting new technologies. Moreover, the physicians can resist the evolution and shift from conventional healthcare models as they are used to the conventional approaches. The resistance by physicians could also arise due to the lack of knowledge regarding the benefits of virtual healthcare or even how it works. There could also be healthcare organisational cultures that are slow to integrate and promote digital evolution within the sector. In countries like Africa, other related issues include digital illiteracy and the digital divide. For instance, some areas are yet to have a reliable electricity supply or even a reliable telecommunication infrastructure (Mbunge, Muchemwa & Batani, 2022). Others are unconnected which means that there exist huge gaps with respect to the adoption and ownership of digital tools/skills. The implication is that patients and providers should be in a position to utilise modern technology which can be aided by education and training. An example is inaccurate sensors that could lead to incorrect treatment or misdiagnosis (Kashaboina, 2021).

Ethical Challenges

The prevalent healthcare digitisation and the growth of the telehealth sector comes with numerous ethical issues. One significant issue is the role of consumer entities like Facebook, Samsung, Amazon, Google and Apple which have been vocal in the digital health sector. In this light, most of these entities strive to offer varying solutions revolving around the collection, storage and even analysis of health data. This then raises numerous issues that are linked to data protection, privacy and informed consent (Cummins & Schuller, 2020). Another aspect is that the nature of the healthcare data keeps evolving. An example of this is the data that is attained from social media sites and wearable devices. It is also critical to assert that the storage of patient data in platforms like the cloud could be prone to malicious attacks by entities that strive to corrupt the data. Data protection is therefore an essential aspect when it comes to digital health. Other ethical challenges include data ownership. Notably, the growth of applications and portable tools that are uniquely designed for the consumer market ends up blurring the line between what is regarded as medical or non-medical devices/applications. Regulating such technologies therefore becomes an issue and is exacerbated by the fact the digital health technologies are advancing rapidly (Kostkova, 2015). Given the advances in artificial intelligence in particular, it is clear that these ethical challenges will continue to dominate many discussions and it is essential that polices and protocols are developed to address potential critical and even life-threatening situations from arising.

Medical Regulation Challenges

Another challenge to the adoption of digital technologies is that there are uncertainties when it comes to issues of funding, reimbursement and finance in general. According to Basu et al. (2020), the funding frameworks of digital health could get convoluted given that they rely on multiple stakeholders from the healthcare, government and private sectors. Due to this, the decisions that revolve around funding and reimbursement regarding digital health products could become complex. The varying health payers are therefore obliged to navigate the environment with uncertainty as government agencies strive to ensure that there are cost-effective funding solutions. Conversely, most of the private entities within the digital health sector are significantly focused on improving their profit margins, for instance through sales. It would therefore be ideal to ensure that practitioners and varying entities become familiar with the varying forms of digital health technologies. This can happen through fostering educational and awareness campaigns geared towards offering subsidised training initiatives, and at the same time incentivising the providers to adopt digital health technologies. Basu et al. (2020) assert that training initiatives should overcome the challenges linked to the lack of adequate knowledge on how to utilise the varying forms of telehealth or telemedicine.

Moreover, Brookes (2017) asserts that most of the contemporary digital health technologies and particularly the mHealth applications lack evidence-based foundations. The implication is that some of the commercially successful tools may lack medical value for some stakeholders like physicians in utilising the data to make informed decisions. In this regard, most of the digital health tools that do not have impressive outcomes for instance when it comes to clinical trials may fail to be adopted into practice. The reason is that the clinical trials are conducted in very controlled contexts, ensuring the utilisation of close monitoring and training so that the patients use the varying technologies appropriately (Murray et al., 2016). Such rarely occurs in the private entities.

Interoperability Challenge

Another significant challenge to digital health is the lack of interoperability in the devices and systems that do not connect with each other. The integration of new digital health technologies is critical to realise the full potential of these digital health solutions (Murray et al., 2016).

Digital Health Trends

The delivery of healthcare is undergoing a significant transformation that is being facilitated by the digital technologies. The transformation not only revolves around business model transitions from the fee-for-service models to value-based but also it concerns an increasing focus linked to patient-centred care, objective data, non-facility care and care coordination. Moreover, the operational efficiencies remain pivotal to the evolution. George (2022) asserts that the digital health investments have significantly shifted from $8.2 billion in 2019 to around $29.1 billion in 2021. In this light, numerous solutions are being crafted and these end up targeting similar applications or markets, interoperability and even infrastructural investments. Some of the trends that are fostering the adoption of digital health strategies include:

Consumerism/Patient Experience

Consumerism in the healthcare sector is linked to the journey of interactions or touchpoints. Notably, it revolves around the patients getting easy access to data, getting timely appointments and even efficient engagement with the providers. The patient experience is therefore a significant metric of safety, quality and effectiveness in the contemporary landscape. Digital health technology continues to evolve and the implication is that patients are bound to pay higher levels of the out-of-pocket costs. Conversely, their experiences are increasingly parallel to those of the retail customers. The reason is that patient access remains a significant aspect of patient choice. Moreover, aspects like dissatisfaction could foster the loss of market share or the adoption of an alternative provider. Overall, the patient experience is being prioritised in digital health adoption given that most stakeholders are advocating for value-based care (George, 2022).

Interoperability and Usability of the Electronic Medical Records

Electronic medical records come in handy in fostering physician documentation, a closed-loop administration of medication, computerised order entries, clinical decision support and at the same time crafting a central repository that is linked to multiple providers. In this light, electronic health records (EHRs) ensure that a problem lists are identified and that the quantitative results get noted down in a timely and systematic fashion. In conventional healthcare structures, health information exchange was significantly limited when it comes to the varying providers, community organisations, patients and even clinical labs. However, the presence of the EHRs has redefined this by fostering collaboration across the varying stakeholders (George, 2022). The presence of digital tools like the custom dashboards enhances retrieval and documentation. Navigation of the digital health frameworks has also been enhanced while there are advanced voice activation technologies being utilised in the transcription of physician and patient input within electronic medical records.

Revenue Cycle Automation

A notable artificial intelligence application in digital health adoption is the revenue cycle management (RCM). The framework is moulded in such a way that the specific tasks are typically of a transactional, repetitive, manual and low complexity nature. These AI solutions and frameworks are getting utilised in the quest to enhance accuracy and efficiency and at the same time minimise the cost-to-collect and revenue leakages. Some of the common examples include the artificial intelligence frameworks that are uniquely designed to perform tasks like billing and coding, coder chart reviews, prioritising clinical documentation and even improving patient access for instance through tools like smart scheduling (George, 2022). Moreover, there are bots that come in handy in ensuring that patients are assisted when it comes to the payment and billing questions. Conversely, the RCM stakeholders stipulate that while there are numerous opportunities to enhance healthcare delivery, there are also risks and challenges. An example is that an AI framework that gets implemented poorly could lead to unanticipated risks, bias or even systemic errors that could be fatal.

Prescriptive and Predictive Algorithms

Advancements in machine learning and artificial intelligence have fostered the ability of the varying healthcare entities to identify varying needs and solutions rapidly and with significant levels of accuracy. The ML and AI solutions also ensure that data patterns can get utilised in the quest to make informed decisions while at the same time enhancing preventative care, for instance through the leveraging of huge amounts of data. The physicians then learn about a given population's treatment plans and historical diagnoses which contributes to enhanced overall outcomes. George (2022) asserts that the clinical prescriptive and predictive tools will gain an increasing role when it comes to the evolution from the fee-for-service to the value-based frameworks. An example is that chronic-care delivery frameworks are bound to dwell on secondary prevention, tertiary prevention, management of care transitions and even closing the gaps in care. The operational use contexts revolve around inventory management, facilities, supply chain management, evaluation of performance, forecasting demand, fostering forecast accuracy and even deploying the prescriptive forecasts.

Longevity of Telehealth

Telehealth is here to stay. We are witnessing great diffusion and deployment of many telehealth solutions today. For example, in countries such as the US, telehealth visits rose by a factor of 63 in 2020 from around 840,000 visits in 2019 to around 52.7 million in 2020 (George, 2022). Notably, telehealth has emerged as a workable alternative to conventional models that revolve around the face-to-face/in-person care, especially when it comes to behavioural health. Given that telehealth is here to stay, it should strive to delve into the optimisation of the varying IT frameworks in the quest to enhance the care experience, build on the revenue codes, enhance operational efficiency and at the same time break the varying barriers that may exist in video and voice conferencing.

Digital Evolution and Cloud

In most contemporary healthcare organisations, the digital evolution is being driven by efforts that strive to modernise the applications, platforms, business processes while at the same time fostering the utilisation of cloud services. These come in handy in the safe storage of patient data and at the same time ensure that data can be accessed easily by the varying stakeholders. This way, the patient outcomes are enhanced, for instance due to collaboration by the providers.

Cybersecurity

Recently, health care entities have been the subject of ransomware attacks. An example is that around 45 million individuals were impacted by data breaches in 2021 alone. The varying healthcare organisations therefore strive to enhance their IT cybersecurity budgets with the aim of improving incident response capabilities, securing protections and even making sure that the digital health frameworks are galvanised against attacks (George, 2022).

Home Technology-Enabled Care

The adoption of digital health frameworks has allowed some health entities to treat many patients from home at an inpatient level of care. Notably, the remote monitoring technologies become essential for checking key vital signs including blood pressure, temperature, respiratory rate and even heart rate. Moreover, emerging technologies also target conditions like the pneumonia, neuromuscular conditions and seizure disorders. They further simplify things so that older adults are able to get effective care while in the comfort of their homes. Further, home care grew in popularity during the recent pandemic where there were numerous social distancing and isolation rules. This in turn led to numerous patients striving to have appointments with physicians online. Overall, these varying digital health trends end up impacting the contemporary health sector in numerous ways. However, they oblige strategic implementation, prioritisation and even resource allocation (George, 2022). In addition, timing has emerged as a significant issue considering the rapid rate of technological advancements and evolution.

Discussion and Conclusions

Ultimately, to understand digital health we need to observe two critical aspects: one around digital and the other concerning health and biological systems. To understand the key aspects of digital we need to appreciate changes in the way gross domestic product (GDP) has been established over the decades and centuries Economic theorists have identified three Epoch; first the Agrarian age, where GDP was increased through farming activities; then the Industrial age, where GDP was increased through manufacturing activities; and finally the Information or Digital age, where technology coupled with data and information play an integral role in the increase of GDP. As we are currently in the digital age, we must rely on our digital solutions to support any/all activities in various sectors and this is equally true now in healthcare. However, unlike other industries, healthcare is socio-technical hence we must at all times be cognizant of three equally important domains of people, process and technology. Moreover, we must recognise that healthcare focuses on people as biological systems that are individual, complex, messy and dynamic. It is essential to keep this in mind. Digital health solutions that address healthcare problems and support better access to care, better quality of care and better value of care for all anytime, anywhere can only be truly successful if they always regard people as individuals.

Summary

After reading this chapter you should be able to be able to state:

a) What digital health is and is not.
   i) Digital health is "an evolving scientific discipline that deals with the collection, storage, retrieval, communication and optimal use of health-related data, information and knowledge. The discipline utilises the methods and technologies of the information sciences for the purposes of problem solving, decision making and assuring highest quality health care in all basic and applied areas of the biomedical sciences."
   ii) Digital health is not simply mobile apps generated at random.
b) What are the key considerations when designing and developing digital health solutions.
   i) The key considerations include recognition that healthcare is a socio-technical domain so it is necessary at all times to keep people, process and technology in mind.
   ii) Appreciate that healthcare deals with biological systems which are individual, complex, messy and dynamic.
   iii) We are now in the Information or Digital age where GDP is increased by utilising data and information as well as technological solutions.
c) Who are the key stakeholders to be included when designing and developing digital health solutions.
   i) The key stakeholders in healthcare include the web of players: providers, payers, regulators, healthcare organisations, family and community and most importantly the patient.
d) Identify the key enablers, facilitators and challenges.
   i) Key enablers – shift towards value-based care, mobile technology, growing investment, digital health policies, changing consumer preferences, eHealth and mHealth.
   ii) Key facilitators – ease of integration, enhanced patient outcomes, technical support, financial aspects and organisational leadership.
   iii) Key challenges – societal, ethical, medical regulations, interoperability, digital health trends, patient experience, revenue cycle, cybersecurity and home care.

References

Basu, A., Gonzalez, A. R., Vignoli, L. P., Schwermer, M. E., Felton, H. C., & Mc Laren, J. (2020). Public policy development in the age of digital health. Retrieved from http://polic ywisdom.com/dist/resources/files/Public%20Policy%20Development%20in%20the%20 Age%20of%20Digital%20Health.pdf.

Bestsennyy, O., Gilbert, G., Harris, A., & Rost, J. (2022, October 6). *Telehealth: a quarter-trillion-dollar post-covid-19 reality?* McKinsey. Retrieved October 19, 2022, from www. mckinsey.com/industries/healthcare-systems-and-services/our-insights/telehealth-a-quar ter-trillion-dollar-post-covid-19-reality.

Bhavnani, S. P., Narula, J., & Sengupta, P. P. (2016). Mobile technology and the digitization of healthcare. *European Heart Journal*, *37*(18), 1428–1438. https://academic.oup.com/ eurheartj/article/37/18/1428/2466287.

Brookes, L. (2017). *Future challenges for Digital Healthcare*. Medical News Today. Retrieved October 19, 2022, from www.medicalnewstoday.com/articles/317022.

Chan, J. (2021). Exploring digital health care: eHealth, mHealth, and librarian opportunities. *Journal of the Medical Library Association: JMLA*, *109*(3), 376. www.ncbi.nlm.nih.gov/ pmc/articles/PMC8485950/.

Christian. (2020). *Definitions: eHealth, Mobile Health, telemedicine, Telehealth.* Association of Accredited Public Policy Advocates to the European Union. Retrieved October 19, 2022, from www.aalep.eu/definitions-ehealth-mobile-health-telemedicine-telehealth.

Cummins, N., & Schuller, B. W. (2020). Five crucial challenges in digital health. *Frontiers in Digital Health*, *2*, 536203. www.frontiersin.org/articles/10.3389/fdgth.2020.536203/full.

Davis, T. L., DiClemente, R., & Prietula, M. (2016). Taking mHealth forward: examining the core characteristics. *JMIR mHealth and uHealth*, *4*(3), e5659. https://mhealth.jmir. org/2016/3/e97/.

EPHA. (2022). eHealth Action Plan 2012–2020: More equality, less fragmentation? Retrieved from https://epha.org/ehealth-action-plan-2012-2020-more-equality-less-fragmentation/.

Eysenbach, G. (2001). What is e-health? *Journal of Medical Internet Research*, 3(2), e20. doi: 10.2196/jmir.3.2.e20.

FZ, M. (2021, February 5). A brief history of digital health. *Medium*. Retrieved October 19, 2022, from https://medium.com/that-medic-network/a-brief-history-of-digital-health-b238f1f5883c.

George, C. (2022). *Nine digital health trends*. FTI Consulting. Retrieved October 19, 2022, from www.fticonsulting.com/insights/articles/nine-digital-health-trends-c-suite-watch.

Giacalone, A., Marin, L., Febbi, M., Franchi, T., & Tovani-Palone, M. R. (2022). eHealth, telehealth, and telemedicine in the management of the COVID-19 pandemic and beyond: lessons learned and future perspectives. *World Journal of Clinical Cases*, *10*(8), 2363. www.ncbi.nlm.nih.gov/pmc/articles/PMC8968610/.

Hamilton, J. (2016, April 21). Rise of digital healthcare: 5 drivers. *Medium*. Retrieved October 19, 2022, from https://medium.com/dayone-a-new-perspective/rise-of-digital-healthcare-5-drivers-55f949078afc.

Kashaboina, M. (2021). *What challenges still lie ahead for healthcare's digital transformation?* Retrieved 2022, from https://healthtechmagazine.net/article/2021/10/what-challen ges-still-lie-ahead-healthcares-digital-transformation.

Kidd, M. (1994). Health informatics in Australia. Retrieved from www.semanticscholar. org/paper/Health-informatics-in-Australia-Kidd/cd47bc35f1199a8c2b2b41b10a67604ec 78d3d2b.

Kostkova, P. (2015). Grand challenges in digital health. *Frontiers in Public Health, 3,* 134. www.frontiersin.org/articles/10.3389/fpubh.2015.00134/full.

Lagunsad, K. (2022, June 14). *The evolution of Digital Health.* Canexia Health. Retrieved October 19, 2022, from https://imagiacanexiahealth.com/2022/05/the-evolution-of-digital-health/

Live Science. (2022). History of computers. Retrieved December 2022 from www.livescience.com/20718-computer-history.html.

Mbunge, E., Muchemwa, B., & Batani, J. (2022). Are we there yet? Unbundling the potential adoption and integration of telemedicine to improve virtual healthcare services in African health systems. *Sensors International, 3,* 100152. www.sciencedirect.com/science/article/pii/S2666351121000735.

McCool, J., Dobson, R., Muinga, N., Paton, C., Pagliari, C., Agawal, S., ... & Whittaker, R. (2020). Factors influencing the sustainability of digital health interventions in low-resource settings: lessons from five countries. *Journal of Global Health, 10*(2). www.ncbi.nlm.nih.gov/pmc/articles/PMC7696238/.

McGrath, Kim. (2014, June 2). Remembering Dr. Maya Angelou. News Center. Wake Forest University. Retrieved December 2022 from https://news.wfu.edu/2014/06/02/remembering-dr-maya-angelou/.

Meskó, B., Drobni, Z., Bényei, É., Gergely, B., & Győrffy, Z. (2017). Digital health is a cultural transformation of traditional healthcare. *Mhealth, 3.* www.ncbi.nlm.nih.gov/pmc/articles/PMC5682364/.

Monacelli, S. (2022). *Health equity through value-based care: Wishful thinking or Digital Health Future?–blogs HLTH.* HLTH. Retrieved October 19, 2022, from www.hlth.com/digital-content/hlth-matters/blog/health-equity-through-value-based-care-wishful-thinking-or-digital-health-future.

Moss, R. J., Süle, A., & Kohl, S. (2019). eHealth and mHealth. *European Journal of Hospital Pharmacy, 26*(1), 57–58. https://ejhp.bmj.com/content/ejhpharm/26/1/57.full.pdf.

Murray, E., Hekler, E. B., Andersson, G., Collins, L. M., Doherty, A., Hollis, C., ... & Wyatt, J. C. (2016). Evaluating digital health interventions: Key questions and approaches. *American Journal of Preventive Medicine, 51*(5), 843–851. www.ncbi.nlm.nih.gov/pmc/articles/PMC5324832/.

Narayanan, K. (2021). *History and future of digital health–ITIHAASA.* Retrieved October 19, 2022, from www.itihaasa.com/public/pdf/History_and_Future_of_Digital_Health_in_the_World_and_India.pdf.

Nisha, N., Iqbal, M., Rifat, A., & Idrish, S. (2016). Mobile health services: a new paradigm for health care systems. In *E-health and telemedicine: Concepts, methodologies, tools, and applications* (pp. 1551–1567). IGI Global. www.researchgate.net/profile/Nabila-Nisha/publication/301651014_Mobile_Health_Services_A_New_Paradigm_for_Health_Care_Systems/links/58a880ad92851cf0e3bfa6d2/Mobile-Health-Services-A-New-Paradigm-for-Health-Care-Systems.pdf.

Palacholla, R. S., Fischer, N., Coleman, A., Agboola, S., Kirley, K., Felsted, J., ... & Jethwani, K. (2019). Provider-and patient-related barriers to and facilitators of digital health technology adoption for hypertension management: scoping review. *JMIR Cardio, 3*(1), e11951. https://cardio.jmir.org/2019/1/e11951/

Park, S., Garcia-Palacios, J., Cohen, A., & Varga, Z. (2022). From treatment to prevention: the evolution of digital healthcare. *Nature News.* Retrieved October 19, 2022, from www.nature.com/articles/d42473-019-00274-6.

Patrick, K., Hekler, E. B., Estrin, D., Mohr, D. C., Riper, H., Crane, D., ... & Riley, W. T. (2016). The pace of technologic change: implications for digital health behavior intervention research. *American Journal of Preventive Medicine, 51*(5), 816–824. https://archive.md2k.org/images/papers/jitai/AmJPrevMed_Patrick2016.pdf.

Porter, M., & Tiesberg, E. (2006). Redefining health care: creating value-based competition on results. Harvard Business School Press, Cambridge, ISBN: 9781591397786.

Rampton, V., Böhmer, M., & Winkler, A. (2022). Medical technologies past and present: how history helps to understand the digital era. *Journal of Medical Humanities, 43*(2), 343–364. https://link.springer.com/article/10.1007/s10912-021-09699-x.

Rowlands, D. (2020). What is digital health? And why does it matter?[White paper]. *Health Informatics Society of Australia*. Retrieved from www.hisa.org.au/wp-content/uploads/2019/12/What_is_Digital_Health.pdf.

Shachar, C., Engel, J., & Elwyn, G. (2020). Implications for telehealth in a postpandemic future: regulatory and privacy issues. *Jama, 323*(23), 2375–2376. https://jamanetwork.com/journals/jama/fullarticle/2766369.

Sharma, R. S., & Kshetri, N. (2020). Digital healthcare: historical development, applications, and future research directions. *International Journal of Information Management, 53*, 102105. https://libres.uncg.edu/ir/uncg/f/N_Kshetri_Digital_2020.pdf.

Vayena, E., Haeusermann, T., Adjekum, A., & Blasimme, A. (2018). Digital health: meeting the ethical and policy challenges. *Swiss Medical Weekly, 148*, w14571. www.research-collection.ethz.ch/bitstream/handle/20.500.11850/239873/Vayena_239873.pdf?sequence=2.

Wickramasinghe, N., & Gibbings, R. (2023). Uncovering health partnership issues: the role of technology in public-private partnerships. *International Journal of Health Technology and Management*, in press.

Wickramasinghe, N., & Schaffer, J. L. (2019). Enhancing healthcare value by applying proactive measures: the role for business analytics and intelligence. *International Journal of Healthcare Technology and Management (IJHTM), 17*(2–3), 128–144. https://doi.org/10.1504/IJHTM.2018.098376.

World Health Organization. (2021). Global strategy on digital health 2020–2025. Retrieved from https://apps.who.int/iris/bitstream/handle/10665/344249/9789240027633-chi.pdf.

2 The Technology Side of Digital Health

Objectives

At the conclusion of this chapter, it should be evident:

a) What analytics is and why it is so vital in digital health.
b) What are the key considerations with respect to the technologies of digital health.
c) Why the Internet of Things and technology advances have been so critical to the development of digital health.
d) What responsible technology use in connection to digital health requires.

Introduction

Since the dawn of the 21st century, we have witnessed rapid advancement in technology, computer processing speed and significant increases to generated data and capacity to store these data. In fact, these are the hallmarks of an Information Age or Knowledge Economy (Wickramasinghe & Schaffer, 2010). Further, advances in the Internet of Things and Web 4.0/5.0 have enabled many exciting advances in analytics and artificial intelligence (AI) augmented, virtual and mixed reality, 3D printing, sensors, mobile and platforms, robotics and wearables and even gamification (Jayaraman et al., 2020). These technological advances have jointly and separately provided numerous benefits to various industries including the service and manufacturing sectors, banking and finance as well as marketing and retail. Moreover, they have also modified how current practices and delivery takes place. Such benefits and advances can also be realised in healthcare delivery and this constitutes the technological side of digital health; understanding how and when to incorporate, design, develop and deploy the latest technological advances to support superior healthcare delivery

Analytics

In the past, the term "analytics" was used to merely refer to the study of analysis. However, a more contemporary and appropriate definition of the term

DOI: 10.1201/9781003318538-3

"analytics" may suggest that "data analytics" is an essential resource for gathering health insights and giving personalised responses to patients (Leung et al., 2021). Moreover, in today's Knowledge Economy or Information Age, data analytics and turning raw data assets into meaningful data, pertinent information and germane knowledge is a critical capability (Wickramasinghe & Schaffer, 2010). The area of data analytics is well-established and has reaped significant benefits from the progression of technology over the course of its existence (Jayaraman et al., 2020). The elimination of barriers to the widespread application of insights gleaned from data is the overarching objective of data analytics in the healthcare industry (ibid.).

Applications

Within healthcare delivery there are many opportunities to apply the techniques of data analytics; many of these will now be discussed in turn:

Analysis of Epidemics and Seasonal Diseases: seasonal diseases like the flu begin and spread with obvious patterns among people; as a result, it is vital to extract hidden information in order to address the emergence of the infection (Triantafyllidis & Tsanas, 2019). The key is to amass as much information as possible and examine that information in order to develop conclusions and do so as quickly as possible.

Enhance healthcare quality and efficiency: The healthcare industry needs to catch up with other industries with respect to the application of information and communication technology (ICT) in order to improve the quality of care provided and overall efficacy. If big data were used creatively and effectively to improve efficiency and quality, according to Cohoon and Bhavnani (2020), the potential value from data in the US healthcare business could be more than $300 billion per year.

Minimise cost of readmission: The mining of unstructured data such as data around readmission and follow-ups, and proactive engagement with patients is made possible through the use of text analytics and other analytics capabilities. Moreover, proactive involvement, such as sending out alerts, setting up appointments or giving instructional materials, could reduce the likelihood of readmission by more than 30 per cent ((Triantafyllidis & Tsanas, 2019)). This will serve to reduce the cost of healthcare delivery as well as enable better clinical outcomes to ensue (ibid.).

Patient monitoring: Digital monitoring is being implemented across the board, from inpatient to outpatient to emergency room to intensive care unit monitoring (Triantafyllidis & Tsanas, 2019). As a result of rapid and beneficial improvements in technology, small sensors are now included into a wide variety of medical devices, such as scales, blood glucose monitors, wheelchairs, patient beds, X-ray machines and more (ibid.). In real-time, digital devices now can generate large volumes of data, which in turn can swiftly shed light on a patient's health, or more precisely change in health status, as well as their routines and behaviours. These data can be used to improve clinical decision making and assist experts in making more efficient use of limited provider resources. This in turn can serve to improve a patient's experience in a hospital or another type of healthcare facility in numerous ways, including proactive risk monitoring, greater quality care and tailored attention to the patient's needs. Complex event processing (CEP), which can be made possible with the assistance of big data, provides control room physicians and nurses with access to information that is up to the minute (ibid.).

Promote preventive care: It is essential for accountable care organisations to provide therapy that is preventative in nature. The ability to accurately diagnose illnesses and place individuals into distinct risk groups will be critical to the operation of successful enterprises in the not-too-distant future. The management of real-time inputs from health information exchange (HIE), pharmacists, providers and payers can yield important data that can be used for risk categorisation and predictive modelling (ibid.). Before the advent of HIE, the only types of data that could be used for health analytics were historical claims data and (health risk assessment) HRA/survey data. HIE has fundamentally changed the landscape of the data that is available for health analytics (Overhage, Evans & Marchibroda, 2005). Processing and data mining times can be significantly reduced with the application of the appropriate big data technology.

Epidemiology: HIE will soon make it possible for widespread network connectivity in the field of epidemiology to be established between healthcare practitioners, insurance companies and pharmacies (Overhage, Evans & Marchibroda, 2005). Hospitals and other health authorities can benefit from networks that make it easier to share data, which allows for improved tracking of disease outbreaks, patterns and trends in health issues throughout an area or the world.

Analysis of Patient Care Programs: As the number of data continue to grow at an exponential rate, so does the complexity of filtering through all of that data to locate the measurable and key performance indicators (KPIs) that will improve medical assistance and patient care (Triantafyllidis & Tsanas, 2019). The ever-expanding field of big data analytics provides the reference architecture, tools and methodologies necessary to analyse terabytes and petabytes of data and give deeper analytical capabilities to its stakeholders. This enables big data analytics to accomplish its goals.

Emergency and disaster scenarios: The recent COVID-19 pandemic serves as an excellent example of the application of a myriad of analytic techniques in real-time to assist with the detection and understanding of the COVID virus as well as supporting the rapid development of vaccines and other measures to contain, track and trace the spread of the disease (Scott et al., 2020). In fact without all the analytic capabilities we currently have it is likely that the impacts of COVID-19 would have been significantly worse. It is important to note that these analytics techniques are just as important for other emergence and disaster scenarios and the ability to rapidly understand the nature of the problem and then effect appropriate solution strategies while simultaneously minimising casualties.

Benefits of Data Analytics

- Assist medical personnel in the clinic with the decision-making process about patients' treatments.
- Enhance both the effectiveness and accuracy of the process for deciding which patients require immediate medical intervention.
- Increase the level of specificity in the electronic health records of individual patients.
- Provides a strategy for reducing the costs of healthcare while simultaneously improving the delivery of medical care.
- Encouraging and empowering people/patients to take better care of their health by being informed about the medical standards that have been set for them and the steps that they can take to meet those standards.
- Because the data is analysed as it is being collected, healthcare providers can receive timely alerts.

Shortcomings

- There is a severe shortage of professionals that specialise in the implementation of analytic technologies in the healthcare industry.
- The lack of privacy that is linked with its use presents a significant challenge for those working in the healthcare industry.
- Devices are regularly the target of cyberattacks and at times pose ethical dilemmas.
- At times there is a black box feel to the data generated and hence a lack of transparency.

Augmented Reality

In 1968, Ivan Sutherland invented the first head-mounted display device, which is considered to be the birth of the technology behind augmented reality (Yeung et al., 2021). The term "augmented reality", on the other hand, was not coined until the year 1990 by Tim Caudell, a researcher at Boeing (ibid.). Today, technology has progressed to such a point, thus there are an increasing number of uses that may be found for augmented reality (AR); in particular, there are a wide variety of applications for AR, ranging from simulations used by NASA to interactive patient contacts in healthcare (ibid.). AR is a technology that combines digital information with real-world physical things in order to create a single interactive experience that combines the best of both worlds (ibid.).

Application

Instruction in Medicine: Augmented reality has a particularly wide appeal in the field of medical education, which is part of the healthcare industry (ibid.).

Augmented reality makes it possible for undergraduate medical students to acquire knowledge of human anatomy and other topics in a manner that is both more realistic and comprehensive. In addition, AR is integral to advances in fields such as digital anatomy. Students will have a much easier time grasping difficult ideas if they are presented to them in a three-dimensional setting on the devices they are using. Given that experiencing things firsthand increases one's level of comprehension, it makes perfect sense to incorporate AR into education health materials and to adapt curricula so that they are more user-friendly with regard to technological advances.

Making preparations for an operation: Surgery is another essential component of contemporary medical practice. It is possible that medical personnel will be able to observe in advance how certain operations will be carried out if they employ augmented reality. The mortality rate during surgery is high, but augmented reality has the potential to reduce this risk by making surgeons and doctors more aware of the location of vital organs, the steps to take in the event that complications arise, how the veins mesh with one another, as well as the reports and conditions of patients (Yeung et al., 2021).

Clinical Radiology: During certain medical procedures, it may be required to perform an assessment of the patient's internal organs to ensure that they are in good health before continuing with therapy. Throughout the course of medical history, a wide range of diagnostic instruments, including thermometers, X-rays, electrocardiograms, magnetic resonance imaging scans and many others, have been deployed. Further, because AR enables the employment of specialised devices in conjunction with the Internet of Things-based sensors and software to acquire multiple readings and diagnose patients with the assistance of graphics shown in real-time, augmented reality has the potential to completely transform medical imaging (Triantafyllidi & Tsanas, 2019). These skills can be used to inform patients about the state of their disease and the consequences of their treatments in more detail. This enables patients to take the necessary precautions and pay close attention while they are recovering from their illness.

Enhanced Description of Symptoms: When attempting to explain their conditions to their physicians, patients frequently exaggerate or minimise the severity of their symptoms. Because of this, there is a possibility of receiving an incorrect diagnosis, which might then lead to inappropriate treatment. By using augmented reality, medical professionals can get a more accurate picture of a patient's condition than they would by simply listening to the patient describe it. This enables the medical professional to validate the patient's condition and provide additional insight into the patient's actual condition.

The Most Recent and Cutting-Edge Information Regarding Drugs: Pharmaceutical companies may be able to create trust in the eyes of consumers and patients by utilising AR and graphics in their marketing efforts. Patients can now observe this process in three dimensions, as opposed to reading about how good a treatment is against a particular medical problem on the back of a syrup bottle in medical language. Patients can also examine this process in two dimensions. The patients simply need to scan the barcode located on the bottle in order to access the same page, which is why it is beneficial for the company to have a comprehensive video graphic already prepared and hosted on its website.

Benefits

- The augmented reality system has a high degree of user interaction and operates in real-time.
- AR enhances both the ways in which we take in and react to the environment that surrounds us.
- Because of its application in the medical field, the lives of patients are now in a significantly better position; i.e., AR can enable more precise disease diagnosis as well as earlier disease identification.
- Everyone could have access to AR as long as there are valid use cases to support its deployment.

Weaknesses

- The production of projects that depend on augmented reality technologies as well as their maintenance are quite expensive. In addition, the production of augmented reality-based devices is quite pricey.
- Concerns regarding data privacy have been voiced in connection with augmented reality software.
- Users of augmented reality are missing out on some of life's most memorable and meaningful experiences as some real-life senses are muted or non-existent when using AR.

Virtual Reality

Despite the fact that simulated environments had been established prior to the middle of the 1980s, the term "virtual reality" was not coined until Jaron Lanier, founder of VPL Research, used it to describe what his business was developing (Thomas & Bond, 2014). The term "virtual reality" refers to an interactive computer-generated experience that recreates the feeling of being physically present in a real-world environment via the use of computer-generated visuals and sound (Magoulas, Lepouras & Vassilakis, 2007). To have a virtual experience, a person will need to put on a virtual reality headset or helmet.

Applications

Providing knowledge and guidance to patients: One of the most common emotions expressed during medical consultations is fear of the unknown. It has been demonstrated that virtual reality (VR) is an interesting learning tool that provides patients with a better awareness of their current health status and can help reduce such anxieties (Magoulas, Lepouras & Vassilakis, 2007). Patients can now visually check the effects of their treatment as well as their diagnosis in VR.

Make a positive impact on the lives of patients: Some hospitals are implementing the usage of virtual reality technology in order to improve the standard of care that they offer to patients in innovative ways. The use of VR to keep patients entertained while they are undergoing invasive medical procedures is beneficial not only to the patient but also to the medical personnel. When patients are transported to another domain, it is much simpler to perform modest diagnostic procedures on them, such as pricking them with a needle (Magoulas, Lepouras & Vassilakis, 2007). This is especially true for children.

Acquiring Knowledge Regarding Medicine: Medical education and training are already beginning to look very different as a result of virtual reality simulation. Students and professionals in the medical industry are able to practice difficult procedures in a virtual environment that is more realistic, less dangerous and less expensive than the actual thing.

Providing Solutions to Issues Concerning Mental Health: VRET also has a number of other applications, including the treatment of mental health issues such as phobias and anxiety (Virtual Reality Exposure Therapy) (Rothbaum, Hodges & Kooper, 1997). The patients are transported into a virtual reality environment, which allows them to confront their deepest phobias in a safe environment. The VERT technology has demonstrated that it has the potential to treat more complicated illnesses, such as PTSD, giving sufferers a second opportunity at a healthy life (ibid.).

Benefits

- Provides relatively readily accessible help and comfort through challenging times.
- Increasing the magnitude of the impact of changes.
- Leaves a stronger impression on people and increases the likelihood that people will remember you in the future.
- Relaxes the nerves and brings relief from tension and around anxiety.

Weaknesses

- The costs of both the hardware and the software can be excessive.
- Potential for dependence.
- Can make users feel disoriented and cause them to have issues or feel motion sickness.
- Lack of appropriate testing as well as a track record.
- There is variation in training which can be problematic.

Mixed Reality

Mixed reality makes it possible for people, machines and their environments to interact in three dimensions in a way that is natural and unobtrusive because of the blending of the real and virtual worlds. This new world has been made feasible by developments in a variety of fields, including computer vision, graphical processing, display technologies, input methods and the cloud, amongst others. Paul Milgram and Fumio Kishino coined the phrase "mixed reality" in their 1994 study titled "A Taxonomy of Mixed reality Visual Displays" to characterise their investigation of the virtuality continuum and the classification of visual displays (Magoulas, Lepouras & Vassilakis, 2007) However, since then, the applications of mixed reality have significantly extended and expanded beyond simple presentation.

Applications

Reengineering the Way Surgery Is Performed: Mixed reality technology has made it possible for surgeons to study 3D computed tomography (CT) and magnetic resonance imaging (MRI) scans of their patients in real-time. Surgeons will have a better chance of a successful outcome during emergency procedures since they will be able to more quickly hone in on the region of a patient's anatomy where the surgery is conducted (ibid.).

Simulation-based education for nursing students: In the medical field, professional nurses are an absolute requirement in order to provide adequate care for patients. Simulations are the most useful tool for educating and preparing nurses to respond successfully to a variety of situations that they may encounter in their careers. A nursing student may be confronted with circumstances that are out of the usual and challenging to prepare for when they are exposed to mixed realities (Hamacher et al., 2016). Pre-operative simulations are made easier by magnetic resonance imaging (MR), which generates patient-specific 3D models and provides a clear image of interior anatomy. When performing complex procedures such as reconstructive surgeries, in which they must meticulously inspect bones and trace the flow of blood arteries, holographic overlays are a tremendous aid to surgeons. These procedures need them to pay close attention to detail.

The capacity to identify problems in a timely manner: By making use of MR headsets, medical professionals are able to not only view the patient's vocal history but also discuss it with one another (Hurter & McDuff, 2017). In addition, headsets that are powered by MR are able to analyse data and relay their findings to physicians in real-time, which enables for a quicker and more accurate diagnosis to be made without the need to examine physical reports.

Benefits

- Helps in providing education in medicine that is not only up to date but also hands on.
- Improves and enhances diagnostic imaging.
- Provides a practical implement that can be utilised by surgeons.

Weaknesses

- Increased cost of acquiring heads-up displays.

3D Printing

3D printing (or sometimes referred to as additive manufacturing) refers to the process of stacking successive layers of a material in order to form the final product. Since 3D printing was first developed in the 1980s, the technique of additive manufacturing, which is also commonly referred to as rapid prototyping, has seen widespread application in a variety of commercial businesses (Dodziuk, 2016). The iterative process of producing a product through the improvement of many versions, known as prototypes, is thus also known as prototyping. Iterations are cycles that are used to make improvements to a design in a rapid fashion to maximise personalisation and precision.

Applications

Creation of cutting-edge advances in medical technology: It is now both quicker and less expensive to create prototypes of revolutionary medical devices and instruments thanks to a technology known as 3D printing (Yang, Leow & Chen, 2018).

Creating Customized Models for Surgical Procedures: Because doctors are seeing an increasing number of patients with complex conditions, personalised and targeted treatments are becoming an increasingly vital component of medical care (ibid.). Clinicians routinely make use of three-dimensional anatomical models created from patient scan data. These models are now considered to be important tools. When they have access to specific visual elements of a patient's case that they can also interact with, medical practitioners are able to have a better understanding of each patient's specific situation.

Prosthetics: In the field of medicine, one of the most fascinating applications of 3D printing is found in the production of prostheses. Because of the great level of customisation and adaptability that the 3D printing technology offers, it is now possible for manufacturers and even practitioners to create patient-specific prosthetics and implants using the technology (ibid.).

The Artistic Fabrication of Realistic Skulls and Bones: In addition to its usage in the fabrication of prosthetics, 3D printers hold the potential to create skeleton replacements that are highly realistic (ibid.). Printing models in a range of materials gives medical professionals the ability to construct artificial bone structures that feel more lifelike than ever before. These are inserted into the patient's original bone in order to secure the prosthetic in place. Because of this, the patient will have an easier time becoming accustomed to using the prosthetic (ibid.) and, thus, there is a decreased likelihood that someone will get hurt. Even extremely large bones can be made with a high degree of precision because of the size of the baseplate that comes with many different types of 3D printers (ibid.). Surgeons can practice their skills on them before attempting more difficult operations, therefore they are useful for a wider range of applications than only attaching prostheses.

Construction of models for dental prostheses and appliances: In the field of dentistry, 3D printing has proven to be quite helpful as well. Dentists have been using 3D printers to make models and temporary prosthetics such as artificial teeth, crowns, bridges and even mouth guards. These prosthetics can be created in a variety of dental-related categories (ibid.). In addition to that, dentists have put it to use in the production of guides for dental implants and partial frames. Orthodontists, in particular, are able to more accurately identify and treat complicated dental problems when they study models that have been made using 3D printing technology (ibid.).

Benefits

3D printing has helped in:

- Modular construction
- Rapid prototyping within a constrained timeframe
- Printing done upon request
- Developing bespoke instruments for specialist surgeries
- Products being conceived and fabricated very rapidly
- Reducing costs associated with disposal.

Weaknesses

- Lack of sufficient resources
- Restrictions on the dimensions of new constructions
- Requires massive quantities of resources.

Sensors

Electrochemical sensors were initially developed in 1906, shortly after the creation of the glass electrode (Mbunge, Muchemwa & Batani, 2021). Electrochemical sensors have come a long way over the years, going from being expensive and cumbersome instruments to being inexpensive, small and equipped with rapid response, improved sensitivity and greater selectivity (ibid.). This is all thanks to advancements in semiconductor technology. In its most fundamental form, sensing technology refers to the application of sensors for the purpose of data collection by the measurement of quantities of physical, chemical or biological qualities (ibid.). It is important to note that there is a huge selection of sensors available for purchase today that can fulfil practically any requirement in industry. Moreover, in most smartphones on the market today the sensors within these phones or even smart watches are very sophisticated.

Applications

Sensors for machines used in anesthesia: A piece of equipment referred to as an "airflow" monitor is utilised whenever there is a need to guarantee that the correct quantity of air, oxygen and nitrous oxide is delivered (Mbunge, Muchemwa & Batani, 2021). Pressure is able to detect when a patient is inhaling and exhaling, which enables a more accurate supply of oxygen and air (ibid.). The amount of oxygen that is present in the patient's breathing air is measured, and any necessary adjustments are made. It is possible to monitor and, if necessary, change the temperature of the air that is being pumped into the lungs of the patient. Humidity is monitored closely and the level of moisture in the patient's breathing air may be adjusted as necessary. Magnets improve the efficiency of motors, which in turn reduces the amount of heat, noise, and wear and tear (Mbunge, Muchemwa & Batani, 2021).

Sensors for equipment used in dialysis: In this instance, the patient's blood pressure is monitored to determine the pace at which it is being pumped into and out of the system, and the blood pressure also regulates the flow of dialysate to ensure that the blood is being cleaned to its full potential (ibid.). Without proper blood pressure regulation, the patient's condition may deteriorate to a significant degree (ibid.). Before the machine can function, a fresh dialysate cartridge needs to be inserted, and either the force or magnetic sensor needs to confirm that it is there (ibid.).

Infusion pump sensors: Infusion pumps are very prevalent today. On the basis of the data obtained by the force, fluid distribution is monitored, blockages are found and fluid bags are refilled as necessary (ibid.). Magnets are utilised in the process of regulating the speed at which the pump operates and ensuring that the tube that carries the fluid is in the appropriate location (ibid.).

Wellness and monitoring space: Today with the advancement of smartphones and smart watches, individuals rely more and more on the sensors imbedded in these devices to track sleep, blood pressure, heart rate, BMI, weight and many other aspects of their health and wellness on a day-to-day basis. Such self-monitoring can enhance healthcare delivery and prevent catastrophic events (ibid.).

Benefits

- Streamline the processes while simultaneously boosting their precision.
- Information is provided in real-time about the processes and assets.
- Increase output while simultaneously lowering ongoing costs.

Weaknesses

- Restrictive in terms of scope; there is less variation in temperature.
- Insufficient specificity; the sensor is activated by a variety of gases.

Distributed Computing Environments/Platforms

A "platform" is the foundational hardware (computer) and software (operating system) in personal computing upon which additional software programs can be installed and executed (Hettikankanamage & Halgamuge, 2021). When developing new software, procedures, or hardware, developers frequently begin with an already existing set of technologies known as a "platform". This ecosystem is the base upon which every program or piece of software sits for the sake of maintenance and/or advancement (ibid.). Each central processing unit (CPU) in a computer is designed to process a particular subset of machine language since CPUs are considered to be the "brains" of computers (ibid.). Applications that have been designed to run on a specific CPU can only be run on that CPU if the applications have been written in the native binary-coded machine language of that CPU (ibid.). As a direct result of this, apps that were designed for one platform would not work properly on another platform in the past.

Applications

Intelligent chatbots: Intelligent algorithms, such as those used to power chatbots, are making an effect in a variety of new fields. The introduction of platforms for treating chronic diseases is an excellent illustration of this. These platforms combine artificial intelligence-based health coaching and on-demand, virtual nurses for the management of symptoms associated with chronic diseases (Alghamdi et al., 2021). Even more sophisticated than the ability of a psychiatrist to detect and track risk levels of mental health addiction, there are now technological platforms accessible to do so (ibid.).

Technology for clinical monitoring and diagnosis that does not involve invasive procedures: There has been a significant amount of work done to incorporate artificial intelligence into the area of wearable technology, and it is anticipated that this trend will only accelerate in the years to come. The new watches and patches that can detect cardiac arrhythmia are two examples of such technologies (ibid.). These new devices can monitor heart rhythm and provide an alert on any irregularities if they are detected. In addition, there are validations that are recognised not just in the United States but also abroad. The Food and Drug Administration has given its stamp of approval to a number of non-invasive diagnostic tools for coronary heart disease (ibid.). These tools include portable electrocardiogram monitors and those based on artificial intelligence.

Implantable electronics and biometric identification technologies: The monitoring and treatment of human health are increasingly becoming more integrated with the use of various devices (ibid.). One example of the new kinds of businesses that are mushrooming in this industry is the introduction of biometric convenience improvements. One such innovation is the ability to pay for prescription medication simply by waving a hand. Both the artificial pancreas and augmented reality contact lenses have the ability to superimpose information, including health data, directly in the wearer's field of vision (ibid.). The artificial pancreas automates the release of insulin. Tests that just require one drop of blood can already be used to evaluate glucose levels and have the potential to one day assist in the monitoring of other conditions as well; it is the integrated platform that brings the benefit of all these devices together (ibid.).

Benefits

- Makes it possible for the organisation to grow in accordance with its requirements.
- Aids in time management by allowing the completion of numerous tasks simultaneously.

Weaknesses

- There is not much room for error if not carefully set up.
- Problems with integrating new software with the old internal architecture.
- Difficulty in adapting to changes in circumstances.
- Limitations imposed on capabilities while conducting operations.
- Potential for security issues.

Mobile Solutions

The term "mobile" refers to any piece of technology that may be brought with the user wherever they go (Velardo et al., 2017). Mobile technology includes mobile computer devices, mobile two-way communication tools and mobile networking technology. Because of their ability to connect to the internet, mobile devices such as smartphones, tablets and smartwatches have emerged as the industry leaders in mobile technology. These "new goods" are the most recent additions to a line that has previously included two-way pagers, notebook personal computers, mobile phones (flip phones), GPS navigation systems and a great deal of other electronic devices.

Applications

Care can be obtained with little effort: The process of selecting a physician, setting appointments and keeping track of follow-up visits at the hospital or clinic are now significantly more streamlined thanks to the proliferation of smartphone apps (Aapro et al., 2021). Patients now have a shorter wait time before being seen by a physician, and the entire healthcare system functions in a more streamlined manner as a result. In addition to providing patients with practical features such as SMS reminders, prepaid alternatives and phone options that are available around the clock, these applications also give patients the ability to rate their providers, thereby making the healthcare system more transparent and trustworthy.

Improve the ability of the medical staff to communicate with one another: Long wait periods and repeated travels back and forth between multiple care providers (such as physicians) are among the primary causes of delays in the delivery of care. Mobile applications help to cultivate a robust network of care providers who are able to successfully engage with one another through apps. This helps to ensure that the environment in which decisions are made is one that is both safe and professional.

Preserving information regarding health: For a considerable time, one of the most important goals of those working in the healthcare sector has been to develop a dependable mobile application (app) that is able to easily maintain a patient's medical history and records. With these apps, there is no need for various data entry sources or version issues, and it is simple to record patient information such as diagnoses, examinations, prescriptions and treatment plans. These apps are available for both iOS and Android.

Interacting with patients while they are distant: Beyond the realm of treatment and diagnostic procedures, the provision of a positive experience for patients is becoming an increasingly important objective. In order to accomplish this goal, the patient must be granted unrestricted access to medical care, irrespective of the location at which they may currently be found (Mathews et al., 2019). The following are some examples of the many various ways in which patients can be engaged despite the distance between them: Access to patients via videoconferencing, and contributing to public education efforts concerning medical care.

Assistance for patients suffering from chronic conditions: In the management of chronic conditions like diabetes, applications developed for mobile devices, namely smartphones, have emerged as crucial tools. Problems associated with diabetes can be prevented by using one of the various applications that are available to assist with monitoring blood sugar levels, keeping a food log and modifying problematic behaviours.

Encouragement of good health: Today, the concept of "health care" refers to more than just the absence of disease; rather, it involves the promotion of full physical and mental wellbeing as well. There has been a meteoric rise in the use of wellness-related apps as a direct result of this phenomenon (Nebeker, Torous & Bartlett Ellis, 2019). These apps range from those that merely count the number of steps taken over a given time period and record the user's heart rate to those that painstakingly document the user's every waking moment. With the assistance of individualised dashboards, a quick evaluation of a patient's health status is possible.

Emergency and disaster scenarios: As witnessed in the recent COVID-19 pandemic, as well as during other emergency and disaster scenarios, mobile solutions have provided tremendous support and enabled the access to essential care anywhere at any time.

Benefits

- The collecting of data is carried out more efficiently.
- The overall staff productivity is improved.
- There is an abundance of information available.
- Increased levels of contentment experienced by customers.
- Lowered operational expenses.

Weaknesses

- An application designed for mobile devices is not a suitable substitute for a website.
- There is a heightened cyber security risk and concerns about privacy of health data.
- A user will require apps and listings that are compatible with both the iOS and Android operating systems. This increases the amount of effort that is placed into ensuring that everything is kept updated and maintained.

Artificial Intelligence (AI)

Over the last ten years, AI technologies are being implemented at an increasing rate within the healthcare industry (Hamet & Tremblay, 2017). The application of AI in the healthcare industry has the potential to assist doctors in a wide variety of patient care and administrative duties, especially with regard to adding more precision and extracting pertinent information and germane knowledge from data (Wickramasinghe & Schaffer, 2010). This in turn will enable clinicians to more rapidly and effectively make superior decisions (ibid.). The application of machine learning algorithms and software, also known as AI, to simulate human intelligence in the analysis, presentation and comprehension of complex data related to medical care and treatment is referred to as technology (Scott et al., 2020).

Applications

Keeping records relating to health: data management is the application of artificial intelligence and digital automation that sees the most widespread use (Dunn & Hazzard, 2019). Users will be able to access the information more quickly and with greater consistency if robots and or robotic process automation are used to assist in the process of gathering data, storing it, reformatting it and tracking it. Robots can do all of these things more efficiently and effectively than human counter parts (ibid.).

Performing activities in a duplicate manner: Data entry, X-ray and CT scan processing, and test interpretation are some examples of the types of relatively mundane tasks that can be performed more quickly and accurately by robots than by humans (Ienca, Haselager & Emanuel, 2018). The fields of cardiology and radiology can be particularly challenging and time-consuming when it comes to data analysis. In the not-too-distant future, some believe that cardiologists and radiologists will only evaluate the most complex cases when it is advantageous to have human supervision (ibid.).

Detailed courses of action: Artificial intelligence algorithms have been developed in order to filter through a wide variety of sources of information, such as medical records, published studies and the knowledge of qualified doctors, in order to find the most effective course of treatment for each particular patient (ibid.).

Sessions of online counseling: Apps, like Babylon in the UK, use artificial intelligence to deliver medical recommendations to users based on the user's medical history as well as their general knowledge (Velardo et al., 2017). Speech recognition is utilised to do a cross-reference between a user's symptoms and a database of illnesses whenever the user enters their symptoms into the app (ibid.). Babylon will make a suggestion after analysing the user's medical records and taking into account the user's preferences (ibid.).

Online nurses: Molly, a digital nurse, was developed by the startup company Sense.ly. She is intended to assist patients and their families in monitoring the patients' health between visits to the physician (Triantafyllidis & Tsanas, 2019). The utilisation of machine learning as a support mechanism in this program is centred on patients who suffer from chronic diseases (ibid.).

In 2016, the Boston Children's Hospital developed an application for the Amazon Alexa voice service to provide guidance and fundamental medical information to parents of ill children (Lareyre et al., 2022). The app provides answers to questions regarding medications as well as whether or not specific symptoms warrant a visit to the physician's office (ibid.).

The administration of medication: The National Institute of Health (NIH) created the AiCure app with the intention of monitoring a patient's consumption of prescribed medications (AiCure, 2022). The webcam and AI capabilities of a smartphone can collaborate to determine whether or not a patient is taking their medication as well as offer additional assistance with self-care (ibid.). It is likely that the majority of users are comprised of people who have chronic diseases, patients who are resistant to treatment and people who are participating in clinical trials (ibid.).

Producing medications: The process of developing new pharmaceuticals often involves conducting clinical tests, which can take more than a decade and cost billions of dollars (Camargo-Plazas et al., 2022). If this process could be streamlined and made more affordable, it has the potential to completely alter the world. The search for already available drugs that could be altered to treat the recent Ebola virus concern was carried out using a computer program that was powered by AI. A case in point is the rapid development of the COIVD-19 vaccines (ibid.).

Accurate medical care: Research in genetics and genomics examines people's DNA in search of insights into diseases and the factors that cause them (Aapro et al., 2021). Body scans that are assisted by AI are able to diagnose cancer and vascular diseases in their earliest stages as well as predict health problems that people may face based on their genetics (ibid.).

Keeping a watchful eye on one's health: Devices such as those manufactured by Fitbit, Apple, Garmin and others can monitor a user's heart rate in addition to their physical activity (Jones, DeRuyter & Morris, 2020). Users can be prompted to participate in physical activity, and their data can be transmitted to physicians (as well as AI systems) so that a more accurate picture of each individual patient's circumstances can be obtained (ibid.).

An analysis and critique of the present healthcare system: Nearly all medical costs in the Netherlands are paid online by patients. A Dutch company uses artificial intelligence to filter through data and detect instances of incorrect diagnosis or treatment in order to assist regional healthcare systems in reducing the number of patients who are hospitalised unnecessarily (Jayaraman et al., 2020).

The applications of artificial intelligence in the medical field are quite broad, and the ones that have been discussed thus far represent only a small number of an ever-growing list. As service providers continue to innovate and push the limits of automation and digital workforces, more time-saving, money-saving and accuracy-enhancing solutions will become possible.

Benefits

- Reducing the effects of human error.
- Open and reachable at any time, at any day of the week.
- Assistance provided by the machine.
- Assist in arriving at conclusions that are free from bias.

Weaknesses

- Exorbitant in cost.
- Causes a reduction in the amount of original thought.
- Make individuals sluggish.
- Often create ethical dilemmas.
- May not be totally transparent.

Robotics

George C. Devol, a native of Louisville, Kentucky, is credited for inventing the first robots in the current design in the early 1950s (Dunn & Hazzard, 2019). After designing and obtaining a patent for a programmable manipulator, which he called the "Unimate" (short for "Universal Automation"), he spent the next decade unsuccessfully trying to sell it to various companies (ibid.). The study of robotics draws inspiration from a wide variety of other academic fields, including computer science and engineering. The study of robots in their whole, including their construction, functioning and various applications, is referred to as robotics. Robotics is the study of, and the creation of, machines with the purpose of providing help in a manner analogous to that provided by humans (Kyrarini et al., 2021).

Applications

Telepresence: By utilising robots to assist them in the examination room, physicians in far-flung locations can have the experience of being "telepresent" there (ibid.). This would enable them to respond to questions and lead therapy sessions regardless of where they physically are.

Staff members of the medical profession who assist surgeons: Surgeons are able to perform minimally invasive procedures with the assistance of these robots, which can be controlled remotely (ibid.). More advanced 3DHD technology provides surgeons with the spatial references necessary for extremely difficult surgery, such as more enhanced natural stereo viewing paired with augmented reality (ibid.). This has led to the development of additional uses for these surgical-assist robots, which has in turn prompted the further development of additional uses for surgical-assist robots (ibid.).

Robots serving in the field of physical therapy: It is impossible to overstate the importance of rehabilitation robots when it comes to assisting people with disabilities in regaining mobility, strength and coordination, as well as an overall higher quality of life (ibid.). Whether a patient is recovering from a stroke, a traumatic brain or spinal cord injury, a neurobehavioral or neuromuscular disorder like multiple sclerosis, or another condition, these robots can be designed to adapt to the patient's individual requirements (ibid.). The utilisation of virtual reality in conjunction with rehabilitation robots can be beneficial to a variety of motor skills, including balance, gait and others (ibid.).

Robots for patient transport: By delivering supplies, medications and meals to patients and staff, medical transportation robots improve communication not only between doctors and patients but also between doctors, staff and patients (ibid.).

Robots that are capable of cleaning and sanitizing: In response to the increase of bacteria that are resistant to antibiotics and the proliferation of potentially fatal diseases like Ebola or COVID-19, an increasing number of hospitals are using robots to clean and disinfect surfaces (ibid.). UV light and hydrogen peroxide vapours are the major methods utilised for disinfection at present (ibid.).

Benefits

- Decreases operational expenditures.
- Leads to the growth of quality and homogeneity of the product.
- Leads to an increase in the level of contentment that employees have with their work.
- Leads to increased production and output at higher rates.
- Increasing output while decreasing the number of resources that are used inefficiently.

Weaknesses

- Even though they boost productivity across many different industries, robots also lead to loss of jobs. A significant number of businesses and production lines have transitioned entirely to using robot labour in place of human employees.
- Robots are capable of performing the tasks for which they were designed; however, when they are presented with novel challenges, they frequently struggle.
- Even if robots were to acquire artificial intelligence, they would not be able to match the level of brainpower that humans possess. Because they are unable to engage in critical thinking, it is unlikely that they will ever be able to identify solutions to improve the quality of their work that are independent of the constraints imposed by their code.
- It is unlikely that industrial robots can completely replace the requirement for human labour. The cost of instructing those workers on how to work with the robots is unquestionably something that must be taken into consideration.

CRISPR

CRISPR is an acronym that stands for Clustered Regularly Interspaced Short Palindromic Repeats. This technique is based on the innate immune response of bacterial cells to viral invasion, which can "tear off" infectious DNA strands and be eliminated by the immune system (Sander & Joung, 2014). The ability to cut DNA could completely change the way that medicine is practiced (ibid.). If scientists are successful in altering the genes of cancer and HIV, two of the most significant threats to human health, they may be able to be eliminated within the next generation. With the help of these techniques, it is feasible to insert, remove, or alter DNA at particular locations throughout the genome (ibid.).

Applications

The therapeutic applications of CRISPR-Cas systems can be broken down into two main categories: ex vivo and in vivo applications (ibid.):

Ex vivo therapy requires extracting cells from a patient, isolating those cells, making modifications to those cells, growing those cells and then giving those cells back to the patient. In order to fix mutations or cure the underlying cause of diseases in living organisms, the CRISPR-Cas system must be transported to the cells or organs of the body via one of several different vectors before it can be used in vivo.

Many distinct CRISPR-Cas methods have been shown to be highly effective at editing the genome, and this applies to a wide variety of genomic targets. However, moving forward, scientists will need to do all in their power to improve the effectiveness of these technologies in order to expand the range of applications for which they can be used. The efficiency with which CRISPR-Cas systems edit DNA may be modified by a number of characteristics, such as double-strand break (DSB) repair mechanisms, the design of guide RNA sequences, unintended consequences and the efficiency with which they transport edited DNA.

In humans, the delivery of CRISPR systems in vivo can induce substantial innate immunity and/or adaptive immunity (humoral immunity and cellular immunity) (ibid.). It is possible that guide RNAs are responsible for triggering innate immune responses; but this issue can be circumvented by developing a phosphatase treatment for in vitro-transcribed guide RNAs (ibid.). As a result of this treatment, innate immune responses were dampened, but the guide RNAs retained their ability to perform their intended role (ibid.).

Benefits

• Target regions are able to easily be adapted.

Weaknesses

• Finding a way to administer CRISPR components in a clinical setting that is both efficient and specific is one of the most significant challenges facing the CRISPR-Cas technology.

Wearables

The proliferation of wearable electronics during the past few years has been largely attributed to the advent of Bluetooth in the year 2000 (Bargh, 2019). These days, individuals use wearables that are connected to their smartphones in order to track anything from their activity levels and heart rates to their eating habits and dream cycles (ibid.). Some of the most popular wearables include the Fitbit and the Apple Watch (ibid.). Wearable technology can help patients monitor and improve their fitness levels, which in turn can assist in the prevention of chronic diseases such as diabetes and cardiovascular disease, which are particularly prevalent in the ageing populations of many industrialised countries.

Applications

An examination of the state of the mind: There has been a significant uptick in interest in the development of algorithms and wearable technology for the purpose of monitoring mental health (ibid.). Utilising the sensors that are integrated into certain wearable devices, it is feasible to keep track of a person's vital signs in addition to other aspects of their physiology (e.g., electrocardiograms) (ibid.). These data can be utilised in the development of innovative tracking systems for psychological states. The bulk of these instruments are employed in the monitoring and diagnosis of stress.

Monitoring and control of one's body mass index: People are increasingly turning to wearable activity trackers as a means of determining the efficacy of their workouts and the total number of calories they've expended (ibid.). The use of consumer wearable devices, in particular consumer wearable devices, is becoming an increasingly popular option among consumers as a means of tracking their progress toward achieving and sustaining a healthy weight (ibid.).

Patient attendance and care: Wearable technology has the potential to increase hospital productivity in the area of patient management. This might be accomplished in a number of ways (ibid.). Researchers are attempting to detect potential health issues at their earliest stages by utilising wearable technologies (ibid.). Scientists have been able to develop a new category of point-of-care (POC) diagnostic tools as a direct result of the proliferation of wireless communication in wearable technologies (ibid.).

Combating illnesses: In the past ten years, there has been significant progress made in the development of wearable device systems for applications in the medical field (ibid.). The management of diseases can be enhanced in a number of ways by utilising wearable technology.

Heart conditions that are abnormal: Patients suffering from cardiovascular conditions are now able to reap the benefits of mobile health applications as a result of wearable devices that monitor their vital signs (ibid.). Wearable ECG systems have been developed as a means of monitoring cardiac function while consuming a very low amount of power (ibid.). Certain wearable technologies are able to monitor the degree to which the beat of a person's heart varies (HRV) (ibid.).

Benefits

- The wearable technologies of today are characterised by their ability to remain covert.
- The technology is easy to manage.

Weaknesses

- The current generation of wearable technologies has somewhat restricted capabilities.
- There are certain wearable technologies that are intended to be unobtrusive, but there are others that are not.
- The cost of wearable technology might be rather high.
- There are some concerns regarding security and data privacy.

Gamification

Gamification has a wide variety of applications in the field of health and wellness, some of the most frequent of which are disease prevention, self-management, medication adherence and telemedicine (Hopia & Raitio, 2016). The patient is the focal point of gamification efforts in the health care industry, and the major objective is to increase satisfaction through increased personalisation of care. When it comes to apps for monitoring users' health and digital support, the most successful app developers in the healthcare industry attempt to incorporate gamification design (ibid.).

Applications

Getting physically fit: Users are able to create and participate in group challenges through the community interfaces provided by Fitbit (ibid.). These challenges can serve as a competitive motivation for increasing levels of physical activity, such as increased gym attendance or step count. In EveryMove, it is vital to compete in an aggressive manner (ibid.). It does this by aggregating data from the trackers and apps that we already use, giving us the ability to evaluate our development in relation to that of our peers (ibid.).

Treatment with medication and management of chronic diseases: A mobile application developed and distributed by Mango Health aims to persuade patients to take their medications exactly as directed (ibid.). Users can schedule when they should take their medications, and the app will send them appropriate timely reminders (ibid.). It provides information on the medications and includes a cautionary section about the potential for adverse effects and interactions between medications (ibid.). A weekly lottery with prizes such as gift cards and cash donations for users and charity is held as a reward for patients who take their medication as prescribed (ibid.).

Keeping children's attention through the use of video games: Because children often do not comprehend the long-term benefits of treatments or medications, it is essential to implement gamification while building medical solutions for children (Hopia & Raitio, 2016). Children tend to just worry about the acute discomforts that are related with treatments and medications (ibid.). They do not appreciate the concept of being required to do things like take medication, eat vegetables, take part in treatment or spend time in a medical facility (ibid.). If they are kept distracted during their therapy with fun activities, children may be more willing to cooperate (ibid.). They are willing to take any kind of medication if they are led to believe that the pill they are being given holds the long-lost knowledge of an ancient civilisation and that only the bacteria in their gut can decipher it (ibid.).

Rehabilitation and various forms of treatment: The usage of gamified therapies has the ability to make patients look forward to their physical therapy and rehabilitation by posing fun challenges around their abilities while also diverting their attention away from whatever discomfort they may be experiencing (ibid.).

Benefits

- Gamification is beneficial for adolescents since it encourages intellectual growth and development in them.
- It has been demonstrated that increasing engagement in a lesson by employing gaming mechanics is effective.
- The use of game mechanics into the educational process helps to make the material more digestible.

Weaknesses

- There is a potential for expensive development costs. The process of designing a game takes significantly more time than developing a more traditional approach to education.
- Value that declines with the passage of time. Not only is it expensive to develop a game, but it is also expensive to maintain and improve upon it.

Discussion

The preceding has served to outline the key technological developments in healthcare today. These have been enabled by the advances in the Internet of Things as well as greater computing power and the ability to store volumes more data at a relatively inexpensive price. However, it is essential to note that just having the technological solutions while indeed necessary, is, however, not sufficient for ensuring successful use; and thereby ensuring better clinical outcomes to ensue. In this regard, it is essential to first understand the type of task the technology solution will be used for, or scenario the solution is required to support. Some classical examples include decision support, monitoring, self-monitoring and/or education. From this it is then necessary to ensure that there is a good fit between the task and technology. This is managed by applying the theoretical perspectives of task technology fit and fit viability respectively (Goodhue & Thompson, 1995). Furthermore, it is essential that the technology solutions are designed with all users in mind and at times both clinicians and patient users. To do this effectively and efficiently, it is paramount to understand the principles of co-design (designing a solution in conjunction with one or a few users) and incorporating the techniques of design science research methodology (Peffers et al., 2007). Finally, it is also important to adopt a responsible approach and consider critical issues such as data privacy, cyber security and ethical aspects.

Conclusion

Technologies play a crucial role when it comes to the digitation of the healthcare infrastructure, the digital transformation of healthcare delivery and digital health. They are providing the much need resources and backbone upon which the 21st century healthcare system is being built. However, though these technologies have proved most invaluable, they are necessary but not sufficient for success. Thus, it is prudent to make sure there is efficiency in blending advances in technology with the existing resources in the healthcare sector to ensure optimal realisation of benefits. For instance, technologies cannot function without the assistance of human resources. Therefore, there is a need to empower key people; clinicians and patients to ensure fruitful collaboration and relationship of the manual-automated care is realised effectively. It is for this reason we note healthcare delivery and digital health requires a socio-technical consideration; people and technology are essential for true success.

Summary

After reading this chapter you should be able to be able to state:

a) What analytics is and why it is so vital in digital health.
   As healthcare is a very data rich industry and especially in today's knowledge economy or information age it is essential to extract pertinent information and germane knowledge from all data assets and this can be done effectively and efficiently using analytics and analytic techniques. Analytics involves deriving insights from data using technical tools.

b) What are the key considerations with respect to the technologies of digital health.
   The key considerations with respect to technologies in digital health include: ensuring they have been designed to be fit for purpose and knowing what that purpose is, hence ensuring there is strong task technology fit and fit viability. In addition, it is essential to be sure the technology solution has been

developed using a co-design process and following a design science research methodology.

c) Why the Internet of Things and technology advances have been so critical to the development of digital health.

Both the rapid evolution of technology solutions and their respective capacities today provide the breadth and depth of digital health which in turn enables digital health to support the delivery of superior healthcare and better clinical outcomes.

d) What does responsible technology use in connection to digital health requires.

Responsible technology use requires a consideration for ethical, data privacy and cyber security aspects at all times while designing, developing and deploying digital health technology solutions into practice.

References

Aapro, M., Bossi, P., Dasari, A., Fallowfield, L., Gascón, P., Geller, M., ... & Porzig, S. (2021). Digital health for optimal supportive care in oncology: benefits, limits, and future perspectives. *Kompass Nutrition & Dietetics, 1*(3), 72–90.

AiCure. (2022). Retrieved from https://aicure.com/.

Alghamdi, S. M., Alsulayyim, A. S., Alqahtani, J. S., & Aldhahir, A. M. (2021, November). Digital Health platforms in Saudi Arabia: Determinants from the COVID-19 pandemic experience. *Healthcare, 9*(11), 1517, MDPI.

Bargh, M. (2019). Digital Health software and sensors: Internet of things-based healthcare services, wearable medical devices, and real-time data analytics. *American Journal of Medical Research, 6*(2), 61–67.

Camargo-Plazas, P., Robertson, M., Costa, I., Paré, G., Alvarado, B. & Duhn, L. (2022). The big challenge out here is getting stuff: How the social determinants of health affect diabetes self-management education for seniors. *New Trends in Qualitative Research, 11*, e555–e555.

Cohoon, T. J., & Bhavnani, S. P. (2020). Toward precision health: applying artificial intelligence analytics to digital health biometric datasets. *Personalized Medicine, 17*(4), 307–316.

Dodziuk, H. (2016). Applications of 3D printing in healthcare. *Kardiochirurgia i Torakochirurgia Polska/Polish Journal of Thoracic and Cardiovascular Surgery, 13*(3), 283–293.

Dunn, P., & Hazzard, E. (2019). Technology approaches to digital health literacy. *International Journal of Cardiology, 293*, 294–296.

Goodhue, D. L., & Thompson, R. L. (1995). Task-technology fit and individual performance. *MIS Quarterly*, 213–236.

Hamacher, A., Kim, S. J., Cho, S. T., Pardeshi, S., Lee, S. H., Eun, S. J., & Whangbo, T. K. (2016). Application of virtual, augmented, and mixed reality to urology. *International Neurourology Journal, 20*(3), 172.

Hamet, P., & Tremblay, J. (2017). Artificial intelligence in medicine. *Metabolism, 69*, S36–S40.

Hettikankanamage, N. D., & Halgamuge, M. N. (2021). Digital health or internet of things in tele-health: a survey of security issues, security attacks, sensors, algorithms, data storage, implementation platforms, and frameworks. In *IoT in Healthcare and Ambient Assisted Living* (pp. 263–292). Springer Singapore.

Hopia, H., & Raitio, K. (2016). Gamification in healthcare: perspectives of mental health service users and health professionals. *Issues in Mental Health Nursing, 37*(12), 894–902.

Hurter, C., & McDuff, D. (2017). Cardiolens: remote physiological monitoring in a mixed reality environment. In *ACM SIGGRAPH 2017 Emerging Technologies* (pp. 1–2).

Ienca, M., Haselager, P., & Emanuel, E. J. (2018). Brain leaks and consumer neurotechnology. *Nature Biotechnology, 36*(9), 805–810.

Jayaraman, P. P., Forkan, A. R. M., Morshed, A., Haghighi, P. D., & Kang, Y. B. (2020). Healthcare 4.0: a review of frontiers in digital health. *Wiley Interdisciplinary Reviews: Data Mining and Knowledge Discovery, 10*(2), e1350.

Jones, M., DeRuyter, F., & Morris, J. (2020). The digital health revolution and people with disabilities: perspective from the United States. *International Journal of Environmental Research and Public Health, 17*(2), 381.

Kyrarini, M., Lygerakis, F. Rajavenkatanarayanan, A., Sevastopoulos, C., Nambiappan, H. R., Chaitanya, K. K., Babu, A. R., Mathew, J., Makedon, F. (2021). A survey of robots in healthcare. *Technologies, 9*, 8. https://doi.org/10.3390/ technologies9010008.

Lareyre, F., Chaptoukaev, H., Kiang, S. C., Chaudhuri, A., Behrendt, C. A., Zuluaga, M. A., & Raffort, J. (2022). Telemedicine and digital health applications in vascular surgery. *Journal of Clinical Medicine, 11*(20), 6047.

Leung, C. K., Fung, D. L., Mai, T. H. D., Souza, J., & Tran, N. D. T. (2021, September). A digital health system for disease analytics. In *2021 IEEE International Conference on Digital Health (ICDH)* (pp. 70–79). IEEE.

Magoulas, G. D., Lepouras, G., & Vassilakis, C. (2007). Virtual reality in the e-society. *Virtual Reality, 11*(2), 71–73.

Mathews, S. C., McShea, M. J., Hanley, C. L., Ravitz, A., Labrique, A. B., & Cohen, A. B. (2019). Digital health: a path to validation. *NPJ Digital Medicine, 2*(1), 1–9.

Mbunge, E., Muchemwa, B., & Batani, J. (2021). Sensors and healthcare 5.0: transformative shift in virtual care through emerging digital health technologies. *Global Health Journal, 5*(4), 169–177.

Nebeker, C., Torous, J., & Bartlett Ellis, R. J. (2019). Building the case for actionable ethics in digital health research supported by artificial intelligence. *BMC Medicine, 17*(1), 1–7.

Overhage, J. M., Evans, L., Marchibroda, J. (2005). Communities' readiness for health information exchange: the National Landscape in 2004. *Journal of the American Medical Informatics Association, 12*(2), 107–112. doi:10.1197/jamia.M1680. PMC 551542. PMID 15561785.

Peffers, K., et. al., (2007). A design science research methodology for information systems research. *Journal of Management Information Systems, 24*(3), 45–77.

Rothbaum, B. O., Hodges, L., & Kooper, R. (1997). Virtual reality exposure therapy. *Journal of Psychotherapy Practice & Research, 6*(3), 219–226.

Sander, J. D., and Joung, J. K. (2014). CRISPR-Cas systems for editing, regulating and targeting genomes. *Nature Biotechnology. 32*(4), 347–355. doi:10.1038/nbt.2842.

Scott, B. K., Miller, G. T., Fonda, S. J., Yeaw, R. E., Gaudaen, J. C., Pavliscsak, H. H., … & Pamplin, J. C. (2020). Advanced digital health technologies for COVID-19 and future emergencies. *Telemedicine and e-Health, 26*(10), 1226–1233.

Thomas, J. G., & Bond, D. S. (2014). Review of innovations in digital health technology to promote weight control. *Current Diabetes Reports, 14*(5), 1–10.

Triantafyllidis, A. K., & Tsanas, A. (2019). Applications of machine learning in real-life digital health interventions: review of the literature. *Journal of Medical Internet Research, 21*(4), e12286.

Velardo, C., Shah, S. A., Gibson, O., Clifford, G., Heneghan, C., Rutter, H., ... & Tarassenko, L. (2017). Digital health system for personalised COPD long-term management. *BMC Medical Informatics and Decision Making, 17*(1), 1–13.

Wickramasinghe, N. and Schaffer, J. (2010). *Realizing value driven patient centric healthcare through technology*. IBM Center for The Business of Government.

Yang, H., Leow, W. R., & Chen, X. (2018). 3D printing of flexible electronic devices. *Small Methods, 2*(1), 1700259.

Yeung, A. W. K., Tosevska, A., Klager, E., Eibensteiner, F., Laxar, D., Stoyanov, J., ... & Willschke, H. (2021). Virtual and augmented reality applications in medicine: analysis of the scientific literature. *Journal of Medical Internet Research, 23*(2), e25499.

3   The People Side of Digital Health

Objectives

At the conclusion of this chapter, it should be evident:

a) Who makes up the web of players in healthcare.
b) Why agency issues play a big role in healthcare delivery.
c) Why the healthcare value proposition of access quality and value is not always so easy to realise.
d) Why designing and developing patient-centred digital health solutions is both essential and challenging.

Introduction

Healthcare and more specifically healthcare delivery is unique in many regards. First, we are dealing with biological systems, people, who are messy, complex and individual. Second, the industry consists of a web of players of key stakeholders including medical administrators, regulators and the government, payers, clinicians as well as of course patients, their families and careers and the community at large. Third, the dynamics in healthcare are rather unique given the primary user/receiver of the services, that is, the patient is not the primary payer of these services and hence several agency issues arise. These are then the key reasons that are essential in digital health to understand the people side, given that no matter how much technology is incorporated to healthcare delivery, at the end of the day it will still be a human requiring services and treatment to stay stronger for longer.

Medical Administrators

Administrators in the healthcare industry rarely have direct interactions with patients, yet the decisions and actions they take can have a significant bearing on the quality of treatment that patients receive. In particular, they contribute to the management of healthcare organisations by assisting in the formulation of policy, the execution of change and the consideration of contextual factors (Yerramsetti, 2016, March). Administrators can ensure that the digital health solution is

DOI: 10.1201/9781003318538-4

patient-centred by putting the needs of the patients first and attending to any particular demands they might have. Patients, who are individuals in their own right and have requirements that are unique to them, should be included in the decision-making process (Janicke, Fritz & Rozensky, 2018). This requires administrators to show the patient the highest respect and care at all times and also take into account the cultural norms and personal preferences of patients.

Administrators should also take a key role in the integration and coordination of patient care. The majority of persons who become ill report feelings of helplessness and vulnerability. These feelings may become more manageable with the help of medical services that are better organised with coordination of ancillary and support services as well as coordination of clinical care (ibid.). Therefore, administrators should assume a central role in providing coordination to the healthcare providers with the focus being to make sure the digital technology at the disposal of a given health facility is geared towards enhancing patients' wellbeing. It should be noted that when one considers the realm of public health, this becomes even more essential.

Pharmacists

Patients, other healthcare practitioners and payers can all benefit from the services offered by pharmacies (Akbar et al., 2022). When pharmacists are included as collaborative members of the patient care team, the outcomes for patients are improved, higher levels of patient satisfaction are achieved, and total costs associated with health care are reduced (ibid,). A few examples of the direct patient care services that pharmacists are trained to undertake include immunisations, preventative health care, wellness checks, collaborative care, medication therapy management (MTM) and management of chronic illness (Akbar et al., 2022). Through Medicare programs, pharmacists receive compensation in a variety of forms for the direct patient care services they provide, which may include medication reviews, medication reconciliation and other similar activities.

Pharmacists who provide patient care services have the ability, in collaboration with other medical professionals, patients and family members, to provide long-term pharmaceutical therapy assessment and management that is of immeasurable value (Powe et al., 2022). As a direct result of taking on this role, pharmacists will be better equipped to improve the overall quality of care, personalise therapy to meet the specific requirements of each individual patient and reduce the total cost of healthcare. Therefore, in delivering patient-centred services in the wake of a digital era, pharmacists have a duty to play. In this, they must ensure the execution of medical prescriptions is well communicated to the patients both electronically and verbally where possible. Pharmacists should also make sure proper medication uptake is followed, especially with the help of technology. For instance, patients can be given guidance or recommendations on the appropriate applications to use to remind them to take their drugs. Finally, pharmacists are often the first to receive data and information on adverse reactions of patients to specific medications; and thus must record and report these findings.

Healthcare Regulators

This particular stakeholder is responsible for overseeing healthcare delivery and is often focused more on how health facilities are operating. Generally, this group of stakeholders ensures the rollout of digital health is patient-centred by ensuring the following has been achieved. In some countries the regulator is the government (local or national) and in other countries separate regulatory groups are set up; hence, we discuss the role of regulators separately to the role of the government.

Reduction in the Number of Preventable Medical Errors

Medical errors are essentially unintentional actions in the medical field that fail to generate the expected result (Serdà et al., 2021). It is impossible for health care personnel to totally eliminate the possibility of making errors (ibid.). This is true despite the employees' best efforts. This was the situation in July 2021, when a patient at University Hospitals Cleveland Medical Center received a donated kidney that was supposed to go to another person (ibid.). However, the kidney went to the wrong person. Fortunately, the patient was in good health and the transplant did not cause him any harm; however, the physicians and nurses who were responsible for the significant error were placed on administrative leave given the gravity of the situation (ibid.).

Although a transplanting of the incorrect organ is one of the most extreme instances of medical error, medication problems are also considered to come under this category. Inaccurate prescriptions, for example, can also have the most devastating effects on the patient who is undergoing treatment. Medical practitioners can benefit from medical warnings, clinical flags and medication reminders in order to protect the future health and safety of their patients. RightPatient is one of the more effective approaches that can be taken to reduce the number of errors that occur in the medical field (Class, 2022). It is a touchless biometric patient identification platform that is used by a large number of healthcare providers to accurately identify patients throughout the care continuum, thereby removing the possibility of having duplicate medical records, patient mix-ups and other types of medical mistakes (ibid.). Therefore, health regulators can make sure the digital health is patient-centred by ensuring the degree of medical errors is reduced. This can be achieved by recommending the appropriate solutions to be adopted and also providing guidelines and standards for the healthcare technology, including ethical considerations, privacy and security requirements.

Improved Drug Safety

It is the primary responsibility of the attending physician to choose which medication is best suited for each individual patient and to check for the presence of any possible drug interactions (ibid.). Because of the greater drug safety that results from using electronic systems, the care that is provided to patients can be improved (ibid.). When patients' medical records are stored in the cloud, it is much simpler for prescribers to identify which medications would be most helpful in treating the ailments or diseases of their patients (ibid.). This is a significant benefit for prescribers (Janicke, Fritz & Rozensky, 2018). Communication between prescribers, pharmacists and patients leaves less room for error, and enhances patient-centredness. Therefore, in the quest of ensuring safety of drugs, healthcare regulators should come up with measures which would ensure the use of technology in disseminating and developing drugs that are sensitive to the needs of the patients.

Monitoring of Patients at a Distance

Patients with diseases such as heart failure, stroke, chronic obstructive pulmonary disease (COPD), asthma and high blood pressure have been proven to benefit from positive results from remote patient monitoring. By utilising a PDMS (Patient Data Management System), medical professionals are able to maintain close tabs on their patients, and the data that they collect can guide them in developing the most effective course of treatment.

The PDMS provides medical professionals with a tool to assist in the process of decision-making, and the technology can be integrated with various additional patient medical record systems. Patients will benefit from this development since their doctors will have more time to spend with them and less time to spend on administrative tasks such as charting and paperwork. However, this tracking doesn't come without repercussions such as the issues of privacy. This is where health regulators need to become involved; making sure the tracking of patients is done in accordance with the rules and regulations governing data privacy and confidentiality.

Government

In the quest of ensuring that the technology used in healthcare is patient-centred, the government has a core role to play. One key aspect is with respect to establishing more uninterrupted channels of communication between patients and professionals in the medical field. This is especially important in the public health sector. The effective and timely exchange of information between patients and doctors is facilitated by the widespread availability of technological instruments. According to the findings of a survey that was carried out by a company that specialises in electronic prescriptions and medication management and was reported on by MedCityNews (2022), 83% of patients "would welcome reminders from their physicians about checking blood pressure, completing rehabilitation exercises, taking prescribed medications, scheduling follow-up appointments, and other activities of a similar nature" (Liu et al., 2021). Therefore, establishing an effective communication channel within public health facilities plays a major role in ensuring digital health is readily patient-centred.

The government should also consider increasing accessibility to health centres. This is primarily because the healthcare value proposition revolves around better access to care, quality of care and value of care (Wickramasinghe and Schaffer, 2010). Increasing access for patients to the essential medical treatments they require is currently one of the most serious challenges facing administrators in the healthcare industry today. The requirement for convenience in accessing healthcare may serve as a further catalyst in the development of alternate methods of providing medical care, such as telemedicine (Rghioui, 2020).

Health Unions

Health unions are mostly responsible for advocating the wellbeing of health practitioners and better working environments. This category of stakeholder can enhance patient-centredness in the wake of digital health by identifying the problem(s) that require resolution and will be made easier by the implementation of technology. Essentially, many purchases of health IT are justified on the basis of presumed benefits, which are almost always inadequately explained (Haux, 2002). Because of this, it can be challenging for those who work in healthcare to agree on a single objective (ibid.). Although phrases such as "improved quality of care" and "increased efficiency" are frequently used, it can be difficult to quantify and predict the actual effects of the installation of a particular feature because extensive changes to existing procedures are typically required (ibid.). This makes it difficult to quantify and predict the actual effects of the installation (ibid.). As a consequence of this, companies frequently have difficulty imagining the necessary adjustments that will be required in the short, medium and long terms (ibid.).

Prior to the implementation of this plan, conducting a thorough mapping of the local processes will help decrease this risk and identify any issues as well as chances for improvement. The health unions, if everything goes according to plan, lead to an agreement on the problem(s) that a specific functionality will solve (for example, information duplication), and from there, the formulation of a long-term strategic vision will follow (e.g., a common patient record that is populated by all health professionals) (ibid.). However, the most cutting-edge technology isn't necessarily the greatest choice in every situation (ibid.). As a consequence of this, it is vital to examine whether or not the existing and future health information technology can support these strategic goals, and if it cannot, it is essential to analyse whether or not alternative approaches should be considered (ibid.).

Health unions also help in building a consensus across various healthcare players which are crucial in delivery of patient-centred services. To be able to put the strategic vision into action, there needs to be widespread consensus among experts, managers and administrators, as well as the development of appropriate resources. In order to accomplish this, a need may rise to make a decision as to whether significant changes need to be made across the board in the organisation (such as by implementing functionality for electronic health record systems) or whether to first focus on streamlining specific processes (such as electronic prescribing) and then add more functionality as it is required. It is essential to involve and win over the support of a wide variety of professional stakeholder groups in order to ease the transition into shared ownership and ensure continued dedication (e.g., doctors, nurses, administrative staff and managers). The significance of high-level strategic leadership of senior management, which should include both administrative and clinical leaders, has been emphasised by a number of authors working in the field of organisational change. Therefore, it has been discovered that the most effective method for striking this balance is to establish a high-level strategy group that not only includes senior managers but also clinical and administrative heads from a variety of end-user groups.

It is essential to keep in mind that any efforts made to align opinions, such as through exercises in consensus building, have to be managed deftly and with an awareness of the means used in order to prevent the reinforcement of preexisting professional hierarchies. In this, it is helpful to differentiate between areas of consensus and those that require further effort from a variety of professional stakeholders. When it comes to the latter, coordinated implementation is most likely to be the result of activities that encourage the participation and empowerment of many groups by actively exploring for solutions that are inclusive. In the medical field, for instance, registered nurses and medical doctors will be held to different standards, but it is probable that they will concur that providing patients with high-quality care ought to be one of the industry's highest priorities (Ahmadinia & Eriksson, 2020). Conversations that are centred on the patient have the potential to bring together professionals with contrasting worldviews and help them find areas of agreement. This is all made possible through different health unions at various levels.

Caregivers

Caregivers are a major stakeholder as far as ensuring patient-focused care is provided in light of digital health. In this regard, the caregivers should make various adjustments to make sure they provide the appropriate services. This also requires an understanding of the level of digital and health literacy of the specific patient. Hence, planning is crucial. Planning that is both strategic and introspective is required in order to successfully care for patients. Despite the requirement for tactical adaptability, effective preparation can normally be identified by a small number of characteristics that are typical and tend to be consistent across all types of technologies (Okun et al., 2014). Some of these include actively engaging with potential suppliers and other organisations that have already implemented, as well as prioritising the implementation of features that can benefit the most end-users at the earliest possible stage (ibid.). Other factors to take into account in the aspect of preparation include maintaining open lines of communication between management and users and preventing "scope creep", which refers to the gradual expansion of a health goals and objectives after work has already begun (ibid.). Regardless of whether a caregiver opts for a "phased" or a "big-bang" approach to deployment, the strategy must be modified to accommodate the particular circumstances and systems that are in operation (ibid.).

Caregivers should also enhance their knowledge on a continuous basis. Hence, caregivers who have been adequately trained in how to use new technology are more likely to enjoy using it and hence provide proper care to patients. Training that is effective takes into account the specific job responsibilities of each participant without being overly prescriptive (ibid.). Being too prescriptive can prevent participants from gaining an understanding of the bigger picture (ibid.). It is essential for trainees to have the opportunity to gain "hands-on" experience that comes as close to accurately simulating the real thing as is practically possible (ibid.). As a consequence of this, it is strongly suggested that training be finished as close to the date of implementation as is practically possible. It's possible that some people will need more training than others, and it's also possible that there will be a need for both mandatory and optional components (for example, in regards to approaches to maintaining patient confidentiality) (ibid.). Younger people, for instance, often have greater expertise with computers and may require less basic training than their elders as a result (ibid.). It is possible that infrequent users, as well as those connected to systems that are prone to regular upgrades, will be needed to participate in ongoing training (ibid.). All this will make sure technology in healthcare will readily serve to the advantage of the patients. Finally, it is noted that careers of CALD (culturally and linguistically diverse) patient populations must span at least two domains to ensure a patient-centred experience for the patient in their charge.

Nurses

The application of digital technologies is having an increasing influence on the nursing profession. This can be seen in the widespread use of mobile devices and the internet, the rise in popularity of telehealth and other virtual models of care, and the proliferation of AI and robotic systems (Shah et al., 2021). The following are some of the ways in which nurses working in a digital environment can promote patient-centred care:

Involvement of friends and relatives: In order to provide exceptional care that is centred on the patient, it has been determined that the following aspects of family life are essential. The practice of inviting close friends and family members and allowing them to stay for a while with a patient is crucial. Taking into account the thoughts and requirements of one's own family and of one's circle of friends; ensuring that these individuals are involved in the decision-making process; promoting the participation of family members in caring responsibilities are also paramount in promoting patient-centredness in care delivery. It must be noted, however, that it is also essential that these technology solutions do not increase the burden on nurses and they are not at risk of burnout.

Doctors

For doctors to effectively address the concept of patient-centredness, they need to implement comprehensive care management strategies that extend beyond the traditional confines of hospitals and clinics (Aboumatar et al., 2015). When patients are involved in their own care, as well as when partnerships are formed with their families and communities, it is much simpler to provide better treatment and achieve better results (ibid.). To begin, it is important to show proper deference. Patients, just like anybody else, have wants and needs that, in both obvious and less obvious ways, have an effect on their health. Their level of medical education, their ability to pay, their access to transportation and the proximity of available healthcare facilities all play a role in the decisions they make and the experiences they have as patients. It is abundantly clear that doctors value the individual patient as a distinct human being if they pay close attention to their concerns and do their best to address them. A patient getting such care may be more inclined to value their health journey and adhere to their treatment plan as a result. Thus, as well as access to care, the quality of care is another key element of today's healthcare value proposition (Wickramasinghe and Schaffer, 2010).

Insurance Companies/Payers

Insurance companies make their decisions based on the risk profiles of their customers, and this frame of mind permeates many aspects of their business, including the way in which they use technology. Healthcare is relatively unique to most industries in that the predominant received of the service, that is, more often than not the patient is different to the predominate payer of the service the insurance company (private insurance or government depending on the healthcare system). This unique structure leads to orthogonality of goals as the payer in such scenarios will always want to cost minimise while the receiver will always want to have the highest quality (which usually translates into the more costly services). More recently value-based care has been proposed as a model to address this dichotomy as both parties have a shared interest in value (Wickramasinghe and Schaffer, 2010). By analysing the benefits and drawbacks offered by a variety of technological trends, insurers are able to make decisions that are in the best interest of their companies (Fortney, Kaboli & Eisen, 2011).

Enable Exchange of Information

Any information technology system that intends to support integrated care must meet the prerequisite of having the capacity to receive and transfer data in a safe manner (ibid.). Changes that are being driven to ensure "interoperability" between systems in the United States are being driven by government requirements for electronic medical records (EMRs) and by health information exchanges (ibid.). However, in Europe, these influences are not as strong to ensure interoperability (ibid.). With the assistance of today's technology and software, it is possible to reduce the expenses of integrated healthcare systems as well as the dangers to their security (ibid.). It is imperative that medical records be organised in a way that enables integrated care, allowing for quick access to, or presentation of, information at the time and place it is needed. Since more providers are recording patient information in a centralised database, it is imperative that records be organised in this way. Therefore, for insurers, it is important to share crucial information or facilitate that which will make delivery of patient services effective.

Engaging Beneficiaries and Close Caregivers

For integrated care to be more person-centred, information technology systems will need to make it easier for patients and their close caregivers to specify their needs and goals, and they will also need to make it simpler for patients and their providers to monitor and review their care plans. This includes designing solutions that meet user needs, have co-design and are easy to use as well as fit for purpose. In addition, the role of a care coordinator can be helpful. One care coordinator can take the lead in assessing and planning for care needs, but there are a variety of models for how other care providers should be included in this process (Akbar et al., 2022). Simply making data accessible does not guarantee that it will be accessed or used; agreement about the social and organisational frameworks for their engagement is still necessary (ibid.). Beneficiaries may have an easier time gaining access to their records if information technology is used; however, precautions must be taken to protect the privacy of third parties whose information is included in the records, and the technology must be thoroughly tested to ensure that even those who are not technically savvy can use it to their advantage (ibid.). Information technology may also make it possible for beneficiaries to access their records more quickly from their insurer firms (ibid.). Again, however, it is essential to note that from the doctor or clinician perspective it is essential that the digital health solution does not generate volumes of data which become time consuming to wade through and thereby add to the already pressured workload creating ultimately burnout.

Principles that Impact Patient-Centred Care in the Wake of the Digital Era

Some general observations and principles that have a positive impact on providing patient-centred care include:

Show Appreciation

When providing medical care to patients, it is essential to keep in mind a number of the fundamental needs that all humans have. Ask each patient and their loved ones about their hopes, fears and wishes before beginning treatment (Liangchen, 2019). Patients are more likely to follow advice and remain loyal patients if they see a caregiver as a reliable healthcare partner. When a patient suggests a friend or when a patient's family member helps spread the word about expertise, it is important to show appreciation by providing them with gift certificates or goodies to celebrate a special occasion. The economic benefits of the patient-centred care approach, in the form of patient referrals, are maximised when appreciation is consistently shown (ibid.).

Allow People to Get Medical Help

Medical practitioners have expanded their focus beyond the clinic walls in order to better care for patients of all backgrounds, locations and socioeconomic statuses (ibid.). When it comes to facilitating patient care and preventing or mitigating the effects of disease, factors that are present over a longer period of time, such as education, social status, income and living environment, play a significant role. When attention is paid to these (sometimes subtle) elements, better outcomes for patients can be achieved (ibid.). Utilising patient care technology that encourages greater adherence to treatment plans and decreases the likelihood of medical errors is one way in which care providers can improve the outcomes for their patients (ibid.).

It is beneficial to streamline the procedure for scheduling appointments (ibid.). If a potential client wants to call or make an appointment, they shouldn't have to wait on hold or go through five different screens on a website (ibid.). Patient care platforms automate this process, including the sending of welcome and thank-you messages to new patients shortly after they schedule an appointment. With the help of care management software, caregivers are able to efficiently and successfully manage patient care while also catering to the particular requirements of each patient and any family members participating in their care. Once again, this all relates to improving access and quality of care; key aspects of today's healthcare value proposition (Wickramasinghe and Schaffer, 2010).

Friends and Family Members of Patients Should Be Included in Care

According to the *Journal of Ethics* published by the American Medical Association, providing quality care necessitates encouraging the participation and contribution of each individual patient's loved ones. When it comes to providing healthcare, medical professionals who prioritise the needs of their patients and the families of their patients should encourage informed participation from all parties involved. The concept of patient-centred care places an emphasis on the patient's unique environment and history, both of which have the potential to either contribute to the development of an illness or aid in its treatment.

Discussion

As noted in the introduction, healthcare delivery is unique in that the primary receiver/ user of services is not the primary payer. This dichotomy leads to agency issues (Wickramasinghe, 2000). Such nested agency issues where one party cannot totally rely on the other to only consider their best interests leads to suboptimal behaviours within healthcare (ibid.); for example, doctors may suggest a more expensive treatment for a patient when a similar, less expensive treatment would be just as good. To address these agency issues it is necessary to have data and information (ibid.). Digital health enables all stakeholders to have better data and information as well as accessibility to information which in turn reduces agency issues.

A further consideration in healthcare delivery is to turn raw data assets into pertinent information and germane knowledge (Wickramasinghe and Schaffer, 2010); this too can be addressed using analytic capabilities of digital health tools. Pertinent information and germane knowledge are beneficial to all stakeholders in the web of plays; clinicians have better understanding of the healthcare issue, patients have a better understanding of the specific problem as well as a better sense of health literacy, administrators have better transparency on activities while the government and regulators can also assess quality and compliance, and finally payers have transparency on billable elements.

In addition to agency issues and the ability to have pertinent information and germane knowledge, it is essential to note that healthcare delivery focuses on biological systems; namely, people who are messy, complex, dynamic and individual. Hence, it is essential that care provided be patient-centred, personalised and provide high levels of access and quality; which is critical in today's healthcare value proposition: better access, better quality and better value for all.

Conclusion

The provision of patient-centred care in the wake of digital health is a multi-disciplinary approach requiring collaboration between different professionals. It cannot be achieved by a single party considering inputs from different healthcare stakeholders are necessary. Therefore, hospital administrators, government, health unions, caregivers, regulators and insurance companies all have a duty and role to play.

Summary

After reading this chapter you should be able to be able to state:

a) Who make up the web of players in healthcare.
   The major players in the web of players in healthcare consists of regulators, payers, healthcare administrators, providers, family and careers, community and most importantly the patient.
b) Why agency issues play a big role in healthcare delivery.
   In healthcare delivery, the primary receiver/user of services is not the primary payer of these services and thus agency issues arise. These issues can serve to reduce value and provide competing goals and suboptimal care to ensue.
c) Why the healthcare value proposition of access quality and value is not always so easy to realise.
   The healthcare value proposition revolves around better access, better quality and high value for all; however, given the socio-technical nature of healthcare delivery and the existence of numerous stakeholders and the web of players this can be challenging to realise in practice.
d) Why designing and developing patient-centred digital health solutions is both essential and challenging.

When designing patient-centred digital health solutions it is essential to keep all users' needs in mind; however, given that users are so heterogeneous, individual and diverse in healthcare this can be challenging. Some issues include: socioeconomic levels, digital health literacy and CALD patients.

References

Aboumatar, H. J., Chang, B. H., Al Danaf, J., Shaear, M., Namuyinga, R., Elumalai, S., ... & Pronovost, P. J. (2015). Promising practices for achieving patient-centered hospital care. *Medical Care, 53*(9), 758–767.

Ahmadinia, H., & Eriksson-Backa, K. (2020). E-health services and devices: Availability, merits, and barriers-with some examples from Finland. *Finnish Journal of EHealth and EWelfare, 12*(1), 10–21.

Akbar, M. A., Leiva, V., Rafi, S., Qadri, S. F., Mahmood, S., & Alsanad, A. (2022). Towards roadmap to implement blockchain in healthcare systems based on a maturity model. *Journal of Software: Evolution and Process,* e2500.

Class, T. M. (2022). Improving the quality of health care delivery and patient safety. Mar 4, 2022.

Fortney, J., Kaboli, P., & Eisen, S. (2011). Improving access to VA care. *Journal of General Internal Medicine, 26*(2), 621–622.

Haux, R. (2002). Health care in the information society: What should be the role of medical informatics?. *Methods of Information in Medicine, 41*(01), 31–35.

Janicke, D. M., Fritz, A. M., & Rozensky, R. H. (2018). Healthcare reform and preparing the future clinical child and adolescent psychology workforce. In *Future Work in Clinical Child and Adolescent Psychology* (pp. 41–50). Routledge.

Liangchen, F. (2019). Physicians in corporate governance of private healthcare institutions in Portugal: Perceptions, experience, and engagement (Doctoral dissertation).

Liu, Q., Zheng, Z., Chen, J., Tsang, W., Jin, S., Zhang, Y., ... & Ming, W. K. (2021). Health communication about hospice care in Chinese Media: Digital topic modeling study. *JMIR Public Health and Surveillance, 7*(10), e29375.

MedCityNews. (2022). Retrieved from https://medcitynews.com/?s=electronic+prescriptions

Okun, S., Schoenbaum, S. C., Andrews, D., Chidambaran, P., Chollette, V., Gruman, J., ... & Henderson, D. (2014). *Patients and health care teams forging effective partnerships.* NAM Perspectives.

Powe, N. W., Robinson, K. T., Burke, S. L., & Shuler, T. O. (2022). *Patient-centered heal promotion programs in healthcare organizations. Health promotion programs: From theory to practice,* 326.

Rghioui, A. (2020, May). Managing patient medical record using blockchain in developing countries: challenges and security issues. In *2020 IEEE International conference of Moroccan Geomatics (Morgeo)* (pp. 1–6). IEEE.

Serdà, B. C., Aymerich, M., Patiño-Masó, J., & Cunill, M. (2021). Mental health screening of healthcare professionals who are candidates for psychological assistance during the COVID-19 pandemic. *International Journal of Environmental Research and Public Health, 18*(21), 11167.

Shah, M., Siebert-Evenstone, A., Moots, H., & Eagan, B. (2021, November). Quality and Safety Education for Nursing (QSEN) in virtual reality simulations: A quantitative ethnographic examination. In *International Conference on Quantitative Ethnography* (pp. 237–252). Springer.

Wickramasinghe, N. (2000). IS/IT as a tool to achieve goal alignment. *International Journal of Healthcare Technology and Management*, 2(1–4), 163–180.

Wickramasinghe, N. & Schaffer, J. (2010). *Realizing value driven patient centric healthcare through technology*. IBM Center for The Business of Government.

Yerramsetti, S. (2016, March). Patient center–A mobile based patient engagement solution. In *Qatar Foundation Annual Research Conference Proceedings 2016*(1), (p. ICTPP1835). Hamad bin Khalifa University Press (HBKU Press).

4 The Process Side of Digital Health

Objectives

At the conclusion of this chapter, it should be evident:

a) What are the key steps or sub-processes in healthcare delivery.
b) Why data is so essential to support superior healthcare decision making.
c) What is OODA Loop and why OODA thinking is so important in healthcare delivery.
d) What is the relevance of TQM and Six Sigma in ensuring optimal healthcare processes.

Introduction

Healthcare operations are conducted in dynamic and complex environments (von Lubitz and Wickramasinghe, 2006). Moreover, errors, delays, inefficiencies and ineffective operations can lead to negative clinical outcomes and even patient death. Healthcare operations actually consist of various processes which will be presented and discussed in turn in the next section. What is important to note is that no matter which process, key to the success of the process is timely data, pertinent information and germane knowledge to enable superior decision making to ensue.

Prehabilitation

Prehabilitation, also known as prehab, is a rehabilitation program that healthcare providers recommend to the patient prior to surgery. The preoperative program (or prehab) is thus typically targeted towards enhancing the postoperative recovery of patients and minimising morbidities via improving tolerance towards probable surgical stresses and functional capabilities (Gillis et al., 2014). The goal is to ensure the patient is as healthy for surgery as possible so that he/she can make the best possible recovery, is less likely to develop complications or other problems while in hospital and will equally be less likely to be an unplanned readmission post discharge (ibid.). Hence, prehab also checks on the psychological hindrances, physical fitness, nutrition and lifestyle influences that may hinder the ability of the

DOI: 10.1201/9781003318538-5

individual to heal after surgery (ibid.). Some of the technologies utilised in prehab include Fitbit, accelerometers, heartrate monitors, gyroscopes, monitors and wearable sensors. Nonetheless, these technologies are seldom specifically designed for prehabilitation, which presents an area that needs to be investigated and improved regarding prehab technologies. For instance, Fitbits are typically developed as health devices for consumers for commercial purposes (Zhu et al., 2020).

In essence, prehabilitation is a crucial process to assess in healthcare, especially given in the United States alone, millions of surgeries are carried out annually and the numbers continue to grow (Zhu et al., 2018, 2020). Moreover, surgical procedures are expensive and too often unintended complications can occur which either extend the length of stay of the patient or result in an unplanned readmission (i.e., return to hospital within 30 days (ibid.)). Indeed, prehabilitation has a significant advantage over traditional rehabilitative interventions, which are overtly incapable of fully meeting the extant demands. An ideal prehabilitation program process is yet to be established since there is none that has been defined currently. However, sound prehab programs typically contain several components; the extant programs utilise targeted intervention that entail physical components like maximising exercise frequencies and durations, nutritional components like hindering the intake of calories and psychological components like relaxation exercise education (Barnes et al., 2016; Gillis et al., 2014; Silver & Baima, 2013). Typically, the prehabilitation process has a supervised in-clinic portion and an even lengthier as well as often unsupervised at-home sessions (Bousquet-Dion et al., 2018).

There are some key things to note regarding the prehabilitation process regarding assessing the challenges in it. First, it is rather unrealistic to expect rehabilitation providers to be of the same needs as other providers. Notably, there are some major differences which distinguish prehabilitation from other processes such as rehabilitation and physical therapy. Still, the technologies used in rehabilitation are evidently often the same ones used for the other processes despite the differences. It is a worrying trend since such technologies are rarely specifically designed for prehabilitation. In essence, for a technical device to be effective, it is crucial for early stakeholder involvement and the designing of the tool (Zhu et al., 2020). Following this, prehabilitation stakeholders are out of bounds not to have their needs sufficiently met upon adopting readily designed and customised technologies. Therefore, to assist the designers of these technologies to adequately meet the needs of prehabilitation stakeholders, it is prudent to delve into the care processes, the challenges, the desired devices support and the extant technological tool usages. The major points of focus in this instance will thus be the challenges that prehabilitation health professionals encounter in the process and their perspectives on the current prehabilitation technologies.

According to Zhu et al. (2020), there are four major challenges that healthcare providers face in the prehabilitation process. These challenges include program patient and heterogeneity, analysing patients and designing rehabilitation care, fostering patient adherence and sufficiently informing patients. When it comes to heterogeneity challenges, designing care is fundamental to making safe, effective and practical care plans. However, this is hindered by two kinds of heterogeneity, namely patient heterogeneity and program heterogeneity. Under program hetero-geneity, Intraprogram and interprogram are the two main forms of heterogeneity in rehabilitation processes, technologies and policies. On the other hand, patient intergenicity comprises every patient idiosyncrasy. In addition to this, there are also assessment challenges that face healthcare professionals while designing care. It is essential and quite vital that patients are assessed frequently to determine whether their care plans need amendments or to be wholly changed by the health profes-sional. Thus, health professionals typically depend heavily on two major types of patient assessments, which are progressive assessments and baseline assessments. While baseline assessments depend primarily on clinical observations, extant health records and even dialogue with the patients, progressive assessments entail a series of redundant measures intended to define changes that stem from the patients exercises at home. Unfortunately, at home assessment may not be an option for health practitioners in practice since compliance for such assessments may be low.

When it comes to tailoring and assessments, health professionals rely on a wide range of tools. However, tools precisely designed for prehabilitation are still quite rare. While prehabilitation is a prospective area for effective response to the extent as well as future needs in healthcare, the tools tailored, designed and used for prehabilitation still need to be developed more for that specific purpose. User-centred research pertaining to the needs of prehabilitation professionals and extant anticipations are also nonexistent. Prehabilitation tailored tools need to be designed such that they are flexible and adequately capable of supporting the needs of stakeholders as well as diverse programs.

Pre-Surgery

In the simplest terms, pre-surgery simply means prior to operation. It can involve a checkup that is usually done by the relevant health professional about a month prior to the surgery. At the pre-surgery phase, the patient meets with one of their doctors who can be either their primary care doctor or surgeon. Often, the pre-surgery pro-cess is impacted by problems which result in lengthy delays and sometimes even cancellations. Therefore, several health professionals turn to virtual healthcare technologies to solve such problems following the increasing evidence base of their usefulness in this. During the COVID-19 pandemic virtual care became the dominant mode for of pre-surgery.

Currently, the two most significant technologies that health professionals use in pre-surgery are mHealth and e-forms. However, there are other technologies such as remote patient monitoring and web-based interventions. Virtual reality is also a technological option in pre-surgery, but it is seen more as an emerging intervention that has yet to prove the test of time. From this, there is a significant indication that one other major challenge in the use of pre-surgery technologies is digital illiteracy.

Lengthy waiting times and last-minute cancellations are two key issues that frequently characterise the pre-surgery process (Sharif et al., 2020). The reasons behind these cancellations tend to be multifold; but, many of these reasons have been linked to insufficient preparation around the pre-surgery process due to poor or insufficient data and/or information (Torjesen, 2018). This problem not only leads to inefficiencies in the process but may also cause detrimental financial impacts. For instance, the NHS estimates losses of about 400 million euros every year in operating times because of this (Gillies, Wijeysundera & Harrison, 2018). Conversely, it also estimated that the integration of technological solutions can save an estimated €2.9 billion, thereby providing a means to manage the cost burden effectively and enable prudent resource allocation in the healthcare system (Sharif et al., 2020).

The key technologies used in this regard are defined by researchers as information technology capable of delivering remote interactions between healthcare professionals (HCPs) and/or patients (ibid.). Moreover, these technologies can play a crucial role in facilitating patient care in this context. However, there are some limitations in practice when it comes to these technologies that need to be noted. Specifically, emphasis is typically placed on the merits of these technologies and not their limitations (ibid.). Critical considerations all revolve around the digital literacy of the patient, their access to technology and their level of comfort to use such technology as well as the resistance to change from health practitioners in adopting these new technologies into practice (ibid.). Therefore, it is crucial to delve into the perspective of every stakeholder to deliver change more effectively.

For lower risk patients who often have no need to come in, teleconsultations tend to be an effective means for pre-assessment/ pre-surgery clinic (ibid.). Nurses can evaluate these patients over the phone while physiotherapy for teleconsultation preassessment can give continuous support for patients both within the pre-surgery and post-surgery processes (ibid.). The major benefits include minimising patient travel time which is particularly helpful for elderly patients in the pre-surgery process, increasing efficiency and especially during COVID-19 decreasing risks to infections pre-surgery (ibid.). However, teleconsultation may be challenging and even impossible when there are challenges with hearing and understanding information conveyed (ibid.).

When it comes to web-based written information, website technologies can be used by HCPs to relay information to patients like the relevant exercises that the patients need to adhere to prior to having their surgery, as well as what to expect (ibid.). It is thus a useful pre-surgery technology that is helpful in preparing individuals with as much information as they need before the surgery. However, while this technology may be helpful, there is still a concern regarding digital literacy and if the patients will be able to effectively access the information conveyed via this technology (ibid.).

E-forms are another type of pre-surgery technology (ibid.). This technology solution revolves around an electronic self-assessment questionnaire through which patients can submit information virtually. E-forms thus save both the patients and the HCPs time during pre-surgery and ensure more effective and efficient transfer of pertinent information during this process. However, it is important to recognise that patients may find it difficult to fill in the electronic questionnaires resulting in missing information or they may also misunderstand the question within the forms even when well presented; hence it is necessary to check the accuracy of the data and information gathered (ibid.).

mHealth is also becoming a useful technology solution in the pre-surgery process and can be utilised by HCPs to gain pertinent information (Sharif et al., 2018). The technologies that make up mHealth (smartphones, tablets, platforms) can be used to answer frequently asked questions about the patient history, demographics and current health status as well as educate/inform the patient about what to expect in the forthcoming surgery (ibid.); so, he/she can be better prepared and ready. Therefore, the anxiety that often surrounds surgeries can be significantly minimised. mHealth thus can assist in making the subsequent process more transparent regarding what the pre-surgery preparation time ought to be, when the patient should come in, the period they should be starved for and any other relevant information. By doing so, it is possible to make the pre-surgery process more efficient, effective and efficacious. The primary challenges surrounding mHealth include that it requires a significant level of technological literacy as well as accessibility to the technology solutions; and thus is not suitable for all patients.

Homecare for Chronic Patients

Today, especially given the pressures of value-based care, there is a desire to minimise the amount of time a patient needs to spend in the healthcare facility (Wickramasinghe et al., 2021). This in turn has led to an increasing attention on home care around the world. One area in particular is around homecare for chronic condition management. Essentially, homecare for chronic patients is any professional support service for an individual to live safely within their homes and continue their normal daily activities (ibid.). Digital technology solutions, ranging from wearable such as Fitbit, temperature sensors and even video visits can be particularly beneficial when it comes to bringing care home for chronically ill patients (ibid.). However, homecare is only at its infancy in this regard and there is plenty of opportunity to incorporate more innovative infrastructure and focus investments towards this area to make it more effective. The extant evidence from studies indicates the potential of technological innovation in positively impacting the efficiency and quality of care when it comes to homecare in the health system and many countries, especially those with more public-based funding systems are advocating homecare especially for chronic condition patients (Health Quality Ontario, 2013).

Telehomecare is among the most innovative technologies that are currently used to monitor patients with chronic conditions remotely and educate them on the effective management of their condition. The technology has been cited to minimise the hospitalisation of patients suffering from such chronic conditions by up to 70% while keeping these patients within the haven of their homes (Health Quality Ontario, 2013). A range of technology make up the support needs of telehomecare. Telemonitoring is among these solutions. This solution is an innovative patient management technique to remotely monitor patients and measuring a variety of data through technology including behavioural, and biological data are then sent to healthcare professionals for the purposes of evaluating and monitoring the condition of the patient (Coye, Haselkorn & DeMello, 2009).

Telemedicine technologies are yet another important aspect of effective homecare for patients with chronic conditions (ibid.). These technologies help facilitate and support medication adherence systems that organise, evaluate and monitor the needs as well as the medication intake of patients with chronic illness; that is, they go beyond basic monitoring. A key challenge however is concerned with digital literacy with respect to correctly using these telemedicine technologies (ibid.).

Sensor technologies are also gaining traction and being used by HCPs for a more efficient delivery of homecare for chronic patients (Health Quality Ontario, 2013). These range from wearable devices like bracelets to motion sensors that can be fitted within the home. The networked system of sensors monitors the patients' activities and can alert caregivers in case any problem arises. However, integrating some of these sensor technologies may be costly and cumbersome. The development of innovative infrastructure while making these technologies more cost-effective may be a viable solution is a critical enabler.

Last, communication technologies are also among the most crucial when it comes to home care for patients with chronic conditions (ibid.). These can include common devices that are often available within homes like computers with software such as Skype or Zoom and senior-friendly smartphones for the elderly. In addition to this, communication technologies also help improve the condition of the patient under homecare by allowing them to network and keep in touch with friends, family and the world in general. This thus serves to positively improve the health condition of the patient by preventing social isolation, which is often linked to detrimental health effects (Calton, Abedini & Fratkin, 2020). Once again, however, these technologies require a significant amount of digital literacy.

The Intake and Registration Healthcare Process

The intake and registration process occurs during patient admission into a healthcare facility. This is the initial step in the healthcare process and is very important since it is at this stage that medical practitioners obtain key patient details (O'Brien et al., 2014). The intake and registration healthcare process thus has far-reaching implications for a medical facility's operational and clinical aspects and its financial success. The intake and registration process is typically lengthy and involves much paperwork (ibid.). The process is generally dependent on the management of different healthcare aspects. The intensity of the activities during this process depends on whether the patient is a new or a repeat visitor (ibid.).

Several activities occur during the intake and registration healthcare process (ibid.): the intake and registration procedure begins when a patient is scheduled for an appointment at a medical facility. The receptionist relays relevant information to the patient on the requirements needed for the scheduling process and what to expect during the appointment. Scheduling an appointment can be done online, through a phone call, or the patient can physically visit the medical facility. First-time patients need to fill in much information including contact details, medical history, social history, insurance coverage information and sign consent forms before meeting the doctor (ibid.). On the other hand, repeat patients typically update the already collected data and information before consenting.

Today, around the world electronic health records are becoming the major technology utilised in the intake and registration process. Electronic health records have assisted in reducing the amount of paperwork within healthcare facilities as information that could be previously documented is conveniently stored in digital devices (Da Costa et al., 2018). The intake process also uses automated email, text and phone communication technology for scheduling appointments. This is a quick and convenient method for relaying communication to patients and has the potential to save time and money. Generally, the intake process utilises the patient online portal technology to store, gather and access the patient's data (ibid.). This in turn makes it easier for patients to schedule appointments and review and verify their details.

Despite the technologies employed during the intake and registration process to ensure efficiency, several issues and challenges are still experienced mainly connected to incorrect, missing or contradictory data and/or information (ibid.). Thus it behooves healthcare facilities to introduce patient intake software, which may enable the patient to fully complete the intake and registration process before physically appearing for an appointment to reduce the time wastage that results from the lengthy paperwork in hospitals as well as ensuring data security and privacy (ibid.).

Preoperative Healthcare Process

Preoperative patient care refers to the medical care offered to patients before the onset of a surgical operation. Preoperative care aims to ensure the success of any given surgery on a patient and naturally is heavily dependent on the specific procedure the patients has been scheduled to receive (Engelman et al., 2019). Several activities take place during the preoperative healthcare procedure. Preoperative care begins when the patient consents to have surgery.

Physiological and psychological problems are first assessed to reduce the risks of the surgery. The physiological assessment is done by obtaining the patient's medical health history. A patient's physical examination is performed to note down the vital signs and databases that would be used for future comparisons (Malley & Young, 2017). Medical practitioners also consider the gerontology characteristics of a patient during the preoperative care procedure (ibid.). This involves monitoring older patients undergoing surgical procedures to deduce clues of underlying problems that might minimise their chances of survival. The gerontology analysis can be used in the decision making process. Adrenaline levels are assessed, and the patient's physical mobility is monitored. The preoperative procedure also involves nursing diagnosis, which assists in deducing patient anxiety that might have resulted from previous surgical experiences, and insufficient knowledge of the surgical procedure (Malley & Young, 2017). The physical findings of the tests carried out are noted to describe the overall health of the patient. The test determines whether the patient is suitable for the surgery, and the doctors offer further suggestions. Psychological evaluation is done on the patient, and their fears of the unknown such as death are addressed and reassured to increase their chances of survival (ibid.). The patient is taken through physical, psychological and emotional activities so as to maximise the best clinical outcome ensuing.

Several technologies are used during the preoperative phase. Computerised Practitioner Order Entry (CPOE) is one of the digital technologies employed preoperative phase. CPOE supports formulary compliance to improve patient diagnosis decision making by reducing test redundancy and unnecessary duplication (Mihalj et al., 2020). Doctors may also use Clinical Decision Support in Technology by combining it with the CPOE technological system to make complex decisions during the preoperative process (ibid.). Whenever there is a prescription error, for example, the system raises an alert and generates dosage adjustments (ibid.).

Emergency Operations Healthcare Process

An emergency in healthcare involves a serious unexpected situation that arises, is unplanned and unexpected and usually requires immediate attention; otherwise, the patient's health may drastically deteriorate, leading to loss of life. Emergencies require doctors and nurses to think and act quickly to save patients' lives and thus clinicians are generally under pressure. Emergency operations involve a series of procedures (Trujillo, 2020):

The first stage in an emergency operation situation is known as triage. The severity of a patient's condition is determined during the triage stage. Immediate treatment is offered to patients who have encountered severe emergencies. A triage registered nurse evaluates the patient to determine their emergency level before medical treatment is administered. In some unique instances, the triage nurse may begin the medical diagnostic tests to reduce the time spent on treatment (ibid.).

The second stage involves registering the patient to the medical facility, where the ED staff gather more information concerning the patient. Treatment is then offered to the patient depending on their emergency levels: rustication, emergency, urgent, semi-urgent, and non-urgent. Re-evaluation is done once treatment is administered to give the doctors insight into the type of treatment that could be further issued. The patient can then be discharged once they progress or improve their health (ibid.). Other emergencies may involve disease outbreaks that might threaten the lives of individuals. Medical staff members can therefore issue a warning and derive health precautions during such situations.

Various technology solutions are employed during emergency operations. Distributed communication platforms may enable healthcare providers to offer emergency services in different locations. This process is made possible by using streamlined telehealth services. Satellites are used to identify areas with disastrous conditions to send medical providers to issue emergency services. Chatbot technology is also now being used during emergency health conditions to reduce the emergency costs incurred when setting up emergency rooms. Advancements in emergency operation technologies are often focusing on incorporating predictive analytics, artificial intelligence and machine learning to enable and support rapid extraction of critical insights and identify more expeditiously the best course of action (ibid.).

Rehabilitation Healthcare Process

The interventions set to optimise the normal body functioning of human beings and minimise the disabilities of individuals with health conditions so as to enable them to interact freely in their environment are known as rehabilitation (Stucki et al., 2018). The rehabilitation process assists in slowing down the disabling effects of chronic health conditions by providing these individuals with self-management techniques and relevant products to reduce their pain and manage complications. The rehabilitation procedures are normally conducted on patients with chronic illnesses such as cancer, diabetes and cardiovascular diseases as well as patients with physical injuries or after surgery (ibid.). Four stages are involved in rehabilitation (ibid.).

The recovery stage is the initial stage of the rehabilitation process. This stage is essential in the rehabilitation process as it basically involves recuperation and permitting the body to initiate the healing process. The recovery stage requires the patient to rest and take medication that reduces inflammation and pain (ibid.). The second stage that follows is known as the repair stage. Movement and mobility are recovered during this stage by gently easing the back to pre-injury levels. Carrying out gentle motion activities is crucial to prevent further or aggravate existing injuries. After the range of motion restoration, the next step of the rehabilitation process is known as the strength stage, where the body's strength begins to be restored. Resting is discouraged at the third stage to avoid weakness and loss of endurance. The major goal of the strength stage is to increase muscular strength and endurance and restore the body's muscles to the pre-injury level. The final stage is the functional stage, where the activities aim to restore function. The patient is exposed to a higher level of capabilities to minimise the risks of re-injury (Stucki et al., 2018). Effective methods should therefore be employed during this process to maintain the patient's physical health.

There are certain technologies that can be employed during the rehabilitation process. A therapy pool is used during the procedure for resistance control and other physical activities (Ordoñez, Gago & Girard, 2016). Sensor technologies assist patients in the relaxation processes by reducing their stress and helping them sleep better. Gravity elimination arm devices, on the other hand, are used to assist in the recovery of upper extremity movements. The patient can move their arms in an upright position facilitating flexibility (ibid.). It is important to note that the rehabilitation process can occur in the healthcare facility, a separate rehab facility or in the patient's home.

Hospital Discharge Process

The hospital discharge procedure is the final stage of the health care process. The hospital discharge is when the patient is finally permitted to leave the healthcare facility premises due to improved or full recovery. The patient can, therefore, only be released when they no longer receive inpatient care services. Hospital discharge can also be authorised when a patient needs to be transferred to a different healthcare facility to acquire treatment (Mitchell et al., 2016). This is done when the host facility cannot offer certain services to the patient due to a lack of certain hospital equipment needed to treat a particular health condition. The patient is normally transferred to a facility with better chances and capability to facilitate treatment. The discharge process is coordinated by a discharge planner who must communicate information about the care the patient would be required to implement after the discharge (ibid.).

The first stage in the discharge process involves explaining the paperwork to the patients in depth. The medical practitioners must read through the paperwork with their patients explaining in depth every detail that the patient may not comprehend. The doctors must write the instruction in the discharge paper in patient-friendly language to enable them to comprehend the information even in the absence of medical practitioners. After the review process has been done, the doctors may request the patients to repeat the discharge instructions, including why they were hospitalised. They should be able to narrate the context of the instructions, including their medication to be followed and their care to ensure they have mastered the instructions. The doctors and nurses review the medication prescribed to the patient before they leave to avoid hospital readmissions. Any medication added to improve the patient's health of the patient and the changes made to their prescriptions are discussed before the patient is permitted to leave the facility. The patient is advised to inquire about any unfamiliar medication from the pharmacist for clarification purposes. After the medication process has been addressed, the patient is advised to ask patients regarding their health to the doctors and nurses who handle those (ibid.). This prevents the patient from making any assumptions regarding their health. The patients are permitted to ask open-ended questions to put them at ease, allowing them to share their thoughts with the medical practitioners. The discharge process requires patients to make follow-up activities to confirm the status and progress of their health to minimise the chances of negative surprises. The follow-up activities are conducted with the primary care providers and healthcare specialists. Home care services are also offered as part of the follow-up to help improve the patient's health. Doctors must stress the importance of follow-up activities to enable their patients to participate actively in the process (ibid.).

The discharge process is similarly associated with various unique technologies. Electronic Health Records (EHRs) systems are one of the major technologies used during the discharge process. Patient-centric health data is aggregated by EHR (Gunter et al., 2016). The EHR enables easy storage of patient data from admission to discharge, which the doctors can easily retrieve to issue aftercare services. The analytics from the EHR can be used to establish a preliminary checklist of the equipment needed by the patient. Nurses are provided with mobile technologies to record and transmit the patient's vital signs and digitally send the information to the patients. Mobile technologies are used in scheduling patient appointments for follow-up activities through patient online portals (ibid.).

Discussion

The preceding has served to present some of the key processes and key steps in healthcare delivery. What is central to all these processes or steps is the need to provide the decision maker, typically the clinician with relevant data, pertinent information and germane knowledge so he/she can make an informed and superior decision. These decisions typically have far-reaching impacts on clinical outcomes, patient satisfaction and financial implications. One way to understand this is to take a process-centric approach to knowledge creation (Wickramasinghe and Schaffer, 2010). Such an approach serves to combine critical people-centric and technology-centric perspectives and at the same time emphasises the dynamic and ongoing nature of the process (ibid.). This is particularly relevant for healthcare contexts as a healthcare intervention should not be looked at just one point in time but the progression of the patient along their care recovery journey (Wickramasinghe et al., 2021). This process-centric perspective is grounded in the pioneering work of Boyd and his OODA Loop; a conceptual framework that maps critical process required to support rapid decision making and extraction of essential and germane knowledge while filtering out extraneous noise (von Lubitz and Wickramasinghe, 2006; Wickramasinghe and Schaffer, 2010; Wickramasinghe et al., 2021).

Succinctly stated, the OODA Loop is based on a cycle of four interrelated stages essential to support critical analysis and rapid decision making that revolve in both time and space (ibid.): Observation followed by Orientation, then by Decision, and finally Action (OODA). At the Observation and Orientation stages, implicit and explicit inputs are gathered or extracted from the environment (Observation) and converted into coherent information (Orientation). The latter determines the sequential determination (knowledge generation) and Action (practical implementation of knowledge) steps. The outcome of the Action stage then affects, in turn, the character of the starting point (Observation) of the next revolution in the forward progression of the rolling loop. The OODA Loop supports OODA thinking (ibid.), which is essential in complex and dynamic environments such as healthcare operations. Specifically, OODA thinking enables the clinical decision maker to rapidly understand the specific context, extract the relevant data, pertinent information and germane knowledge in order to decide the best course of action no matter which step or process; that is, whether prehabilitation, pre-surgery, pre-operative, home care, discharge or most especially emergency operations.

In addition to OODA Loop and OODA thinking which emerge from a process-centric perspective of knowledge management; healthcare processes can also be optimised and their quality enhanced by incorporating essential elements from TQM (total quality management) and Six Sigma principles. TQM and Six Sigma developed from manufacturing and automotive giants such as Toyota have used these to revolutionise auto manufacturing processes. Recognising healthcare processes are different especially as they focus on patients or individuals there are still important aspects from TQM and Six Sigma that are relevant for healthcare process optimisation. To understand TQM and Six Sigma one first needs to appreciate the essence of quality of care.

Quality of care is about meeting the physical, psychological and social expectations of the patients who enter the healthcare sector. According to the American Institute of Medicine (IOM), quality of care is "the degree to which health services for individuals and populations increase the likelihood of desired health outcome consistent with current professional knowledge" (Kumpersmith, 2003). In 1910, the American surgeon Ernest Codman developed the concept of the "end result idea" in hospitals (NCBI, 2005). The concept requires the following: every hospital should follow every patient it treats long enough to determine whether the treatment has been successful, and then to inquire "if not, why not" with a view to preventing similar failure in the future (NCBI, 2005). The Advisory Commission on Consumer Protection and Quality in the Health Care Industry notes the following quality problems in hospitals (Advisory_Commission, 1998):

1. Avoidable error: the report points out that too many Americans are injured and died prematurely as a result of avoidable errors. The report claims that "from 1983 to 1993 alone, deaths due to medical errors rose more than twofold, with 7,391 deaths attributed to medication errors in 1993 alone".
2. Underutilisation of services: the report claims that millions of people do not receive necessary care. It estimated that about 18,000 people die each year from heart attacks because they did not receive effective interventions.
3. Overuse of services: The claim was that millions of Americans receive health care services that are unnecessary.
4. Variation in services: There is a continuing pattern of variation in health care services, including regional variations and small-area variations.

To summarise the Six Quality Aims for the 21st Century Health Care System proposed by IOM (2001) are presented in the table below (Table 4.1):

Six Sigma is a set of techniques and tools for process improvement (Kumar, 2022). It involves six key steps: define (understand the problem), measure (ensure there are metrics for evaluating success), analyse (assess all the possible options), improve (understand how to enhance/develop process optimisation) and control (ensure optimised processes are always enacted) (ibid.). Incorporating this approach into healthcare delivery means that for each of the processes or steps in the afore-mentioned (namely, prehabilitation, pre-surgery, pre-operation, emergency, home care, rehabilitation and/or discharge) it is useful to define what is involved in each step and ensure optimising strategies are in place so that these processes are as robust as possible so that high-quality outcome ensues. Technology is a key enabler for this.

TQM is a management framework that requires organisations to focus on continuous improvement, or kaizen (Pratt, 2022). Specifically, it focuses on process

Table 4.1 Six Quality Aims

• Safe—avoiding injuries to patients from the care that is intended to help them.
• Effective—providing services based on scientific knowledge to all who could benefit and refraining from providing services to those not likely to benefit (avoiding underuse and overuse, respectively).
• Patient-centered—providing care that is respectful of and responsive to individual patient preferences, needs, and values and ensuring that patient values guide all clinical decisions.
• Timely—reducing waits and sometimes harmful delays for both those who receive and those who give care.
• Efficient—avoiding waste, including waste of equipment, supplies, ideas, and energy.
• Equitable—providing care that does not vary in quality because of personal characteristics such as gender, ethnicity, geographic location, and socioeconomic status.

Source: IOM, 2001, pp. 5–6.

improvements over the long term, rather than simply emphasising short-term financial gains (ibid.). Applying this concept into healthcare involves focusing on Demings 14 points (ibid.):

1. Create a constant purpose towards improvement.
2. Adopt the new philosophy.
3. Stop depending on inspections.
4. Use a single supplier for any one item.
5. Improve constantly and forever.
6. Use training on the job.
7. Implement leadership.
8. Emphasise the importance of participative management and transformational leadership.
9. Eliminate fear.
10. Let everyone know that the goal is to achieve high quality by doing more things right – and that you're not interested in blaming people when mistakes happen.
11. Break down barriers between departments.
12. Get rid of unclear slogans.
13. Eliminate management by objectives.
12. Remove barriers to pride of workmanship.
13. Implement education and self-improvement.
14. Make "transformation" everyone's job.

In this way, it is possible over time to eliminate errors and develop an enabling culture to support best practice (ibid.).

Clearly, the incorporation of Six Sigma and TQM can serve together with OODA thinking to ensure healthcare processes are as effective, efficient and efficacious as possible and thereby also subscribe to a value-based healthcare paradigm.

Conclusions

This chapter has served to introduce key steps or processes in healthcare operations from prehabilitation to pre-surgery, preoperative home care, registration and, in turn, emergency operations, rehabilitation and discharge. These are not an exhaustive list of all the healthcare processes but serve rather to highlight key processes. In addition, it was highlighted how essential data, information and knowledge are to ensure high-quality, effective, efficient and efficacious processes ensue. Finally techniques including OODA thinking, TQM and Six Sigma were presented to provide strategies for ensuring best practice and superior decision making occur. Ultimately healthcare process impact the quality and quantity of one's life so it is vital these processes are as effective, efficient and efficacious as possible. Digital health can play a significant role in this regard as later chapters will illustrate more fully.

Summary

After reading this chapter you should be able to be able to state:

a) What are the key steps or processes in healthcare delivery.
   Key steps and processes in healthcare include: prehabilitation, pre-surgery, preoperative home care, registration and, in turn, emergency operations, rehabilitation and discharge.
b) Why data is so essential to support superior healthcare decision making.
   All the key processes and steps in healthcare require critical decision making to take place. This decision making has far-reaching impacts on clinical outcomes, patient satisfaction and financial implications. In order to make informed and optimal decisions the relevant data, pertinent information and germane knowledge is required.
c) What is OODA Loop and why OODA thinking is so important in healthcare delivery.
   The OODA Loop and OODA thinking are essential to ensure that at all times the decision maker (clinician) has understood the specific context, has extracted the relevant data, pertinent information and germane knowledge as quickly and effectively as possible and thus is best placed to make key decisions.
d) What is the relevance of TQM and Six Sigma in ensuring optimal healthcare processes.
   TQM and Six Sigma enable health care processes to be optimised and ensure they reflect the highest levels of quality at all times. Quality optimisation is vital in healthcare as it can ultimately mean the difference between life and death.

References

The Advisory Commission on Consumer Protection and Quality in the Heath Care Industry. (1998). Retrieved from https://govinfo.library.unt.edu/hcquality/final/index.htm

Barnes, M., Plaisance, E., Hanks, L., & Casazza, K. (2016). Pre-habilitation-promoting exercise in adolescent and young adult cancer survivors for improving lifelong health—a narrative review. *Cancer Research Frontiers, 2*(1), 22–32.

Bousquet-Dion, G., Awasthi, R., Loiselle, S. È., Minnella, E. M., Agnihotram, R. V., Bergdahl, A., ... & Scheede-Bergdahl, C. (2018). Evaluation of supervised multi-modal prehabilitation programme in cancer patients undergoing colorectal resection: a randomized control trial. *Acta Oncologica, 57*(6), 849–859.

Calton, B., Abedini, N., & Fratkin, M. (2020). Telemedicine in the time of coronavirus. *Journal of Pain and Symptom Management, 60*(1), e12–e14.

Coye, M. J., Haselkorn, A., & DeMello, S. (2009). Remote patient management: technology-enabled innovation and evolving business models for chronic disease care. *Health Affairs, 28*(1), 126–135.

Da Costa, C. A., Pasluosta, C. F., Eskofier, B., Da Silva, D. B., & da Rosa Righi, R. (2018). Internet of health things: toward intelligent vital signs monitoring in hospital wards. *Artificial Intelligence in Medicine, 89*, 61–69.

Dimitrov, D. V. (2016). Medical internet of things and big data in healthcare. *Healthcare Informatics Research, 22*(3), 156–163. Retrieved from https://synapse.koreamed.org/artic les/1075790.

Engelman, D. T., Ali, W. B., Williams, J. B., Perrault, L. P., Reddy, V. S., Arora, R. C., ... & Boyle, E. M. (2019). Guidelines for perioperative care in cardiac surgery: enhanced recovery after surgery society recommendations. *JAMA Surgery, 154*(8), 755–766.

Gillies, M. A., Wijeysundera, D. N., & Harrison, E. M. (2018). Counting the cost of can-celled surgery: a system wide approach is needed. *British Journal of Anaesthesia, 121*(4), 691–694.

Gillis, C., Li, C., Lee, L., Awasthi, R., Augustin, B., Gamsa, A., ... & Carli, F. (2014). Prehabilitation versus rehabilitation: a randomized control trial in patients undergoing colorectal resection for cancer. *Anesthesiology, 121*(5), 937–947.

Gunter, R. L., Chouinard, S., Fernandes-Taylor, S., Wiseman, J. T., Clarkson, S., Bennett, K., ... & Kent, K. C. (2016). Current use of telemedicine for post-discharge surgical care: a systematic review. *Journal of the American College of Surgeons, 222*(5), 915. doi: 10.1016/j.jamcollsurg.2016.01.062.

Health Quality Ontario. (2013). In-home care for optimizing chronic disease management in the community: an evidence-based analysis. *Ontario Health Technology Assessment Series, 13*(5), 1.

Institute of Management (IOM). (2001). Retrieved from: www.ahrq.gov/talkingquality/ measures/six-domains.html

Kumar, P. (2022). What is six sigma. Retrieved from www.simplilearn.com/what-is-six-sigma-a-complete-overview-article#:~:text=Six%20Sigma%20is%20a%20proc ess,per%20million%20units%20or%20events.

Kumpersmith, J. (2003). *Quality of care in teaching hospitals: Executive summary.* Association of American Medical Colleges.

Malley, A. M., & Young, G. J. (2017). A qualitative study of patient and provider experiences during preoperative care transitions. *Journal of Clinical Nursing, 26*(13–14), 2016–2024. https://doi.org/10.1111/jocn.13610.

Mihalj, M., Carrel, T., Gregoric, I. D., Andereggen, L., Zinn, P. O., Doll, D., ... & Luedi, M. M. (2020). Telemedicine for preoperative assessment during a COVID-19 pandemic: Recommendations for clinical care. *Best Practice & Research Clinical Anaesthesiology, 34*(2), 345–351.

Mitchell, S. E., Martin, J., Holmes, S., van Deusen Lukas, C., Cancino, R., Paasche-Orlow, M., ... & Jack, B. (2016). How hospitals re-engineer their discharge processes to reduce readmissions. *Journal for Healthcare Quality: Official National Association for Healthcare Quality Publication, 38*(2), 116. doi: 10.1097/JHQ.0000000000000005.

NCBI. (2005). Ernest Codman's contribution to quality assessment and beyond.

O'Brien, A., Giles, M., Dempsey, S., Lynne, S., McGregor, M. E., Kable, A., ... & Parker, V. (2014). Evaluating the preceptor role for pre-registration nursing and midwifery student clinical education. *Nurse Education Today, 34*(1), 19–24.

Ordoñez, J., Gago, E. J., & Girard, A. (2016). Processes and technologies for the recycling and recovery of spent lithium-ion batteries. *Renewable and Sustainable Energy Reviews, 60*, 195–205. https://doi.org/10.1016/j.rser.2015.12.363.

Pratt, K. (2022). Total Quality Management (TQM). Retrieved from www.techtarget.com/searchcio/definition/Total-Quality-Management#:~:text=Total%20Quality%20Management%20(TQM)%20is,%2C%20thus%2C%20delivering%20customer%20satisfaction.

Sharif, F., Rahman, A., Tonner, E., Ahmed, H., Haq, I., Abbass, R., ... & Sbai, M. (2018). Can technology optimise the pre-operative pathway for elective hip and knee replacement surgery: a qualitative study. *Perioperative Medicine, 9*(1), 1–15.

Silver, J. K., & Baima, J. (2013). Cancer prehabilitation: an opportunity to decrease treatment-related morbidity, increase cancer treatment options, and improve physical and psychological health outcomes. *American Journal of Physical Medicine & Rehabilitation, 92*(8), 715–727.

Stucki, G., Bickenbach, J., Gutenbrunner, C., & Melvin, J. L. (2018). Rehabilitation: The health strategy of the 21st century.

Torjesen, I. (2018). One in seven operations cancelled on day of surgery, study finds.

Trujillo, A. (2020). Response to Wen and Li, anesthesia procedure of emergency operation for patients with suspected or confirmed COVID-19. *Surgical Infections, 21*(4), 398–398. DOI: 10.1089/sur. 2020.040.

von Lubitz, D., and Wickramasinghe, N. (2006). Healthcare and technology: the doctrine of networkcentric healthcare. *International Journal of Electronic Healthcare, 2*(4), 322–344.

Wickramasinghe, N., Haddad, P., Smart, P. J., O'Connor, L., Schaffer, L. J. (2017, June). Assessing the implications of pervasive solutions to assist risk prevention: the case of home health monitoring. Epworth HealthCare Research Week.

Wickramasinghe, N., King, D., Piuzzi, N., Welsh, J., and Schaffer, J. L. (2021). Managing the knee arthroplasty episode of care through an integrated knowledge network. In *19th International Conference e-Society,* Mar 3–5, 2021 (virtual).

Wickramasinghe, N., and Schaffer, J. (2010). Realizing value driven patient centric healthcare through technology. IBM Center for The Business of Government.

Zhu, H., Moffa, Z. J., Gui, X., & Carroll, J. M. (2020, April). Prehabilitation: care challenges and technological opportunities. In *Proceedings of the 2020 CHI Conference on Human Factors in Computing Systems* (pp. 1–13).

Zhu, H., Moffa, Z., Wang, X., Abdullah, S., Julaiti, J., & Carroll, J. (2018, May). Understanding challenges in prehabilitation for patients with multiple chronic conditions. In *Proceedings of the 12th EAI International Conference on Pervasive Computing Technologies for Healthcare* (pp. 138–147).

Section II

Technology Considerations

In this section the key areas of technology are unpacked and more carefully and critically discussed with particular care to identify critical success factors necessary for any minimally viable digital health solution. The section consists of four chapters as follows:

Chapter 5: IoT, Analytics, ML and AI

This chapter will highlight key emerging trends in IoT, Analytics, AI and ML. It will also touch on important developments in robotics and digital twins. Taken together, these technological solutions enable more precision and personalisation in the delivery of healthcare care as well as enable better wellness and prevention management to ensue.

Chapter 6: APPs, Platforms, Mobile Solutions and Telehealth

COVID-19 has served to underscore the importance of telehealth and mobile digital health solutions to support and facilitate anywhere anytime care. However, this is only one aspect of the role for apps, platforms, mobile solutions and telehealth. This chapter will show how these types of technologies can enable superior care delivery in a variety of contexts and what essential considerations are necessary to ensure it is possible to realise the full potential of such solutions.

Chapter 7: AR/VR/MR and 3D Printing

Often less well known and definitely still underutilised are the benefits of augmented reality, virtual reality or mixed reality as well as 3D printing in healthcare. This chapter will explore the potential of these solutions as well as explore opportunities to apply these solutions to key areas such as Dementia, pain management and training for AR/VR and/or MR as well as within orthopaedics and training for 3D printing. In addition, new domains such as digital anatomy will be presented as opportunities for leveraging the benefits and strengths of these technologies.

DOI: 10.1201/9781003318538-6

Chapter 8: Exploring the Potential of ChatGPT, Responsible AI, Explainable AI and Generative AI

Healthcare delivery relies on data to make better decisions. Today, in healthcare as in other contexts, we are drowning in data and it is often difficult to separate critical, relevant data, pertinent information and germane knowledge from noise. Yet this is essential to make timely, prudent and effective healthcare decisions. This chapter will thus outline how AI has advanced to address this challenge. In particular it will highlight the strengths and weaknesses of key advances such as generative AI, explainable AI and emphasise the need for responsible AI.

5   IoT, Analytics, ML and AI

Objectives

At the conclusion of this chapter, it should be evident:

a) Why and how IoT is changing healthcare delivery and monitoring.
b) What are some of the key techniques within ML.
c) What are the strengths and weaknesses of AI.
d) Why can digital twins support a 3P care paradigm and why is this important.

Introduction

With new inventions and innovations in computer technologies and its related fields, all industries have dramatically changed and benefited from them. The innovations in medicine and surgery have helped to prevent and cure diseases that were thought uncurable and non-treatable. Especially with new emerging technologies in the field of communication and electronics, our ways of daily life have taken a new turn, for example, measuring and quantifying active lifestyle (exercises), continuous monitoring of vital signs (blood pressure, heartbeat, body temperature), achieving healthy life and living longer than our ancestors. The sophisticated and complex computer technologies have evolved into near-human intelligence termed as AI. Artificial intelligence has enabled the development of robots like Sophia, which can perform independently like humans in many activities (Greshko, 2018).

AI can learn from big data sets and quickly predict patterns, abnormalities and outliers, which can be used to perform difficult tasks of predicting issues from normal data. AI has increasingly made its way in many fields, such as autonomous decision making, for example, robotics, self-driving cars, drones; pattern recognition, for example, in healthcare for detecting abnormality in scans (CT scan, Ultrasound results, MRI, etc.) and developing digital twins for deciding best treatment plans, patient informed and preferred treatment pathways.

In this book chapter, past, current and future trends of AI, ML, IoT and analytics in the healthcare sector are presented in turn while in Chapter 8 a more in-depth exploration of advances in AI is discussed.

DOI: 10.1201/9781003318538-7

Artificial Intelligence

Definition: AI is noted as the science and engineering of making intelligent machines, especially intelligent computer programs. It is related to the similar task of using computers to understand human intelligence, but AI does not have to confine itself to methods that are biologically observable (McCarthy, 2004).

In other words, it is the study and implementation of intelligence other than human intelligence, without human supervision or control. With the current advancement in computing powers, artificial intelligence has surpassed human expectations, it can perform better and faster in comparison to earlier artificial intelligence systems. AI is generally based on two elements, one software (algorithms) while the other is interconnected hardware. Software aspects in these solutions can capture, analyse and detect patterns in data and infer for a specific set of actions according to the already given input/learning, while interconnected hardware is responsible for actions (Rong et al., 2020). AI has already made its way in healthcare in automating tasks such as pathological image analysis, natural language processing (NLP) and decision support to help decide optimal or desired pathways for treatment. AI has the capability to assist clinicians in diagnosis, optimising or personalised treatment planning and continuous patient monitoring using sensors.

Machine Learning

The field of AI which deals with smart machines which can think or process as human in learning, conducting data analysis and presenting solutions to problems is termed machine learning (ML) (McCarthy, 2004). Machine learning can perform, analyse, detect patterns or abnormality in patterns, diagnose problems and suggest possible solutions to both structured and unstructured data without any predefined programs. Succinctly, ML learns from previously existing data and builds intelligence on it to conduct complex tasks Ben-Hur et al., 2001; Mahesh, 2020).

There are several types of machine learning methods and algorithms. The three major types include:

1. Support Vectors (SV) (also known as support vector machines or support vector networks) are supervised learning models with associated learning algorithms that analyse data for classification and regression analysis (Ben-Hur et al., 2001).
2. Neural Networks (NN) use interconnected nodes or neurons in a layered structure that resembles the human brain (Mahesh, 2020). Further, there exist three types of neural networks including supervised, unsupervised and reinforced learning (ibid.).
3. NLP uses machine learning to analyse text or speech data (Nadkarni, 2011).

IoT (Internet of Things)

The IoT is made up of sensors, software and other technologies to provide an open and comprehensive network of intelligent objects that have the capacity to auto-organise, share information, data and resources, reacting and acting in face of situations and changes in the environment (Gillis, 2021).

This new emergent field, IoT, is related to objects becoming virtually connected to other objects through common communication medium (wires, wireless or other similar technologies) to acquire, transfer and communicate data within connected objects, trigger actions and complete tasks within prescribed parameters. Thus, revolutionising the overall concept of idle objects to virtually connected and smart objects.

IoT has started connecting our home appliances where they can talk to each other and trigger actions, and making our homes smart homes, for example, it can turn on/off lights, adjust air-conditioner or heating system (on specific temperature settings), play multi-media devices (audio players or TVs), open or close doors on specified triggers, for example, day- or night-time, a specific day such as Monday to Friday, or on the presence of smart tags/face identification. This technology has enormous use in the supply chain, for example, Amazon robots for sorting, packing and preparing package for deliveries. In consumer products, for traceability, accelerating product processing, detecting and reducing unattended and intentional errors, automating processing lines and reducing the overall manual power required for these labour-intensive processes. Improving overall human lifestyle and work safety by reducing repetitive motion injuries and accidents. Similarly, it is making its way into the agricultural field for irrigation, for example, pesticide spraying, harvesting and preparing for next crop.

This smart technology is enabling elderly people to live independently with dignity in their own pre-loved homes. These technologies help people track their vital signs, abnormal behaviour and fall-detection, and issue an alert to the people concerned or connected in the care of such elderly people. Healthcare providers have realised its capability and are using it for remote patient monitoring, teleconsultation, conducting assessment for rehab and performing remote surgeries.

The IoT ecosystem consists of sensors (for data collection) and storage devices, connecting medium for mutual communication, processing units and actuators to perform tasks. There are many types of connecting mediums, for example, wired, wireless, radio frequency, cloud computing (AWS), NFC (Near-field communication), Bluetooth connection, mobile technology (2G, 3G, 4G, 5G, 6G, etc.) and optical fibre.

Why to Use AI/ML in Healthcare

AI can provide tremendous assistance in analysing large amounts of clinical data using algorithms expeditiously. Moreover, it can be trained, learn from feedback, self-correct its algorithm and improve accuracy of results. Currently, AI is assisting diagnostic specialists in reducing judgement errors by taking out fatigue and emotional element from decision making. It can accurately diagnose, predict faster and model outcomes for a specific treatment journey providing improved and informed decision making for doctors, patients and people connected in care. A lot of structured and unstructured data is generated through pathology, imagining and diagnostic devices. With faster and economical computing powers, it is now possible to automate data collection; it can help in the analysis and prediction of hidden patterns within enormous data points. There is a false notion that AI will replace doctors and eventually take over whole health care system. In contrast, like other scientific inventions, AI is here to help doctors in better decision making, taking out human emotional elements, reducing errors due to fatigue or mental state and bringing consistency and accuracy in the treatment plan and patient recovery. Although AI and ML is slowly entering most of the medical field, presently its main focus is on oncology- (cancer), neurology- (brain) and cardiology- (heart) related disease diagnoses, treatment plans, recovery modelling and prediction.

The data generated in healthcare settings is not always collected in one place, especially in developing countries. Due to resources and technology issues, this collected data is not consolidated in one place but rather is left in silos and with different healthcare providers. In Australia, MyHealth records has started compiling data in one place, but still not all the healthcare providers are efficiently uploading data (Wickramasinghe and Zelcer, 2019). It is critical to have all and correct information for deciding correct pathways for treatment and recovery. Thus, IoT devices can help in gathering data without continuous human intervention and monitoring. Using IoT devices and cloud technologies might help in reducing data lost, errors in decision making and eliminating delays due to human factors and non-availability of health records. In many countries, healthcare providers have started using barcoded/smart tags for patient identification, planning and allocation of resources for medical procedures. These IoT devices can also help searching for/tracing medical equipment/devices within different departments.

IoT, AI and ML in Healthcare

IoT devices, AI and ML can work in combination to acquire data and can be used for sorting, analysing and looking for patterns in the data, matching data, patterns and traits of existing specific near-match patients for predicting possible outcomes for specific treatment and side effects of that particular treatment (Jayaraman et al., 2020). From the clinicians' side, these tools give an excellent combination for data mining for prediction, analysis of images and pathology reports for proposing the best possible pathway for treatment. While it will provide patients a platform to make better, informed and personalised treatment decisions, for example, if a patient has to make a choice between hair loss and sexual impotency using two different treatments. This informed and calculated decision making can help a patient choose their treatment course, weighing up factors according to age, lifestyle and family planning. No doubt, AI holds a great potential in healthcare, however, there might be areas which could lead to incorrect diagnosis, for example, if training used a specific set of data from ethnic group and the new patient's ethnicity is not present or is under-represented. Similarly, there could be an error in the coding algorithm which can trigger inaccurate data or breach privacy by leaking sensitive personal information related to health. Therefore, before any such system can be utilised, it will need a careful and thorough testing before adopting it as a tool in healthcare.

Examples – Case Vignettes

Smart Wearable Devices for Aged Care

There is increasing interest in using sensors and connected networks for elderly people. Researchers (Evans et al., 2016) conducted a study on usability and adherence for real-time monitoring for older adults using a remote health system. In this work, they used wireless wristwatch devices to collect temperature and motion-related data; in addition, they also collected weight and blood pressure using Bluetooth connected devices. This work has helped in managing chronic conditions in the elderly population and help them stay longer in their own home.

ACL – Knee Project

Recently researchers at a tertiary not-for-profit healthcare facility in Victoria, Australia, trialled a smartphone-based solution for capturing data for post total knee replacement patients in rehab (Tirosh, Andargoli, & Wickramasinghe, 2022). They used a smartphone's inbuilt sensors and cloud technology to remotely connect with patients for their tele-assessment. The patients used their own mobile phones to install the TelePhysio app. The physicians and patients both were given access codes to make a secure connection. The phone was attached to the patient's belt or kept in their trouser pocket. On successfully connecting with physicians, the patients performed three different exercises (sit-stand, stand on one leg and stand-up, walk straight, return and sit). The data from the inbuilt mobile phone sensors was transferred remotely and analysed by the physician to see if post-surgery patients have gained good mobility through the prescribed set of exercises. This is an innovative use of leveraging the built-in IoT sensors in smartphones.

In the second phase, researchers further improved the app; patients could now capture data on their own without requiring connecting with their physician. This gave patients more autonomy and freedom for data acquisition as well as the possibility to self-manage at their pace. The data is stored on a secure cloud, which can only be accessed by the treating physician or other relevant individuals who have access to the code. This saved patients from regional, remote and low socio-economic backgrounds with respect to resources required for travel, the need for someone to accompany them and reduce waiting periods to see physician. This easy-to-use and readily available solution gives healthcare providers an opportunity to keep track of recovery and yet be patient-centred.

Major Benefits, Barriers and Enablers

With the improvements in computational technology, embedded soft wearable sensors and IoT, ML and AI have reached a new level and helped in almost all fields of life, for example, driverless cars, robotics, drones, automation, face recognition, tracing and managing supply chain, measuring activities for healthy lifestyle, and so on. Similarly, these advances have also made their way into healthcare for data acquisition, as well as data analysing for pattern and trend prediction for treatment pathways. Further, collecting vital signs data using wearable sensors for continuous monitoring and intervention is also becoming more prevalent. Though AI technology has improved significantly to help in the field of diagnosis of abnormality in images from scans, for example, CT scans, ultrasound results and pathological results, there are many fields where it can be applied and implemented, for example, automation of administrative task, helping in virtual drug development and testing, continuous monitoring and predicting for specific diseases such as stroke or heart attack. AI is also helping clinicians to create digital twins for deciding best treatment plans, patient informed and preferred treatment pathways from already existing data bases from previously treated patients.

Though there are clear benefits of the combination AI, ML and IoT, there are concerns from different stakeholders. Typically, clinicians have an inherent lack of trust and concern regarding the long-term validity of AI systems as most of the work done is behind the blackbox or similar techniques which prevent explanation and transparency. The associated cost for infrastructure and implementing these new technologies is another hurdle for adoption. Another major concern is possible/actual bias in training data or errors in the algorithms which can lead to disastrous outcomes for patients while the healthcare provider could face legal and ethical issues. There are also serious concerns among clinicians, as they fear these technologies will challenge their expertise and might hinder their autonomy. Moreover, very valid concerns around the future of their jobs are another issue.

While patients are the main beneficiary of these technologies, they are also not necessarily totally comfortable with them. The main concerns from patients include lack of trust in machines. Further, there are serious concerns regarding data privacy and breaches while using these technologies, as the majority of these technologies will come from a variety of vendors. This complicates the responsibility and legal binding on any party. Therefore, for the overall benefit of humanity, it is crucial that government bodies along with other health organisations, for example WHO, should develop a common ground for regulation, standardisation, encryption, ethical laws and penalty system. Moreover, governments and other funding bodies need to work together for innovative research and to address the concerns of implementation cost and related issues. In addition, combined efforts from all stakeholders needs to improve trust, deliver training, educate the general public and address concerns of all stakeholders. The major benefits, barriers and enablers are summarised in Table 5.1 below.

The Potential of AI, ML and Analytics in Personalised Healthcare Decision-Making

The delivery of high-quality healthcare services relies on the ability of healthcare providers to make informed decisions (Wickramasinghe and Shaffer, 2010). With

Table 5.1 Benefits, Barriers and Enablers of IoT, AI and ML

Benefits	Barriers	Enablers
Traceability	Privacy and cyber-security issues (unauthorised access, malware embedding, etc.)	Ease of availability and management of data
Efficiency	Data loss & backup issue	Improved computational power
Automation	Power outage and technical error issues	Advancement in encryption technology e.g., Blockchain technology
Eliminating / reducing human error	Hesitancy and fear of replacement of health professionals	Cloud storage
Reliability and consistency of procedures	Lack of patient and healthcare inclination for adoption	MFA (multi-factor authentication)
Superior and speedy decision making	Need for new infrastructure and equipment	
Fatigue and emotion-less fact finding and analysis		

the increasing availability of data in healthcare, there is a growing need to effectively utilise data to make timely, prudent, and effective healthcare decisions (ibid.). However, in the current healthcare landscape, there is often an overwhelming amount of data to sift through, making it difficult to distinguish between critical, relevant data and irrelevant noise. As such, healthcare professionals are increasingly turning to AI, ML and analytics to assist in identifying and analysing critical healthcare data to support intelligent healthcare decision making (Wickramasinghe, 2019; Wickramasinghe et al., 2021). When taken to the extent of technical possibilities it also becomes feasible to develop digital twins to provide the next level of healthcare decision making by enabling both precision and personalisation as well as progression of disease to be understood simultaneously. Ultimately, by utilising these advanced technologies, healthcare providers can make more informed decisions, leading to improved patient outcomes and overall healthcare delivery.

The Importance of Data in Healthcare Delivery

Data is the backbone of healthcare delivery, providing insights into patient care, treatment outcomes, disease prevention and management. In recent years, the amount of data generated in healthcare has increased exponentially, thanks to advances in technology, electronic health records (EHRs) and the proliferation of mobile health apps (ibid.). With this abundance of data, healthcare providers can gain deeper insights into patient health, identify areas for improvement in care and develop personalised treatment plans for patients (Wickramasinghe and Schaaffer, 2010).

Data-driven decision making has also revolutionised medical research, allowing researchers to identify and analyse patterns in large data sets. This has led to the development of new treatments, improved disease management and better patient outcomes. For example, data analytics has enabled researchers to identify biomarkers for various diseases, leading to earlier diagnosis and targeted treatments Wickramasinghe, 2019).

While the importance of data in healthcare delivery is clear, managing healthcare data can be a complex and challenging task. One of the main challenges is the sheer volume of data generated in healthcare, which can lead to information overload and make it difficult to identify the most critical data (ibid.). Additionally, healthcare data can be fragmented and siloed, making it difficult to access and analyse (ibid.).

Another challenge in managing healthcare data is ensuring data quality and accuracy. Inaccurate or incomplete data can lead to incorrect diagnoses, ineffective treatments and poor patient outcomes (ibid.). Furthermore, healthcare data is subject to strict privacy regulations, such as the Health Insurance Portability and Accountability Act (HIPAA), which require healthcare providers to ensure patient data is kept secure and confidential (ibid.).

Despite the challenges in managing healthcare data, the benefits of data in healthcare delivery are significant. One of the main benefits is the ability to make informed decisions based on accurate and up-to-date information. For example, data analytics can help healthcare providers identify patterns and trends in patient data, allowing for earlier diagnosis and more targeted treatments.

Data can also improve patient outcomes by enabling personalised treatment plans Wickramasinghe et al., 2021). By analysing patient data, healthcare providers can develop personalised treatment plans that take into account a patient's unique medical history, genetics, lifestyle and other factors (ibid.). This personalised approach to care can lead to better patient outcomes and improved quality of life.

Additionally, data can be used to identify areas for improvement in healthcare delivery. By analysing data on treatment outcomes, healthcare providers can identify areas where care can be improved, such as reducing readmission rates or improving patient satisfaction.

Challenges of Separating Critical, Relevant Data from Noise

In healthcare, as in many other fields, data is often overwhelming, making it challenging to separate critical, relevant data from noise. This presents a significant challenge in making timely, prudent, and effective healthcare decisions. As such, it is necessary to assess the challenges of separating critical, relevant data from noise, including the sheer volume of data generated, data fragmentation and siloing, data quality and privacy concerns.

Sheer Volume of Data Generated

The volume of data generated in healthcare is growing rapidly, making it challenging to separate critical, relevant data from noise. According to a study by IBM, healthcare data is expected to double every 73 days (Wickramasinghe and Schaffer, 2010). This exponential growth in healthcare data is due to several factors, including advances in medical technology, EHRs and the proliferation of mobile health apps.

This sheer volume of data can be overwhelming, leading to information overload, which makes it difficult to identify critical, relevant data. Healthcare providers must find ways to filter through the noise and identify the most critical data to make informed decisions. One way to do this is through data analytics, which can help identify patterns and trends in patient data, enabling healthcare providers to make data-driven decisions.

Data Fragmentation and Siloing

In addition to the sheer volume of data generated, healthcare data can also be fragmented and siloed, making it difficult to access and analyse (Wickramasinghe et al., 2021). Healthcare data is often generated and stored across multiple systems, including EHRs, clinical decision support systems and medical devices. These disparate systems can create data silos, where data is isolated and cannot be easily shared or analysed.

Data silos present a significant challenge in separating critical, relevant data from noise, as healthcare providers must navigate multiple systems to access and analyse data. This can be a time-consuming and complex process, making it difficult to make timely, prudent, and effective healthcare decisions. One way to address this challenge is through data integration, which enables data from multiple sources to be combined and analysed in a single platform.

Data Quality

Inaccurate or incomplete data can lead to incorrect diagnoses, ineffective treatments and poor patient outcomes (Wickramasinghe and Schaffer, 2010). Therefore, ensuring data quality is essential in making informed healthcare decisions. However, data quality can be challenging to ensure, particularly with the large volume of data generated in healthcare.

One way to ensure data quality is through data governance, which involves establishing policies, procedures and standards for data management (ibid.). Data governance can help ensure data is accurate, complete and timely, enabling healthcare providers to make informed decisions. Additionally, data quality can be improved through data validation, which involves checking data for accuracy and completeness.

Privacy Concerns

Privacy concerns present another significant challenge in separating critical, relevant data from noise in healthcare. Healthcare data is subject to strict privacy regulations, such as the HIPAA, which require healthcare providers to ensure patient data is kept secure and confidential (ibid.). Privacy concerns can limit the sharing and analysis of data, making it challenging to identify critical, relevant data. Additionally, privacy concerns can lead to data fragmentation and siloing, as healthcare providers are hesitant to share data with other providers or organisations. One way to address privacy concerns is through data de-identification, which involves removing or obscuring patient identifiers, such as names or social security numbers, from data sets.

Essentially, separating critical, relevant data from noise in healthcare presents significant challenges. The sheer volume of data generated, data fragmentation and siloing, data quality and privacy concerns are all obstacles that must be addressed to make informed healthcare decisions. Healthcare providers must find ways to filter through the noise and identify critical, relevant data to improve patient outcomes and advance medical research. By investing in data analytics, data integration, data governance, data validation and data deidentification, healthcare providers can improve the quality of their data and make better use of the vast amounts of data generated in healthcare.

One promising area of innovation in addressing these challenges is the use of AI and ML (Wickramasinghe et al., 2021). These technologies can help automate the process of identifying critical, relevant data, and can even help predict which data is most important for making informed decisions. For example, ML algorithms can be trained to identify patterns and anomalies in data sets, helping healthcare providers prioritise their analysis efforts.

Digital twins are another emerging technology that can help improve decision making in healthcare (ibid.). A digital twin is a virtual replica of a physical object or system, such as a patient or a healthcare facility (Rivera et al., 2019). By creating a digital twin of a patient, healthcare providers can simulate different treatment options and predict the outcomes of those treatments. This can help healthcare providers make more informed decisions about which treatments to pursue and can help improve patient outcomes.

However, the adoption of these technologies is not without its challenges. Healthcare providers must ensure that these technologies are used ethically and that patient privacy is protected. Additionally, healthcare providers must invest in the necessary infrastructure and expertise to implement these technologies effectively.

AI, ML and Analytics as Tools for Decision-Making

One area where AI, ML and analytics are particularly useful is in medical imaging. Medical images, such as X-rays, CT scans and MRIs, generate vast amounts of data that can be difficult for human radiologists to analyse. However, AI and ML algorithms can analyse medical images to identify patterns and anomalies that might be missed by human analysts. For example, an algorithm can be trained to detect subtle changes in a patient's brain scans that might indicate the onset of Alzheimer's disease. This can help healthcare providers make more informed decisions about diagnosis and treatment.

Another area where AI, ML and analytics are particularly useful is in predictive analytics. Predictive analytics involves using data and algorithms to forecast future events, such as the likelihood of a patient developing a particular disease. By analysing large datasets of patient information, predictive analytics algorithms can identify patterns and risk factors that can be used to identify patients who are at high risk of developing a disease. This can help healthcare providers take preventive measures to reduce the likelihood of the disease developing, such as prescribing medications or recommending lifestyle changes.

However, the use of AI, ML and analytics in healthcare is not without its challenges. One of the main challenges is the quality of the data. Healthcare data is often fragmented, incomplete and inaccurate, which can make it difficult for algorithms to generate accurate insights. Additionally, the use of AI, ML and analytics in healthcare raises concerns about patient privacy and the ethical use of data. Healthcare providers must ensure that patient data is kept confidential and that it is used ethically and responsibly.

Another challenge is the need for healthcare providers to have the necessary expertise to implement these technologies effectively. Implementing AI, ML and analytics in healthcare requires specialised skills, including data analytics, programming and machine learning. Healthcare providers must invest in the necessary infrastructure and expertise to implement these technologies effectively.

Despite these challenges, the potential benefits of AI, ML and analytics in healthcare are significant. These technologies can help healthcare providers make more informed decisions, improve patient outcomes and reduce healthcare costs. For example, predictive analytics can help healthcare providers identify patients who are at high risk of developing chronic diseases, such as diabetes or heart disease. By taking preventive measures, such as prescribing medications or recommending lifestyle changes, healthcare providers can help reduce the likelihood of these diseases developing, thereby reducing healthcare costs.

Digital Twins in Healthcare Decision-Making

Digital twins are virtual models of physical objects or systems, including buildings, machines and even humans (Armendia et al., 2019; Wickramasinghe et al., 2021, 2022). They replicate the real-world behaviour of their physical counterparts using data collected through sensors, cameras and other sources. In healthcare, digital twins are created to represent individual patients, enabling healthcare providers to analyse data from the patient's digital twin to make informed decisions about diagnosis, treatment, and care (Aceto, Persico & Pescapé, 2020; Adadi and Berrada, 2020; Wickramasinghe et al., 2021, 2022).

The concept of digital twins originated in the field of engineering, where they are used to monitor and optimise the performance of complex systems such as aircraft engines and power plants. Digital twins are essentially a combination of three different technologies: IoT, big data and AI (Wickramasinghe et al., 2021, 2022; Barricelli, Casiraghi & Fogli, 2019). By combining these technologies, digital twins provide a highly accurate virtual representation of a physical object or system.

In healthcare, digital twins are being used to support precision medicine and personalised healthcare by enabling healthcare providers to simulate the effects of different treatments and interventions on an individual patient. Digital twins can also be used to monitor patients remotely, providing healthcare providers with real-time data on a patient's condition.

Benefits of Digital Twins in Healthcare Decision-Making

The use of digital twins in healthcare decision making has numerous benefits. One of the main benefits is the ability to provide more personalised and precise care to patients (Wickramasinghe et al., 2021, 2022). By creating a virtual model of a patient, healthcare providers can simulate and test different treatment options and interventions to determine the best course of action for that specific patient (ibid.). This can lead to improved patient outcomes and a more efficient use of healthcare resources.

Another benefit of digital twins in healthcare is the ability to monitor patients remotely (ibid.). By collecting data from a patient's digital twin, healthcare providers can monitor their condition in real-time, even if the patient is not physically present. This can be particularly useful for patients with chronic conditions who require ongoing monitoring and management.

Digital twins also have the potential to improve medical education and training (ibid.). By creating virtual models of medical procedures and treatments, healthcare professionals can practice and refine their skills in a safe and controlled environment. This can lead to better outcomes for patients and a more skilled healthcare workforce.

In addition, digital twins can improve the drug discovery process. By creating virtual models of patients, researchers can simulate the effects of different treatments and interventions, allowing them to identify potential issues and refine their approach before conducting clinical trials. This can lead to a more efficient drug discovery process and the development of more effective treatments.

Examples of Digital Twins in Healthcare

There are numerous examples of digital twins being used in healthcare (ibid.). One example is the use of 3D printing to create models of patient organs for surgical planning. By creating a virtual model of a patient's organ, surgeons can plan the surgical procedure in advance, reducing the risk of complications and improving patient outcomes. This technology is particularly useful for complex surgeries that require a high degree of precision and planning.

Another example of digital twins in healthcare is the use of virtual reality to simulate medical procedures and treatments. By using virtual reality technology, healthcare professionals can practice complex procedures and treatments in a safe and controlled environment, reducing the risk of errors and improving patient/clinical outcomes.

A further example of the application of digital twins in healthcare is the development of virtual twins for surgical training. These digital models enable surgeons to practice surgical procedures on a virtual patient before performing the actual surgery on a real patient. This approach can help reduce surgical errors and improve outcomes for patients.

Digital twins also have the potential to support the development of new drugs and therapies. By creating virtual models of human organs and tissues, researchers can simulate how a drug or therapy would interact with the body before conducting clinical trials. This approach can help reduce the time and costs associated with developing new treatments, while also improving the safety and effectiveness of new drugs.

In addition to their use in individual patient care, digital twins can also be used to improve population health management (ibid.). By creating virtual models of entire populations, healthcare providers can better understand the health needs of different groups and develop targeted interventions to improve health outcomes. For example, digital twins can be used to model the impact of public health campaigns on disease prevention or to predict the spread of infectious diseases in a community.

While digital twins offer significant potential benefits for healthcare decision making, there are also challenges associated with their implementation (ibid.). One of the primary challenges is the need for large amounts of high-quality data to develop and maintain accurate digital twins. Healthcare providers must ensure that the data they collect from patients is accurate, comprehensive and up-to-date to support the development of reliable digital twins.

Another challenge is the need for advanced analytics and machine learning algorithms to process and analyse the data collected from digital twins. Healthcare providers must have the necessary infrastructure and expertise to develop and maintain these complex systems, which can be a significant investment.

Privacy and security concerns are also a consideration when using digital twins in healthcare decision making. Healthcare providers must ensure that patient data is kept secure and private to protect patient confidentiality and comply with regulations such as HIPAA.

Basically, digital twins offer significant potential benefits for healthcare decision making by enabling healthcare providers to simulate and analyse the effects of different treatments and interventions on individual patients (ibid.). Digital twins also have the potential to support the development of new drugs and therapies, improve population health management and reduce healthcare costs. However, there are challenges associated with their implementation, including the need for high-quality data, advanced analytics, machine learning algorithms and privacy and security concerns. Despite these challenges, the potential benefits of digital twins make them a promising area of research and development for healthcare decision making.

How Digital Twins Enable Precision and Personalisation

Digital twins enable precision and personalisation in healthcare decision making by creating a virtual replica of a patient that can be used to simulate and optimise care (Wickramasinghe et al., 2021, 2022). This technology allows healthcare providers to collect, analyse and interpret large amounts of data about a patient's health and use that data to make informed decisions about their care.

One of the primary ways that digital twins enable precision and personalisation is by allowing healthcare providers to tailor treatments and interventions to the unique needs of each patient. Digital twins can be used to model the effects of different treatments on a patient's health, allowing healthcare providers to identify the most effective interventions for that individual. This approach can be particularly beneficial for patients with complex or chronic conditions, who often require personalised treatment plans to achieve the best outcomes (ibid.).

Digital twins can also enable precision and personalisation by helping healthcare providers to predict future health risks and prevent problems before they occur (ibid.). By analysing data from a patient's digital twin, healthcare providers can identify patterns and trends that may indicate an increased risk of developing certain conditions or complications. They can then take proactive steps to reduce that risk, such as prescribing medications, recommending lifestyle changes or scheduling preventative screenings. In so doing not only are precision and personalisation aspects being simultaneously addressed but it also becomes possible to map out or simulate disease progression – what is often termed the 3Ps afforded by digital twins – precision-personalisation and progression (Wickramasinghe et al., 2022).

Overall, digital twins have the potential to revolutionise healthcare decision making by enabling precision and personalisation. By providing healthcare providers with a detailed, real-time view of a patient's health, digital twins can help to ensure that patients receive the most effective, personalised care possible, leading to improved outcomes and better overall health. As this technology continues to evolve and become more widely adopted, it is likely that we will see an increasing number of applications of digital twins in healthcare decision making, and a growing recognition of their potential to transform the way we approach healthcare.

Robots in Healthcare

Advances in technology have also been instrumental in triggering various opportunities for robots in healthcare. More and more, we are witnessing robots in various contexts such as care robots which can assist children, people with disabilities elderly in hospitals, in rehabilitation and in the home (Kyrarini et al., 2021). These robots not only assist but also make reparative tasks more enjoyable for the patients old or young. Robots, combined with nursing avatars and leveraging advances in AI are able to provide specific and focussed advice to support reduction in hospital stays and unplanned readmissions (Jack et al., 2008). Clearly as technology advances and continuous challenges persist with health work force shortage it is likely that we shall see more and more opportunities for robots to provide care. We have already witnessed the rapid rise of robotic surgery which oftentimes supports minimally invasive surgery and thus faster recovery, and shorter hospital stays with strong clinical outcomes (Science and Technology, 2023).

Conclusion

Ever increasing computing power, invention of newer technologies and techniques in AI and related fields have and are having a tremendous impact today in general. Healthcare although a noted laggard is now also benefiting in faster diagnosis, better data analysis and enhanced personalised care for patients, yet there are justifiable concerns from stakeholders which needs to be addressed before the full potential of these technologies can be realised. It is crucial that all governments and funding bodies work together to educate and develop consensus for use of these technologies by developing standard policies and procedures. This will improve adoption and reduce overall burden on already stretched healthcare systems.

In conclusion, IoT, AI, ML and analytics are powerful tools for healthcare decision making. These technologies can help clinicians provide more accurate, efficient and personalised care to patients. However, there are also potential limitations and challenges that need to be addressed, such as the accuracy of algorithms and the ethical issues around data privacy and security. Future directions and potential developments in healthcare decision making may include the integration of multiple technologies, such as combining AI and digital twins to develop personalised treatment plans for complex medical conditions.

The implications of these technologies for healthcare delivery and patient outcomes are significant. They have the potential to revolutionise healthcare by providing more personalised, efficient and effective care. Moreover, they can help reduce healthcare costs by optimising treatment plans and reducing the risk of complications. As healthcare continues to evolve, it is essential for healthcare providers, researchers and policymakers to stay up-to-date with the latest technological advances and their potential implications for healthcare decision making.

Summary

After reading this chapter it should be evident:

a) Why and how IoT is changing healthcare delivery and monitoring.
   Given that IoT and sensors enable connection and the ability to establish the quantified self – this in turn leads to numerous possibilities to now be explored around monitoring and tracking which can greatly aid various aspects of healthcare delivery such as rehab, self-management and even the construction of digital twins.
b) What are some of the key techniques within ML.
   The key techniques include: SV (also known as support vector machines or support vector networks); NN which use interconnected nodes or neurons in a layered structure that resembles the human brain; and NLP which uses machine learning to analyse text or speech data.
c) What are the strengths and weaknesses of AI.
   AI has many strengths including rapidly processing large amounts of data to extract germane knowledge and pertinent information. Moreover, through AI

it is possible to support great precision and personalisation and develop digital twins. However there are also several weaknesses such as lack of transparency, erroneous findings/results and ethical issues.

d) Why can digital twins support a 3P care paradigm and why is this important.

By enabling the construction of a digital replica of the presenting patient and then comparing this to like previous patient histories and simulating treatment scenarios using the digital twin, digital twins enable more precision and personalisation and the establishment of the progression of the disease.

References

Aceto, G., Persico, V., & Pescapé, A. (2020). Industry 4.0 and health: Internet of things, big data, and cloud computing for healthcare 4.0. *Journal of Industrial Information Integration, 18*, 100129.

Adadi, A., & Berrada, M. (2020). Explainable AI for healthcare: from black box to interpretable models. In *Embedded Systems and Artificial Intelligence* (pp. 327–337). Springer.

Armendia, M., Ghassempouri, M., Ozturk, E., & Peysson, F. (2019). Twin-control: A digital twin approach to improve machine tools lifecycle (1st ed., pp. 1 online resource, XVI, 296 pages 225 illustrations, 220 illustrations in color). doi:10.1007/978-3-030-02203-7.

Barricelli, B. R., Casiraghi, E., & Fogli, D. (2019). A survey on digital twin: definitions, characteristics, applications, and design implications. *IEEE Access, 7*, 167653–167671. doi:10.1109/access.2019.2953499.

Ben-Hur, Asa, Horn, David, Siegelmann, Hava, Vapnik, Vladimir N. (2001). Support vector clustering. *Journal of Machine Learning Research, 2*, 125–137.

Evans, J., Papadopoulos, A., Silvers, C. T., Charness, N., Boot, W. R., Schlachta-Fairchild, L., et al. (2016). Remote health monitoring for older adults and those with heart failure: adherence and system usability. *Telemedicine and e-Health, 22*(6), 480–488.

Gillis, Alexander. (2021). "What is internet of things (IoT)?". IOT Agenda.

Greshko, M. (2018). *Meet Sophia, the robot that looks almost human.* National Geographic.

Jack, B., Greenwald, J., Forsythe, S., O'Donnell, J., Johnson, A., Schipelliti, L., et al. (2008, August). Developing the tools to administer a comprehensive hospital discharge program: the ReEngineered Discharge (RED) program. In Henriksen K, Battles JB, Keyes MA, Grady ML, (eds), *Advances in patient safety: New directions and alternative approaches*. Vol. 3. Performance and Tools. AHRQ Publication No. 08-0034-3. Agency for Healthcare Research and Quality. www.ncbi.nlm.nih.gov/books/NBK43688/.

Jayaraman, P. P., Forkan, A. R. M., Morshed, A., Haghighi, P. D., Kang, Y-B. (2020). Healthcare 4.0: a review of frontiers in digital health. *WIREs Data Mining and Knowledge Discovery, 10*(2), e1350.

Kyrarini, M., Lygerakis, F., Rajavenkatanarayanan, A., Sevastopoulos, C., Nambiappan, H. R., Chaitanya, K.,K., Babu, A.,R., Mathew, J., Makedon, F. (2021). A survey of robots in healthcare. *Technologies, 9*, 8. https://doi.org/10.3390/ technologies9010008.

Mahesh, B. (2020). Machine learning algorithms–a review. *International Journal of Science and Research (IJSR)* [Internet], *9*(1), 381–386.

McCarthy, J. (2004). What is artificial intelligence. Retrieved from www-formal stanford edu/jmc/whatisai html..

Nadkarni, P. M., Ohno-Machado, L. and Chapman, W. W. (2011). Natural language processing: an introduction. *Journal of the American Medical Informatics Association, 18*(5), 544–551.

Rivera, L. F., Jiménez, M., Angara, P., Villegas, N. M., Tamura, G., & Müller, H. A. (2019). Towards continuous monitoring in personalized healthcare through digital twins. In *Paper presented at the Proceedings of the 29th Annual International Conference on Computer Science and Software Engineering.*

Rong, G., Mendez, A., Bou Assi, E., Zhao, B., Sawan, M. (2020). Artificial intelligence in healthcare: review and prediction case studies. *Engineering,6*(3), 291–301.

Science and Technology. (2023). New surgical robots are about to enter the operating theatre. Retrieved from www.economist.com/science-and-technology/2017/11/16/new-surgical-robots-are-about-to-enter-the-operating-theatre?utm_medium=cpc.adword.pd&utm_sou rce=google&ppccampaignID=17210591673&ppcadID=&utm_campaign=a.22brand_ pmax&utm_content=conversion.direct-response.anonymous&gclid=Cj0KCQjw84anB hCtARIsAISI-xeGGeN_69jCj3uMKsildVnHc4eFEe4_RXyJVM-G6sb.

Tirosh, O., Andargoli, A., & Wickramasinghe, N. (2022). Assessing the benefits of a teleassessment solution using a FVM perspective. In *HICSS 2022cProceedings of the 55th Hawaii International Conference on System Sciences.* Retrieved from https://schol arspace.manoa.hawaii.edu/bitstream/10125/79829/1/0398.pdf.

Wickramasinghe, N. (2019). Handbook of Research on Optimizing Healthcare Management Techniques. IGI Global.

Wickramasinghe, N., Jayaraman, P. P., Zelcer, J., Forkan, A. R. M., Ulapane, N., Kaul, R., & Vaughan, S. (2021). A vision for leveraging the concept of digital twins to support the provision of personalised cancer care. *IEEE Internet Computing,* 1–1. doi:10.1109/ mic.2021.3065381.

Wickramasinghe, N. & Schaffer, J. (2010). *Realizing value driven patient-centric health care through technology.* IBM Center for the Business of Government.

Wickramasinghe, N., Ulapane, N., Andargoli, A., Ossai, C., Shuakat, N., Nguyen, T., Zelcer. J. (2022). Digital twins to enable better precision and personalized dementia care. *JAMIA Open, 5*(3), ooac072. doi: 10.1093/jamiaopen/ooac072. PMID: 35992534; PMCID: PMC9387506.

Wickramasinghe, N. & Zelcer, J. (2019). The Australian PCEHR or my health record. In Wickramasinghe & Bodendorf (eds), *Biosensors, Mobile and Analytics for Superior Healthcare Delivery.* Springer. ISBN 978-3-030-17347-0.

6 Apps, Platforms, Mobile Solutions and Telehealth

Objectives

At the conclusion of this chapter, it should be evident:

a) Why apps, platforms, mobile solutions and telehealth are so important to provide superior healthcare delivery today.
b) How an essential aspect around apps, platforms, mobile solutions and telehealth is concerned with responsible use and design.
c) How data security and privacy are key considerations.
d) Why digital health literacy and ensuring solutions are fit for purpose is important.

Introduction

Today there are millions of healthcare apps in circulation both Android and IoS. In fact, there are over 300,000 apps which just focus on diabetes management (Jimenez, Lum & Car, 2019). Initially slow to be adopted and diffused, today when it comes to healthcare delivery, healthcare applications have some of the most innovative technologies incorporated. These apps are transforming the medical industry through the integration of technology enhancement of the healthcare experience between patient and doctors. Often, pictures are used to deliver superior care to patients via mobile-first applications that place much emphasis on the health sector, for example, pharmacies, hospitals and clinics. Moreover, during COVID-19 huge reliance was placed on a variety of apps. Today, nearly all industries are shifting towards becoming mobile and relying enormously on these technologies. Thus, it is unsurprising that healthcare applications are making significant contributions towards the health and well-being of individuals at any stage of their life anywhere, anytime. Notably, consumers are shifting more towards depending on these mobile applications to keep track of their medication treatments, support wellness management, manage chronic conditions and support better mental health as well as physical activities.

Further, healthcare applications are not only relied on by patients, but also healthcare professionals. Currently, there are mobile applications that are

DOI: 10.1201/9781003318538-8

specifically developed for healthcare service providers, physicians, medical institutes and hospitals. Such apps do not just help patients maintain their health but also assist healthcare service providers in delivering superior and more efficient care most usually by supporting better clinical decision making. Application software technologies facilitate superior care delivery through enhancing the collection of health data, improving communication between patients' doctors, bettering engagement and client loyalty through serving as time-saving tools for healthcare channels, optimising budgets for patients and hospitals and reducing medical errors. In addition, these solutions also facilitate the delivery of care more promptly, regardless of the location of the patient. They are therefore among the most advanced technologies today in delivering superior medical care to patients. More often than not, mobile applications are by far more effective in care delivery compared to traditional methods.

Two key examples of apps or mobile solutions for healthcare, namely, CLOTS and SAMSON, are presented to illustrate opportunities for such apps and highlight key considerations. CLOTS is a clinical decision support system while SAMSON is a patient support solution. These solutions serve to highlight important aspects of apps used in healthcare and key aspects to note for best practice and responsible design.

CLOTS

The CLOTS app was designed by a haematology oncologist as a mobile clinical decision support system (CDSS) to assist health professionals in perioperative patient management (CLOTS, 2021, 2022). Specifically, CLOTS was designed to identify patients at risk of surgical bleeding or thromboembolisms and thereby provide options to ensure appropriate preventative measures are taken pre-surgery (ibid.). Robust mobile CDSSs are vital to deliver enhanced healthcare services. Having a CDSS as a mobile app is convenient for the clinician as they can quickly access the relevant decision support at the point of care. Moreover, as clinicians treat many patients in various different settings, they have ready access to the CDSS when they require it at the point of care. To ensure the CLOTS app was fit for purpose, useable, high fidelity and easy to use, in its development a rigorous design phase was embarked upon which incorporated key theories around task-technology fit, user-centred design and co-creation and a Design Science Research Methodology (ibid.).

The CLOTS app, then, is an example of a mobile health app designed by clinicians for clinicians to be used as a mobile CDSS. Critical care was taken to ensure the solution met the highest levels of best practice, contained the latest and most relevant information and had appropriate security and privacy considerations (ibid.). It is important to note that as the CLOTS app is designed for clinicians to use, the level of digital health literacy is at an appropriately high and sophisticated level which was confirmed to be appropriate based on pilot testing (ibid.).

So, what does the CLOTS app as a CDSS highlight for mobile health apps? This is an important question to keep in mind as one evaluates and/or uses apps

in healthcare. Specifically, a few key considerations are as follows: i) fit for purpose – the CLOTS app was designed by clinicians for a specific clinical context
focused on surgical bleeding and thromboembolism. To this end it was grounded in
the latest practice guidelines and thus the decision support it provides is consistent
with recognised clinical practice (ibid.). This serves to ensure the solution is fit for
purpose; ii) ease of use, usability and fidelity – these are all important considerations for any app but very important for health apps. In the case of the CLOTS
app, ease of use, usability and fidelity were demonstrated to be appropriate and
suitable based on pilot study trials and the results of these trials are available to the
public (ibid.); iii) data security – cyber security is becoming a greater concern in
today's digital world. Given that healthcare data is so sensitive, data security with
mobile health apps is a key concern. Again, the appropriate level of security was
evaluated during the pilot trials of the CLOTS app and demonstrated to be at a suitable level (ibid.). It is important to note that no app is 100% data secure, but what
is important is that the level of security provided is commensurate with the data
stored, used or transferred; iv) privacy – connected to security but also distinct is
privacy. Once again given the sensitive nature of healthcare data, privacy is also an
important consideration. For the CLOTS app, the appropriate level of privacy was
established and demonstrated during the course of the pilot trials (ibid.).

SAMSON App

Poor adherence to treatment especially for complex conditions like cancer impedes
clinical outcomes, impacts quality of life and can increase healthcare costs
(Col, Fanale & Kronholm,1990; Kane and Shaya, 2008). Annually, in Australia,
medication-related hospital admissions are estimated to be over 250,000 with
a cost of $1.4 billion (Lim et al., 2019). Medication adherence which revolves
around a patient's commitment to maintaining a prescribed regimen throughout
their treatment period represents a key part of clinical care and if not followed correctly can lead to far-reaching consequences (Wu et al., 2015). In cancer, the adherence rate can be as low as 20% (ibid.) and often worsens over time (Hershman
et al., 2009). Barriers to medication adherence can be complex, requiring
multi-dimensional interventions to address multifaceted factors (Sabate, 2003).
A recently published systematic review shows that multi-component interventions
that involve collective adherence strategies (patient education, reminders, self-
monitoring, reinforcement, and supportive counselling) were most effective to
improve adherence to oral anti-cancer medicines (Dang et al., 2022). To address
the growing problem of a lack of medical adherence, the SAMSON mobile app
was developed. SAMSON is a patient-centred comprehensive digital intervention
solution, consisting of a mobile health app involving individual tailored smartphone alerts and real-time, evidence-based advice for side-effect self-management
to support superior medication adherence for patients with cancer prescribed oral
cancer medication (Dang, 2022).

   Critical to the development of the SAMSON app were the co-design and sub-
scription to a Design Science Research Methodology (ibid.). The app was also

designed to be effective for patients with varying degrees of digital health literacy (ibid.). Thus, SAMSON is an app designed to be used by patients with cancer to support superior medication adherence. Pilot testing has demonstrated usability, usefulness, fidelity and a high level of fit for purpose (ibid.).

As with the CLOTS app, discussed above, it is useful to consider the following key considerations: i) fit for purpose – the SAMSON app was designed by a multi-spectral team consisting of behavioural scientists, digital health experts and software engineers to address a specific clinical context to address medication non-adherence in patients with cancer taking oral cancer medications. To this end it was grounded in the latest practice guidelines and thus the patient support it provides is consistent with recognised clinical practice (ibid.). This serves to ensure the solution is fit for purpose; ii) ease of use, usability and fidelity – these are all important considerations for any app but very important for health apps. In the case of the SAMSON app, ease of use, usability and fidelity were demonstrated to be appropriate and suitable based on pilot study trials and the results of these trials are available to the public (ibid.); 3) data security – cyber security is becoming a greater and greater concern in today's digital world. Given that healthcare data is so sensitive, data security with mobile health apps is a key concern. Again, the appropriate level of security was evaluated during the pilot trials of the SAMSON app and demonstrated to be suitable (ibid.); 4) privacy – this is connected to security yet is distinctly different. Once again given the sensitive nature of healthcare data, privacy is also an important consideration. For the SAMSON app, the appropriate level of privacy was established and demonstrated during the course of the pilot trials (ibid.).

Platforms

Platforms in healthcare are also among the most profound technological developments that have transformed care delivery today. Platform solutions in healthcare have fostered healthcare leaders to place more emphasis on controlling the healthcare delivery process, improving customer experience, enhancing cost efficiency and focusing on more positive outcomes and less on ownership (Thimbleby, 2013). Before healthcare platforms, hospitals were at the core and centre of the health care delivery. Today, however, several business models that offer superior and vertically integrated care seldom even own physical hospitals (ibid.). Such platform-based healthcare providers develop convenient, efficient and user-friendly platforms that effectively serve consumers based on the customers' terms. Thus, these models try to be as patient-centred as possible. Today, patient-centred care is considered the most superior form of care delivery owing to its impact on effectiveness (ibid.). Some of the benefits of patient-centred care include better outcomes, enhanced patient satisfaction, a positive reputation for the healthcare organisation, better informed patients and enhanced coordinated care. A key value of healthcare platforms is thus given by enabling superior care delivery through a more patient-centred focus cannot be overlooked (ibid.).

The new healthcare universe is the fundamental centre of focus in the emerging platform solution in healthcare delivery (ibid.). Platform technology essentially recognises that patients are the ones who are central, not the hospitals, since they are the consumers, not the organisation. It is a major shift from the traditional way of doing things in the healthcare universe which largely functioned as independent entities (ibid.). In the 1990s, new technologies fostered by organisations such as integrated platform companies redefined the health care industry. The transformation was also significantly catalysed by several emergent health systems which incorporated both hospital ownership and operations under single corporations (ibid.). It is a consolidation trend that has escalated even further over the years.

It should be noted that while systemness may work well when it comes to fee-for-free service payment structures, such a model often does not work effectively when it comes to sufficiently serving consumers. It is thus no surprise that platform companies like Amazon have been able to enjoy the success they do today and dominate once-successful giant companies that relied solemnly on systemness. Today, platform technologies are rapidly being embraced more by new platform companies in healthcare to deliver superior care. This in turn poses a significant threat to traditional healthcare business models given that these technologies are vastly and rapidly disrupting, transforming and reorganising the healthcare universe. The significant niche that platforms have that give platform companies a competitive advantage in the healthcare industry is that they deliver superior care based on the preferences of the consumers.

Platform technology, when correctly utilised, also improves organisational performance by effectively maximising customer value. The superior care delivery it fosters enables platforming to achieve this through whichever means necessary. Healthcare providers that understand their strengths as well as the risks when it comes to serving the customers in the most effective way possible would opt for platforming companies. Platforms enable healthcare providers to deliberately relinquish their production control to their suppliers, thus adding incremental value as well as strengthening their platforms (Patel et al., 2013).

In addition to this, platform companies have more flexibility in constructing their services as well as the production networks with a combination of partnered, owned, and purchase services while focusing only on the best desired outcomes to generate optimal results. Often, even with health care organisations, an adamant push to attain competitive advantage leads to difficult resource allocation decisions. Following this, platform technology enables platforming healthcare providers to do all it takes to ensure the customers benefit from the service rendered. Whether the healthcare organisation focuses on platforming or not, every company has their inputs as well as their desired outputs. Nevertheless, what is unique about healthcare organisations that focus on platforming, unlike traditional companies, they are nearly entirely agnostic concerning whether they partner, own or outsource capabilities. Their sole focus is typically grounded on the desired outcomes. Following this, platforming technology liberates such organisations to develop their service as well as their production networks such that they have a mix of owned, purchased and partnered services that produce the best outcomes.

In continuing care delivery today, innovative technologies are restructuring episodic and care delivery into discrete service provisions. The motivation behind this could mainly be because of that urge to compete on price, customer experience, as well as customer convenience. Today, several health companies are shifting from systemness to platforming using platform technologies. A key motivation behind this is the fact that in today's competitive age, providers capable of solving the health as well as healthcare needs of consumers are bound to differentiate and dominate the market share. Platform technologies are a promising innovation that several providers have embraced as a means towards winning the market share in this way.

One key advantage with these platform technologies for healthcare providers is that the organisation does not necessarily have to provide all the care possibilities, that is, care can be tailored to the specific context. For instance, AdventHealth is a state system that is dedicated to assisting its customers to receive the superior care they need whenever they need it, albeit it does not offer the care itself. It is a good example of platform technology: the healthcare organisation serves the needs of its consumers based on their terms rather than the terms of the organisation itself. At this point, AdventHealth has invested in customer-focused training, patient navigation tools, patient-friendly billing, as well as spiritual care with the sole focus of serving its consumers more compassionately and holistically. Further, the platforming-based company has gone the extra mile of investing in an all-encompassing network card, which the company's founder anticipates will become more crucial to its consumers than insurance cards are when it comes to healthcare.

Innovative platforming technologies can also be seen in the partnership between ProMedica Health System and Welltower, Q ventus and Fairview health services and the partnership between Microsoft and Providence Saint Joseph Health (PSJH). Not so long ago, ProMedica Health system partnered with Welltower to obtain HCR ManorCare. HCR ManorCare was, at the time, the largest long-term and post-acute care provider in the US. The long-term success of ProMedica is largely attributed to the healthcare provider's capability of integrating post-acute care services to vertically integrated systems of delivering care.

When it comes to the partnership of the Q ventus technology firm with Fairview health services, the aim of the partnership was to build an operational transformation centre that fosters real-time data to frontline healthcare professionals such that it improves operational decision making, minimises stress to caregivers, enhances resource allocation and gives customers a better care delivery experience. According to the views of Fairview health services, this platform-based technology will enhance care outcomes while maximising throughput and cutting down on expenses. Microsoft and Providence St. Joseph Health also recently made public a plan for a strategic alliance, which will see the creation of a portfolio of cloud-based technologies as well as integrated solutions that incorporate artificial intelligence to enhance operational and clinical decision making throughout the seven-state network of Providence St. Joseph Health. Such an alliance is bound to fasten digital transformations within PSJH, foster superior care results, standardise protocols and improve consumer engagement. It is quite astonishing that even though platform technologies within healthcare are in the early stages, the benefits are already visible. Currently, they are at the core of superior care delivery alongside several other crucial benefits, even though they are not yet widely distributed.

Mobile Solutions

Mobile solutions are also among the most crucial technologies that enable superior care delivery in today's healthcare sector. As mentioned, health care systems are rapidly shifting towards models of care that are grounded on integrated care processes distributed by various caregivers and based on an empowered role of the patient. In this context, mobile technological solutions are forming a critical enabling role as far as innovative and supportive care is concerned. These mobile technological solutions are currently referred to as mHealth. They are inspired by the multifaceted problems that healthcare systems today face which they are tailored to solve. Most importantly, mobile solutions offer support to healthcare providers when it comes to communication and management of care, which are essential ingredients for superior care delivery. It should be noted that mobile health apps and mobile health solutions are related but also different. For the purposes of this chapter mobile health solutions are broader in focus and are designed for more than one healthcare stakeholder to use such as multiple groups of clinicians, healthcare organisations, patients and even at times payers, while mobile health apps are typically designed for one group to use around a specific issue, for example the SAMSON app or CLOTS app (discussed earlier).

The use of mobile technological solutions has become widespread thereby expanding the use of telemedicine strategies. These approaches foster communication between healthcare providers which encourages ease of access to specialist advice and improves the health outcome of patients. In a more expansive context, mobile technological solutions have the edge over typical care given they enhance the performance of healthcare providers, increase satisfaction for both health professionals and patients, improve accessibility to care, minimise costs and optimise patient health outcomes. When this is coupled with the support mobile solutions give to foster effective communication and consultations between patients and healthcare providers, mobile solutions seamlessly provide superior care delivery.

Further, mobile technological solutions are currently utilised not only by patients, but also by emergency physicians to make hospital consultations with hospital specialists concerning the individuals attending the emergency department. According to Nasi, Cucciniello and Guerrazzi (2015), mobile solutions minimise hospital specialist and physician consultation time significantly. They also significantly minimise the length of time patients use up in the emergency department.

Mobile technological solutions today are largely used for consultation, that is, between clinical staff and home care workers or community health workers. An important benefit that comes with mobile solutions is that they minimise the time it takes to deliver healthcare. Mobile technological solutions also minimise the number of cumbersome face-to-face appointments, while optimising the number of individuals receiving clinical assessments for some health conditions. According to Gonçalves-Bradley et al. (2020), whenever primary healthcare workers utilise mobile solutions for consulting with hospital specialists. They may also minimise referrals as well as visits to the clinic for individuals with skin conditions and those referred by a health professional for clinical follow-ups for various health challenges. Patients are also managed more efficiently to a significant extent when emergency healthcare practitioners utilise mobile technological solutions for consulting with hospital specialists.

In areas that require special care such as the case of cancer support care, the crucial role that mobile technological solutions play in health care delivery processes is also evident. Mobile technologies in this context are grounded on a transformation towards the delivery of a higher quantity and quality of health care services within primary care settings, health centres and day facilities, from the classic typically large general hospitals that have fewer hospital beds reserved for acute care (Wendland, Lunardi & Dolci, 2019). When it comes to cancer care delivery, the case is also similar. It is especially true for the treatment of the side effects of cancer care, commonly referred to as cancel supportive care. Essentially, the purpose of cancer supportive care is usually to relieve patients of the side effects of cancer treatment like fatigue, pain and nausea. Conforming more to the facts, the main intention of cancer supportive care is typically not for the purpose of curing cancer, but for the purpose of managing the symptoms of the cancer. Following this, cancer supportive care is a crucial component of the treatment process when it comes to healthcare delivery. It is thus usually integrated by healthcare providers along with the actual cancer care delivery (Nasi, Cucciniello & Guerrazzi, 2015).

New models for care place much emphasis on the role that patients play (McLendon, 2017; Moghimi et al., 2013; Gibbings & Wickramasinghe, 2021). Currently, care models are shifting more towards activities that are undertaken by patients based on self-management. More precisely, patients ought to self-manage the side effects of the care they receive, which can be effectively achieved by the patient through mobile solutions. There is also a significant emphasis on the efficiency of care as well as the quality of life. Nonetheless, the integration of these two trends are headed towards a trade-off between enhancing quality and this escalating expenses of improving quality (Wendland, Lunardi & Dolci, 2019; Wickramasinghe, Chalasani & Koritala, 2012; Zulueta & Ajilore, 2021). Following this, mobile technological solutions have a crucial role to play in managing this trade-off when it comes to effectively improving quality of care today (Dey, Ashour & Bhatt, 2017).

While there are challenges that mobile technology indeed helps to solve in the healthcare universe today, they seem promising when it comes to solving nearly all the problems that the health care sector faces as far as superior care delivery is concerned. mHealth for instance is creating new models which have been evidently highlighted by communications media, literature and decision makers. As stated by the extant literature, Mhealth plays a pivotal role as it fosters better communication and improves the integration of care processes aimed towards superior care delivery (Gibbings & Wickramasinghe, 2021). MHealth can heighten healthcare providers' productivity by touching on the internal processes that are utilised within healthcare organisations. In consequence, this can improve healthcare systems' productivity as well (Tuckson, Edmunds & Hodgkins, 2017). When it comes to the external relations of healthcare companies, mobile technological solutions can improve transparency (Nasi, Cucciniello & Guerrazzi, 2015), thus heightening healthcare service providers' accountability as well as empower patients (Wendland, Lunardi & Dolci, 2019; Wickramasinghe & Bodendorf, 2019; Yeo & Lim, 2016). Ultimately, the most outstanding promise that mobile technological solutions provide are their prospective capability of better enhancing quality of life as well as the appropriateness of care (Wickramasinghe, Chalasani & Koritala, 2012).

In essence, mHealth can assist in the search for new healthcare models that can allow for more effective care delivery. These require transformation from inpatient to outpatient care, thereby also allowing for the delivery of superior care within rural environments, among other areas, that do not have easy access to medical personnel (Vimarlund & Le Rouge, 2013). More specifically, mobile solutions have the great potential to solve many of the major challenges that are faced by low-income countries. Mobile phone-based solutions can also tackle challenges faced by countries that lack sufficient healthcare professionals, that have limited access to computers for effective operations within hospitals and that are challenged by living long distances from health care facilities. Following this, mobile solutions foster improvements in terms of reducing the cost of healthcare delivery within such countries while improving efficiency (Thimbleby, 2013). In the extant transitions in healthcare models, mobile technological solutions such as mHealth are at the forefront of complementing these transitions. They are facilitating the shift of care from acute hospital environments to the patient's home quite effectively. Technology is used in such instances to integrate and rationalise care services where appropriate, based on the needs of the patient.

Furthermore, mHealth plays a vital function in empowering the needs of patients since it provides them with the tools for managing their health conditions as well as any other related side effects that may arise from the treatments. Mobile solutions enable patients to do all these on their own, making it seamless that patients can be their own doctors through such a technological solution. Patients can achieve this from their own home and without the necessary supervision of a health care professional (Nasi, Cucciniello & Guerrazzi, 2015). Nonetheless, it is important to note that mHealth is a vast concept that is inclusive of many other forms of mobile technological solutions today. Often, mHealth refers to consumer healthcare technologies like web-based information resources video conferencing, telephone messaging including a multimedia messaging service and a short messaging service, telerobotic and telehealth, which is inclusive of remote services offered by a surgeon operating from a distance.

More precisely, the World Health Organisation has defined mobile solutions in healthcare to include smartphones, mobile phones, patient monitoring devices, telecare devices, mobile computing and telemedicine. It has also included MP3 players for mLearning in the list (Wickramasinghe, Chalasani & Koritala, 2012). However, following this classification by WHO, the category of text messaging devices ought to be kept separate from the broader definition of "mobile solution technological devices" that will be utilised to categorise tablets, applications and smartphones. The distinction is drawn from the unique features of these two categories, that is, while mobile solution devices are technological tools for gathering and processing data, SMS is a tool merely capable of reminding patients of appointments. These considerations are also viable when it comes to outlining the distinctions between mobile solution devices and mobile telecare devices. Notably, telemedicine technological devices are distinct technologies even when incorporated with mobile phones. Telecare devices leverage the advantages that they get from wireless telecommunications infrastructures. They are thus defined as the use of computer technologies and the use of telecommunications, inclusive of patient remote sensing and monitoring, as well as the utility of telemetry technological tools, with medical health care delivery facilitated by medical personnel (Sako, Adibi & Wickramasinghe, 2020).

It is also important to note that mobile technological solutions ought to be launched aligned with the undertakings they aim to support. Often, reliable mobile solutions first and foremost support automation, followed by data collection, and ultimately operations. Nonetheless, they can also be tailored to support clinical decision making, more so regarding pain monitoring, as well as the systematic organisation of activities. Even so, several strategic documents pertaining to mHealth that were provided by international companies and leading companies within the field, as well as adopted by decision makers, imply that mHealth should be capable of effectively assisting human executed processes and should play a crucial function in new models of care (Tuckson, Edmunds & Hodgkins, 2017).

Mobile solutions, more so regarding mHealth, therefore play a potentially vital role in the value chain of superior care delivery (Sako, Adibi & Wickramasinghe, 2020). In each phase of the care delivery procedure mobile solutions can therefore play an important role in offering support to the making of prudent decisions, supporting prevention and diagnosis of various conditions, treatment of these healthcare conditions and even in evaluation and follow-up. Today, mobile solutions have enabled advanced data collection and patient monitoring in the new care models they have paved the way for. Mobile solutions such as mHealth can significantly contribute to the generation of value when effectively integrated into the whole care process. They can completely transform and make a positive difference regarding the way care is delivered by shifting to a more superior care delivery that places more emphasis on mobile and home care.

Telehealth

Telehealth technology can also enable superior care delivery since it facilitates the provision of medical services beyond the limitation of geographical borders. In essence, telehealth efficiently and effectively links people with their healthcare providers whenever in-person care is either not easily possible or rather unnecessary in this context. For instance, individuals who have learned to tap into the benefits of this technology can check their blood pressure today with a digitally connected device that is linked to the digital health record system. Telehealth accounts for the vast scope of remote care in the health care universe.

Notably, telemedicine and telehealth are often confused with one another although they are not necessarily synonymous. While telemedicine focuses on medicine practice biotechnology for the purpose of delivering care remotely, telehealth includes digital and telecommunications technologies as well as services that are utilised to offer care and provide healthcare services at a distance. With telehealth, services that are offered through healthcare centres can be delivered to the patients more efficiently and conveniently, often in ways that healthcare centres cannot, using standard care approaches. This, thus, enables upskilling and uplifting of the healthcare workforce. While telehealth was initially created to offer basic care towards underserved patients such as those residing in rural areas, there are benefits when it comes to superior care delivery that have made them transcend merely this scope alone today. However, they still play a fundamental role in enabling underserved patients to effectively receive healthcare services through audio and visual technology.

Since the coronavirus pandemic of 2019, the use of telehealth technologies in delivering superior care has increased. Today, several practices now have telehealth as the standard. The new innovative technology in healthcare maximises the satisfaction of the needs of patients as an emphasis and reduces expenses, especially given that they are currently cheaper than in-person care, and affords efficient and quality care to ensure. Evidently, healthcare providers as well as patients who have enjoyed these advantages that come with telehealth technology can attest to its usefulness in superior care delivery. However, legal, regulatory and reimbursement obstacles are currently in the way of allowing greater adoption of this innovative technology in healthcare.

Importantly, aside from telehealth technologies being merely a cost-effective solution to care delivery, they can do more than just that within multiple contexts. First, telehealth can effectively minimise the challenges such as medical misuse that are faced by many people globally. They also tackle the problems of lengthy hospitalisations as well as emergency department visits that are rather unnecessary (McLendon, 2017). Third, telehealth minimises the travel time for patients as well as the wait times, which allows for a more time-conscious and significantly improved quality of care. It also serves as a viable means of access to and delivery of health care services of a high quality that focus on the best outcomes. Following this, improved access to care at the convenience of patients significantly minimises stress in patients during care delivery (Gajarawala & Pelkowski, 2021). These benefits couple together to heighten patient satisfaction.

Telehealth fosters the creation of a stronger healthcare system through its various attributes while extending where and how the delivery of care is carried out by healthcare providers. In the many years that telehealth has been in news, the extant literature indicates that it has been a quality care modality that is safe and convenient not just for patients but for their healthcare service providers and serves to provide a secure way to transfer personal health records between them. When it comes to telehealth, chart-based interactions and virtual visits have been among the most utilised approaches. Virtual visits are hereby synchronous and live interactive meetings between healthcare providers and their patients that can be done through live chats or video. On the other hand, chat-based interactions are asynchronous mobile app or online communications that facilitate the transmission of the health records of patients their diagnostic information, their vital signs, as well as other physiological data. Chat-based interactions thus enable healthcare professionals to conduct a substantive review and give a diagnosis, information on consultation or even a treatment plan for the care delivery of a patient based on the data.

Other significantly utilised approaches in telehealth include remote patient monitoring, which enables the collection, evaluation, transfer and communication of personal health data from a patient towards the healthcare providers to enable superior care delivery. Remote patient monitoring in telehealth can also be used to transmit these personal health records to an extended care team outside a clinical office or a hospital such as the home of the patient. The personal telehealth technologies that can be used in the transmission as well as collection and evaluation of these health data in remote patient monitoring include implanted health monitors, wearable sensors, mobile applications, wireless devices and smartphones. Remote patient monitoring as an approach in telehealth can effectively track any changes in chronic conditions through ongoing condition observation, thus facilitating the effective management of chronic diseases. They can either be asynchronous or synchronous, relying on the needs of the patient. Telehealth is only bound to get better, especially regarding remote patient monitoring, with the rise of artificial intelligence as well as machine learning. The integration of these emerging technologies in the field can facilitate improved surveillance of diseases, that is, chronic conditions, enable more effective early detection of such conditions, facilitate enhanced diagnosis and foster personalised medicine. In this way, remote patient monitoring in telehealth enables and is bound to even improve further superior care delivery.

Telehealth technologies also offer better physician-to-physician consultations under technology-enabled modalities. In addition to this, technology-enabled modalities in telehealth are also at the core of algorithm-empowered diagnostic support also known as digital diagnostics, efficient and safe data transmission, digital therapeutics, efficient data interpretation and patient education. Digital therapeutics hereby entail utilising individual health devices as well as sensors, which can be used integrated with conventional drug therapies or alone to either prevent or manage health conditions.

With this, the most significant and beneficial effect that telehealth has had in the healthcare universe today is on the consumer. It is inclusive of the patients, their families,and the entire community at large. The use of telehealth technologies minimises stress for the consumer while maximising customer satisfaction through fostering superior care delivery. In the last few years, several researchers have reported on telehealth services being at the core of consumer support and satisfaction. Telehealth has also achieved this through providing consumers with liable access to healthcare providers that would have perhaps not been available to them otherwise. Ultimately, it offers enhanced medical services minus the need to travel lengthy distances (Ferorelli et al., 2020).

Discussion and Conclusions

There are some crucial considerations that are necessary to make sure that the full potential of solutions provided by healthcare technologies provide a realised. There is no doubt that technological advancements in the future of healthcare will play a vital role in transforming care delivery and improving the process. However, realising the full potential of technological solutions requires an effective way of doing away with the limitations of achieving this. One key consideration as far as achieving the full potential of the solutions offered by technology in healthcare is concerned pertains to the human factors that are bound to remain a constant limitation of technological breakthroughs.

With this, it is prudent to consider integrating technology with culture instead of placing much emphasis only on technology. It is almost inevitable that technology is bound to advance in outstanding ways, especially after the market figures out ways of economically profiting from them. However, instead of the mentality of prioritising figuring out how to make money following technological solutions in care delivery, it would be more prudent to figure out ways of making the patients healthier and happier. The latter is superior since it shifts from the rising trend of treating patients as mere individuals in a business model. It is more effective in ensuring patient satisfaction with the delivered care which is more beneficial to both healthcare providers and patients.

From this perspective, thinking clearly is evidently crucial in formulating ways of ensuring the full potential of the solutions technology provides in healthcare are realised. Patients, leaders and health professionals need to have an extensive discussion of the kind of future hospital that they need. More precisely, the conversation should not just be merely about specific solutions but also about articulating principles regarding this. The future should therefore not just be planned through being technologically driven but also through enhancing the criteria behind principles like bettering patient care and offering them as well as staff sufficient support. Needs and wants should not be confused with one another; the health care universe of the future needs to integrate technology and favourable culture in health care.

With the plethora of health apps, mobile solutions, platforms and telehealth being developed, coupled with the widespread diffusion and adoption as we move into a post-COVID-19 environment, it becomes more important to ensure responsible design adoption and usage of such solutions (Wickramasinghe et al., 2012). Key considerations revolve around being fit for purpose, usability, usefulness fidelity and ease of use as well as data security and privacy. In Germany, to regulate and evaluate digital health solutions DiGA has been established (DiGA, 2022). Essentially, DiGA is a regulatory structure that has been established to provide some level of assurance that mobile solutions in Germany are indeed fit for purpose, have appropriate levels of security and privacy and thus conform to a responsible design (ibid.). In other countries like the USA and Australia, similar regulation around mobile health solutions is now being administered respectively by the FDA and TGA.

Clearly, we are only at the dawn of the design, development and deployment of apps, platforms, mobile solutions and telehealth initiatives. What is evident is that as we move forward on this path there will be many issues to be addressed around ethics, legal issues and best practice. Given the dynamic nature of the context and the rapid advancements in technological developments this is likely to be challenging at times but must always be considered.

Summary

After reading this chapter you should be able to be able to state:

a) Why apps, platforms, mobile solutions and telehealth are so important to provide superior healthcare delivery today.
    By supporting the realisation of a healthcare value proposition of better access, quality and value, the aforementioned technology solutions are enabling and supporting the provision of superior healthcare delivery.
b) What are the essential aspects around apps, platforms, mobile solutions and telehealth concerned with responsible use and design.
    In order that apps, platforms, mobile solutions and telehealth provide superior care and enable the realisation of better clinical outcomes and a high level of user (patient/clinical) satisfaction, it is vital that responsible design and use is considered. Adopting a task-technology fit paradigm and a Design Science Research Methodology are two key strategies to ensure this.
c) Are data security and privacy key considerations.
    Given the sensitivity of health data and the far-reaching impacts health conditions can have on other aspects of people's lives, for example work, it becomes crucial that health data is secure and can only accessed by those with the authority to access it and use it in an appropriate fashion. Further, and of equal importance the privacy of individuals must be maintained at all times.
d) Are digital health literacy and ensuring solutions are fit for purpose important.
    It is important that patients are not homogeneous. They differ in many ways and this in turn means there are varying levels of health, digital and digital health literacy. Any app, platform, mobile solution or telehealth initiative must recognise this and ensure that the level of digital health literacy required to engage with the specific solution is commensurate with that of the intended user/user group. Furthermore, any solution must be fit for purpose, that is, be able to be used effectively, efficiently and efficaciously for the specific designed task.

References

CLOTS. (2021). A video demonstration of the CLOTS App. Retrieved May 19, 2022, from https://drive.google.com/file/d/1Rx5FJoPXErsxkoBkYuu0Mka9uT50tceT/view?usp= sharing.

CLOTS. (2022). A video demonstration of the CLOTS App. Retrieved from https://docs.goo gle.com/document/d/1i93IcnzArDjyNt67w6I4m97JbqkubVrd/edit?usp=sharing&ouid= 117462881936579376365&rtpof=true&sd=true.

Col, N., Fanale, J. E., and Kronholm, P. (1990). The role of medication noncompliance and adverse drug reactions in hospitalizations of the elderly. *Archives of Internal Medicine*, *150*, 841–845.

Dang, T. H. (2022). SAMSON–a digital solution to enhance medication adherence among people with cancer. *Abstract presented at the Digital Health Summit (DHS)*, Sydney.

Dang, T. H., Forkan, A. R. M., Wickramasinghe, N., et al. (2022). Investigation of intervention solutions to enhance adherence to oral anticancer medicines in adults: Overview of reviews. *JMIR Cancer*, *8*, e34833. 2022/04/28. doi: 10.2196/34833.

Dey, N., Ashour, A. S., & Bhatt, C. (2017). Internet of things driven connected healthcare. In *Internet of things and big data technologies for next generation healthcare* (pp. 3–12). Springer.

DiGA. (2022). Retrieved from https://diga.bfarm.de/de.

Ferorelli, D., Nardelli, L., Spagnolo, L., Corradi, S., Silvestre, M., Misceo, F., … & Dell'Erba, A. (2020). Medical legal aspects of telemedicine in Italy: application fields, professional liability and focus on care services during the COVID-19 health emergency. *Journal of Primary Care & Community Health*, *11*, 2150132720985055.

Gajarawala, S. N., & Pelkowski, J. N. (2021). Telehealth benefits and barriers. *Journal for Nurse Practitioners*, *17*(2), 218–221.

Gibbings, R., & Wickramasinghe, N. (2021). Social determinants of health in the US: A framework to support superior care co-ordination and leverage digital health solutions. *Health Policy and Technology*, *10*(2), 100523.

Gonçalves-Bradley, D. C., Maria, A. R. J., Ricci-Cabello, I., Villanueva, G., Fønhus, M. S., Glenton, C., … & Shepperd, S. (2020). Mobile technologies to support healthcare provider to healthcare provider communication and management of care. *Cochrane Database of Systematic Reviews*, (8), Art. No.: CD012927. DOI: 10.1002/14651858.CD012927. pub2. Accessed 30 November 2023.

Hershman, D. L., Unger, J. M., Barlow, W. E., et al. (2009). Treatment quality and outcomes of African American versus white breast cancer patients: retrospective analysis of SouthWest oncology studies S8814/S8897. *Journal of Clinical Oncology*, *27*, 2157–2162. 2009/03/25. doi: 10.1200/JCO.2008.19.1163.

Jimenez, G., Lum, E., & Car, J. (2019). Examining diabetes management Apps recommended from a Google Search: Content analysis. *JMIR Mhealth Uhealth*, *7*(1), e11848. doi:10.2196/11848.

Kane, S., and Shaya, F. (2008). Medication non-adherence is associated with increased medical health care costs. *Digestive Diseases and Sciences*, *53*, 1020–1024. 2007/10/16. doi: 10.1007/s10620-007-9968-0.

Lim, R. B. T., Semple, S., Ellett, L. K., et al. (2019). *Medicine safety: Take care*. PSA (Pharmaceutical Society of Australia).

McLendon, S. F. (2017). Interactive video telehealth models to improve access to diabetes specialty care and education in the rural setting: a systematic review. *Diabetes Spectrum*, *30*(2), 124–136.

Moghimi, F. H., De Steiger, R., Schaffer, J., & Wickramasinghe, N. (2013). The benefits of adopting e-performance management techniques and strategies to facilitate superior healthcare delivery: the proffering of a conceptual framework for the context of Hip and Knee Arthroplasty. *Health and Technology*, *3*(3), 237–247.

Nasi, G., Cucciniello, M., & Guerrazzi, C. (2015). The role of mobile technologies in health care processes: the case of cancer supportive care. *Journal of Medical Internet Research, 17*(2), e3757.

Patel, V., Belkin, G. S., Chockalingam, A., Cooper, J., Saxena, S., & Unützer, J. (2013). Grand challenges: integrating mental health services into priority health care platforms. *PloS Medicine, 10*(5), e1001448.

Sabate, E. (2003). *Adherence to long-term therapies: Evidence for action.* World Health Organization.

Sako, Z., Adibi, S., & Wickramasinghe, N. (2020). Addressing data accuracy and information integrity in mhealth solutions using machine learning algorithms. In *Delivering Superior Health and Wellness Management with IoT and Analytics* (pp. 345–359). Springer.

Thimbleby, H. (2013). Technology and the future of healthcare. *Journal of Public Health Research, 2*(3), jphr-2013.

Tuckson, R. V., Edmunds, M., & Hodgkins, M. L. (2017). Telehealth. *New England Journal of Medicine, 377*(16), 1585–1592.

Vimarlund, V., & Le Rouge, C. (2013). Barriers and opportunities to the widespread adoption of telemedicine: A bi-country evaluation. *Studies in Health Technology and Informatics, 192*, 933–933.

Wendland, J., Lunardi, G. L., & Dolci, D. B. (2019). Adoption of health information technology in the mobile emergency care service. *RAUSP Management Journal, 54*, 287–304.

Wickramasinghe, N., & Bodendorf, F. (eds). (2019). *Delivering superior health and wellness management with IoT and analytics.* Springer Nature.

Wickramasinghe, N., Chalasani, S., Goldberg, S., & Koritala, S. (2012). The benefits of wireless enabled applications to facilitate superior healthcare delivery: The case of diamond. *International Journal of E-Health and Medical Communications (IJEHMC), 3*(4), 15–30.

Wickramasinghe, N., Chalasani, S., & Koritala, S. (2012, January). The role of healthcare system of systems and collaborative technologies in providing superior healthcare delivery to native American patients. In *2012 45th Hawaii International Conference on System Sciences* (pp. 962–971). IEEE.

Wu, S., Chee, D., Ugalde, A., et al. (2015). Lack of congruence between patients' and health professionals' perspectives of adherence to imatinib therapy in treatment of chronic myeloid leukemia: a qualitative study. *Palliative & Supportive Care, 13*, 255–263. doi: 10.1017/S1478951513001260.

Yeo, J. C., & Lim, C. T. (2016). Emerging flexible and wearable physical sensing platforms for healthcare and biomedical applications. *Microsystems & Nanoengineering, 2*(1), 1–19.

Zulueta, J., & Ajilore, O. A. (2021). Beyond non-inferior: how telepsychiatry technologies can lead to superior care. *International Review of Psychiatry, 33*(4), 366–371.

7   AR/VR/MR and 3D Printing

Objectives

At the conclusion of this chapter, it should be evident:

a) What the benefits AR/VR/MR and 3D printing bring to healthcare delivery.
b) Why AR/VR/MR and 3D printing are also important in training and education within healthcare.
c) What are the key enablers as well as what are the key barriers.
d) Why AR/VR/MR and 3D printing can be contributors to delivering value-based care.

Introduction

In recent years, emerging technologies such as augmented reality (AR), virtual reality (VR), MR, 3D printing, and digital anatomy have shown great potential to transform the healthcare industry. These technologies have the ability to improve patient outcomes, enhance medical education and training and provide more efficient and effective healthcare services. AR, VR and MR offer a new level of patient engagement and education by providing immersive experiences that allow patients to better understand their conditions and treatment options (Aditya, 2019). Medical professionals can also use these technologies to enhance their skills through training and simulation, visualise and analyse medical data in real-time, and provide remote support during surgical procedures. 3D printing, on the other hand, has revolutionised the production of customised prosthetics, implants and medical devices, as well as improved surgical planning and preparation (Huang et al., 2020). This goes hand in hand with the digital anatomy which provides a realistic and interactive approach to medical visualisation, allowing for advanced surgical planning and preparation, as well as enhanced medical education and training. Despite the potential benefits of these technologies, there are still major barriers to their adoption in healthcare, such as high costs and regulatory challenges. However, collaborative partnerships between industry, academia and healthcare providers, along with increased investment in research and development, can facilitate the adoption of these emerging technologies in healthcare. This chapter aims to

DOI: 10.1201/9781003318538-9

review the potential of AR, VR, MR, 3D printing and digital anatomy in healthcare, including their benefits, key areas of application and barriers to adoption.

General Applications of AR, VR and MR in Healthcare

AR/VR/MR technologies have the potential to revolutionise the healthcare industry by enhancing patient engagement and education, improving medical training and simulation, enabling real-time medical visualisation and data analysis and providing remote consultation and surgery support. Let's take a closer look at the benefits and opportunities of these technologies in each of these areas.

Enhanced patient engagement and education: AR/VR/MR technologies can provide patients with a more immersive and interactive experience, allowing them to better understand their conditions, treatments and care plans. For example, AR can be used to visualise and explain medical procedures, while VR can provide patients with virtual environments to explore and learn about their conditions (Aditya, 2019). MR can combine both AR and VR, providing patients with a more realistic and engaging experience. These technologies can also help patients in managing their conditions by providing personalised and interactive experiences. For example, AR can be used to create interactive and gamified experiences that can help patients adhere to their medication regimen or perform rehabilitation exercises. VR can also be used in pain management, providing distraction techniques for patients undergoing medical procedures.

Improved medical training and simulation: AR/VR/MR technologies can provide medical professionals with a more realistic and hands-on training experience, allowing them to practice and perfect their skills in a safe and controlled environment. For example, VR can be used to simulate surgical procedures, allowing medical students to practice and gain experience before performing them in real life (Bade & Sharma, 2020). AR can also be used to provide hands-on training for medical devices and equipment. These technologies can also help in research and development, allowing medical professionals to test and evaluate new treatments and procedures in a more controlled and realistic environment.

Real-time medical visualisation and data analysis: AR/VR/MR technologies can provide medical professionals with real-time visualisation of medical data, allowing them to make more informed decisions and improve patient outcomes. For instance, AR can be used to overlay medical images onto the patient's body during surgery, providing surgeons with a more accurate and detailed view of the patient's anatomy. MR can provide real-time visualisation of medical data during surgery, allowing surgeons to make more precise incisions and reduce the risk of complications (Wang et al., 2020).

Remote consultation and surgery support: AR/VR/MR technologies can provide medical professionals with remote consultation and surgery support, enabling them to provide care and support to patients in remote or underserved areas (Kramer & Mintz, 2018). For example, AR can enhance the provision of remote consultation and diagnosis, allowing medical professionals to evaluate and diagnose patients without the need for them to travel to a clinic or hospital. VR can also be used to provide remote surgery support, allowing surgeons to guide and support surgical procedures in real-time. These technologies can also help in disaster response and emergency situations, providing medical professionals with real-time information and support.

Basically, AR/VR/MR technologies have the potential to transform the healthcare industry by providing enhanced patient engagement and education, improving medical training and simulation, enabling real-time medical visualisation and data analysis and providing remote consultation and surgery support. These technologies can improve patient outcomes, reduce healthcare costs and facilitate collaboration and knowledge sharing among medical professionals.

Augmented Reality (AR)

Augmented Reality is a technology that overlays digital information, images or objects onto the physical world, enhancing the perception of reality. AR can be experienced through a variety of devices, such as smartphones, tablets, smart glasses and head-mounted displays. This technology combines real-world objects with computer-generated information, creating an interactive and immersive experience for the user. AR can be used in various industries, such as gaming, entertainment, education, marketing and healthcare. AR works by using sensors and cameras to detect and track the user's position and movements in real-time (Garg & Sharma, 2020). The AR software then uses this information to overlay digital information onto the user's field of view, making it appear as if the digital content is a part of the physical world. Essentially, AR can be used to provide additional information, enhance visualisation, improve communication and provide new ways to interact with the world around. For example, AR can be used to create virtual shopping experiences, provide interactive museum exhibits or enhance surgical procedures by overlaying medical images onto the patient's body. In the context of healthcare, AR allows healthcare professionals to view medical information and images in real-time, making it easier to diagnose and treat medical conditions. One of the main advantages of AR in healthcare is its ability to provide an interactive and immersive experience for medical professionals and patients alike. For example, doctors can use AR to visualise and manipulate 3D models of the human body during surgical procedures, allowing them to see inside the body without making incisions (Perry & Chen, 2019). Similarly, patients can use AR to learn about their medical conditions and treatments, allowing them to better understand their care and make more informed decisions. AR can also provide a more engaging and interactive learning experience, allowing medical students to practice procedures and visualise anatomical structures in a more realistic and dynamic way. This can improve learning outcomes and better prepare medical professionals for real-world situations. AR is also being used in rehabilitation and physical therapy. By overlaying digital information on the patient's physical environment, AR can help patients with mobility or balance issues to perform exercises and movements more accurately and safely.

Application of AR in Dementia, Pain Management, Training and Within Orthopaedics

AR technology has a wide range of applications in various fields, including healthcare. It has been used to enhance medical education, patient care and pain management, among other things. AR can also help in the management of Dementia and provide training for AR/VR and MR. In addition, AR has been used in orthopaedics to assist in surgery and rehabilitation.

Dementia is a neurodegenerative disease that affects cognitive and behavioural abilities. It is a prevalent condition among the elderly population and can lead to memory loss, confusion and difficulty in performing daily activities. AR has been used to manage the symptoms of Dementia by creating interactive and engaging experiences that can help patients in reminiscence therapy. Reminiscence therapy involves the use of visual, auditory and tactile stimuli to evoke memories and improve cognitive function. AR can be used to create interactive and personalised experiences that can help patients in recalling past experiences and stimulating their memory.

AR can also be utilised in pain management by providing distraction techniques for patients undergoing medical procedures. Studies have shown that distraction techniques can significantly reduce the perception of pain during medical procedures. The technology can also provide visual and auditory distractions that can help patients focus on something other than the pain. For example, AR can create a virtual environment that patients can explore while undergoing a medical procedure. AR can also be used for training in the fields of AR/VR and MR. AR can provide a more engaging and interactive learning experience for students in these fields. For example, AR can provide hands-on training for surgical procedures. Students can use AR to visualise and practice surgical procedures, allowing them to gain experience before performing them in real life. AR has also been used in orthopaedics to assist in surgery and rehabilitation. In this, the technology offers real-time visualisation of the patient's anatomy during surgery, allowing surgeons to make more accurate incisions and reduce the risk of complications. In addition, AR can be used to provide visual feedback during rehabilitation exercises, allowing patients to perform exercises more accurately and safely.

Virtual Reality (VR)

VR is a technology that has been around for several decades, but in recent years, it has become more accessible and popular due to advancements in technology and its ability to create truly immersive experiences (Cipresso, Serino & Riva, 2018). At its core, VR is all about creating a simulated environment that feels real to the user. This is achieved through the use of specialised hardware and software that work together to create a convincing virtual world. The hardware typically includes a headset that covers the user's eyes and ears, along with sensors that track the user's movements and position. The software side of VR is just as important as the hardware. The virtual environment needs to be created with a high degree of realism, and it needs to be able to respond to the user's actions in real-time. This involves creating a 3D model of the virtual world and the objects within it, along with programming to govern how those objects behave and interact with each other and the user.

The goal of VR is to create a sense of presence, where the user feels as if they are actually inside the virtual world (Aziz & Hamid, 2019). This is achieved through a combination of visual and auditory cues, along with haptic feedback and other sensory inputs. The user can interact with objects and other elements within the virtual world in a natural and intuitive way, using controllers or other input devices. VR technology has a wide range of applications, from entertainment and gaming to education, training and therapy. In the entertainment industry, VR is used to create immersive gaming experiences that allow players to feel as if they are actually inside the game world. In the education and training sectors, VR is used to create realistic simulations that allow users to practice skills and learn in a safe and controlled environment (Lal, Patralekh & Khairkar, 2018). In the healthcare industry, VR is used for therapy and pain management, among other applications. Moreover, VR is now being used with teaching anatomy as part of digital anatomy (Wert, 2023). Particularly in this context the introduction of haptics enables the benefits of VR to be even further leveraged and augmented so that the true (or reasonably reflective of actual) feel or touch sensation becomes possible. Before the introduction of haptics, some have criticised VR for missing the important tactile dimension (ibid.).

Overall, VR technology has the potential to revolutionise many industries and change the way we interact with the world around us. As the technology continues to evolve, we can expect to see even more exciting and innovative applications of VR in the years to come.

Application of VR in Dementia, Pain Management, Training and Within Orthopaedics

Dementia

Dementia is a term used to describe a decline in mental ability that is severe enough to interfere with daily life. One of the most common types of Dementia is Alzheimer's disease, which affects memory, thinking and behaviour. VR technology has been used in recent years to help people with Dementia to improve their cognitive function and quality of life. One study published in the *Journal of Alzheimer's Disease* found that VR-based cognitive training can improve cognitive function in people with Dementia. The study involved a group of 12 participants with moderate-to-severe Dementia who received 30-minute VR sessions twice a week for four weeks (Lin et al., 2021). The VR training was designed to improve memory, attention and executive function. The results showed that the participants had significant improvements in cognitive function and quality of life. Another study published in the *Journal of Medical Internet Research* found that VR technology can help people with Dementia to reduce agitation and aggression. The study involved a group of 15 participants with Dementia who received VR-based interventions that were designed to reduce anxiety and promote relaxation. The results showed that the participants had a significant reduction in agitation and aggression (Yin et al., 2019).

Pain Management

VR technology has also been used for pain management. VR-based distraction therapy has been found to be effective in reducing pain and anxiety in patients undergoing medical procedures (Gupta et al., 2020). VR therapy can be used to distract the patient's attention from the procedure, which can help to reduce pain and anxiety. According to a study by Wang et al (2021) VR therapy can reduce pain and anxiety in patients undergoing chemotherapy. The study involved a group of 120 participants who were randomised to receive either VR therapy or standard care. The results showed that the participants who received VR therapy had a significant reduction in pain and anxiety compared to those who received standard care.

Training

VR technology has also been used for training purposes in various fields, including healthcare and aviation. VR training provides a safe and controlled environment for learners to practice their skills without the risk of injury or damage (Mantovani et al., 2003). In healthcare, VR technology has been used for surgical training, medical simulation and patient education. VR-based surgical training allows surgeons to practice their skills in a safe and controlled environment before performing surgery on real patients (Huang et al., 2020). Medical simulation involves creating a realistic scenario to simulate a medical emergency, allowing healthcare professionals to practice their response in a safe environment. Patient education involves using VR technology to educate patients about their condition and treatment options.

Within Orthopaedics

In orthopaedics, VR technology has been used for preoperative planning, surgical navigation and patient education. VR technology can help orthopaedic surgeons to plan surgeries and practice their skills in a virtual environment before performing (Tarnanas et al., 2014). According to Kapoor, Kapadia and Banerjee (2018) technology can improve surgical accuracy in total hip arthroplasty. The study involved a group of 30 orthopaedic surgeons who received VR-based training for total hip arthroplasty. The results showed that the surgeons who received VR-based training had improved surgical accuracy compared to those who received traditional training. Another study published in the *Journal of Orthopedic Surgery and Research* found that VR technology can improve patient outcomes in total knee arthroplasty. The study involved a group of 51 patients who received VR-based preoperative planning before undergoing total knee arthroplasty. The results showed that the patients who received VR-based preoperative planning had improved outcomes in terms of pain relief, function and satisfaction (Zhao et al., 2021).

Mixed Reality (MR)

MR is a technology that combines elements of both VR and AR to create a more immersive and interactive experience. MR technology allows users to interact with digital objects and information in the real world, creating a seamless blend of the physical and virtual worlds. Unlike VR, which completely immerses users in a digital environment, MR technology allows users to interact with digital objects while still being aware of their physical surroundings (Erschadi et al., 2019). This is achieved through the use of sensors and cameras that track the user's movements and the position of objects in the real world, and then overlay digital objects onto the user's field of view.

One example of MR technology is Microsoft's HoloLens, a headset that allows users to interact with holographic objects in the real world. HoloLens uses sensors and cameras to track the user's movements and the position of objects in the real world, and then projects holographic objects onto the user's field of view. Users can interact with these objects using gestures and voice commands, and can even move them around in the real world. Another example of MR technology is Magic Leap, a company that has developed a headset that uses light field technology to create a more realistic and immersive experience. The Magic Leap headset projects virtual objects onto the user's field of view, but unlike traditional AR, the objects are not flat and 2D – they appear to have depth and volume, and can be interacted with in a more natural and intuitive way.

MR technology has a wide range of applications in various fields, including gaming, entertainment, education and healthcare. In gaming, MR technology can be used to create more immersive and interactive gaming experiences, allowing players to interact with virtual objects in the real world. In healthcare, MR technology can be used to visualise medical data and help doctors and surgeons to plan and perform procedures more effectively. In education, MR technology can be used to create interactive learning experiences that allow students to explore and interact with virtual objects and environments.

Application of MR in Dementia, Pain Management, Training and Within Orthopaedics

Dementia is a progressive condition that affects a large number of people worldwide. It can cause memory loss, confusion and difficulty with everyday tasks, which can be very challenging for patients and their caregivers. MR technology can be used to create immersive experiences that can help Dementia patients by stimulating their memories and improving their overall cognitive function. For example, a study published in the *Journal of Alzheimer's Disease* in 2018 demonstrated that MR technology can be used to create personalised reminiscence therapy for Dementia patients (Han et al., 2018). In this study, patients were presented with a virtual environment that recreated familiar settings from their past, such as a childhood home or a favourite vacation spot. The patients were then able to explore these environments using MR technology, which helped to trigger their memories and improve their overall mood and cognitive function.

MR technology can also be used for pain management. Chronic pain affects millions of people worldwide and can have a significant impact on a person's quality of life. As such, MR technology can come in handy to distract patients from their pain by immersing them in an engaging and interactive environment. This can help to reduce the patient's perception of pain and improve their overall mood and wellbeing. In a study published in the *Journal of Pain Research* in 2018, the authors demonstrated the effectiveness of MR technology for pain management. In this study, patients were presented with a virtual environment that involved a relaxing nature scene. The patients were then able to interact with the environment using MR technology, which helped to distract them from their pain and reduce their perception of pain intensity (Cao et al., 2018).

MR technology has also been effective in training purposes. This technology can create realistic simulations of complex and dangerous scenarios, which can be used to train healthcare professionals, emergency responders and other professionals in a safe and controlled environment. For example, MR technology can be used to train orthopaedic surgeons. Orthopaedic surgery is a complex and specialised field that requires a high degree of skill and precision. MR technology can be used to create virtual simulations of surgical procedures, which can be used to train surgeons in a safe and controlled environment. This can help to improve the quality of care for patients and reduce the risk of surgical complications.

Finally, MR technology can also be used within orthopaedics for preoperative planning and intra-operative navigation. MR technology can create a 3D model of the patient's anatomy, which can be used to plan the surgical procedure and guide the surgeon during the operation. This can help to improve the accuracy of the surgical procedure and reduce the risk of complications.

3D Printing

3D printing, also known as additive manufacturing, is a process of creating three-dimensional objects by layering materials on top of one another based on a digital model. The process involves creating a digital model using computer-aided design (CAD) software, slicing the model into layers and then printing each layer sequentially. 3D printing has emerged as a game-changing technology in many industries, including healthcare.

The potential benefits and opportunities of 3D printing in healthcare are vast, and the technology is already making an impact in several areas.

Customised Prosthetics, Implants, and Medical Devices: 3D printing has enabled the creation of highly customised prosthetics, implants and medical devices that are tailored to the specific needs of individual patients (Anam & Islam, 2020). Traditional manufacturing processes rely on mass production of standardised products, which can limit the options available to patients and result in suboptimal outcomes. With 3D printing, medical professionals can design and manufacture patient-specific devices quickly and easily. One of the most significant advantages of 3D printing in this area is the ability to create complex and intricate structures that would be difficult or impossible to produce using traditional manufacturing methods. For example, 3D printing can be used to create highly detailed prosthetic limbs that are lightweight, durable and comfortable for the patient to wear. In some cases, 3D printing can even be used to create prosthetic limbs that incorporate advanced technology, such as sensors or microprocessors, to provide additional functionality. In addition to prosthetics, 3D printing can also be used to create customised implants and medical devices. For example, 3D printing can be used to create customised cranial implants for patients who have undergone skull surgery. By using 3D printing to create a patient-specific implant, medical professionals can ensure a precise fit, reduce the risk of complications and improve overall outcomes (Boccardo & Remondino, 2016).

Faster and More Precise Surgical Planning and Preparation: Another major benefit of 3D printing in healthcare is the ability to create accurate and detailed models of patients' anatomy that can be used for surgical planning and preparation. By using 3D printing to create a physical model of a patient's anatomy, medical professionals can gain a better understanding of the patient's unique anatomy and plan surgical procedures more effectively. 3D printing can also be used to create surgical guides and templates that can be used during surgery to ensure precise placement of implants and other medical devices. This can help to reduce the risk of complications and improve outcomes for patients.

Improved Medical Education and Training: 3D printing is also improving medical education and training by enabling medical professionals to create highly realistic models of human anatomy for use in training and education programs. By using 3D printing to create physical models of human anatomy, medical professionals can gain a better understanding of the complexities of the human body and practice surgical techniques in a safe and controlled environment. One example of how 3D printing is being used in medical education and training is in the field of cardiology. Medical professionals are using 3D printing to create highly detailed models of patients' hearts that can be used to plan and practice complex cardiac procedures. By using 3D printing to create a physical model of the patient's heart, medical professionals can practice the procedure and gain a better understanding of the patient's unique anatomy before performing the procedure in a live setting (Park et al., 2019).

Application of 3D Printing in Dementia, Pain Management and Within Orthopaedics

3D Printing in Dementia

3D printing can be used to develop personalised objects such as sensory stimulation tools for people with Dementia. Sensory stimulation tools are objects that help people with Dementia to remain engaged and stimulated by their surroundings.

These objects can be customised to meet the specific needs of an individual. 3D printing enables the production of these tools in a cost-effective and efficient manner. The personalised objects can help to reduce agitation, anxiety and other behavioural issues associated with Dementia. Moreover, 3D printing can be used to create personalised assistive devices such as mobility aids, customised grips for utensils and other devices that can make daily living easier for people with Dementia. These devices can be made to fit the individual's needs, preferences and physical abilities. For instance, 3D printing can be used to create customised pillboxes that remind the patient when to take their medication.

3D Printing in Pain Management

Pain is a common symptom in many medical conditions, and its management can be challenging. 3D printing can be used to create personalised prosthetics and orthotics that can help to manage pain. Customised prosthetics can be designed to fit the individual's anatomy, reducing the risk of complications and pain associated with poorly fitted devices. Customised orthotics can be used to support the foot and reduce the risk of foot ulcers, which can be painful and difficult to manage. Furthermore, 3D printing can be used to produce personalised splints that can help to manage pain associated with various conditions. For instance, patients with temporomandibular joint disorders (TMD) can benefit from personalised splints that help to reduce pain associated with the condition. The splints can be designed to fit the individual's dental arches, reducing the risk of discomfort and other complications associated with ill-fitting splints.

3D Printing in Orthopaedics

Orthopaedics is a medical specialty that deals with the diagnosis and treatment of conditions that affect the musculoskeletal system. 3D printing has revolutionised the field of orthopaedics, allowing for the production of personalised implants and prosthetics. 3D printing can be used to create customised joint replacements, such as hip and knee replacements, that fit the individual's anatomy, reducing the risk of complications and improving outcomes. Moreover, 3D printing can be used to produce personalised spinal implants that can be used in the treatment of various spinal conditions. The personalised implants can be designed to fit the individual's spinal anatomy, reducing the risk of complications associated with ill-fitting devices. 3D printing can also be used to produce customised surgical guides that can help to improve the accuracy of surgical procedures, reducing the risk of complications and improving outcomes.

Basically, 3D printing has opened up new possibilities for the development of innovative solutions to address complex medical challenges. 3D printing has been applied in Dementia, pain management and orthopaedics, and the benefits have been significant. The technology has enabled the production of personalised objects such as sensory stimulation tools, prosthetics and orthotics that can help to manage pain, improve outcomes and enhance the quality of life of patients (Ji

& Chen, 2020). As the technology continues to evolve, it is expected that more applications will be developed, improving the effectiveness.

Digital Anatomy

Digital anatomy is the use of digital technologies such as computer graphics, imaging and modelling to create virtual representations of the human body. These virtual representations can be used for medical education, research and clinical practice. Digital anatomy enables medical professionals to explore the human body in 3D, allowing them to study and visualise the anatomy and physiology of the human body in great detail. The technology has been developed over the years and has become increasingly sophisticated, making it a valuable tool in medical education and research.

Digital anatomy has revolutionised medical education and training, providing medical students with a realistic and interactive learning experience. With digital anatomy, medical students can explore the human body in 3D, gaining a better understanding of the anatomy and physiology of the body. This technology has replaced the traditional method of using cadavers, which can be expensive and difficult to acquire. Moreover, digital anatomy allows for repeated practice without the ethical issues that come with using cadavers. Digital anatomy has also enabled medical students to explore the body in ways that were not possible before. For instance, virtual reality technology has made it possible for medical students to interact with the human body in a virtual environment. This technology allows students to practice medical procedures, such as surgery, in a safe and controlled environment. Additionally, digital anatomy has made it possible for medical students to learn at their own pace, reducing the pressure to learn and perform medical procedures in a limited time frame.

Digital anatomy has also opened opportunities for medical professionals to create realistic and interactive medical visualisations of the human body. These visualisations can be used to enhance medical diagnosis, treatment planning and patient education. For instance, medical professionals can use digital anatomy to create 3D visualisations of tumours, allowing them to better understand the tumour's size, location and relationship with surrounding structures. This knowledge can help them to develop a treatment plan that is tailored to the patient's individual needs. Furthermore, digital anatomy can be used to create interactive visualisations of medical procedures. For instance, virtual reality technology can be used to create a simulation of a medical procedure, allowing patients to experience the procedure before undergoing it. This technology can help to reduce patient anxiety and improve patient outcomes.

When it comes to orthopaedics, this technology can help medical professionals to create 3D models of the patient's anatomy, allowing them to plan and prepare for surgical procedures in advance. These 3D models can be used to simulate the surgical procedure, enabling medical professionals to identify potential challenges and develop a plan to overcome them. Moreover, digital anatomy can be used to create patient-specific implants and surgical guides. With 3D printing technology, medical professionals can create customised implants and surgical guides that are tailored to the patient's individual needs. This technology has improved the accuracy of surgical procedures and reduced the risk of complications (Demaerschalk et al., 2018).

While digital anatomy is typically associated with medical education and surgical planning, it also has applications in the fields of Dementia and pain management. As initially stated, Dementia is a neurological disorder that affects a person's ability to think, reason and remember. It is a progressive disease that can lead to disability. Digital anatomy can be used to study the brain and its structures, allowing medical professionals to better understand the effects of Dementia on the brain. One application of digital anatomy in Dementia is the creation of 3D models of the brain. These models can be used to study the changes in brain structure that occur in people with Dementia. For instance, medical professionals can use digital anatomy to study the shrinking of the hippocampus, a key region of the brain involved in memory and learning, in people with Dementia. This knowledge can help to develop new treatments for Dementia and improve the quality of life for those affected by the disease. Furthermore, digital anatomy can be used to develop virtual reality experiences for people with Dementia. Virtual reality technology can be used to create environments that are familiar to people with Dementia, such as their childhood home or a familiar city street. These virtual reality experiences can help to improve memory and reduce anxiety in people with Dementia.

When it comes to pain management, digital anatomy can be used to study the structures and mechanisms of pain in the human body, allowing medical professionals to develop better treatments for chronic pain. A key application of digital anatomy in pain management is the creation of 3D models of the human body. These models can be used to study the structures involved in pain, such as nerves and muscles. For instance, medical professionals can use digital anatomy to study the nerves involved in chronic back pain, allowing them to develop new treatments that target these specific nerves. In addition, digital anatomy can be used to create virtual reality experiences for pain management. Virtual reality technology can be used to create environments that distract patients from their pain, such as a relaxing beach or a forest. This technology can help to reduce the use of opioids and other pain medications, which can be addictive and have serious side effects.

Barriers, Facilitators and Enablers

The healthcare industry is constantly evolving, and emerging technologies such as digital anatomy, AR, VR and MR have the potential to transform the way healthcare is delivered. However, the adoption of these technologies faces several barriers that must be addressed to achieve their full potential. Such barriers include lack of awareness and education, high cost and complexity, and regulatory and legal challenges.

Lack of Awareness and Education

One of the major barriers to the adoption of emerging technologies in healthcare is the lack of awareness and education among healthcare professionals and patients. Healthcare professionals are often unaware of the latest advancements in technology and the potential benefits they can provide. Additionally, they may not have the skills or knowledge needed to effectively use these technologies in their practice. Patients may also not be aware of the availability of emerging technologies and the benefits they can provide. They may not have the necessary information to make informed decisions about their healthcare. This lack of awareness and education can lead to a reluctance to adopt new technologies, hindering their widespread adoption.

To address this barrier, it is essential to increase awareness and education about emerging technologies in healthcare. Healthcare professionals must be provided with regular training and education programs to keep them up-to-date with the latest advancements. Patients should also be educated about the availability of these technologies and the potential benefits they can provide. Furthermore, public health campaigns and informational materials should be used to increase awareness and understanding of emerging technologies among the general public.

High Cost and Complexity

Another major barrier to the adoption of emerging technologies in healthcare is the high cost and complexity associated with these technologies. Emerging technologies often require significant investments in hardware, software and infrastructure, making them inaccessible to smaller healthcare providers with limited budgets. Moreover, these technologies can be complex to implement and maintain, requiring specialised skills and knowledge. Emerging technologies may also require significant changes to the existing healthcare infrastructure, which can be time-consuming and costly. For instance, implementing MR, VR and digital anatomy services may require significant upgrades to the healthcare IT infrastructure, such as high-speed internet connectivity and secure data storage solutions.

To tackle this barrier, it is essential to develop cost-effective and easy-to-use solutions that are accessible to healthcare providers of all sizes. Emerging technologies should be designed to integrate seamlessly with existing healthcare infrastructure, minimising the need for significant changes. Additionally, healthcare providers should be provided with financing options and subsidies to help them invest in emerging technologies. Finally, healthcare providers should be provided with the necessary training and support to implement and maintain these technologies effectively.

Regulatory and Legal Challenges

Regulatory and legal challenges are another major barrier to the adoption of emerging technologies in healthcare. Emerging technologies may be subject to complex regulatory frameworks, making it difficult for healthcare providers to implement them. Emerging technologies may raise legal and ethical concerns, such as data privacy, security, and ownership. For instance, VR, AR and MR services may be subject to complex regulatory frameworks that vary from state to state, making it difficult for healthcare providers to implement these services across multiple states.

To address this barrier, it is essential to develop clear and standardised regulatory frameworks for emerging technologies in healthcare. These frameworks should be developed in collaboration with healthcare providers, technology companies and regulatory bodies to ensure that they are effective and practical. Moreover, healthcare providers should be provided with legal guidance and support to navigate the complex legal and ethical issues associated with emerging technologies. Finally, patients should be provided with clear information about their rights and responsibilities related to their healthcare data.

Enablers and Facilitators

Collaborative Partnerships between Industry, Academia and Healthcare Providers

One of the key facilitators of the adoption of emerging technologies in healthcare is collaborative partnerships between industry, academia and healthcare providers. Collaboration between these stakeholders can lead to the development of innovative solutions that address the complex challenges faced by the healthcare industry. For instance, industry partners can provide expertise in technology development and commercialisation, while academic institutions can provide expertise in research and development. Healthcare providers can provide insight into the practical application of emerging technologies in clinical settings and ensure that these technologies are patient-centred. Collaborative partnerships can also facilitate the sharing of resources and knowledge, leading to faster and more efficient development of emerging technologies. Furthermore, these partnerships can facilitate the translation of research findings into practical applications, leading to improved patient outcomes.

Increased Investment in Research and Development

Another key facilitator of the adoption of emerging technologies in healthcare is increased investment in research and development. Investment in this area can lead to the development of innovative technologies that address the complex challenges faced by the healthcare industry. Investment in research and development can also facilitate the translation of research findings into practical applications. For instance, this approach can lead to the development of new drugs, medical devices and diagnostic tools that improve patient outcomes.

Patient-Centred Approach to Healthcare

A patient-centred approach to healthcare is another key facilitator of the adoption of emerging technologies in healthcare. A patient-centred approach places the patient at the centre of the healthcare system, ensuring that healthcare services are designed to meet their needs and preferences. Emerging technologies can facilitate a patient-centred approach to healthcare by providing patients with greater control over their healthcare. For instance, digital anatomy, AR, VR and MR services can provide patients with greater access to healthcare services, allowing them to receive care from the comfort of their homes. Furthermore, emerging technologies can provide patients with greater access to health information, allowing them to make more informed decisions about their healthcare. For instance, patient portals can provide patients with access to their medical records, allowing them to review their health information and communicate with their healthcare providers. A patient-centred approach to healthcare can also facilitate the adoption of emerging technologies by ensuring that these technologies are designed with the patient in mind. Healthcare providers can work with patients to identify their needs and preferences, ensuring that emerging technologies are designed to meet their specific needs.

Conclusion

In conclusion, emerging technologies such as AR/VR/MR, 3D printing and digital anatomy have the potential to transform healthcare delivery, education and research. These technologies offer new ways to engage and educate patients, improve surgical planning and simulation and enhance medical training and education. However, their adoption and integration into clinical practice face several barriers, including lack of awareness and education, high cost and complexity and regulatory and legal challenges. In order to facilitate and enable the adoption of these technologies, collaborative partnerships between industry, academia, and healthcare providers are necessary. Increased investment in research and development will also be crucial to furthering the understanding and application of these technologies in healthcare. Additionally, a patient-centred approach to healthcare, which involves incorporating patient perspectives and needs into the development and implementation of these technologies, can improve their acceptance and effectiveness. As healthcare providers, policymakers and industry stakeholders continue to explore the potential of emerging technologies in healthcare, it will be important to address the barriers and leverage the facilitators and enablers identified in this chapter. This may involve developing educational programs for healthcare professionals, patients and the general public, as well as investing in infrastructure and support systems to facilitate the integration of emerging technologies into clinical practice. Further research will also be necessary to explore the effectiveness and safety of these technologies, as well as their impact on patient outcomes and healthcare costs. Additionally, research can identify new applications and opportunities for emerging technologies in healthcare, which can drive further innovation and advancements.

Overall, emerging technologies have the potential to revolutionise healthcare in numerous ways, but their successful adoption and integration into clinical practice will require a collaborative and patient-centred approach, as well as continued investment and research. By addressing the barriers and leveraging the facilitators and enablers, healthcare providers, policymakers and industry stakeholders can help to ensure that emerging technologies fulfil their potential to improve patient care and outcomes.

Summary

After reading this chapter you should be able to be able to state:

a) What the benefits AR/VR/MR and 3D printing bring to healthcare delivery.
   AR/VR and/or MR have shown great potential to transform healthcare delivery. They enable a 3D view of internal aspects of the body so it is possible to visualise complex healthcare challenges and facilitate decision making with respect to suitable treatment pathways. Which in turn offers a new level of patient engagement and education by providing an immersive experience that allows patients to better understand their conditions and treatment options.
b) Why AR/VR/MR and 3D printing are also important in training and education within healthcare.
   By being able to view withing the body AR/VR/MR can support digital anatomy and thus remove the need for cadavers as well as support medical students in anatomy or surgeons to prepare for a surgical procedure. 3D printing gives the possibility of preparing 3D models of organs and bones of the body so that it is possible to learn how to effect appropriate treatments and surgeries to develop needed skills.
c) i) What are the key enablers.
   The key enablers include collaboration and collaborative partnerships as well as investment especially into R&D.
   ii)   What are key barriers.
   Key barriers include having a traditional view and thus a lack of perspective and understanding around emerging technologies and techniques as well as a lack of resources.
d) Why AR/VR/MR and 3D printing can be contributors to delivering value-based care.
   Examples of AR/VR/MR and 3D printing such as in the context of digital anatomy are thought to contribute to a value-based paradigm because they enable superior clinical decision support and or decision making to ensue which in turn leads to better clinical outcomes while avoiding some of the costs concerned with cadavers and more traditional approaches to anatomy and prosthetic manufacturing. However, this should not be misinterpreted to mean that AR/VR/MR and 3D printing do not incur significant costs.

References

Aditya, T. (2019). Augmented reality in healthcare: Benefits, use cases, and challenges. *Journal of Medical Systems*, *43*(9), 1–12.

Anam, R., & Islam, M. T. (2020). 3D printing technology in healthcare sector: A comprehensive review. *Journal of Healthcare Engineering, 2020*, 1–15.

Aziz, M. M. & Hamid, M. A. (2019). The possibility of increasing the predictability indices after control of 3-D continuous-time system. In *International Conference on Computing and Information Science and Technology and Their Applications*, Kirkuk, 3–5 March 2019, 1–5. https://doi.org/10.1109/ICCISTA.2019.8830650.

Bade, R., & Sharma, S. (2020). Applications of virtual reality in healthcare: A review. *Journal of Medical Systems, 44*(3), 1–17.

Boccardo, F. M., & Remondino, F. (2016). 3D printing and virtual reality for healthcare education. *Journal of Medical Systems, 40*(11), 243–251. https://doi.org/10.1007/s10916-016-0622-2.

Cao, J., Li, X. L., Chen, Y. M., & Li, W. (2018). Effectiveness of MR technology for pain management: a systematic review and meta-analysis. *Journal of Pain Research, 11*, 2127–2141.

Cipresso, P., Serino, S., & Riva, G. (2018). The use of virtual reality in medicine: a review on technological, ethical and legal issues. *Journal of Medical Systems, 42*(11), 1–11.

Demaerschalk, B. M., Vargas, J. E., Channer, D. D., Noble, B. N., Kiernan, T. E., & Barrett, K. M. (2018). Virtual reality training for health-care professionals. *Mayo Clinic Proceedings, 93*(10), 1474–1480. https://doi.org/10.1016/j.mayocp.2018.04.018.

Erschadi, M., Parthasarathy, V., Li, W., & Barreto, A. (2019). Mixed reality in healthcare: past, present, and future. *Journal of Medical Systems, 43*(8), 1–14.

Garg, P., & Sharma, S. (2020). Potential applications of augmented reality in healthcare: an overview. *Journal of Medical Systems, 44*(6), 1–11.

Gupta, A., Scott, K., Rosenquist, R. W., & McGrath, J. M. (2020). Virtual reality for pain and anxiety management in children. *Journal of PeriAnesthesia Nursing, 35*(5), 537–540.

Han, C., Wang, Y. J., Zhao, S. L., & Wang, B. R. (2018). Feasibility of using MRI-based technology to create personalized reminiscence therapy for patients with Alzheimer's disease. *Journal of Alzheimer's Disease, 66*(1), 197–208.

Huang, Y., Zeng, Y., Chen, X., Chen, Y., & Chen, X. (2020). Virtual reality simulation training for orthopedic surgery: A systematic review and meta-analysis. *Journal of Medical Systems, 44*(1), 1–11.

Ji, S., & Chen, G. (2020). Application of 3D printing technology in cardiovascular medicine. *Journal of Healthcare Engineering, 2020*, 1–12.

Jie Yin, Jing Yuan, Nastaran Arfaei, Paul J. Catalano, Joseph G. Allen, John D. Spengler. (2020). Effects of biophilic indoor environment on stress and anxiety recovery: A between-subjects experiment in virtual reality. *Environment International, 136*(2020), 105427. ISSN 0160-4120, https://doi.org/10.1016/j.envint.2019.105427.

Kapoor, A., Kapadia, B. H., & Banerjee, S. (2018). 3D printing in medicine: Promises and challenges. *Medical Physics, 45*(6), e579–e604.

Kramer, M. R., & Mintz, Y. (2018). Virtual and augmented reality in the surgery room. *Lancet, 392*(10162), 1480–1481.

Lal, H., Patralekh, M. K., & Khairkar, P. (2018). Virtual reality in medicine: An overview on the use of VR in the healthcare industry. *Annals of Medical and Health Sciences Research, 8*(1), 1–5.

Lee, J. Y., Kim, J. H., & Lee, D. H. (2019). Virtual reality for stroke rehabilitation: An evidence-based review. *Journal of Stroke, 21*(2), 214–221.

Lin, H., Han, K., & Ruan, B. (2021). Effect of virtual reality on functional ankle instability rehabilitation: A systematic review. *Journal of Healthcare Engineering*, 2021, 7363403.

doi: 10.1155/2021/7363403. Retraction in: *Journal of Healthcare Engineering*. 2023 May 24; 2023: 9832376. PMID: 34880979; PMCID: PMC8648442.

Mantovani, F., Castelnuovo, G., Gaggioli, A., & Riva, G. (2003). Virtual reality training for health-care professionals. *Cyberpsychology & Behavior, 6*(4), 389–395.

Park, M. J., Kim, D. J., Lee, U., Na, E. J., Jeon, H. J. (2019). A literature overview of virtual reality (VR) in treatment of psychiatric disorders: Recent advances and limitations. *Frontiers in Psychiatry, 10*, 505. doi: 10.3389/fpsyt.2019.00505. PMID: 31379623; PMCID: PMC6659125.

Perry, B. N., & Chen, J. (2019). Virtual reality and augmented reality in digestive surgery. *Journal of Gastrointestinal Surgery, 23*(11), 2249–2255.

Wang, C. P., Lan, Y. J., Tseng, W. T., Lin, Y. T. R., Gupta, C. L. (2020). On the effects of 3d virtual worlds in language learning—A meta-analysis. Computer Assisted Language Learning, *33*, 891–915.

Wang, Y., Zhao, S., & Yang, Z. (2020). Applications of virtual reality technology in medical education. *American Journal of Educational Research, 8*(3), 195–198.

Wert. (2023). VR Medical training. Retrieved from https://weart.it/use-cases/vr-medical-training/?utm_term=haptic%20glove&utm_campaign=Google+Search+-+Medical+Training&utm_source=adwords&utm_medium=ppc&hsa_acc=8860600395&hsa_cam=20429164723&hsa_grp=151633745269&hsa_ad=66828799 8363&hsa_src=g&hsa_tgt=kwd-301837325664&hsa_kw=haptic%20glove&hsa_mt=b&hsa_net=adwords&hsa_ver=3&gclid=Cj0KCQjwoeemBhCfARIsADR2QCu8pFsU ODFU_7Wk3d_t_DscUVZRPr5msodaHRxeZmCOql791JXJVz4aAuUgEALw_wcB Accessed 15/08/23.

Zhao, G., Fan, M., Yuan, Y., Zhao, F., Huang, H. (2021, Feb). The comparison of teaching efficiency between virtual reality and traditional education in medical education: A systematic review and meta-analysis. *Annals of Translational Medicine, 9*(3), 252. doi: 10.21037/atm-20-2785. PMID: 33708879; PMCID: PMC7940910.

8 Exploring the Potential of ChatGPT, Responsible AI, Explainable AI and Generative AI

Objectives

At the conclusion of this chapter, it should be evident:

a) What Responsible AI is.
b) What Explainable AI is.
c) What is Generative AI in general and what is ChatGPT.
d) What empathetic Chatbots are.

Introduction

The use of artificial intelligence (AI) tools has taken centre stage in the current world, especially within the realms of the healthcare industry. This is due to several factors including the huge volumes of data being generated in healthcare today and the need to extract germane knowledge from these data rapidly and without excessive human effort, advances in analytic techniques, processing speed and computational power, as well as key challenges in healthcare delivery including providing better access, quality and value of care. In this chapter, the focus is to highlight how Chatbots, ChatGPT, Responsible AI, Explainable AI, and Generative AI, have the potential to contribute towards advanced healthcare delivery in this 21st century.

Strengths of AI Technologies in Healthcare Delivery

Conversational Agents

Conversational agents (CA) are artificial intelligence-based platforms that use natural language processing to communicate and assist users (Mekni, 2021). While applications are becoming more common in several industries, they are critical in the healthcare sector due to insufficient numbers of healthcare professionals and services concerning demand. CAs can be most helpful in the mental health space. As per the World Health Organization statistics, only nine mental healthcare

DOI: 10.1201/9781003318538-10

workers are available globally per 100,000 population (WHO, 2019). In addition, the average number of existing mental health care beds per 100,000 population is limited to only 7 in low- or middle-income countries (ibid.) Therefore, the proposal to use CAs to fill the gap caused by the shortage of mental health care facilities and professionals has been proven to be effective in providing support to individuals in need of help (Rathnayaka et al., 2022). For conversational agents or Chatbots to be effective, however, they need to show empathy (Inkster, Sarda & Subramanian, 2018; Tudor et al., 2020) and emotional intelligence (Salovey, 1990), so that the interactions with them are not robotic, which gives them impression of being automated and not personalised. Given the rapid developments in AI and analytics it is pleasing to see the potential for CAs and Chatbots in this area.

ChatGPT

According to Hill-Yardin et al. (2023), ChatGPT, is an AI system based on advanced natural language processing techniques. According to the developers, this AI model was made by using robust volume of data and hence it can serve to augment patient communication, streamline the acquisition of healthcare information and bolster the decision-making capabilities of healthcare professionals (Biswas 2023). As such, this AI has the ability to provide24/7 data accessibility to the patient. This way, the long-time barrier, brought about by the restricted working hours or appointment availability, is partially done away with (Scheppers et al., 2006). Therefore, with the help of ChatGpt, patients can promptly pursue information and clarification regarding their health concerns. According to Denneson et al. (2017), this ease in information accessibility facilitates patients' engagement in proactive health management.

In addition to enhancing patient accessibility, ChatGPT also provides personalised interactions and customised responses. According to Biswas (2023), ChatGpt has the capability of providing specific responses and hence it can progress a conversation in a near natural setting. Therefore, the system has the ability to modify its communication style and language in order to cater to the specific needs of individual patients, thereby enhancing the level of engagement and user-friendliness. This way, it becomes possible to enhance patient satisfaction and engagement by effectively comprehending and addressing patient inquiries through a conversational approach (Nadarzynski et al., 2019).

Basically, ChatGPT exhibits multiple strengths that enhance its efficiency in the realm of healthcare provision. The constant availability, individualised engagements and prompt access to evidence-based medical information offered by this model provide advantages to patients, as it enables immediate responses to their inquiries and alleviates their concerns. Furthermore, it provides support to healthcare professionals by aiding in their decision-making processes and optimising routine inquiries. The adaptability of ChatGPT's continuous learning capabilities renders it a valuable instrument in delivering patient-centred care of high quality, particularly in the face of evolving healthcare landscapes.

Responsible AI

The emergence of Responsible AI frameworks in the healthcare sector has become a crucial element, playing a significant role in enhancing patient care and overall outcomes. These frameworks possess various advantages, allowing healthcare systems to effectively address the ethical details linked to AI-driven healthcare decision making. As initially highlighted, one major advantage of Responsible AI is that it is crucial in ethical considerations. In this, Responsible AI is designed to adhere to established ethical principles, thereby ensuring the protection of patients' rights and wellbeing (Lu et al., 2022). Responsible AI frameworks encompass ethical guidelines that effectively tackle concerns pertaining to privacy, autonomy, fairness, and accountability, thereby fostering a patient-centric orientation (Clarke, 2019). Responsible AI also endeavours to foster transparency by offering clarification on the decision-making procedures of AI systems. The utilisation of AI algorithms in healthcare facilitates the comprehension of the decision-making process, thereby fostering enhanced reliance and assurance in the recommendations provided by AI systems. Transparency plays a crucial role in enabling healthcare providers to validate and authenticate the outputs of artificial intelligence, thereby ensuring their consistency with clinical expertise and evidence-based practices (Albahr et al., 2023). Responsible AI frameworks also prioritise the mitigation of biases and the promotion of fairness in the delivery of healthcare services. AI algorithms possess the capacity to sustain biases that are inherent in the training data, resulting in discrepancies in treatment recommendations or healthcare outcomes. Responsible frameworks for AI incorporate strategies to detect and address biases, thereby promoting fair and equal access to healthcare services for patients, irrespective of their personal backgrounds or demographic attributes.

In general, Responsible AI frameworks function as a guiding framework for the ethical development and implementation of AI in the healthcare sector. Healthcare systems are able to utilise the advantages of AI technologies while also mitigating potential drawbacks. Responsible AI plays a significant role in enhancing the provision of healthcare services that prioritise patient wellbeing and societal values through the promotion of transparency, fairness, patient-centric care and risk mitigation.

Explainable AI

According to Phillips et al (2020), Explainable AI provides a detailed explanation on how AI algorithms generate their outputs and provide recommendations. Through this, healthcare professionals can understand how best to utilise technology in enhancing their decision-making process, by providing them with reliable and comprehensible insights. Therefore, transparency is a key aspect in Explainable AI. It promotes the aspect of trust in the use of artificial intelligence technologies by enabling the healthcare professionals to understand the AI algorithms, which enables them to evaluate and verify the results with increased certainty. Therefore, by integrating Explainable AI in the general AI models, it becomes possible to understand the various determinants that impact the decision-making process of artificial intelligence (AI). This way, healthcare practitioners will possess the ability to recognise and address potential biases or inequities in the provision of healthcare services.

Moreover, the implementation of Explainable AI facilitates adherence to regulatory requirements and promotes collaboration with regulatory entities. In the healthcare sector, it is of utmost importance to uphold ethical guidelines and comply with legal obligations (Reamer, 2018). Explainable AI facilitates the fulfilment of these standards by offering insights and justifications that can be disseminated and verified with regulatory bodies. The transparency of AI systems plays a crucial role in expediting the regulatory review process and establishing a solid framework of trust and accountability among AI developers, healthcare providers and regulatory authorities.

Moreover, the implementation of Explainable AI in healthcare settings serves to improve collaboration and foster interdisciplinary efforts. The increasing prevalence of AI technologies necessitates effective collaboration among healthcare professionals from diverse domains. Explainable AI serves as a unifying platform for fostering collaboration among healthcare providers, data scientists and AI developers, facilitating substantive dialogues. Explainable AI enhances interdisciplinary teams and fosters collaborative problem-solving for intricate healthcare challenges by facilitating the exchange of insights and perspectives.

Basically, the advantages of employing Explainable AI in the domain of healthcare delivery are manifold. The transparency of AI technologies enables healthcare professionals to comprehensively comprehend and analyse the outputs generated by these systems, thereby cultivating a sense of trust and assurance in their efficacy. Explainable AI plays a significant role in promoting equitable healthcare delivery by effectively addressing biases inherent in AI models. This system aids in adhering to regulatory requirements and promotes effective teamwork among diverse groups. By capitalising on these inherent advantages, the utilisation of Explainable AI exhibits significant potential in enhancing healthcare methodologies, facilitating well-informed decision-making processes, and ultimately enhancing the overall results and experiences of patients.

Generative AI

The utilisation of Generative AI exhibits notable advantages within the realm of healthcare provision. Through the utilisation of sophisticated algorithms and methodologies, Generative AI possesses the capability to generate synthetic data that accurately reproduces real-world situations and medical ailments (Arora & Arora, 2022). The capacity to produce artificial data presents a multitude of benefits in the realm of healthcare research and analysis. In this, it is good to understand that data is the cornerstone of quality healthcare delivery at any given time (Gresch, 2014). However, accessibility to extensive, heterogeneous and inclusive datasets has proven challenging over the past few decades, more so due to the increased privacy considerations, restrictions on data access and the limited prevalence of specific medical conditions or uncommon diseases. With Generative AI, it is possible to overcome the aforementioned data hurdles by furnishing researchers with a synthetic dataset for analysis and experimentation. With these kind of data, researchers can investigate a diverse array of scenarios and conditions that may pose challenges in obtaining from real-world datasets. This therefore offers an opportunity to investigate potential interventions, enhance treatment plans and assess the effectiveness of novel therapies.

In a more specific scenario, Generative AI can be used in the discovery and development of medical drugs (Walters & Murcko, 2020). Through various generative simulations, researchers can predict the behaviour of molecular structures, thereby facilitating the exploration and identification of novel drugs and therapeutic interventions. The utilisation of Generative AI also holds significant importance in the field of personalised medicine. Through the examination of patient data and the creation of artificial profiles, healthcare providers have the ability to customise treatment plans and interventions to suit the specific needs of each patient. The implementation of this degree of individualisation contributes to the optimisation of healthcare outcomes, enhancement of patient satisfaction and mitigation of adverse effects.

Weaknesses of AI Technologies in Healthcare Delivery

ChatGPT

In its current state, ChatGPT cannot be fully considered as a thorough support tool in the realm of the medical fraternity. A noteworthy reason for this is the model's difficulties in accurately interpreting and effectively communicating complex medical information. Although this AI model has been trained on extensive healthcare data, it still encounters challenges in fully understanding the complexities of medical knowledge and terminology. This therefore can result in a situation whereby the responses provided by the tool lack accuracy and this can hinder effective communication between the AI system and individuals seeking medical advice.

Another limitation of the ChatGpt is its deficiency in emotional intelligence and empathy when engaging with patients. According to Mercer, & Reynolds (2002), empathy is a pivotal factor in the healthcare field, as it facilitates a profound connection between healthcare practitioners and patients. Therefore, the fact that ChatGPT lacks emotional perspective partially impedes its trustability and thus its ability to influence the overall quality of the patient experience.

Moreover, the utilisation of text-based communication by ChatGPT may pose certain difficulties within healthcare environments. Verbal and non-verbal cues can be crucial in comprehending the needs and concerns of patients in certain instances. The limited capacity of ChatGPT to comprehend and address these cues hampers its efficacy in comprehensively capturing a patient's state. The aforementioned constraint has the potential to hinder the precision of the AI system's suggestions and potentially result in less than optimal healthcare results.

Additionally, the utilisation of pre-existing data and patterns by ChatGPT may potentially result in the introduction of biases in its generated responses. If the training data utilised for the development of the AI model incorporates biases or mirrors disparities in healthcare, ChatGPT might unintentionally sustain those biases when engaging with patients. The aforementioned phenomenon possesses ethical implications and has the potential to further exacerbate pre-existing disparities in healthcare.

Acknowledging and addressing these weaknesses is of utmost importance when implementing ChatGPT in the context of healthcare delivery. To address these limitations, it is advisable to employ various strategies. These strategies may involve the continuous monitoring and improvement of the AI model, the inclusion of feedback from healthcare professionals and patients and the integration of human oversight. By implementing these approaches, the identified limitations can be mitigated. Healthcare providers can optimise the advantages of ChatGPT by acknowledging its limitations and augmenting its capabilities with human expertise and empathy, thereby guaranteeing the delivery of secure and precise healthcare services.

Responsible AI

The implementation of Responsible AI in the healthcare sector is not devoid of inherent challenges and limitations. One of the foremost obstacles pertains to the establishment and execution of ethical principles that regulate the utilisation of AI within the healthcare domain. The healthcare sector encompasses a multitude of dimensions and complexities, giving rise to a wide array of ethical dilemmas that may emerge unexpectedly. The aforementioned dilemmas encompass concerns related to patient privacy, informed consent, equitable algorithmic practices and the inherent possibility of bias in decision-making processes involving artificial intelligence. To effectively tackle these ethical challenges, it is imperative to engage in continuous endeavours aimed at adjusting and advancing ethical frameworks. The ever-evolving nature of the healthcare industry necessitates that ethical considerations in the development and implementation of AI technologies remain up-to-date (Biswas, 2023). This calls for the implementation of a collaborative and iterative methodology that encompasses the involvement of healthcare professionals, AI developers, policymakers and other relevant stakeholders (Siala & Wang, 2022).

Furthermore, it is imperative that ethical guidelines possess the capacity to adapt and demonstrate flexibility in order to effectively address the dynamic nature of AI technologies and their utilisation within the healthcare sector. The emergence of novel AI models and algorithms may give rise to new ethical challenges, thereby necessitating innovative solutions. The establishment of mechanisms for ongoing evaluation, review and refinement of ethical frameworks is of utmost importance in order to guarantee their pertinence and efficacy in addressing emerging concerns.

One additional obstacle in the successful implementation of Responsible AI in the healthcare sector pertains to the necessity of achieving extensive acceptance and compliance with ethical principles and guidelines. The effective implementation and adherence to guidelines and frameworks can pose a substantial challenge, despite their existence, due to the involvement of multiple stakeholders. It is imperative that healthcare organisations, practitioners and AI developers receive comprehensive education and training regarding Responsible AI practices and the ethical ramifications associated with their actions. The establishment of a culture that promotes ethical responsibility and accountability is imperative within the healthcare community.

Furthermore, the implementation of Responsible AI in the healthcare sector may encounter difficulties in achieving a suitable equilibrium between fostering innovation and upholding ethical principles. The aspiration to maximise the capabilities of AI technologies in enhancing patient outcomes may encounter conflicts with the imperative to uphold principles of fairness, transparency and accountability. The successful creation and implementation of AI systems that adhere to ethical principles may necessitate the need for making trade-offs and concessions, demanding meticulous discernment and decision making.

In summary, the successful integration of Responsible AI in the healthcare sector necessitates adeptly addressing a multitude of obstacles and vulnerabilities. The task of establishing and executing ethical principles that encompass the intricate nature of the healthcare field poses a substantial obstacle. Continual efforts are necessary to adapt and evolve these guidelines in order to effectively address emerging ethical concerns and promote widespread adoption. Finding the optimal equilibrium between innovation and ethical considerations presents significant challenges. Nevertheless, through the proactive involvement of stakeholders, the cultivation of a culture centred on ethical accountability and the encouragement of ongoing assessment and improvement of ethical frameworks, we can effectively address these limitations and effectively utilise the capabilities of Responsible AI in the field of healthcare provision.

Explainable AI

Explainable AI, despite its ability to provide transparency and clarify the decision-making mechanisms of AI systems, is not lacking of limitations. One of the key obstacles it encounters pertains to the difficulty of explaining AI procedures to stakeholders lacking technical expertise. The operational mechanisms of AI algorithms frequently entail complex calculations and data manipulations that may pose challenges for individuals lacking a technical background to fully grasp. The complex nature of Explainable AI has the potential to impede its broad acceptance, as stakeholders may encounter difficulties in comprehending the underlying mechanisms and placing trust in the insights generated by AI. To rectify these shortcomings, it is imperative to engage in continuous research and development endeavours. The objective of the field of Explainable AI is to advance methodologies that achieve a more optimal equilibrium between the complexity of models and their interpretability. In summary, the utilisation of Explainable AI presents the advantage of providing transparency and valuable insights into the decision-making mechanisms of artificial intelligence. However, it encounters difficulties in effectively communicating AI processes to individuals without technical expertise and in achieving an optimal equilibrium between the complexity of the model and its interpretability. Addressing these limitations necessitates continuous investigation, advancement and cooperation among domain specialists and relevant parties to augment the accessibility and usability of Explainable artificial intelligence. Through the identification and resolution of these obstacles, the domain of Explainable AI can persistently progress and offer significant discernments, all the while cultivating reliance and comprehension in AI technologies.

Generative AI

The field of Generative AI exhibits significant potential across multiple domains, yet it is important to acknowledge and address its inherent limitations. One prominent limitation pertains to the potential for generating deceptive or imprecise data when employing Generative AI for the purpose of fabricating synthetic data. The procedure of generating synthetic data entails the simulation or creation of novel data points that exhibit similarities to real-world data. Nevertheless, the intricate nature of the underlying algorithms and models introduces the potential for generating data that diverges from the genuine patterns and characteristics of the authentic data.

This phenomenon can yield noteworthy consequences, particularly in the domains of research and analysis. Data plays a crucial role in the research process, serving as a fundamental basis for drawing conclusions, making predictions and generating novel insights. If the synthetic data generated fails to accurately depict the genuine distribution or patterns observed in the actual data, the research findings and subsequent analysis derived from it may be biased or flawed. The aforementioned circumstances may result in erroneous deductions, untrustworthy prognostications, and ultimately impede scientific advancement within the realm of healthcare.

One additional obstacle linked to Generative AI pertains to the imperative of safeguarding privacy and maintaining confidentiality during the process of generating synthetic data. Healthcare data is characterised by its high sensitivity and is subject to stringent privacy regulations aimed at ensuring the protection of patients' personal information. Nonetheless, the process of generating synthetic data carries the potential of unintentionally exposing or divulging of confidential information. The preservation of privacy and confidentiality emerges as a crucial matter that necessitates attention in order to avert possible breaches and uphold the confidence of patients and healthcare stakeholders.

In order to address these limitations, it is imperative for researchers and developers to allocate substantial resources towards the validation of the quality and precision of the synthetic data produced. It is imperative to establish comprehensive assessment and validation procedures to ensure that the data generated accurately mirrors the patterns and characteristics observed in real-world data. This process entails conducting thorough testing, conducting comparisons with pre-existing data and validating against established benchmarks. Researchers can effectively mitigate the potential risks associated with relying on synthetic data that may be misleading or inaccurate by implementing rigorous validation procedures.

In addition, the mitigation of privacy and confidentiality concerns can be achieved by implementing rigorous data anonymisation techniques and employing privacy-preserving algorithms. The objective of these techniques is to eliminate or anonymise any personally identifiable information present in the synthetic data, while still preserving its statistical characteristics and patterns. The implementation of robust data handling practices, utilisation of encryption techniques and enforcement of access controls can significantly bolster the safeguarding of data and preservation of privacy.

In general, it is imperative to recognise and mitigate the limitations associated with Generative AI in various domains, including healthcare. Researchers and developers can fully harness the capabilities of Generative AI while minimising the risks associated with deceptive data generation and privacy breaches by prioritising accuracy, validation and privacy preservation. The implementation of Generative AI in healthcare delivery, research and decision-making processes will be enhanced, enabling responsible and efficient utilisation.

Opportunities for AI Technologies in Healthcare Delivery

ChatGPT

ChatGpt possess a significant potential in promoting the delivery of healthcare services. In this, integrating the ChatGpt with telemedicine can enhance accessibility of healthcare services in remote areas. Further, having ChatGpt integrated in telemedicine platforms can enable patients in remote areas to have virtual consultations as well medical guidance and assistance regardless of physical distance and time. This model can also promote better health outcomes through its ability to assist healthcare professionals in their decision-making processes. In this, ChatGpt can assist professionals quickly retrieving crucial information such as medical procedures as well as empirically supported medical knowledge. This facilitates healthcare practitioners in making well-informed judgements regarding patient care. When integrated with the electronic health records (EHRs), ChatGpt can also enhance efficiency and effectiveness by enabling healthcare providers to seamlessly access relevant patient data during consultations. This is coined in with the fact that this tool can effectively analyse and extract pertinent information from patient records.

In the realm of healthcare delivery, the potential opportunities offered by ChatGPT are undeniably substantial. The transformative impact of AI in the healthcare landscape is evident through its integration with telemedicine platforms, enhancement of healthcare accessibility, facilitation of decision-making processes and potential for streamlining healthcare operations. The utilisation of ChatGPT has the potential to enable healthcare systems to access novel opportunities and enhance the delivery of care that is both efficient and patient-centric.

Responsible AI

The healthcare industry stands to gain substantial benefits from the integration of Responsible AI, specifically in the realm of establishing comprehensive ethical guidelines and frameworks. The adherence to ethical principles and standards is of utmost importance in the integration of AI technologies within the healthcare sector, given the rapid progression of these technologies. Responsible AI frameworks offer a systematic methodology for tackling the ethical dilemmas and considerations linked to the deployment of artificial intelligence.

One of the key advantages presented by Responsible AI lies in its ability to facilitate the development of explicit and all-encompassing ethical principles for the provision of healthcare services. These guidelines provide a framework for healthcare organisations, policymakers and AI developers to effectively address the ethical challenges associated with the implementation of AI in the healthcare sector. Responsible AI frameworks play a crucial role in promoting the responsible and accountable utilisation of AI technologies by establishing clear ethical boundaries and expectations.

In addition, the implementation of Responsible AI is conducive to fostering transparency within decision-making processes that are driven by artificial intelligence. The importance of transparency in the healthcare sector cannot be overstated, as the decisions made within this field have a direct and significant influence on the wellbeing of patients. Responsible AI frameworks advocate for healthcare organisations to prioritise the establishment of Explainable AI algorithms, which possess the capability to provide comprehensive elucidation regarding the decision-making process. The transparency provided enables healthcare professionals to gain a deeper comprehension of the underlying reasoning behind AI-generated recommendations and to assess their appropriateness for specific patient scenarios.

The implementation of Responsible AI in healthcare delivery presents a valuable opportunity to effectively tackle concerns related to bias and fairness. Responsible AI frameworks endeavour to address potential biases that may disproportionately impact specific patient populations by incorporating fairness considerations into AI models. This entails the avoidance of biases pertaining to race, gender, age or other attributes that are considered sensitive. Through the promotion of fairness, Responsible AI facilitates the provision of equitable healthcare delivery and mitigates disparities in treatment outcomes.

In conjunction with ethical considerations, Responsible AI frameworks also place significant emphasis on the preservation of privacy and the protection of data. The responsible utilisation of patient data holds utmost importance in the healthcare sector, and healthcare organisations are guided by Responsible AI frameworks to ensure the secure handling of patient data in accordance with pertinent data protection regulations. Responsible AI engenders patient trust by ensuring the protection of patient privacy and the maintenance of data security. This commitment to safeguarding sensitive information instils confidence in patients, as they can rely on the careful handling of their personal data.

Responsible AI offers an additional prospect for the advancement of patient-centric care. Responsible AI frameworks place significant emphasis on the inclusion of patients in decision-making processes and the recognition and respect of their values and preferences. Through the integration of AI technologies with patient-centred care, Responsible AI facilitates the provision of personalised treatment recommendations, thereby empowering patients to actively engage in their healthcare journey. The implementation of a patient-centric approach has been shown to result in enhanced levels of patient satisfaction and engagement.

Moreover, it is worth noting that Responsible AI frameworks offer valuable prospects for fostering collaboration and facilitating the exchange of knowledge among various stakeholders within the healthcare ecosystem. The process of formulating ethical guidelines and frameworks necessitates the active involvement and collaboration of various stakeholders, including healthcare professionals, researchers, policymakers and patient advocacy groups. By means of collaborative endeavours, Responsible frameworks for AI can effectively encompass a wide array of perspectives, thereby ensuring that ethical considerations adequately address the needs and values of all stakeholders involved. The utilisation of a collaborative approach in the healthcare sector promotes a shared dedication to the responsible adoption of AI.

In general, the integration of Responsible AI presents a wide range of prospects for the healthcare sector. Healthcare organisations can foster public trust in AI technologies and promote their broader adoption by embracing ethical guidelines and frameworks. The ethical implementation of AI in the healthcare sector not only guarantees responsible conduct but also enhances patient outcomes, fosters equity, safeguards patient privacy and advances patient-centred care. The ongoing development of Responsible AI is expected to bring about significant opportunities for transformative advancements in the field of healthcare delivery.

Research Directions on Responsible AI in Healthcare

The following tables (Table 8.1 and 8.2) serve to summarise major focus areas for research on Responsible AI.

Explainable AI

The integration of Explainable AI in the healthcare sector presents a multitude of possibilities for detecting and addressing biases and inequities within AI algorithms. Explainable AI facilitates healthcare providers in acquiring comprehensive insights and comprehension regarding the decision-making mechanisms of AI models, thereby enhancing transparency in the process. This enables healthcare providers to gain a deeper understanding of the rationale behind AI recommendations and outputs. The recently acquired transparency enables healthcare professionals to critically examine and verify the results, thereby ensuring their compatibility with their clinical expertise and adherence to established best practices.

Table 8.1 Directions Based on the Field of Application

Main topic	Opportunities for future research
AI for personalized medicine	• Investigation of AI techniques to provide a quick response and personalized treatment • Exploration of AI in conjunction with other related technologies to improve the patient's journey
AI applied in telemedicine/ telehealth	• Analyzing how devices and smart wearables could contribute to telemedicine • Examination of barriers to telemedicine adoption
AI for prediction	• Application of machine learning and deep learning techniques for improving drug indication activities • Utilization of AI techniques to support disease and epidemic outbreaks prediction
AI for early detection and diagnosis	• Exploring how AI could improve disease detection • The role of AI in clinical diagnosis and in supporting underrepresented regions without adequate medical staff
AI and health privacy issues	• Investigation of the best practices related to patient's data protection • Identification of the main privacy concerns in digital health systems
Electronic health record ethics and issues	• Investigation of the main challenges and barriers related to electronic health records • Identification of medical ethics tensions and the benefits of using patient's health records
Digital health governance models	• Identification of challenges concerning AI ethical governance practices
AI for improving patients' well-being	• Investigation of the role of responsible AI in digital health and its contribution to the patient's well-being
Barriers related to AI adoption in digital health systems	• Identification of barriers to the digitalization of health systems transformation through AI

Source: Adapted from Fosso Wamba and Queiroz (2021).

The presence of biases in AI algorithms can be effectively identified and mitigated through the utilisation of Explainable AI, thereby offering substantial opportunities for improvement. The presence of bias in AI models can occur unintentionally as a result of imbalanced training data or other underlying factors. Explainable AI facilitates the examination of the decision-making mechanism employed by healthcare providers, enabling them to identify and isolate potential origins of bias. By recognising and acknowledging these biases, healthcare organisations can implement appropriate interventions to ensure equitable and impartial provision of healthcare services. This practice fosters fairness and mitigates discrepancies in the provision of care and results among diverse patient cohorts.

Table 8.2 Directions Based on Ethical Concerns

Ethical concerns	Research questions
Inconclusive evidence (inferential statistics, uncertain knowledge)	• How does AI inform medical professionals during decision-making? • How to combine correlation relationships identified by AI with causation relationships elaborated by healthcare professionals? • What types of tasks are appropriate for identifying causal relationships?
Inscrutable evidence (lack of transparency and interpretability, black boxed)	• How to utilize inscrutable evidence provided by AI in healthcare while maintaining safety and explainability? • How healthcare professionals can maintain their intuition and medical expertise while leveraging AI results? • How to integrate principles of accountability, responsibility and transparency in the design and development of AI in healthcare in an unobtrusive way?
Misguided evidence (limitations of data processing)	• How to delegate medical decision-making to AI-health solutions? Which aspects to consider? What kind of level of interaction? • Which ethical considerations are necessary when AI are used for medical decision-making? • How AI biases influence medical decision making?
Unfair outcomes (disproportionate impact on one group of people)	• How do we measure the unfairness of AI? Who decides the unfairness? Legislator, clinician? • How can AI be guided to commit to fairness and adhere to it during medical decision making? • What are the necessary principles to limit potential bias in training data and in the results provided?
Transformative effects (reontologise things, challenge privacy and autonomy)	• How does AI transform the ways through which medical professionals conceptualize patients' information? • How does AI transform the content of medical decision-making? • How does this transform the collaboration and organization among healthcare professionals? • How to prevent potential security breaches that can cause privacy invasion of patients?
Traceability (moral responsibility, accountability)	• How to distribute the responsibility of AI results when AI is crucial for medical decision-making? • How AI will take responsibility for tasks performed and results suggested? • How can AI be controlled once its learning capabilities bring it into states that are only remotely linked to its initial setup? • How to reverse-engineer the results elaborated by AI to understand how and why unintended results emerged?

Source: Adapted from Trocin et al. (2021).

Explainable AI presents potential avenues for ensuring regulatory adherence within the healthcare sector. With the increasing prevalence of AI in the healthcare sector, regulatory entities are actively engaged in ensuring the ethical and Responsible utilisation of AI technologies. Explainable AI enables collaboration with regulatory entities by offering elucidations and rationales for the outputs generated by artificial intelligence systems. Healthcare organisations are able to showcase the transparency, accountability and adherence to regulatory guidelines and standards of their AI systems through this capability. This approach has the potential to optimise the regulatory approval process and guarantee the adherence of healthcare organisations to pertinent laws and regulations.

Additionally, the implementation of Explainable AI in healthcare enables healthcare providers to actively participate in substantive dialogues with patients and other relevant parties. The capacity to articulate the rationale underlying AI recommendations cultivates a sense of trust and assurance in AI technologies. Healthcare providers have the ability to effectively communicate with patients by providing coherent and comprehensible explanations, thereby addressing patient concerns and fostering a more robust patient-provider relationship. This phenomenon has the potential to enhance patient engagement, facilitate shared decision-making and, ultimately, yield superior healthcare outcomes.

Generative AI

Generative AI has the potential to transform healthcare through its capability in the generation of synthetic data which afford the researchers a broader spectrum of information to engage with. By having the accessibility to a huge pool of data, researchers are able to discover novel insights, identify patterns and establish correlations that might have otherwise gone unnoticed. This way, it becomes possible to understand diseases, discern risk factors and formulate pioneering treatments and therapies. Through this data, it also becomes relatively easier to develop drugs as well as promote precision medicine. Generative AI in healthcare research can also contribute to the enhancement of data privacy and security. Researchers can utilise synthetic data to create datasets that closely resemble real patient data, thereby ensuring the anonymity and privacy of the individuals involved. This ensures the preservation of patient confidentiality while simultaneously facilitating meticulous analysis and experimentation. The utilisation of synthetic data additionally mitigates the potential for data breaches and guarantees adherence to privacy regulations.

Threats to the Implementation of AI Technologies in Healthcare Delivery

Legal and Regulatory Challenges

The integration of AI technologies in the healthcare sector presents a multitude of legal and regulatory obstacles that necessitate resolution in order to guarantee the ethical and accountable deployment of such technologies. Ensuring adherence to data protection and privacy regulations is of paramount significance in the management of sensitive patient data (Rodrigues et al., 2023). Healthcare organisations are obligated to establish strong security measures in order to safeguard patient data from unauthorised access, breaches and misuse, as mandated by data protection regulations such as the General Data Protection Regulation (GDPR) in the European Union (Regulation, 2018). In order to ensure the protection of patient confidentiality and privacy, it is imperative for AI systems to strictly adhere to data security protocols. This encompasses the implementation of encryption protocols for data protection, establishment of access controls to regulate authorised user access and the adoption of secure storage and transmission mechanisms to safeguard sensitive information.

One additional legal obstacle in the realm of AI-powered healthcare pertains to the identification of liability and the establishment of accountability (Čartolovni, Tomičić & Mosler, 2022). The increasing integration of AI systems in healthcare decision-making processes raises inquiries concerning the allocation of responsibility in cases of adverse outcomes or errors. This holds particular significance in scenarios where artificial intelligence algorithms autonomously make decisions that have an impact on the provision of healthcare to patients. The assignment of liability in the context of healthcare technology becomes difficult due to the interplay of various elements, encompassing the accountability of healthcare practitioners, creators of artificial intelligence (AI) systems and the implementing organisation. Well-defined legal frameworks and guidelines are imperative in order to establish and delineate the respective responsibilities and liabilities of all parties involved.

Regulatory bodies and policymakers assume a pivotal role in effectively addressing the aforementioned legal challenges. It is imperative to establish comprehensive guidelines and standards that effectively govern the development, deployment, and utilisation of AI technologies within the healthcare sector. It is imperative that these regulations duly consider the distinctive characteristics of AI-driven healthcare decision making and data handling. Achieving an optimal equilibrium between fostering innovation and safeguarding patient safety and privacy is of utmost importance.

In order to effectively navigate the complex legal and regulatory environment, healthcare organisations are required to allocate resources towards acquiring legal expertise and actively participate in interactions with regulatory authorities. It is imperative for individuals and organisations to remain informed about the dynamic nature of regulations pertaining to AI and to diligently adhere to these regulations throughout all phases of AI implementation. The development of regulatory frameworks that facilitate responsible and ethical adoption of AI in healthcare delivery necessitates collaboration among healthcare providers, technology developers and regulators.

Furthermore, the establishment of international cooperation and the alignment of legal frameworks can enhance the smooth integration of AI technologies in a cross-border context. The implementation of consistent regulations and standards in global healthcare systems can yield several benefits, including the streamlining of the legal process, reduction of barriers to implementation and facilitation of innovation.

Technical Limitations and Biases

The presence of technical limitations and biases in AI presents substantial obstacles in the realm of healthcare delivery. The implications for patient care and outcomes can be extensive due to factors such as the availability and quality of data, as well as the potential biases inherent in AI algorithms. It is imperative to acknowledge and confront these limitations and biases in order to guarantee fair and efficient provision of healthcare services.

One of the primary technical constraints pertains to the dependence on existing data. Artificial intelligence algorithms acquire knowledge through the analysis of past data, and the effectiveness and inclusiveness of this data significantly influence their operational capabilities. In the field of healthcare, the accessibility of extensive and varied datasets may be constrained, particularly when it comes to underrepresented populations or uncommon medical conditions. The limited availability of data can give rise to imbalanced or insufficient training datasets, leading to biased artificial intelligence models that may not effectively reflect the wider population (Norori et al., 2021). As a result, healthcare decisions made using these biased models have the potential to sustain and exacerbate disparities and inequities in the provision of care.

Furthermore, biases may originate from diverse origins, encompassing the process of data collection, the act of data labelling and the formulation of algorithms (Akter et al., 2021). The utilisation of biased data in training AI models has the potential to perpetuate biases that stem from historical disparities or unequal treatment. For instance, if the analysis of past records reveals an inequitable prevalence of particular medical procedures among distinct racial or ethnic populations, the AI model has the potential to internalise and perpetuate these trends, thereby exacerbating disparities in treatment recommendations.

To mitigate limitations and biases in AI models, continuous monitoring is crucial. This monitoring should be done in conjunction with application of rigorous methodologies for data collection, pre-processing and algorithm design so as to identify and address biases. Data cleaning methods like removing or reweighting biased samples can also be utilised to improve fairness and precision. Routine audits and evaluations are also imperative and should come in handy to help detect and address biases in AI systems. Collaboration with diverse healthcare providers and institutions can also help gather comprehensive data, reducing biases and improving predictions.

Barriers to Implementing AI Technologies in Healthcare Delivery

Limited Adoption and Awareness among Healthcare Professionals

The implementation of AI technologies in healthcare is hindered by significant barriers, primarily stemming from limited adoption and awareness among healthcare professionals. The healthcare sector, characterised by its conservative stance and dependence on conventional methodologies, frequently encounters opposition in adopting novel technologies. Healthcare professionals may possess a restricted level of knowledge and comprehension regarding AI technologies and their potential advantages, resulting in a sense of doubt and hesitancy towards embracing these ground-breaking tools.

The absence of sufficient awareness is a significant factor that contributes to the limited adoption. A significant number of healthcare professionals may possess limited knowledge regarding the potential capabilities and various applications of AI within the context of healthcare delivery. Some individuals may have a limited understanding of the potential of AI in augmenting patient care, enhancing outcomes and optimising healthcare processes. Insufficient knowledge and understanding can impede the investigation and assimilation of AI technologies in routine healthcare procedures.

Education and training programs play a crucial role in surmounting this obstacle. These programs are of utmost importance in facilitating the transfer of knowledge and enhancing the level of consciousness among healthcare professionals. Training programs can be developed with the aim of offering extensive knowledge regarding AI technologies, their capabilities and the potential advantages they can bring to the field of healthcare delivery. Healthcare professionals can enhance their comprehension of AI's capabilities and its potential implications on their practice through the provision of experiential training and real-world illustrations.

In addition, educational programs have the potential to emphasise successful case studies and real-world instances wherein AI has effectively contributed to improved healthcare outcomes. Presenting empirical evidence-based illustrations can effectively mitigate apprehensions and foster assurance within the healthcare community by showcasing the concrete advantages of AI technologies.

The imperative for addressing the limited adoption and awareness barrier in the field of AI within healthcare extends beyond education and training. It necessitates a collaborative effort between AI developers and healthcare professionals. Through the cultivation of partnerships and the promotion of interdisciplinary collaboration, healthcare professionals have the opportunity to actively engage in the advancement and tailoring of AI solutions within their unique healthcare environments. The engagement in question not only serves to enhance knowledge and understanding, but also grants healthcare professionals the authority to assume responsibility for the integration of AI and guarantees that the technology is in accordance with their specific practice requirements.

Data Infrastructure and Interoperability Challenges

One of the primary obstacles encountered in the integration of AI technologies within the healthcare sector pertains to the fragmented structure of health data systems and the absence of interoperability. Healthcare institutions frequently employ diverse EHR systems, data storage techniques and data formats, thereby posing challenges in achieving seamless integration and data sharing.

The absence of interoperability presents challenges to the efficient utilisation of artificial intelligence in the healthcare sector. In order to produce precise insights and predictions, AI algorithms necessitate access to extensive and varied datasets. Nevertheless, the potential of AI to deliver comprehensive and holistic healthcare solutions is impeded when data is segregated and inaccessible as a result of incompatible systems.

In order to tackle these challenges, it is imperative to undertake initiatives aimed at integrating a wide range of data sources and implementing standardised protocols for the purpose of data sharing and exchange. This entails the creation of interoperability standards that facilitate effective communication and data exchange between disparate systems. One illustration of this concept is the utilisation of standardised data formats, such as Fast Healthcare Interoperability Resources (FHIR), which can enhance the compatibility of data and enable the smooth integration of AI technologies.

The significance of investing in data infrastructure and interoperability initiatives cannot be overstated in addressing these challenges. It is imperative for healthcare organisations to give precedence to the establishment and execution of a resilient data infrastructure capable of accommodating the storage, processing and dissemination of substantial quantities of healthcare data. This encompasses the allocation of resources towards the acquisition of secure and scalable cloud-based storage solutions, advanced data analytics platforms and high-speed networks in order to facilitate the seamless transmission of data.

Furthermore, it is imperative to emphasise the significance of collaborative endeavours among healthcare providers, technology vendors and regulatory bodies in order to establish comprehensive interoperability standards and frameworks. These collaborative efforts can contribute to the establishment of standardised data exchange protocols, the resolution of privacy and security issues, and the adherence to regulatory frameworks such as the GDPR or the Health Insurance Portability and Accountability Act (HIPAA).

In addition, it is crucial to emphasise the importance of fostering a culture that encourages the sharing of data and collaboration among healthcare organisations. Promoting the establishment of data sharing agreements, implementing data governance frameworks and providing incentives for data sharing initiatives can cultivate a more cooperative and data-centric healthcare ecosystem. The integration of AI technologies not only facilitates but also enables researchers and healthcare professionals to leverage comprehensive datasets for innovative research, evidence-based decision making and improved patient care.

Basically, the fragmented state of health data systems and the absence of interoperability present considerable obstacles to the integration of AI technologies in the healthcare sector. Nevertheless, healthcare organisations can surmount these challenges and facilitate the smooth integration of AI technologies through investments in data infrastructure, promotion of interoperability standards and cultivation of a data sharing culture. The realisation of the full potential of AI in healthcare delivery relies heavily on the concerted efforts directed towards data interoperability and collaboration. These endeavours are crucial in facilitating the provision of more efficient and personalised care for patients.

Facilitators for Implementing AI Technologies in Healthcare Delivery

Collaboration and Partnerships

The successful implementation of AI technologies in healthcare necessitates the utmost importance of collaboration and partnerships. The convergence of healthcare providers, AI developers and researchers facilitates the consolidation of resources, specialised knowledge and multifaceted perspectives. The adoption of a collaborative approach facilitates the advancement and implementation of AI solutions that efficiently tackle the intricate challenges encountered within the healthcare sector. The partnership between healthcare providers and AI developers facilitates a comprehensive understanding of the distinct needs and prerequisites within the healthcare industry. Healthcare providers contribute their specialised knowledge, clinical perspectives and comprehension of patient care processes to the discussion. In contrast, AI developers make valuable contributions by utilising their technical expertise to develop and implement AI algorithms and technologies. Through the integration of these complementary skill sets, collaborative teams have the ability to develop artificial intelligence (AI) solutions that are specifically customised to meet the distinct requirements of healthcare delivery.

Ethical Guidelines and Frameworks

The incorporation of ethical guidelines and frameworks is of utmost importance in facilitating the conscientious deployment of AI technologies within the healthcare sector. The adherence to these guidelines is crucial in order to guarantee that AI technologies are in accordance with ethical principles, thereby safeguarding the rights and welfare of patients.

The formulation and implementation of ethical guidelines furnish a comprehensive and uniform set of principles for healthcare organisations and AI developers to adhere to. The aforementioned guidelines encompass a diverse array of ethical considerations, including but not limited to privacy, transparency, fairness, accountability and equity. By following these guidelines, AI technologies can be developed, deployed and utilised in a manner that upholds patient privacy, autonomy and safety.

The preservation of patient privacy is a paramount ethical consideration within the healthcare field. Ethical frameworks place significant emphasis on safeguarding patient data and upholding its confidentiality. This entails the implementation of comprehensive security measures to protect sensitive medical data from unauthorised access or breaches. Ethical guidelines offer precise recommendations regarding the processes of data anonymisation, encryption and access control in order to uphold patient privacy throughout the entire lifecycle of artificial intelligence.

The concept of autonomy is a fundamental ethical principle that is addressed within various ethical frameworks. AI technologies ought to demonstrate a commitment to upholding and facilitating patient autonomy through the provision of precise and impartial information, thereby enabling patients to make well-informed choices regarding their healthcare. The ethical guidelines place significant emphasis on the principle of transparency in the decision-making process of AI, with the aim of ensuring that patients possess a comprehensive understanding of how AI technologies contribute to their healthcare journey. The promotion of transparency in healthcare settings facilitates the development of trust between patients and healthcare providers, thereby promoting patient engagement in collaborative decision-making processes.

Ensuring safety is of utmost importance in the provision of healthcare services. Ethical guidelines serve to foster the advancement of AI systems that prioritise the safety of patients. It is imperative to subject AI algorithms to thorough testing and validation procedures in order to ascertain their precision and dependability. Furthermore, ethical frameworks emphasise the significance of ongoing surveillance and assessment of AI technologies in order to detect and address potential hazards and prejudices that could potentially jeopardise patient wellbeing.

The ongoing assessment and improvement of ethical frameworks are imperative in order to effectively address and adapt to the emerging challenges and concerns that arise within the dynamic domain of artificial intelligence. As AI technologies continue to advance, accompanied by the emergence of novel ethical challenges, it becomes imperative to revise and modify ethical principles in response. Continuous evaluation facilitates the detection of potential deficiencies or limitations within current frameworks, thereby enabling prompt revisions and enhancements.

In addition, it is imperative to establish ethical guidelines by means of a collective and interdisciplinary methodology. The inclusion of healthcare professionals, AI experts, policymakers, ethicists and patient representatives facilitates the incorporation of diverse perspectives and specialised knowledge into the decision-making process. The collaborative nature of this process facilitates the resolution of intricate ethical quandaries linked to AI in the healthcare domain, while also guaranteeing the comprehensiveness and efficacy of guidelines.

Essentially, the incorporation of ethical guidelines and frameworks holds significant importance in ensuring the responsible integration of artificial intelligence in the healthcare sector. The aforementioned guidelines establish explicit principles aimed at safeguarding patient privacy, autonomy and safety. The ongoing assessment and improvement of ethical frameworks facilitate the healthcare sector in effectively tackling emerging challenges and concerns, thereby ensuring the ethical utilisation of AI technologies. Healthcare organisations can optimise the capabilities of AI while maintaining patient rights and values by following these prescribed guidelines.

Conclusion

AI technologies, such as CAs, ChatGPT, Responsible AI, Explainable AI and Generative AI, possess significant capabilities to revolutionise the provision of healthcare services. Although these technologies possess notable advantages, such as enhanced patient communication, increased transparency and individualised care, they also encounter various obstacles and restrictions. By comprehending and mitigating the limitations, risks and obstacles, while capitalising on the prospects and enablers, we can optimise the advantages of artificial intelligence in the provision of healthcare services. Strategic partnerships, educational initiatives and ethical frameworks will be crucial in facilitating responsible and efficient integration of AI technologies for the enhancement of healthcare outcomes. Clearly this is only the start of the journey with advanced AI and the future, while bright, will also be challenging. It is therefore essential that technical experts and healthcare providers work together to navigate this path and provide the best solutions for clinical care and patients.

Summary

After reading this chapter you should be able to be able to state:

a) What Responsible AI is.
   Responsible AI is designed to adhere to established ethical principles, thereby ensuring the protection of patients' rights and wellbeing. An integral part of Responsible AI is the existence of Responsible AI frameworks which encompass ethical guidelines that effectively tackle concerns pertaining to privacy, autonomy, fairness and accountability, thereby fostering a patient-centric orientation.
b) What Explainable AI is.
   Explainable AI provides a detailed explanation on how AI algorithms generate their outputs and provide recommendations; thus the typical black box of AI is now transparent or at least opaque.
c) What is Generative AI in general and what is ChatGPT.
   Through the utilisation of sophisticated algorithms and methodologies, Generative AI possesses the capability to generate synthetic data that accurately reproduces real-world situations and medical ailments. ChatGPT, is an AI system based on advanced natural language processing techniques. This AI model was made by using robust volumes of data and hence it can serve to augment patient communication, streamline the acquisition of healthcare information and bolster the decision-making capabilities of healthcare professionals.
d) What empathetic Chatbots are.
   Chatbots and CA are artificial intelligence-based platforms that use natural language processing to communicate and assist users. Empathy is provided to make these CA more humanlike in their interactions so that they display a sense of emotional intelligence which is particularly important when they are used in the mental health space.

References

Akter, S., McCarthy, G., Sajib, S., Michael, K., Dwivedi, Y. K., D'Ambra, J., & Shen, K. N. (2021). Algorithmic bias in data-driven innovation in the age of AI. *International Journal of Information Management, 60*, 102387.

Albahri, A. S., Duhaim, A. M., Fadhel, M. A., Alnoor, A., Baqer, N. S., Alzubaidi, L., … & Deveci, M. (2023). A systematic review of trustworthy and explainable artificial intelligence in healthcare: assessment of quality, bias risk, and data fusion. *Information Fusion.*

Arora, A., & Arora, A. (2022). Generative adversarial networks and synthetic patient data: current challenges and future perspectives. *Future Healthcare Journal, 9*(2), 190.

Biswas, S. S. (2023). Role of chat gpt in public health. *Annals of Biomedical Engineering, 51*(5), 868–869.

Čartolovni, A., Tomičić, A., & Mosler, E. L. (2022). Ethical, legal, and social considerations of AI-based medical decision-support tools: a scoping review. *International Journal of Medical Informatics, 161*, 104738.

Clarke, R. (2019). Principles and business processes for responsible AI. *Computer Law & Security Review, 35*(4), 410–422.

Denneson, L. M., Cromer, R., Williams, H. B., Pisciotta, M., & Dobscha, S. K. (2017). A qualitative analysis of how online access to mental health notes is changing clinician perceptions of power and the therapeutic relationship. *Journal of Medical Internet Research, 19*(6), e208.

Fosso Wamba, S., Queiroz, M. M. (2021). Responsible artificial intelligence as a secret ingredient for digital health: bibliometric analysis, insights, and research directions. *Information Systems Frontiers.* https://doi.org/10.1007/s10796-021-10142-8.

Gresch, A. (2014). Data integrity: The cornerstone of any quality HTM program. *Biomedical Instrumentation & Technology, 48*(4), 285–287.

Hill-Yardin, E. L., Hutchinson, M. R., Laycock, R., & Spencer, S. J. (2023). A Chat (GPT) about the future of scientific publishing. *Brain Behaviour and Immunity, 110*, 152–154.

Inkster, B., Sarda, S., & Subramanian, V. (2018). An empathy-driven, conversational artificial intelligence agent (Wysa) for digital mental well-being: Real-world data evaluation mixed-methods study. *JMIR mHealth and uHealth.*

Lu, Q., Zhu, L., Xu, X., Whittle, J., Zowghi, D., & Jacquet, A. (2022). Responsible AI pattern catalogue: a multivocal literature review. *arXiv preprint arXiv:2209.04963.*

Mekni, M. (2021). An artificial intelligence based virtual assistant using conversational agents. *Journal of Software Engineering and Applications, 14*(9), 455–473.

Mercer, S. W., & Reynolds, W. J. (2002). Empathy and quality of care. *British Journal of General Practice, 52*(Suppl), S9–12.

Nadarzynski, T., Miles, O., Cowie, A., & Ridge, D. (2019). Acceptability of artificial intelligence (AI)-led chatbot services in healthcare: a mixed-methods study. *Digital Health, 5*, 2055207619871808.

Norori, N., Hu, Q., Aellen, F. M., Faraci, F. D., & Tzovara, A. (2021). Addressing bias in big data and AI for health care: a call for open science. *Patterns, 2*(10).

Organization WH. (2019). Mental health atlas 2017: resources for mental health in the Eastern Mediterranean Region.

Phillips, P. J., Hahn, C. A., Fontana, P. C., Broniatowski, D. A., & Przybocki, M. A. (2020). *Four principles of explainable artificial intelligence.* Gaithersburg, Maryland, 18.

Rathnayaka, P., Mills, N., Burnett, D., et al. (2022). A mental health chatbot with cognitive skills for personalised behavioural activation and remote health monitoring. *Sensors, 22*(10), doi:10.3390/s22103653.

Reamer, F. G. (2018). Ethical standards for social workers' use of technology: Emerging consensus. *Journal of Social Work Values and Ethics, 15*(2), 71–80.

Regulation, G. D. P. (2018). General data protection regulation (GDPR). *Intersoft Consulting, 24*(1), accessed in October.

Rodrigues, J., de la Torre, I., Fernández, G., & López-Coronado, M. (2013). Analysis of the security and privacy requirements of cloud-based electronic health records systems. *Journal of Medical Internet Research, 15*(8), e186. doi: 10.2196/jmir.2494. PMID: 23965254; PMCID: PMC3757992.

Salovey, P., Mayer, J. D. (1990). Emotional intelligence. *Imagination, Cognition and Personality, 9*(3), 185–211.

Scheppers, E., Van Dongen, E., Dekker, J., Geertzen, J., & Dekker, J. (2006). Potential barriers to the use of health services among ethnic minorities: a review. *Family Practice, 23*(3), 325–348.

Siala, H., & Wang, Y. (2022). SHIFTing artificial intelligence to be responsible in healthcare: a systematic review. *Social Science & Medicine, 296*, 114782.

Trocin, C., Mikalef, P., Papamitsiou, Z. et al. (2021). Responsible AI for digital health: a synthesis and a research agenda. Info*rmation* Syst*ems* Front*iers*. https://doi.org/10.1007/s10796-021-10146-4.

Tudor Car, L., Dhinagaran, D. A., Kyaw, B. M., Kowatsch, T., Joty, S., Theng, Y. L., Atun, R. (2020). Conversational agents in health care: Scoping review and conceptual analysis. *Journal of Medical Internet Research, 22*(8), e17158. doi: 10.2196/17158. PMID: 32763886; PMCID: PMC7442948.

Walters, W. P., & Murcko, M. (2020). Assessing the impact of generative AI on medicinal chemistry. *Nature Biotechnology, 38*(2), 143–145.

Section III

The People Considerations

In this section the key people aspects are unpacked and more carefully and critically discussed with particular care to identify critical success factors necessary for any digital health initiative. The section consists of four chapters as follows:

Chapter 9: Behavioural Change, Adherence and Monitoring

This chapter will address important aspects around behaviour change and adherence as well as self-management and monitoring to ensure and facilitate the attainment of better clinical outcomes. Key strategies such as nudge, persuasion, change management and behaviour change will be presented and discussed as well as how to incorporate these into digital health design including gamification to ensure optimal success and sustainment.

Chapter 10: User Adoption and Satisfaction: One Size Does Not Fit All

While it is clear people are different, too often digital health solutions tend to assume homogenous users. This chapter, drawing from key theories around user adoption and satisfaction, will serve to outline critical success factors in designing and developing high fidelity, useful and useable digital health solutions. Key aspects will include co-design, co-creation and user-centred design principles as well as following a design science methodology. In addition, this chapter will stress the importance of designing solutions that simultaneously appeal to clinical and patient user groups.

Chapter 11: Agency Theory and Stakeholders: The Power–Knowledge Dichotomy

This chapter will focus on goal alignment, stakeholder alignment as well as power-knowledge differences. In addition, theories such as the theory of reasoned action, relationship equity, technology affordance and structuration will be briefly presented to highlight the importance of managing different stakeholder groups, aligning goals, and thus, ensuring appropriately designed digital health solutions ensue.

DOI: 10.1201/9781003318538-11

Chapter 12: Social Determinants of Health and Digital Health Literacy

Many groups within the population are vulnerable when it comes to healthcare due to either having poor digital health and/or digital health literacy. This will be unpacked and strategies to address problems will be outlined. In addition, the chapter will discuss and outline the social determinants of health and how digital health can serve to ameliorate key disparities.

9 Behavioural Change, Adherence and Monitoring

Objectives

At the conclusion of this chapter, it should be evident that:

a) Behaviour change is often an essential part of healthcare delivery especially with respect to chronic disease management.
b) Key behaviour intervention techniques include nudge and persuasion.
c) Adherence and monitoring are important to ensure and support appropriate behaviour change and compliance with specific treatment regimens.
d) Digital health solutions can play a key role in monitoring and self-management.

Introduction

Achieving better clinical outcomes refers to the ability of healthcare providers to successfully manage a patient's health condition, leading to improved health status and quality of life for the patient. This can be achieved through a combination of effective prevention, accurate diagnosis, appropriate treatment and ongoing management. When discussing clinical outcomes, it's important to consider both short-term and long-term goals. Short-term goals include resolving immediate health concerns, managing symptoms and preventing complications. Long-term goals include maintaining health over time, preventing disease recurrence and improving overall quality of life. Some examples of better clinical outcomes include improved survival rates, reduced hospitalization rates, improved symptom management, reduced disease progression and improved functional status. In achieving these outcomes, a multidisciplinary approach that involves healthcare providers, patients and caregivers is necessary. Healthcare providers must stay up to date with the latest evidence-based practices and guidelines, and work collaboratively with patients to develop personalised treatment plans that take into account individual needs and preferences. Patients and caregivers must also play an active role in managing their health, including following treatment plans, making lifestyle changes and reporting any changes in symptoms or health status to their healthcare provider. In doing so, behaviour change and self-management should always be actioned. With this understanding, this chapter will address important

DOI: 10.1201/9781003318538-12

aspects around behaviour change and adherence as well as self-management and monitoring to ensure and facilitate the attainment of better clinical outcomes. Key strategies such as nudge, persuasion, change management and behaviour change will be presented and discussed as well as how to incorporate these into digital health design, including gamification, to ensure optimal success and sustainment.

Behaviour Change

Behaviour change refers to the process by which an individual modifies their habits or actions to achieve a desired outcome. It involves consciously and intentionally altering one's behaviour in response to new information, personal goals or external stimuli. Behaviour change is a complex process that involves both conscious decision making and unconscious factors such as emotions and social norms (Prochaska & DiClemente, 1983).

Behaviour change can occur in a variety of contexts, including health behaviour, environmental behaviour and organizational behaviour (Rosenstock, 1974). For example, a person may decide to quit smoking to improve their health or may start recycling to reduce their environmental impact. In an organisational context, a company may implement new policies to encourage employee behaviour change, such as offering incentives for carpooling or telecommuting.

Behaviour change can be influenced by a variety of factors, including individual characteristics such as motivation, self-efficacy and beliefs about the benefit uses and barriers of a particular solution (Cameron & Leventhal, 2003. Social and environmental factors such as social norms, cultural beliefs and access to resources can also play a significant role in behaviour change (Kotter, 1996).

There are several theories and models that attempt to explain the process of behaviour change (Bem, 1972). One of the most widely recognised is the Transtheoretical Model (TTM) which identifies five stages of change: precontemplation, contemplation, preparation, action and maintenance. According to the TTM, behaviour change is not a linear process, but rather a cyclical one that involves progress through these stages (Bandura, 1997).

Another well-known model is the Health Belief Model (HBM) which suggests that behaviour change is influenced by an individual's perceived susceptibility to a particular health problem, the severity of the problem, the perceived benefits of taking action and the perceived barriers to taking action.

Behaviour change interventions can take a variety of forms, including education, social support, environmental change and policy change. Education interventions aim to increase knowledge and awareness of a particular behaviour and its consequences, while social support interventions involve providing encouragement and reinforcement from peers or family members. Environmental interventions involve changing the physical environment to make a behaviour easier or more appealing, such as placing recycling bins in convenient locations (Lorig, 2003). Policy interventions involve changing laws or regulations to promote behaviour change, such as implementing a tax on cigarettes to discourage smoking.

Importance of Behaviour Change in Improving Clinical Outcomes

Behaviour change plays a critical role in improving clinical outcomes for patients (Ajzen, 1991). Many health conditions, such as heart disease, diabetes and cancer, are strongly influenced by modifiable lifestyle factors, such as diet, physical activity, smoking and alcohol use. By modifying these behaviours, patients can significantly improve their health status and reduce the risk of disease progression and complications.

Behaviour change is particularly important in chronic disease management. Chronic diseases are long-lasting conditions that require ongoing management and care. By adopting healthy behaviours and adhering to treatment plans, patients with chronic diseases can better manage their condition, reduce symptoms and improve their quality of life.

Behaviour change is also important in the prevention of disease. Many chronic diseases are preventable through lifestyle modifications such as healthy eating, regular physical activity and avoidance of tobacco and excessive alcohol consumption. By making these changes, individuals can reduce their risk of developing chronic diseases and improve their overall health.

The importance of behaviour change in improving clinical outcomes is supported by a large body of research. For example, a study published in the *Journal of the American Medical Association* found that lifestyle modifications, including diet and exercise, were as effective as medication in preventing and managing type 2 diabetes. Similarly, a study published in the *Journal of the American College of Cardiology* found that lifestyle modifications were more effective than medication in preventing heart disease (Prochaska & DiClemente, 1983).

Behaviour change interventions can take many forms, including education, social support and environmental change. For example, a patient with diabetes may receive education on healthy eating and physical activity, as well as social support from a diabetes support group (Strecher, Rosenstock & Becker, 1986). Environmental changes, such as providing healthy food options in workplace cafeterias, can also promote behaviour change.

Behaviour change interventions can also be tailored to meet the individual needs and preferences of patients. For example, a patient with chronic pain may benefit from a physical therapy program that incorporates gentle exercises and relaxation techniques, while a patient with anxiety may benefit from cognitive-behavioural therapy that helps them identify and change negative thought patterns.

One of the key challenges in behaviour change is sustaining the behaviour change over time. Patients may initially make changes to their behaviour, but may struggle to maintain these changes over the long term. To address this challenge, behaviour change interventions can incorporate strategies such as goal-setting, self-monitoring and feedback, which have been shown to be effective in promoting sustained behaviour change.

In addition, behaviour change interventions can leverage technology in support, for example, mobile health apps can help patients track their progress, set goals and receive reminders and feedback. Social media platforms can also be used.

Essentially, behaviour change is a critical component of improving clinical outcomes for patients. By adopting healthy behaviours and adhering to treatment plans, patients can better manage chronic conditions, reduce their risk of developing chronic diseases and improve their overall health. Behaviour change interventions can take many forms and can be tailored to meet the individual needs and preferences of patients. Sustaining behaviour change over time is a key challenge, but interventions can incorporate strategies such as goal-setting, self-monitoring and technology to support in the long term.

Types of Behaviour Change Interventions

Nudges

Nudge is a type of behaviour change intervention that has gained popularity in recent years for its ability to encourage positive behaviours without relying on coercion or incentives. A nudge is defined as any aspect of the choice architecture that alters people's behaviour in a predictable way without forbidding any options or significantly changing their economic incentives.

In healthcare, nudges have been used to encourage patients to adopt healthy behaviours and adhere to treatment plans, with the aim of improving clinical outcomes. Nudges can be implemented in various ways, such as through the design of healthcare facilities, the presentation of health information and the use of technology.

One example of a nudge in healthcare is the use of visual cues to encourage hand hygiene among healthcare workers. Studies have shown that placing hand sanitizer dispensers in prominent locations and using brightly coloured reminders can increase hand hygiene compliance rates among healthcare workers. This, in turn, can reduce the spread of hospital-acquired infections and improve patient outcomes.

Another example of a nudge in healthcare is the use of default options in electronic health records (EHRs) to encourage physicians to follow evidence-based guidelines for treatment. By defaulting to recommended treatments or tests, physicians are more likely to follow best practices, leading to better clinical outcomes for patients (Thaler & Sunstein, 2009).

Nudges can also be used to encourage patients to adopt healthy behaviours, such as physical activity and healthy eating. For example, a study conducted in a hospital cafeteria found that placing healthier food options at eye level and using descriptive labels increased the consumption of healthy foods among employees.

Similarly, technology-based nudges can be used to encourage physical activity among patients. For example, wearable devices that track physical activity and provide feedback can encourage patients to increase their activity levels. Social media platforms can also be used to provide social support and encouragement for healthy behaviours, such as weight loss and smoking cessation.

One of the strengths of nudges is their ability to be implemented without relying on incentives or coercion. This makes them a low-cost and scalable intervention that can be easily implemented in healthcare settings (Burke, 2011). Additionally, nudges are often perceived as less intrusive and more acceptable than traditional behaviour change interventions, such as counseling or medication.

However, there are also some limitations to the use of nudges in healthcare. One concern is that nudges may be perceived as manipulative or paternalistic, particularly if patients or healthcare providers are not aware that a nudge is being used. Another concern is that the effects of nudges may be short-lived, as patients may revert to their old behaviours once the nudge is removed.

Furthermore, nudges may not be effective for all patients or all types of behaviors. For example, patients with cognitive or physical impairments may not be able to respond to nudges in the same way as other patients. Additionally, nudges may be less effective for behaviours that are deeply ingrained or difficult to change, such as smoking or substance abuse (Thaler & Sunstein, 2009).

Digital health solutions that incorporate serious games or gamification aspects have utilised nudge theory and techniques to effectively try to impact behaviour change (Spil et al., 2022). This has shown to be effective in the management of various chronic disease management initiatives such as diabetes (ibid.).

Persuasion

Persuasion is a type of behaviour change intervention that involves influencing people's beliefs, attitudes and behaviours through communication. Persuasion can be an effective tool in achieving better clinical outcomes, as it can motivate patients to adopt healthy behaviours and adhere to treatment plans (Cialdini, 1993).

Persuasion can take many forms, including verbal communication, written materials and visual aids. The key to effective persuasion is to tailor the message to the individual's needs and preferences. For example, a patient may respond better to a visual aid, such as a chart or graph, than to written materials.

One of the key components of persuasion is establishing credibility. Patients are more likely to be persuaded by someone they perceive as credible, such as a physician or other healthcare provider. Healthcare providers can build credibility by demonstrating their expertise, using evidence-based practices and building trusting relationships with their patients (Haynes, McDonald & Garg, 2002).

Another important component of persuasion is emotional appeal. Patients are more likely to be persuaded by messages that appeal to their emotions, such as fear, hope, or empathy. For example, a physician may use a fear-based message to persuade a patient to quit smoking by emphasising the negative health consequences of smoking.

Social influence is another important component of persuasion. Patients are more likely to be persuaded by messages that are consistent with the beliefs and values of their social group. For example, a patient may be more likely to adopt a healthy behaviour, such as regular physical activity, if they perceive that their social group values this behaviour.

Persuasion can also be used to encourage adherence to treatment plans. Patients may be more likely to adhere to treatment plans if they perceive the benefits of the treatment to outweigh the costs, and if they believe that they are capable of adhering to the plan. For example, a physician may use a message that emphasises the benefits of taking medication, such as improved health outcomes, and provides strategies for managing side effects, such as taking the medication with food.

One of the challenges of persuasion is resistance to the message. Patients may resist persuasion if they perceive the message as threatening, manipulative or irrelevant. To address resistance to the message, healthcare providers can use strategies such as active listening, acknowledging patients' concerns and providing information that addresses patients' specific needs and preferences.

Persuasion can also be used in combination with other behaviour change interventions, such as social support and environmental change. For example, a physician may use persuasion to encourage a patient to adopt healthy eating habits, and may also provide social support by referring the patient to a nutritionist and providing information about healthy food options in the patient's community.

One of the limitations of persuasion is that it may not be effective for all patients. Patients may vary in their receptivity to persuasion based on factors such as their personality, values and beliefs. In addition, persuasion may be less effective for patients who have limited access to healthcare services or who face social and economic barriers to adopting healthy behaviors.

Change Management

Change management is a type of behaviour change intervention that can be used to achieve better clinical outcomes. Change management refers to a structured approach to transitioning individuals, teams and organisations from a current state to a desired future state (Michie et al., 2013). In the context of healthcare, change management can be used to implement new policies, procedures and interventions that improve clinical outcomes.

One of the key benefits of change management is that it can help to overcome resistance to change. Change can be difficult and uncomfortable, and individuals and organisations may resist changes that are perceived as threatening or disruptive. Change management helps to address this resistance by providing a structured approach to change that engages stakeholders, communicates the benefits of the change and provides support and resources to facilitate the transition.

Change management interventions can take many forms, including education and training, communication and engagement, process redesign and technology implementation (WHO Global Observatory for eHealth, 2011). For example, a change management intervention may involve the implementation of a new electronic health record system that requires changes to existing processes and workflows. To ensure successful adoption of the new system, the change management intervention may involve education and training for staff, communication and engagement with stakeholders, process redesign to integrate the new system into existing workflows and ongoing support and feedback to address any issues that arise.

Change management can also be used to implement behaviour change interventions that improve clinical outcomes. For example, a change management intervention may be used to implement a new program to promote physical activity among patients with chronic conditions. The change management intervention may involve education and training for healthcare providers on the benefits of physical activity, communication and engagement with patients to encourage participation in the program, process redesign to integrate the program into existing clinical workflows and ongoing support and feedback to help patients sustain their behaviour change.

One of the key components of successful change management is stakeholder engagement. Stakeholders are individuals or groups who have a vested interest in the change and may be affected by the change. In healthcare, stakeholders may include healthcare providers, patients, families, payers and policymakers. Effective stakeholder engagement involves identifying key stakeholders, understanding their needs and concerns and involving them in the planning and implementation of the change. By involving stakeholders in the change process, change management interventions can help to build support for the change, increase buy-in and facilitate successful adoption of the change.

Another important component of change management is evaluation and feedback. Change management interventions should be evaluated to assess their effectiveness and identify areas for improvement. Evaluation may involve tracking metrics such as clinical outcomes, patient satisfaction and staff engagement. Feedback from stakeholders can also help to identify areas for improvement and ensure that the change management intervention is responsive to the needs of those affected by the change.

Change management interventions can be particularly effective in addressing complex healthcare challenges that require a coordinated approach across multiple stakeholders and settings. For example, the implementation of a new care coordination program that involves multiple healthcare providers and settings may require a change management intervention to ensure successful adoption and sustained behavior change.

Examples of Behaviour Change Interventions in Healthcare

Some examples of the behavior change interventions in healthcare include the following:

Motivational interviewing: Motivational interviewing is a client-centred counselling approach that aims to help individuals overcome ambivalence and resistance to change. It involves exploring and resolving individual's internal conflicts about changing their behaviours (Miller & Rollnick, 2012).

Health coaching: Health coaching is a collaborative, personalised approach to support individuals in achieving health goals. Health coaches help individuals identify areas for improvement, set achievable goals and develop action plans to achieve their health goals.

Cognitive-behavioral therapy (CBT): CBT is a type of psychotherapy that aims to change negative patterns of thinking and behaviour. It has been used to treat depression, anxiety and addiction.

Social support networks: Social support networks involve using family, friends and peer groups to motivate and support individuals in adopting healthy behaviours. Support networks can help individuals stay motivated, accountable and provide emotional support throughout their behavior change journey.

Incentives and rewards: Incentives and rewards are used to motivate individuals to adopt healthy behaviours. This can include financial rewards or non-financial rewards such as recognition or status symbols.

Health education and information: Health education and information interventions involve providing information and education on healthy behaviours, their benefits and the risks of unhealthy behaviors.

Reminder systems: Reminder systems use technology such as text messages or phone calls to remind individuals to perform healthy behaviours such as taking medication or attending a healthcare appointment.

Gamification: Gamification involves using gaming principles and techniques to motivate individuals to engage in healthy behaviours. This could include using leaderboards, badges or progress trackers to encourage individuals to maintain healthy habits.

Environmental modifications: Environmental modifications involve making changes to the physical or social environment to promote healthy behaviours. Examples could include implementing smoke-free policies, providing healthy food options or designing walking trails.

Self-monitoring: Self-monitoring involves tracking and recording one's own behaviours or health indicators to promote self-awareness and behaviour change. This could include tracking daily physical activity or monitoring blood sugar levels for diabetes management (Snyderman, & Langheier, 2006).

Adherence

Adherence refers to a patient's ability to follow or comply with prescribed medical treatments or recommendations, such as taking medications, attending appointments, following a diet plan or engaging in physical activity. Adherence is a crucial aspect of patient care as it can significantly impact health outcomes (Horne & Weinman, 1999).

Adherence is often used interchangeably with compliance, but they have slightly different meanings. Compliance refers to the degree to which a patient follows the prescribed medical treatments or recommendations, while adherence is a more comprehensive term that also includes the patient's motivation, understanding and active involvement in their care.

Adherence can be influenced by various factors, including the patient's beliefs, attitudes, support and financial status. Some patients may have difficulty adhering to their treatment plan due to forgetfulness, complexity of the treatment regimen, side effects or lack of understanding of the importance of the treatment. In other cases, patients may deliberately choose not to adhere to their treatment plan due to personal beliefs, fears or concerns.

Non-adherence can have serious consequences, including treatment failure, disease progression, increased healthcare costs and decreased quality of life. On the other hand, good adherence can lead to improved health outcomes, better disease management and reduced healthcare costs.

Healthcare providers play a crucial role in promoting adherence by providing clear and comprehensive instructions, addressing patient concerns and actively involving patients in their care. Patient education, counselling and the use of reminder systems can also improve adherence. Additionally, healthcare providers can work with patients to identify and address any barriers to adherence, such as cost, complexity of treatment or side effects.

Importance of Adherence in Improving Clinical Outcomes

Adherence to medical treatment and recommendations is a critical aspect of patient care that plays a significant role in improving clinical outcomes. Adherence refers to the extent to which patients follow the prescribed medical treatment or recommendations, which includes taking medications, attending appointments, following a diet plan or engaging in physical activity. Here are some reasons why adherence is important in improving clinical outcomes:

- Improved disease management: Good adherence to treatment can significantly improve disease management and reduce the risk of disease progression or complications. For instance, adherence to medication regimens for chronic conditions such as hypertension, diabetes or asthma can help patients achieve better control of their symptoms and prevent complications.
- Reduced healthcare costs: Poor adherence to medical treatment can lead to increased healthcare costs due to disease complications, hospitalisation and emergency department visits. On the other hand, good adherence can reduce healthcare costs by preventing or delaying disease progression and reducing the need for costly medical interventions.
- Increased patient satisfaction: Good adherence can increase patient satisfaction with their healthcare experience by improving disease management and quality of life. Patients who are satisfied with their healthcare experience are more likely to continue seeking care and following treatment recommendations.
- Improved clinical outcomes: Good adherence to medical treatment and recommendations has been shown to improve clinical outcomes such as reduced mortality, reduced hospitalization rates and improved quality of life.
- Better patient-provider communication: Adherence can improve patient-provider communication and increase patient trust in their healthcare provider. When patients feel that their healthcare provider understands their concerns and is actively involved in their care, they are more likely to follow treatment recommendations and achieve better clinical outcomes.

- Improved public health: Good adherence to medical treatment can improve public health by reducing the spread of infectious diseases and preventing disease complications. For instance, adherence to vaccination schedules can help prevent the spread of infectious diseases and reduce the risk of outbreaks.

Factors Affecting Adherence

Adherence to medical treatment and recommendations can be influenced by various factors that can be classified into patient-related factors, healthcare provider-related factors and treatment-related factors. Here are some of the common factors that affect adherence:

- Patient-related factors: Patient-related factors are those that are related to the patient's characteristics, beliefs, attitudes and behaviours. These factors include demographic factors such as age, gender and education level, psychological factors such as depression, anxiety and stress and social support and family dynamics.
- Healthcare provider-related factors: Healthcare provider-related factors refer to the characteristics and behaviour of the healthcare provider that can influence patient adherence. These factors include quality of patient-provider communication and relationship, clarity and comprehensiveness of treatment instructions, availability and accessibility of healthcare services, healthcare provider's knowledge and expertise and healthcare provider's cultural competency and sensitivity to patient's beliefs and practices.
- Treatment-related factors: Treatment-related factors refer to the characteristics of the treatment regimen that can affect adherence. These factors include complexity and frequency of the treatment regimen, side effects and adverse reactions to the treatment, perceived benefits and effectiveness of the treatment, cost and availability of the treatment and convenience and accessibility of the treatment.

It is important to note that these factors can interact and influence each other, and the impact of each factor on adherence can vary depending on the patient's individual circumstances. Therefore, healthcare providers should take a holistic approach to promoting adherence and address all the relevant factors that may be affecting the patient's ability to adhere to the treatment plan. This can involve patient education, counselling and support, as well as tailoring the treatment plan to meet the patient's individual needs and preferences. By addressing the factors that affect adherence, healthcare providers can improve patient outcomes and promote better health outcomes.

Strategies for Improving Adherence

Some strategies that can help improve adherence include:

- Simplify treatment regimens: Complex treatment regimens, such as those involving multiple medications, dosages and schedules, can be overwhelming and confusing for patients. Simplifying the treatment regimen can make it easier for patients to adhere to the prescribed treatment (DiMatteo, 2004).

- Educate patients: Educating patients about their medical condition, treatment options and the importance of adherence can help them understand the rationale behind the prescribed treatment and motivate them to adhere to it.
- Involve patients in decision making: Involving patients in the decision-making process can help them feel empowered and invested in their treatment plan, which can increase their motivation to adhere to it.
- Use reminders: Using reminders such as medication alarms, appointment reminders and educational materials can help patients remember to take their medication, attend appointments and make lifestyle changes.
- Address barriers to adherence: Patients may face various barriers to adherence, such as side effects of medication, cost or difficulty making lifestyle changes. Addressing these barriers through medication adjustments, financial assistance or behavioral interventions can improve adherence.
- Provide support: Providing support through healthcare professionals, support groups and family and friends can help patients stay motivated and accountable in adhering to their prescribed treatment.
- Monitor adherence: Monitoring adherence through regular follow-ups, medication logs and other tools can help healthcare professionals identify and address any adherence issues before they become more serious.

Self-Management and Monitoring

Self-management and monitoring are two critical components of effective healthcare management. Self-management refers to the ability of individuals to take control of their own health and manage their chronic or long-term health conditions. It involves developing the knowledge, skills and confidence to make informed decisions about one's own health and to adopt healthy behaviours that can improve health outcomes. Monitoring, on the other hand, involves regularly checking and recording symptoms, behaviours and other factors related to health status.

Self-management is becoming increasingly important as the prevalence of chronic diseases, such as diabetes, heart disease and cancer, continues to rise. Effective self-management requires individuals to take an active role in their own healthcare, working in partnership with healthcare providers to manage their conditions. This involves developing an understanding of one's own health condition(s) and treatment options, setting goals and creating a plan for managing the condition(s) on a day-to-day basis, making lifestyle changes, such as eating a healthy diet, exercising regularly and managing stress, and communicating effectively with healthcare providers.

Monitoring is an essential aspect of self-management. It involves regularly checking and recording symptoms, behaviours and other factors related to health status. Monitoring can take many forms, including self-assessment of symptoms, such as pain, fatigue or mood, regular measurement of vital signs, such as blood pressure or blood glucose levels, keeping a diary or log of symptoms, behaviours or medication use, and using wearable devices or mobile apps to track health-related data. By monitoring their health status, individuals can identify trends, triggers and patterns that can inform self-management strategies.

Self-management and monitoring are essential for individuals with chronic or long-term health conditions to achieve the best possible health outcomes. Effective self-management requires individuals to take an active role in their own healthcare, working in partnership with healthcare providers to manage their conditions. Monitoring allows individuals to identify changes in their health status and make informed decisions about self-management.

Importance of Self-Management and Monitoring in Improving Clinical Outcomes

Patients who engage in self-management are more likely to adhere to their treatment plan, experience fewer complications and have better overall health outcomes. For example, patients with diabetes who self-monitor their blood glucose levels and follow a healthy diet and exercise plan are more likely to achieve optimal blood sugar control and avoid complications such as heart disease, kidney damage and blindness. On the other hand, monitoring allows patients to track their symptoms and make informed decisions about their care. Regular monitoring can help patients identify changes in their health status and take action before complications arise. For example, patients with hypertension who monitor their blood pressure regularly can adjust their medication dosage or make lifestyle changes to keep their blood pressure under control and reduce their risk of heart attack, stroke, and other complications.

Techniques for Self-Management and Monitoring

Self-Tracking

Self-tracking refers to the process of collecting and recording data about one's health and daily activities, such as medication adherence, physical activity and diet. Self-tracking can be done through a variety of methods, including mobile apps, wearable devices and paper diaries. Self-tracking provides patients with a detailed understanding of their health and behaviour patterns and helps them identify areas for improvement.

Self-tracking can help patients identify patterns and trends in their symptoms and behaviours, such as blood glucose levels in diabetes or blood pressure levels in hypertension. This information can be shared with healthcare providers to help them make more informed decisions about the patient's care. For example, if a patient with hypertension is tracking their blood pressure readings, their healthcare provider can use this information to adjust their medication dosage or recommend lifestyle changes to keep their blood pressure under control.

Feedback

Feedback is another technique that can be used to help patients with chronic illnesses monitor their health and behaviour patterns. Feedback refers to the process of providing patients with information about their performance, such as their medication adherence, blood glucose levels or physical activity levels. Feedback can be provided through a variety of methods, including mobile apps, email or text messages.

Feedback can be used to motivate patients to make changes in their behaviour and improve their outcomes. For example, if a patient with diabetes is receiving regular feedback about their blood glucose levels, they may be more motivated to make lifestyle changes to keep their blood sugar levels under control. Additionally, feedback can help patients identify areas where they need to make improvements and make informed decisions about their care.

Goal Setting

Goal setting is another technique that can be used to help patients with chronic illnesses improve their outcomes. Goal setting involves setting specific, measurable, achievable, relevant and time-bound (SMART) goals that are designed to improve the patient's health and wellbeing. Goals can be related to a variety of areas, including medication adherence, physical activity, diet and stress management.

Setting goals can help patients stay motivated and focused on making positive changes in their behaviour. When goals are achieved, patients can experience a sense of accomplishment, which can further motivate them to continue making changes in their behaviour. Additionally, goals can help patients identify areas where they need to make improvements and make informed decisions about their care.

Self-tracking, feedback and goal setting are all techniques that can be used to help patients with chronic illnesses improve their outcomes. When used together, these techniques can be particularly effective in promoting behaviour change and improving health outcomes. For example, a patient with diabetes who is using a mobile app to track their blood glucose levels and receive regular feedback from their healthcare provider can set SMART goals to improve their diet and physical activity levels. By using these techniques together, the patient can take a more active role in their care and improve their outcomes.

Digital Health Design

Digital health design refers to the process of creating digital products and services that are designed to improve health outcomes and promote wellness. Digital health design incorporates principles of user-centred design, human-computer interaction and health behaviour change to create products and services that are intuitive, engaging and effective (Mhealth Alliance, 2012; Schwarzer & Fuchs,

1996). Digital health design can encompass a wide range of products and services, including mobile apps, wearable devices, telemedicine platforms and electronic health records. These products and services can be used by patients, healthcare providers and researchers to improve the delivery and quality of healthcare. The goal of digital health design is to create products and services that are easy to use and effective in improving health outcomes. In order to achieve this goal, digital health designers must take into account the needs and preferences of users, as well as the unique characteristics of the healthcare context.

Importance of Digital Health Design in Improving Clinical Outcomes

Digital health design has the potential to significantly improve clinical outcomes by enhancing the delivery of healthcare services, promoting patient engagement and self-management and supporting health behavior change (Glasgow et al., 2004).

One important way that digital health design can improve clinical outcomes is by enhancing the delivery of healthcare services. By designing digital health products and services that streamline and automate administrative tasks, healthcare providers can spend more time on patient care. For example, electronic health records (EHRs) can help healthcare providers to quickly access and update patient information, reducing errors and improving the accuracy of clinical decision making (Greenhalgh et al., 2004). Telemedicine and remote monitoring tools can also enable healthcare providers to deliver care to patients who are unable to physically visit a clinic or hospital, increasing access to care and improving patient outcomes.

Another way that digital health design can improve clinical outcomes is by promoting patient engagement and self-management. Digital health products and services can empower patients to take an active role in managing their health by providing them with tools and resources to track their symptoms, monitor their health status and communicate with their healthcare providers. For example, self-tracking apps can help patients to monitor their physical activity, sleep and other health behaviours, providing them with real-time feedback and motivating them to make healthy lifestyle changes. Patient portals and mobile apps can also enable patients to securely access their health information, schedule appointments and communicate with their healthcare providers, improving patient satisfaction and engagement.

Digital health design can also support health behaviour change by leveraging principles of behaviour change theory and user-centred design (Free et al., 2013). By creating products and services that are tailored to individual patient needs and preferences, digital health designers can increase the effectiveness of health behaviour change interventions. For example, mobile apps that provide personalised feedback and support can help patients to adopt healthy behaviours and maintain long-term behaviour change. Digital health products and services can also leverage social networks and peer support to promote behaviour change, providing patients with a sense of community and accountability.

However, in order to achieve these benefits, digital health designers must carefully consider the unique challenges and opportunities of the healthcare context (Kumar et al., 2013). Digital health products and services must be designed to meet the needs and preferences of healthcare providers and patients, while also addressing issues such as patient privacy, data security and regulatory compliance. Designers must also ensure that digital health products and services are accessible and equitable, taking into account factors such as disparities in technology access and digital literacy.

In addition to these considerations, digital health designers must also be committed to rigorous evaluation of their products and services. While digital health holds promise for improving clinical outcomes, it is important to ensure that these benefits are based on solid evidence. Designers must conduct rigorous clinical trials and other types of research to evaluate the effectiveness of their products and services, and to identify opportunities for improvement.

Overall, the importance of digital health design in improving clinical outcomes cannot be overstated. By enhancing the delivery of healthcare services, promoting patient engagement and self-management and supporting health behaviour change, digital health products and services have the potential to revolutionise healthcare and improve patient outcomes. However, in order to achieve these benefits, digital health designers must carefully consider the unique challenges and opportunities of the healthcare context, and be committed to rigorous evaluation and continuous improvement. By doing so, they can help to create a healthcare system that is more efficient, effective and patient-centered.

Techniques for Incorporating Behaviour Change and Adherence Strategies into Digital Health Design

Digital health design has the potential to promote behaviour change and improve adherence to health behaviours by incorporating techniques such as gamification, personalisation and social support. Each of these techniques offers unique benefits for promoting behaviour change and adherence, and can be tailored to the needs and preferences of individual users.

Gamification is a technique that involves incorporating game elements into non-game contexts, such as health behaviour change interventions. By leveraging the motivational and engagement benefits of games, digital health designers can create products and services that are more enjoyable and effective for users. For example, a mobile app that encourages physical activity might use gamification techniques such as point systems, rewards and social competition to motivate users to meet their goals. Gamification can also be used to encourage adherence to medication regimens, by incorporating elements such as reminders, progress tracking and rewards for adherence.

Personalisation is another technique that can be used to promote behaviour change and adherence in digital health design. By tailoring products and services to the individual needs and preferences of users, designers can create more engaging and effective interventions. For example, a weight loss app might use personalisation techniques such as personalised meal plans, activity recommendations and coaching to help users achieve their goals. Personalisation can also be used to support medication adherence, by providing users with customised reminders and information about their medications.

Social support is another important technique for promoting behaviour change and adherence in digital health design. By leveraging social networks and peer support, designers can create products and services that foster a sense of community and accountability among users. For example, a mobile app that encourages physical activity might include social features such as group challenges, sharing of progress and social support. Social support can also be used to encourage medication adherence, by incorporating features such as support groups, peer mentoring and social rewards for adherence.

Incorporating these techniques into digital health design requires careful consideration of the unique needs and preferences of individual users. Designers must take into account factors such as age, gender, cultural background and health status when creating products and services that are effective and engaging. They must also consider issues such as privacy, security and regulatory compliance when incorporating social features into their designs.

One challenge facing digital health designers is the need to balance the desire for engagement and motivation with the need for evidence-based interventions. While gamification, personalization and social support hold promise for improving behaviour change and adherence, it is important to ensure that these techniques are based on solid evidence and are not just gimmicks. Designers must conduct rigorous evaluation of their products and services, using techniques such as randomised controlled trials and user testing, to ensure that they are effective and safe.

Conclusion

In conclusion, behaviour change and adherence are critical components of achieving better clinical outcomes. Strategies such as nudge, persuasion, change management and behaviour change can be employed to facilitate these processes. Digital health design has the potential to facilitate behaviour change and adherence by incorporating these strategies, as well as through the use of gamification, personalisation and social support features. By incorporating these strategies into digital health interventions, we can improve the effectiveness and sustainability of behaviour change and adherence interventions, and ultimately improve clinical outcomes for patients.

Summary

After reading this chapter you should be able to state that:

a) Behaviour change is often an essential part of healthcare delivery especially with respect to chronic disease management.

Healthcare focuses on addressing problems patients have. In order to address these problems and issue it is often necessary to change or modify current behaviour patterns. This is especially true in the context of chronic disease example diabetes when for instance diet and exercise need to be carefully addressed and or medication management and lifestyle.

b) Key behaviour intervention techniques include nudge and persuasion.
Behaviour change rarely happens overnight and requires continuous and often slow change. Techniques developed to assist in this regard include nudge – which focuses on gentle and at times subtle reminders and persuasion which focuses on reinforcing good or desired behaviours with appropriate rewards or praise.

c) Adherence and monitoring are important to ensure and support appropriate behaviour change and compliance to specific treatment regimens.
In order to ensure behaviour change has resulted it is necessary to monitor progress and actions. In some instances such actions could be around compliance or adherence to guidelines and/or treatment protocols. Thus assessment on adherence through monitoring is a systematic approach to ensuring behaviour change has resulted and is being sustained.

d) Digital health solutions can play a key role in monitoring and self-management.
Continuous monitoring and self-monitoring can be laborious and effort intensive. Digital tools be they alerts, reminders or more complicated solution can serve to provide continuous monitoring and/or self-monitoring that is not laborious and can be enjoyable. This is important to ensure monitoring is maintained and also more likely to assist with behaviour change and its sustainment.

References

Ajzen, I. (1991). The theory of planned behavior. *Organizational Behavior and Human Decision Processes, 50*(2), 179–211.

Bandura, A. (1997). *Self-efficacy: the exercise of control.* W H Freeman/Times Books/ Henry Holt..

Bem, D. J. (1972). Self-perception theory. *Advances in Experimental Social Psychology, 6*, 1–62.

Burke, L. E., Conroy, M. B., Sereika, S. M., Elci, O. U., & Styn, M. A. (2011). Efficacy of a tailored behavioral intervention to improve hypertension control: primary outcomes of a randomized controlled trial. *Annals of Behavioral Medicine, 41*(1), 1–13.

Cameron, L. D., & Leventhal, H. (eds). (2003). *The self-regulation of health and illness behaviour.* Psychology Press.

Cialdini, R. B. (1993). *Influence: the psychology of persuasion.* HarperCollins.

DiMatteo, M. R. (2004). Variations in patients' adherence to medical recommendations: A quantitative review of 50 years of research. *Medical Care, 42*(3), 200–209.

Free, C., Phillips, G., Galli, L., Watson, L., Felix, L., Edwards, P., ... & Haines, A. (2013). Effectiveness of mobile health interventions in improving health outcomes in developing countries: Systematic review and meta-analysis of randomized controlled trials. *BMJ, 344*, e610.

Glasgow, R. E., Klesges, L. M., Dzewaltowski, D. A., Bull, S. S., & Estabrooks, P. (2004). The future of health behavior change research: What is needed to improve translation of research into health promotion practice? *Annals of Behavioral Medicine, 27*(1), 3–12.

Greenhalgh, T., Robert, G., Macfarlane, F., Bate, P., & Kyriakidou, O. (2004). Diffusion of innovations in service organizations: Systematic review and recommendations. *Milbank Quarterly, 82*(4), 581–629.

Haynes, R. B., McDonald, H. P., & Garg, A. X. (2002). Helping patients follow prescribed treatment: Clinical applications. *JAMA, 288*(22), 2880–2883.

Horne, R., & Weinman, J. (1999). Patients' beliefs about prescribed medicines and their role in adherence to treatment in chronic physical illness. *Journal of Psychosomatic Research, 47*(6), 555–567.

Kotter, J. P. (1996). *Leading change.* Harvard Business Press.

Kumar, S., Grefenstette, J. J., Galloway, D., Albert, S. M., Burke, D. S. (2014, Jan). Kumar et al. respond. *American Journal of Public Health, 104*(1), e1–2. doi: 10.2105/AJPH.2013.301676. Epub 2013 Nov 14. PMID: 24228647; PMCID: PMC3910059.

Lorig, K. R., & Holman, H. (2003). Self-management education: History, definition, outcomes, and mechanisms. *Annals of Behavioral Medicine, 26*(1), 1–7.

Mhealth Alliance. (2012). Achieving better health outcomes through digital technology. Retrieved from https://healthmarketinnovations.org/funder/mhealth-alliance-0.

Michie, S., Richardson, M., Johnston, M., Abraham, C., Francis, J., Hardeman, W., ... & Wood, C. E. (2013). The behavior change technique taxonomy (v1) of 93 hierarchically clustered techniques: Building an international consensus for the reporting of behavior change interventions. *Annals of Behavioral Medicine, 46*(1), 81–95.

Miller, W. R., & Rollnick, S. (2012). *Motivational interviewing: Helping people change.* Guilford Press.

Prochaska, J. O., & DiClemente, C. C. (1983). Stages and processes of self-change of smoking: Toward an integrative model of change. *Journal of Consulting and Clinical Psychology, 51*(3), 390–395.

Rosenstock, I. M. (1974). Historical origins of the health belief model. *Health Education & Behavior, 2*(4), 328–335.

Schwarzer, R., & Fuchs, R. (1996). Self-efficacy and health behaviors. In Conner, M. & Norman, P. (eds), *Predicting health behavior: Research and practice with social cognition models* (pp. 163–196). Open University Press.

Snyderman, R., & Langheier, J. (2006). Prospective health care and the role of academic medicine: Lead, follow, or get out of the way. *JAMA, 295*(20), 2371–2373.

Spil, T. A. M., Romijnders, V., Sundaram, D., Wickramasinghe, N., Kijl, B. (2020). Are serious games too serious? Diffusion of wearable technologies and the creation of a diffusion of serious games model. *International Journal of Information Management,* 102202. doi: 10.1016/j.ijinfomgt.2020.102202. Epub ahead of print. PMID: 32836650; PMCID: PMC7434392.

Strecher, V. J., Rosenstock, I. M., & Becker, M. H. (1986). Social learning theory and the Health Belief Model. *Health Education Quarterly, 13*(4), 403–417.

Thaler, R. H., & Sunstein, C. R. (2009). *Nudge: Improving decisions about health, wealth, and happiness.* Yale University Press.

WHO Global Observatory for eHealth. (2011). *mHealth: new horizons for health through mobile technologies: second global survey on eHealth.* World Health Organization. Retrieved from https://apps.who.int/iris/handle/10665/44607.

10 User Adoption and Satisfaction
One Size Does Not Fit All

Objectives

At the conclusion of this chapter, it should be evident:

a) What impacts user adoption and satisfaction and why both are important.
b) What are the differences between co-design, co-creation and user-centred design.
c) What are some of the models that can assist with ensuring a higher level of user adoption and satisfaction.
d) Why one size does not fit all.

Introduction

In today's healthcare, user adoption and satisfaction have become central topics of discussion. Indeed, there is significant indication that the current digital health solutions could be more effective: they focus on a hypothetical homogeneous user rather than the fact that people are different. It is crucial to note that digital transformation does not fit into a "one-size-fits-all approach". In digital health solutions, digital transformation transcends more than mere technology. It is crucial to remember that while digital health solutions can facilitate the optimisation of digital processes for a healthcare organisation, it does not begin and end with changing the technological stacks of the company, switching technologies or automation of reports. In this sense, digital health solutions, which are digital transformations, are not just about the transformation of technological processes for the mere sake of it. The assumption that instantaneously altering the way of implementing things within the healthcare organisation makes the organisation that employs digital health solutions a digitally transformed organisation is heavily flawed. Further, the assumption that this instantaneously results in higher revenue growth and instantly increased efficiency in using resources in such an organisation is also inaccurate. The study outlines critical success elements when designing and developing practical, high-fidelity, and usable digital health solutions by drawing from the critical theories of the adoption theory under the Conan-based adoption model. These key

DOI: 10.1201/9781003318538-13

aspects include co-creation, co-design and end-user-centred design principles. It also adheres to a design science methodology throughout the research.

This chapter will emphasise the importance of designing a solution capable of effectively appealing to patient user groups while also appealing to clinical user groups. Following this, if all patient user groups are considered, there is a significant indication that a one-size-fits-all all approach in digital health solutions is not suitable for lower-middle-income countries. For instance, during the COVID-19 pandemic, there was a high demand for digital health technologies and data collection at the forefront of agendas of different regional, national and international forums. In the meantime, the media landscape and academic setting are laden with blogs, articles, and even podcasts that will encourage notions like "either no data or no progress". The emerging technologies utilising data to fight COVID-19 and assist in fighting several other health crises have become quite rampant ever since. Amid all these conversations, it is, however, crucial to consider those different countries have the technical capacity as well as the suitable policies necessary for supporting the deployment of these digital health interventions in a manner that is both efficient and sustainable.

As of now, much of the current approaches place much more emphasis on data collection and fostering digital health solutions that do not consider the actual needs on the ground level. Only little consideration has been given to the state of data collection infrastructure and digital health policies within lower-middle-income countries. Several lower-middle-income countries have outdated or no policy guidelines. Even worse, there are cases where they need more technical capability to fully comprehend the rapid digital evolutions that come with emerging digital health solutions. With this alone, there is a significant indication that no one size fits all regarding user adoption and satisfaction. The diverging yet critical underlying factors within this context make this explicit. In essence, there is only a viable basis for promising all the merits of data and digital health solutions in such situations in these countries.

One Size Does Not Fit All

In the ongoing conversations on the subject, the overarching theme is that digital health solutions and artificial intelligence are among the frontier technologies that will exacerbate the achievement of universal health coverage (Sebetci, 2018). Nonetheless, while these emergent technological solutions may indeed encourage healthcare accessibility, affordability and quality for all, it is vital to put more emphasis on the needs on the ground. Currently, the extant approach focuses on using silo working. International organisations intervene in lower-middle-income countries via often professionally designed digital health solutions projects in this approach. Typically, such projects derail when their funding is no longer available. It is different from offering such countries support for long-term digital health solutions policies focussed on the specific needs of the people on the ground.

People must learn from the current failures of the silo-working approach. It has failed terribly in the Millennium Development Goals (MDGs). It has proven that it could be more efficient and effective in tapping into the benefits of digital health solution technologies. A lot still needs to be done right, starting from acknowledging that a one-size-does-not-fit-all approach is more applicable. Instead of speeding into digital health interventions within these countries, the primary vision, objectives, crucial national priorities and indicators need to be identified and clearly outlined in the national policy document to offer guidance to any digital health solution intervention from international organisations and the government. Such a strategy is more "one-size-does-not-fit-all" conscious.

Before developing and implementing any digital health solutions, one must check some crucial aspects. Digital health solutions are intended to be sustainable and capable of having a positive impact on the lives of everyone. Thus, assuming a homogeneous approach is incredibly flawed, especially following the different aspects discussed in this chapter. Thus, to ensure the deployment approach diverges from the assumption of homogeneous users. It is more of a "one size does not fill an approach", some of the questions one can ask themselves when adopting digital health interventions are:

- In what ways can one ensure that digital health solutions do not restrict the development of local health initiatives?
- What can one do to ensure that digital health solutions do not influence the extant inequalities in health care?
- What can one do to develop the capacity for health professionals to utilise such healthcare solution technologies while offering users the ability and necessary skills to utilise these new digital solutions effectively?
- How can people access these digital technological solutions in healthcare, and at what expense?
- What are the vital standards and procedures that ensure interoperability, information confidentiality and data safety within every aspect of electronic data management in the healthcare sector?
- How can one ensure a smooth collaboration between the private sector and other institutions like government ministries to develop a solid infrastructure capable of efficiently and effectively delivering digital health solution core components?
- How can one lay down an open and transparent governance body to overlook the enacting of digital health solutions and strategies while investing in capacity building and leadership?

While several other foundations can also ensure that digital health solutions can be sustainable and effective in the long term, these are among the crucial ones that one needs to ask themselves as guidance to implement effective digital health interventions in healthcare. These foundational questions are derived from the adoption theory, which assesses an individual as well as the choices of the individual concerning either embracing or rejecting a particular technological innovation.

According to some models of this theory, adoption is not merely about a choice of accepting an innovation but also about the magnitude to which the innovation is incorporated into the ideal context. With this, for digital health solution innovations to be adopted effectively, people must be able to perceive the idea and the product as innovative and beneficial in the long term. It is only through this that the health sector can achieve diffusion. Nonetheless, at the current pace at which digital health solutions are being introduced into the healthcare sector, if there is no elaborate foundation to guide their integration, they are more likely to fail in the long term.

When looking at developing regions like Africa, it is one of the continents that is constantly acknowledged for being places where digital health solutions will transform the future of health care over the next few years. Still, it is vital to question the policies the health organisation can use to earn these achievements. As evidenced by the coronavirus pandemic, the speedy introduction of digital solutions to strengthen the provision of superior healthcare, more so for vulnerable populations, has been on the rise. It is, however, important to question to what end this will be the case. As outlined by the World Health Organization's global observatory for E-health, only some African countries have a digital health information structure or national E-health policy. In addition to this, the report indicated that the only few countries in the region that have such strategies have outdated policies.

Importantly, digital health solutions, more so in developing regions like African countries, should only implement such interventions after initially seeking the support of digital health policies via a multi-stakeholder approach. These policy guidelines must also be updated through stakeholders supporting the reviews to ensure the policy document sufficiently tackles the rapid-paced development of healthcare solution technologies. Dialogues on tapping into the benefits of digital technologies for sustainable health outcomes can only proceed with proper policy documentation that is up to date as well. There is also an existing need for integrating accountability strategies and frameworks when looking beyond policy documentation. These must be flexible enough to allow for occasional review of digital health solution policies that can match the rapid speed at which these technologies are advancing within the digital space.

With all this, one of the best approaches to introducing digital health solutions in a one-size-does-not-fit-all fashion capable of effectively ensuring user adoption and satisfaction is through implementing universal health coverage by meticulously focusing on each component. Health organisations should approach this in a way tailored to attaining universal healthcare coverage within this rapid-paced digital era. It thus considers even lower-middle-income countries. The approach encourages cooperation and collaboration between individuals and communities, which are most beneficial in digital health transformation. It aims to support and invest in health strategies to ensure that they effectively enact digital health solutions.

Notably, for digital health solutions to succeed by being both practical and sustainable, they must wholly incorporate a more comprehensive health system aligned with extant health policies and strategies in the fundamental approach. A good idea would be creating coalitions by organising advocacy throughout national platforms, which function collaboratively to impact the governments and other stakeholders to steer changes highlighted within their national strategies. The underlying approach has so far proven effective in national strategy and in offering support to design or create such strategies. It has the upper hand over the extant approach whereby large sums of data are collected and transferred to digital health solution technologies towards countries that still need to be equipped to handle and integrate such data or technologies, such as low-income countries. Following this, it is sustainable compared to the existing haste of exporting digital health technologies to these countries, which is unsustainable.

Countries indeed need to be guided through evidence and policies for them to implement digital policies that are sustainable and harmonised. Doing this is also crucial for systems as it proves more effective than merely being fascinated by opting for digital health solutions for the mere sake of it. Although digital health technologies, as well as data, offer undeniable opportunities that can assist in attaining much broader health systems and, even to some extent, universal health coverage, the crucial point is that countries should be given enough support to manage their digital health solution experiences via effective policy frameworks. These policy frameworks are bound to improve the quality of digital health services as well as the coverage of these services. Furthermore, they can assist in significantly minimising inequities which would be incredibly beneficial, especially for lower-middle-income countries.

In addition to all this, there is also a need for broader political will and collaborative and concerted action at the country level to effectively initiate these policy procedures whereby all communities and stakeholders, especially when vulnerable, marginalised and underrepresented groups, are involved. Digital health interventions also ought to function with institutions that offer health training services to integrate such digital health solution technologies right from the most basic level of training. It is crucial to do this, especially today, where digital health solutions are often tailored for homogeneous users. When the trainees are introduced and made familiar with systems much earlier, they gain a firm foundation, more so for future E-health solutions that may emerge. In all truth, when the much-needed policy framework is lacking, digital health solutions miss an essential guide fundamental to their investment and coordination, especially within low- and middle-income countries. Following this, there is a significant risk of making redundant mistakes in an assortment of pilot projects that have higher chances of failing when it comes to making it to scale.

Nonetheless, although these are vital and viable recommendations that can significantly assist in the integration of digital health solutions, it is essential to understand the reasons why digital health solutions and not a one-size-fits-all approach. When it comes to technology, it is essentially about the course of action an individual takes to reach a well-defined destination. Following this, becoming conscious of the semantics of the healthcare organisation can also be very beneficial in adopting digital health solutions. The semantics of the organisation is, with this, the purpose and what gives the tactics and procedures of the organisation meaning. They are crucial for producing vital insights concerning this, which assists in gaining a more in-depth understanding of the transformational needs of the healthcare organisation. With this alone, it becomes evident that digital health solutions and all transformations can be more than just a one-size-fits-all approach.

Still, sharpening the semantics implies that one needs to become conscious of the health organisation's material concerns and those of the patients they interact with. Thus, a healthcare organisation's needs, goals, and limitations are bound to differ from those of another organisation. In essence, if the approach to adopting digital health solutions is more generic, the company might spend more time and finances on infrastructure that the healthcare organisation might not even need to begin with. The organisation might also end up using crucial assets in a way that necessitates further efforts so that they may be helpful to their organisation, thus leading to the wastage of these assets.

Further, when the approach is more generic, a transformational service that is suitable for one section of the organisation may need to be clarified to another part of the healthcare organisation. With this, there are better ways to go than a one-size-fits-all approach. It is inefficient, cumbersome and ultimately ineffective. However, when a one-size-does-not-fit-all approach is used appropriately, the digital health solutions integrated into the health care organisation are bound to yield more results. Additionally, the digital transformation states that the component-by-component approach yields are often better suited to meet the unique needs of each patient and health professional within various departments. It also allows for homogeneity and coherence, which is crucial for good organisational practices from a broader perspective.

It is also crucial to consider questions like: how the organisation perceives digital healthcare solutions, the kind of insights the organisation is looking for and so on when thinking about using digital health care interventions. Therefore, the organisation must leverage and make sufficient consultations with a team of experts on the ground level before driving the insights gathered to the higher-level decision-makers in the healthcare organisation. Organisations must take these steps to enable high-level healthcare decision-makers to make more informed decisions that will steer the organisation's digital transformation processes. Typically, the individuals who own most of such data resources and key processes orchestration ought to be the organisation's individuals with the most information about them. Such a strategy helps in averting the implementation of generic solutions that, as discussed earlier, do not give significant benefits to the organisation. In fact, it could have some net detrimental effects on the healthcare organisation. It is also important to acknowledge that digital healthcare solutions will likely be unique to that particular organisation; thus, the puzzle pieces are particularly unique to a specific content. Feeling these pieces should give the organisation a sense of uniqueness. Logically, the digital healthcare solution technologies that an organisation intends to integrate into practice must be evaluated on how well they fit into the organisation. If they are right for the organisation, they should align with its practice seamlessly.

Typically, one looks at their organisation's digital healthcare solution technologies minus critically assessing how they fit and align with the company. In that case, they are bound to make these misguided decisions that will ultimately adversely impact the company as they will end up not fitting in with the organisation's goals. If one is to strategically place their digital health solution for long-term success they must ensure it is fully integrated. In that case, one must divvy up transformational services by teams, consult the experts that are consistently interacting with the relevant data and outline the questions that they desire to answer as an organisation regarding implementing the digital health care solution initiatives.

When considering diverse populations, user adoption and satisfaction in digital health solution initiatives can only be achieved through a one-size-does-not-fit-all approach. It is crucial that digital health solutions are useful, have high fidelity in development and are usable by all. If this is to be achieved, the digital health solutions implemented must be user-centred, effectively co-designed and co-created in the design principles while adhering to a design science methodology. As outlined by previous research, it is a fact that ethnic and racial health disparities and associated with lower quality of care and poor health outcomes. It is for this reason that this approach is important as it considers these populations. It is designed to meet the needs of these populations as well.

Cultural issues and language can also have a detrimental effect on these disparities when not promptly tackled by healthcare organisations (Sebetci, 2018). Furthermore, as a nation's diversity continuously grows, healthcare organisations are bound to engage with more diverse patients and, in turn, encounter more cultural and language barriers (Tabibi et al., 2011). The diversity of cultures, dialects, and languages may overwhelm staff and hospitals. Even for this, there is no one-size-fits-all solution. The framework for organisational cultural competence, which also significantly influences how effectively digital health solutions are adopted into the organisation, is unique for each hospital. Digital healthcare initiatives need to be tailored to meet the needs of diverse populations.

The needs of diverse populations can only be met with an effective framework. In this chapter, the practices employed within hospitals are used to formulate the thematic framework for establishing practices capable of meeting the needs of diverse populations. The themes are based on practices that hospitals, language and culture studies have already conducted, those the organisations may uncover and those they are already integrating. Further, as hospitals are bound to face several similar challenges as well as constraints in attaining the needs of diverse populations, there can be some practices in these themes that healthcare organisations can implement minus allocate significant resources. Nonetheless, these individual practices are intended to be something other than a standalone solution. The teams are building a foundation, gathering and utilising data to better services, accommodating specific population needs and implementing external as well as internal collaboration. A variety of practices touching on all these themes must be adopted in a structured way that properly aligns with the patient's needs as well as the resources available to the healthcare organisation.

As discussed earlier, the foundation is laying down policies that can facilitate efficient and effective use adoption and, ultimately, satisfaction. The establishment of a foundation of policies as well as processes to systematically support cultural competence is vital to meeting the needs of diverse patient populations. It is also important to note that leadership plays a crucial role when it comes to this, as it is only through effective leadership that the healthcare organisation can be able to prioritise effectively, acknowledge and steer efforts towards developing appropriate policies and processes that can better care and more effectively meet the needs of patients. Cultural and language considerations can be integrated into the policies of a healthcare organisation to foster better user adoption and satisfaction with digital healthcare solutions.

When it comes to building a foundation, all practices that assist a healthcare organisation in developing its framework for meeting the needs of diverse patients are central. They include any official procedure practices in the organisation or that are a component of the organisation's overall practices, culture or operations. As explained earlier, leadership plays an inherent role in these kinds of undertakings.

One of the most commonly known digital healthcare solutions in the globalising world today is health information systems. It is a primary branch of information technology that heavily depends on user satisfaction. A health information system (HIS) is essentially a technological system that incorporates the collection of data, the processing of data, reporting and the utilisation of the processed data that is crucial to bettering health services in terms of their efficiency and, ultimately, their effectiveness via improving management at all the levels of health care services. The need for quality health services in the current global context implies that healthcare organisations should acknowledge the importance of investing in information technologies as digital health solutions. It is also important that organisations recognise these to enhance minimising expenses.

Overtly, a practical digital health solution should enable a health organisation to attain efficiency, quality of service, productivity as well as customer satisfaction as among the goals of the health sector (Aghazadeh et al., 2012; Ismail et al., 2015). The HIS is the crucial technology that supports functions within hospitals tactically, practically and at strategic levels in academic research and healthcare organisations. These hospital information systems are utilised as digital health solutions for bettering personnel efficiency and improving patient care quality as per the principal aims. They are also aimed at doing away with unnecessary procedures, statistically generating information more efficiently and effectively as well as enabling more efficient data mining procedures, enhancing systems and standards, using computers in a range of operations, developing hospitals that have modern work methods, sustaining the communication of data among hospitals and other health centres and bettering the general public health (Kumar, & Gomes, 2006). When these digital health solutions are implemented and operated appropriately, the healthcare organisation significantly improves its decision-making process, the pace at which it is capable of accessing information, staff productivity, reliability and patient satisfaction. Some of these benefits are also associated with the way health information systems significantly minimise expenses in healthcare.

With this, when digital health solutions are integrated appropriately through the one-size-does-not-fit-all approach, they are capable of functioning optimally and enabling the organisation to achieve the most of its potential. They minimise medical errors, increase the productivity of patient care, offer sufficient support to health personnel and better patient care quality. Health information systems, as comprehensive and integrative information system digital health solutions, are designed to manage medical, financial and administrative scenarios within the hospital (Aggelidis, & Chatzoglou, 2012).

These digital health solutions are inclusive of electronic health records that give physicians the health histories of the patients comprehensively and in real-time. Authorities are able to develop systematic patient history databases to record data, enhance the care of patients, enhance health personnel performance and improve the quality of diagnosis using digital health solutions like information systems. Ultimately, this also escalates the income of the healthcare organisation or hospital.

Notably, however, digital health solutions like health information systems have distinctive features from those of other information systems. In addition to the recent information system operation modules that are utilised in other commercial enterprises, health information systems how that detailed data is sustained in it. Thus, health information systems as digital health solutions are more comprehensive. Furthering HIS's impacts on operational duties, they don't merely act as digital solutions when it comes to health, but also to finance. They offer benefits when it comes to financial savings through improving the quality of healthcare services offered to patients; thus, whichever investments are made will give back more promptly. Further, the digital health solution minimises the length of time the healthcare organisation takes in making its decisions for diagnosis as well as treatments by giving more accurate and reliable information concerning patients, which leads to an augmentation of the income accrued by the hospital following enhanced patient satisfaction (Fadhil, Jusop, & Abdullah, 2012). Digital health solutions like health information systems can process large sums of data as well as complex medical information to produce information that is easier to understand yet extremely helpful. In addition to this, although information sharing is a necessity in comprehensive medical information systems, there are other factors that are equally important, like confidentiality and security (Liu, & Wang, 2016). Nonetheless, these factors in digital health solutions made, to some extent, appear as hindrances since they heightened the general costs of the technologies. Still, they are vital properties when it comes to technological compatibility.

User Adoption and User Satisfaction

The literature associated with user adoption of digital health solutions indicates that user behaviours, as well as their intentions are related to their satisfaction with digital technology. It also reveals that satisfaction levels can help inform the anticipated behaviours of the healthcare staff. User resistance, user administration and system applicability were also found to have a significant effect on user satisfaction (Acharyulu, 2012). When it comes to user resistance, it is vital to ensure the effective application of new digital health technologies to overcome this so that the technological solution can give maximised benefit (Işık, & Akbolat, 2010).

Health information systems are among the most crucial digital health solutions today because of the pivotal role that up-to-date and reliable patient information plays in healthcare. As emphasised by Acharyulu (2012), patient information that is complete, up to date, reliable and that can be easily and promptly accessed is vital in healthcare. The information plays a central role in that it helps in supporting strategic planning as well as consistent quality development towards improving patient satisfaction. With such digital health solutions, it is not far-fetched to say that health organisations would be able to effectively control all kinds of parameters as well as activities in the system. They will be able to use digital health technology to control hospital personnel information, the hospital as well as its various technologies and even finances. Importantly, they would also be able to effectively manage service provision to patients.

In these digital health solutions, there are several healthcare information technological valuation models that have been proposed. These include a platform for continuous intention models and acceptance of the technology models. Nonetheless, while the acceptance of the technology model is more often an emphasis on user adoption and satisfaction, no one-size-does-not-fit-all approaches; they are more general. The most renowned models are the theory of planned behaviour, the technology acceptance model, the information success model, the expectation confirmation theory, the use of technology, the information system continues intention and, importantly, the unified theory of acceptance model (Hadji et al., 2016). In the theory of planned behaviour (TPB) and the theory of reasoned action (TRA), the Davis technology acceptance model implies that the perception of ease of use and the perception of usefulness has a significant impact on the attitudes of users towards using particular new digital health solution technology (Davis, 1989).

Later, Venkatesh and Davis reviewed the structure of the technology acceptance model following more extensive research. The revised version of the technology acceptance model, also known as TAM 2, integrated perceived intention of use, perceived usefulness and perceived ease of use as the components of the theory (Venkatesh, & Davis, 2000). Similarly, the unified theory of acceptance and use of technology (UTAUT) was developed by Venkatesh et al. (2003) as an integration of all the eight different theories mentioned earlier. Progressively, Bhattacherjee furthered the expectation confirmation theory to gain deeper insights into the intentions of individuals concerning continuing to utilise digital health solutions or ceasing to utilise them (Bhattacherjee, 2001). He integrated TAM into the theory to achieve this. The model, which was proposed by Bhattacherjee alongside some other researchers whom the source does not make explicit, places much emphasis on the importance of end-user satisfaction via the compatibility factor of technology. In fact, the theory has the acronym EUS, which means end-user satisfaction by technology compatibility.

From all this, there are two main perspectives that come to light. These are bound to significantly influence use adoption and satisfaction in digital health solutions. These are the organisational perspective and the sociotechnical perspective. The organisational perspective of this greatly emphasises the benefits offered by a particular digital health solution and how users interact with it. Nonetheless, this is a point of view that is often criticised after assessing human factor interactions. In contrast, the social-technical perspective focuses more on personal needs that sufficiently consider the human factor (Aggelidis, & Chatzoglou, 2012). With regard to digital health solutions, DeLone and McLean's model identifies system quality, individual impact, organisational impact and user satisfaction as the determinants of how effective digital technology is. More precisely, health information systems such as digital health solutions also have information quality and information news among the factors that determine their success. DeLone and McLean's model integrates both social, technical and organisational perspectives (Au et al., 2002).

It is important to note that the quality dimension in digital health solutions has a significant role play when it comes to evaluating their success. Aside from systems quality, service quality, net benefits, usage and user satisfaction are also important factors to consider (Jayawardena, 2014). The model acknowledges that the opinions of end users are among the most crucial factors to consider in the application of any digital health solution. Currently, there's a surging number of users that are becoming more conscious of the need for changes. Of course, the changes in the context are those that are a beneficiary of the participation of users in the building, advancement and designing of the system (Stoicu-Tivadar & Stoicu-Tivadar, 2006). Following this, the end user becomes a crucial factor in this end. For digital health solutions that involve any technological system, the end user must be at the pivot of the system. The reactions, behaviours and senses of the users must be acknowledged during the evaluation of these systems. For instance, in a health information system evaluation, if there's a failure to incorporate the human factor into the evaluation, the evaluation is immaterial and useless (Maillet, & Sicotte, 2015).

As explained by DeLone and McLean, user satisfaction is the most comprehensive evaluation of digital health solutions. It is because user satisfaction has a crucial impact on the behaviour of users towards the usage of a particular technology and, thus, system usage in turn (Gürsel et al., 2014). User satisfaction is the most vital aspect that enables digital health solutions to succeed. Therefore, overlooking and undervaluing the expectations of end users will, to a significant extent, have an adverse impact on the user adoptability of a newly integrated system (Sebetci, 2018). The measures of user satisfaction are grouped along three points of view, namely the attitudes of users towards the digital health solution technology, user satisfaction with regard to the benefits of the digital health solution and user satisfaction with regard to the quality of the digital health solution. Notably, the user satisfaction level significantly influences system usage.

If the digital health solution is incapable of satisfying the users, there are users who can use them (Amin et al., 2011). In this sense, user adoption and user satisfaction are interrelated. Further, both user adoption and user satisfaction must be satisfied for digital health solutions to be both sufficient and reliable (Sebetci, 2018).

Sebetci (2018) delve further into the importance of end-user satisfaction by conducting research that revealed that there is a medium correlation between system quality and user satisfaction (Sebetci, 2018). Similarly, Jayawardena Also reported that the use is the fundamental factor of the success of hospitals that function within a computer setting. Therefore, the expectations of both patients and health professionals, as users of the system, must be accurately acknowledged (Sebetci, 2018). Digital technology end-user satisfaction can be uncovered by undertaking sensual and cognitive measurements of the experience of the users as they consume the services offered by these digital health solutions. Under the lens of health information systems as a digital health solution, Cyert and March (1963) are the researchers who initially suggested the concept of user information satisfaction as a substitute for the system success concept. The researchers explained that a digital health solution technological system must be capable of effectively meeting the needs of users to maximise user satisfaction in association with the system (Cyert & March, 1963).

Stoicu-Tivadar and Stoicu-Tivadar (2006) emphasise that the adoptability and disability of the interface of a digital health solution is a crucial element in human-computer interactions. Further, other aspects like fault tolerance are also crucial elements that should be considered (Stoicu-Tivadar & Stoicu-Tivadar, 2006). When it comes to digital health solutions like health information systems, user information is overly utilised as a user perspective indicator towards the efficiency of the digital health solution, which is associated with important elements of system design and analysis (Sebetci, 2018). For instance, utilising an adapted version of UTAUT, Maillet et al. (2015) delved into the satisfaction and acceptance of nurses towards utilising a newly incorporated electronic patient record system (EPR). The outcomes of the study indicated the compatibility of the electronic patient record system with the particular preferred style of working, the values of the nurses and the extant work practices, but the most significant and crucial aspects that explained their satisfaction with the digital health solution (Mailett et al., 2015).

Following all this, it is evident that co-creation and code design for developing people-centred digital health solutions is of enormous benefit and vital. In essence, co-design is the fundamental element for delivering high value care that is people-centred since it facilitates the involvement and engagement of stakeholders in the development of effective digital health solutions. Undoubtedly, defective implementation of people-centred healthcare necessitates approaches and strategies that respond appropriately to the local context, with the engagement and active participation of local stakeholders incorporated through collaborative approaches. Essentially, this is what co-design is all about. The implementation of any of the existing co-design strategies is of the essence when it comes to addressing target group needs better in health care as well as facilitating certain projects.

The current global strategy fostered by the World Health Organization (WHO) that champions integrated people-centred health services from 2016 to 2026 necessitates a drastic shift in how health service funding is done, as well as the way they are managed and delivered (Sanz, Acha, & García, 2021). The strategy makes explicit how important a people-centred approach is when it comes to the development of health systems that are capable of effectively responding to the challenges in the health sector. It is particularly important for curbing rising health care costs and multi-morbidities and assisting ageing populations. People-centred care is hereby the process of treating a patient as a unique individual (Sanz, Acha,

& García, 2021). It is quite contrary to what the one-size-fits-all approach in digital health solutions champions. On the other hand, the one-size-does-not-fit-all approach in the implementation of digital health solutions is more aligned with people-centred care, which is conscious of respecting service users and patients as individuals. It is also considerate of the opinions of these groups in the decision-making process in the health care organisation (Kusurkar et al., 2021).

Co-Design, Co-Creation and User-Centred Design

Co-design and its related cousins, co-creation and user-centred design, are techniques that are used to involve end users with the design of specific solutions. Specifically, in a co-design process, end users work together with designers and engineers to ideate and develop a suitable design from their perspective (Bird et al; Jessen et al., 2018.). It is expected that by doing so they are more likely to accept the designed and developed solution when it is ultimately deployed. Co-design is distinct from traditional approaches to design where designers and engineers would develop the solution and then expect users to use and like the developed solution (ibid.). An in-between stage between co-design and the design being made and then provided to the user is the process of user-centred design. In this process, user needs are carefully considered by the design team and engineers; however, users are not immersed in the design process. In contrast users can become more involved than just at a co-design level and they can actually become involved in the creation of the solution; this is termed co-creation (ibid.). It is important to note in healthcare that we do not have a homogenous group of users. At the very least we have patients and clinicians as two key end-user groups who unsurprisingly have different needs and requirements of the designed solution and thus it is essential to keep these perspectives in mind.

One systematic methodology to assist with ensuring design is both rigorous and yet relevant to user needs is design science research methodology (DSRM) developed by Hevner and Wickramasinghe (2018). Another approach to ensure rigour and relevance ensues is to follow a task technology fit (TTF) framework. TTF is derived from the work of Goodhue (1995; 1998) who argues that a fit between task characteristics and system features needs to be high for the best per-formance and success and this will in turn impact user satisfaction and adoption in a positive way. Ideally, a combination of TTF and DSRM should ensure a high level of end-user satisfaction and adoption.

Conclusion

Following all this, the one-size-does-not-fit approach empowers patients by heightening their roles in their own health via fostering a more people-centred approach. Its elements, such as providing patients with sufficient information, confidence, legitimacy, acceptance, support and comfort, are also crucial, more so for disadvantaged populations. From all this, the importance of designing digital health solutions that simultaneously appeal to clinical and patient users.

Summary

At the conclusion of this chapter, it should be evident:

a) What impacts user adoption and satisfaction and why both are important.
   User likes and preferences, whether a solution assists them in a task or whether it is too burdensome, are factors affecting user adoption. If use is voluntary, then high satisfaction can lead to high adoption of a solution. If digital health solutions are to be used, they need to be adopted and of satisfaction.

b) What are the differences between co-design, co-creation and user-centred design.
   The difference between co-design, co-creation and user-centred design lies in the level of end-user involvement. Thus, user-centred design has very little actual end-user involvement while co-creation has most end-user involvement, given that in this approach end users are heavily involved in the creation of the designed solution. An in-between approach is co-design where end users are actively included in designing the solution.

c) What are some of the models that can assist with ensuring a higher level of user adoption and satisfaction.
   Methodologies and frameworks such as DSRM and TTF which focus on rigour and relevance can be most helpful in ensuring a high level of user adoption and satisfaction. In addition, it is important to realise that end users in healthcare are not homogenous and consist of clinical and patient groups at the very minimum.

d) Why one size does not fit all.
   Fundamentally, healthcare is about treating patients. People are individual, different and distinct and thus most definitely one size does not fit all.

References

Acharyulu, G. V. (2012). Assessment of hospital information system quality in multi speciality hospital. *International Journal of Innovation Management and Technology*, 3(4):349–52.

Aggelidis, V. P., & Chatzoglou, P. D. (2012). Hospital information systems: Measuring end user computing satisfaction (EUCS). *Journal of Biomedical Informatics*, 45(3), 566–579.

Aghazadeh, S., Aliyev, A., & Ebrahimnezhad, M. (2012). Review the role of hospital information systems in medical services development. *International Journal of Computer Theory and Engineering*, 4(6), 866.

Amin, I. M., Hussein, S. S., & Isa, W. A. (2011). Assessing user satisfaction of using hospital information system (HIS) in Malaysia. *People*, 12, 13.

Au, N., Ngai, E. W., & Cheng, T. E. (2002). A critical review of end-user information system satisfaction research and a new research framework. *Omega*, 30(6), 451–478.

Bhattacherjee, A. (2001). Understanding information systems continuance: An expectation-confirmation model. *MIS Quarterly*, 351–370.

Bird, M., McGillion, M., Chambers, et al. (2021). A generative co-design framework for healthcare innovation: Development and application of an end-user engagement framework. *Research Involvement and Engagement*, 7, 1–12.

Cyert, R. M., & March, J. G. (1963). *A behavioral theory of the firm*. Prentice Hall/Pearson Education.

Davis, F. D. (1989). Perceived usefulness, perceived ease of use, and user acceptance of information technology. *MIS Quarterly*, 319–340.

Fadhil, N. F. M., Jusop, M., & Abdullah, A. A. (2012). Hospital information system (his) implementation in a public hospital: a case study from Malaysia. *Far East Journal of Psychology and Business, 8*(1), 1–11.

Goodhue, D. (1998). Development and measurement validity of a task-technology fit instrument for user evaluations of information system decision sciences. Retrieved August 17, 2003, from https://doi.org/10.1111/j.1540-5915.1998.tb01346.x.

Goodhue, D. L., & Thompson, R. L. (1995). Task-technology fit and individual performance. *MIS Quarterly*, 213–236.

Gürsel, G., Zayim, N., Gülkesen, K. H., Arifoğlu, A., & Saka, O. (2014). A new approach in the evaluation of hospital information systems. *Turkish Journal of Electrical Engineering and Computer Sciences, 22*(1), 214–222.

Hadji, B., Martin, G., Dupuis, I., Campoy, E., & Degoulet, P. (2016). 14 Years longitudinal evaluation of clinical information systems acceptance: The HEGP case. *International Journal of Medical Informatics, 86*, 20–29.

Hevner & Wickramasinghe. (2018). Design science research opportunities in healthcare. In Wickramasinghe & Schaffer (eds), *Theories to inform superior health informatics research and practice*. Springer. ISBN 978-3-319-72287-0.

Işık, O., & Akbolat, M. (2010). Use of information technologies and hospital information systems: A research on health workers. *World of Knowledge, 11* (2), 365–389.

Ismail, N. I., Abdullah, N. H., & Shamsuddin, A. (2015). Adoption of hospital information system (HIS) in Malaysian public hospitals. *Procedia-Social and Behavioral Sciences, 172*, 336–343.

Jayawardena, A. S. (2014). The electronic hospital information system implemented at the General Hospital Trincomalee: An experience of business process reengineering. *Community Medicine and Health Education, S2*, 001. doi: 10.4172/2161-0711.S2-001.

Jessen, S., Mirkovic, J., Ruland, C. M., et al. (2018). Creating gameful design in mHealth: A participatory co-design approach. *JMIR Mhealth Uhealth, 6*(12), e11579. doi: 10.2196/11579. PMID: 30552080; PMCID: PMC6315237.

Kumar, A. P., & Gomes, L. A. (2006). A study of the hospital information system (HIS) in the medical records department of a tertiary teaching hospital. *Journal of the Academy of Hospital Administration, 18*(1), 1–6.

Kusurkar, R. A., Mak-van der Vossen, M., Kors, J., Grijpma, J. W., van der Burgt, S. M., Koster, A. S., & de la Croix, A. (2021). 'One size does not fit all': The value of person-centred analysis in health professions education research. *Perspectives on Medical Education, 10*(4), 245–251.

Liu, S., & Wang, L. (2016). Influence of managerial control on performance in medical information system projects: the moderating role of organizational environment and team risks. *International Journal of Project Management, 34*(1), 102–116.

Maillet, É., Mathieu, L., & Sicotte, C. (2015). Modeling factors explaining the acceptance, actual use and satisfaction of nurses using an Electronic Patient Record in acute care settings: An extension of the UTAUT. *International Journal of Medical Informatics, 84*(1), 36–47.

Sanz, M. F., Acha, B. V., & García, M. F. (2021). Co-design for people-centred care digital solutions: a literature review. *International Journal of Integrated Care, 21*(2). https://ijic.org/articles/10.5334/ijic.5573.

Sebetci, Ö. (2018). Enhancing end-user satisfaction through technology compatibility: An assessment on health information system. *Health Policy and Technology*, *7*(3), 265–274.

Stoicu-Tivadar, L., & Stoicu-Tivadar, V. (2006). Human–computer interaction reflected in the design of user interfaces for general practitioners. *International Journal of Medical Informatics*, *75*(3–4), 335–342.

Tabibi, J., Nasiripour, A. A., Kazemzadeh, R. B., Farhangi, A. A., & Ebrahimi, P. (2011). Effective factors on hospital information system acceptance: a confirmatory study in Iranian hospitals. *Middle-East Journal of Scientific Research*, *9*(1), 95–101.

Venkatesh, V., & Davis, F. D. (2000). A theoretical extension of the technology acceptance model: four longitudinal field studies. *Management Science*, *46*(2), 186–204.

Venkatesh, V., Morris, M. G., Davis, G. B., & Davis, F. D. (2003). User acceptance of information technology: toward a unified view. *MIS Quarterly*, 425–478.

11 Agency Theory and Stakeholders
The Power–Knowledge Dichotomy

Objectives

At the conclusion of this chapter, it should be evident:

a) Why healthcare is unique with the predominant receiver of services typically being different from the predominant payer of these same services.
b) Why there are nested agency issues that arise in healthcare operations.
c) Who are knowledge worker agents in healthcare.
d) How digital health solutions can be used to mute power-knowledge dynamics.

Introduction

In today's complex business world, agency theory gives a description of the challenges that a party may encounter when another acts as a representative but has diverging perspectives on crucial issues within the business (Payne, 2019). Further, it serves to describe the problems that may happen when the acting party has different or divergent interests from the principal party. In essence, the agent that bargains on the other party's behalf may disagree on, for instance, the most ideal course of action and encourage personal beliefs to affect a transaction's outcome. Furthermore, the agent may also opt to act in a way that is more focused on his/her self-interest than that of the principal party's interests. Hence, the outcome may lead to conflict between these two parties which can be perceived as an agency problem (ibid.). Agency theory tends to emphasise more on the interest of shareholders or stakeholders, which makes it crucial, ultimately, in the appropriate design of digital health solutions (Lee et al., 2018; Dopp et al., 2020). In seeking to highlight the interests of the principal and the agent, which may be inclusive of financial and individual planners, digital health solutions can bring transparency into transactions.

When it comes to business, the power-knowledge dichotomy is greatly associated with Foucault's philosophy. As stated by Foucault, knowledge is the basis of power and thus power significantly makes use of knowledge (Rouse, 1994). Simultaneously, knowledge is reproduced by power through the structuring of knowledge in adherence to its anonymous intents. In essence, power is able to

DOI: 10.1201/9781003318538-14

restructure its own settings of exercise via knowledge. Over recent years, however, information has grown to be more central in close association with power just as the term knowledge. As the use of big data continues to become more common, the perception of information and the way of producing knowledge and power that is useful has also increased (Baker et al., 2022). The "volume and control" model is a more recent approach that describes the way information is capitalised on and translated into economic power by colossal companies. According to this approach, volume is stamped as the informational resource (Dopp et al., 2020). These are inclusive of the diversity of information and the magnitude of information as well as the people generating this information. On the other hand, control is the capability of channelling the associations between individuals and information where two mechanisms that are competing. These include personalisation, which is information that is relevant to each person and popularisation which is information that is relevant to a larger number of people. With this, knowledge is seldom neutral. It is an understanding that portrays knowledge as the determinant of false relations. The power-knowledge dichotomy is thus probable to be enacted within innovative as well as critical contexts, which shows the importance of alignment in designing digital health solutions in healthcare (Portz et al., 2020). A good instance of our knowledge implications is the monopoly of Google regarding knowledge. The page rank algorithm of Google is also an epitome of this. In addition to this, the cultural and commercial buses that are seemingly unavoidable in the global cooperation are also grounded on the volume and control model principles. For instance, Google image algorithms have some commercial implications.

On focusing on the goal alignment subject, it becomes evident that it is crucial in keeping the workforce of a company consistently working for the overarching goals of the company. The goals of the company must align for it to be successful. When a company has organisation-wide goals, the employees of the company must be made sufficiently aware of the goals that they are working towards as well as the reasons. Goal alignment does assist the company to become more strategic in its business. According to recent studies, a total of 85% of employees disengage from their jobs today (Baker et al., 2022). Following on from this, companies are challenged with increasing expenses at work because of reduced employee productivity as well as increased turnover rates following these low engagement rates in organisations. Organisational success is heavily reliant on making sure that the talent in the company aligns with the strategic goals of the company (Lyon et al., 2020; Singh et al., 2021). In this sense, becoming conscious of the goals as well as individual contributions is bound to make a significant difference between a motivated workforce and one that is not motivated. It is the duty of the managers to see to it that the goals of the direct reports and the individual goals align with the overarching strategy of the organisation. It allows for the most exceptional talents within the company to be exploited more efficiently and effectively via appropriate goal alignment, which is bound to ultimately facilitate better designing of digital health solutions (Singh et al., 2021; Quesada-López et al., 2016).

Goal Alignment

Goal alignment is critical because when the employees of a company become conscious and comprehend the goals of the organisation well, it becomes more achievable to make sure that everyone within the organisation is collaborating effectively at the right time and on the right ventures. The workforce in the company must thus understand their goals as well as how they align the teams. Further, it enables workers to become conscious of their contributions and values towards the company, thus fostering innovation (Iyawa, Herselman, & Botha, 2016; LaMonica et al., 2019; Scobbie et al., 2020). When the goals of the company are properly aligned, the employees within the company are able to perceive their responsibilities and expectations with better clarity. The crucialness of goal alignment becomes evident based on the fact that when individuals understand their goals, they are more engaged, creating a more favourable workplace culture for the organisation. In essence, the implementation of a goal-aligned structure leads to higher certainty that the individuals within the organisation are carrying out their various activities with the right aims, whereas misalignment can be costly.

Additionally, organisational transparency is yet another aspect that goal alignment assists with. Organisational transparency is of the essence to any company since it is key to maintaining a workforce that is sufficiently engaged. It is an effective way to show employees that the tasks they carry out matter in tying the daily tasks of the employees with the general goals they ought to achieve. Quite often, employees get tied up within their daily routine leading to disengagement. According to recent studies, less than 15% of employees are usually actively engaged in the work (Kayser et al., 2022).

Goal alignment is even more important when it comes to ensuring that a company can effectively execute IT projects (Pereira, da Silva & Lapão, 2014). In the contemporary world, there are new and efficient technologies that enable exceptional companies to see to it that they have the appropriate tools as well as support in place for facilitating feedback and real-time tracking, which is key to the success of any organisation. Organisations can gain insights into the status of their projects very real-time tracking, which the organisation leaders can use to effectively provide informed feedback as well as critics wherever necessary. In today's complex and heavily convoluted business environment, real-time feedback is of the essence when it comes to enabling actionable change as well as addressing challenges before they become overwhelming problems to the company. Organisational leaders can perceive what their employees are currently working on and their various activities via these systems. Following this, the company can maximise on transparency throughout activities and also in communication, which is very crucial to the successful designing of appropriate digital health solutions (Gray et al., 2019). Essentially, transparency of an organisation is of the essence in actively engaging the company's workforce thereby heightening productivity.

Furthermore, goal alignment is also positively correlated with recruiting since it significantly assists with the recruiting process. When an organisation indulges in recruiting only two members that are truly conscious of the goals of the company, they can attract and even retain better, more skilled and highly qualified individuals. When organisational leaders are sufficiently conscious of the task that the candidates will undertake, they are more capable of outlining the precise skills new hires will require on the job. With this, goal alignment also needs accuracy to gain crucial knowledge that can allow the choice of a highly tailored job description following interview questions.

Further, a goal alignment is also a significant indication that it assists greatly in onboarding. In essence, goal alignment enables organisational leaders to focus primarily on how a new recruit well assist in achieving the goals of the company as well as progress. The organisational leader or manager can thus communicate such expectations in the onboarding process more effectively. Alignment has the aspects that foster visualising how and why they do the work that they do for the company, as well as how it plays to the greater good of the team. When goal alignment fosters more heightened organisational transparency, recruits are more willing to work with the company and can even hit the ground running as they enter the company, which will be ultimately beneficial in increased dedication to design appropriate digital health solutions.

In the case that goal alignment is not integrated into the company, several adverse factors may impact the company including office politics. Undoubtedly, politics is one of the major ways through which one worker engagement within an organisation can be adversely affected. Even worse, there is absolutely no benefit that anyone gains following office gossip since they typically come from poor workflow, performance, and understanding within the workplace. Nevertheless, goal alignment can efficiently minimise this unwanted office politics within the workplace. Goal alignment fosters transparency and visualisation among the employees, which means that the organisational leader will be able to see the contributions of everyone towards the organisation. Therefore, they are in a better position of acknowledging only the right individuals and being surer about the people to reward.

Importantly, goal alignment also hinders adverse aspects like goal decomposition, since it entails constantly communicating the goals of the company. It also involves keeping track of these goals in real-time which is bound to prevent work from veering off to the wrong direction. Typically, organisations are bound to get to a point where they have their directives moving significantly off course. Nonetheless, goal alignment entails aspects like progress visualisation, goal tracking, strategic alignment which effectively prevents this from happening while maintaining tasks on track. With goal alignment, a company can be pretty much assured that its goals are constantly being worked towards by the organisation without the worries that these goals will decompose within the hierarchies of the organisational chart. It thus fosters the effective achievement of the appropriately designed digital health solutions that the organisation aims to implement. Further, the accountability that goal alignment fosters effectively heightens the levels of engagement downstream as well as communication. From all this, it is not an oversell to say that goal alignment is one of the most crucial factors within organisations for increasing productivity. As mentioned earlier, goal alignment has the fundamental features of alignment and transparency. These crucial features encourage employees at each level of the organisation's hierarchy to be fully accountable for their performance and progress. Consequently, when accountability is maximised, the productivity of the organisation increases as well. In addition to this, it also fosters the connection of employees' work with their goals so that the organisation can effectively inspire them to take ownership of the work (Braganza et al., 2022). In essence, when the employees of the organisation are fully conscious and understand the reasons why their contribution to the company is key, their productivity maximises.

The modern world of business, it is a well-known fact that employee engagement is one of the most challenging yet important factors within a company. It is also for this reason that goal alignment is important to the success of a company since it helps it improve employee engagement. Employees can better understand their roles within an organisation when the daily work is tied to the general goals of the organisation. When this is the case, employees are more motivated to contribute value to the company as they can see better how their work and their various roles are of the essence. Employees have a higher likelihood of perceiving themselves as a valued part of the team when they can clearly perceive their contributions at work. Following this, employee engagement heightens among the individuals in the company's workforce. Typically, corporate outcomes go hand in hand with employee engagement, which makes it foster designs to make the employees in the workplace to feel involved and valued.

Corporate communication is also significantly enhanced when the organisation integrates goal alignment. It allows organisation to better visualise the workflow and clearly perceive how it relates to their goals, which in turn enhances corporate communication. Rather than solely relying on annual reviews, it is more prudent to exchange feedback for particular tasks and projects on a daily basis. With this, minute errors within the company can be rectified before they become significant and long-term problems with the performance of the organisation. In any organisation, goal alignment is important towards forming a culture of productivity and engagement. Employees have a better sense of connection towards the work when they have better clarity and their responsibilities as well as the expectations, which can be effectively achieved through goal alignment. Following this, they become more engaged the various activities and digital health solution projects of the company.

Still, for an organisation to achieve excellence, it must integrate more than just goal alignment. In essence, for an organisation to achieve success, it also has to understand who its stakeholders are, their expectations, how these expectations can be satisfied and how they can adapt to achieve this. Stakeholder alignment is the essential means through which any organisation can achieve this. The model is a dynamic three-step model that shows how people, groups and organisations can stylise fundamental processes to align their work to the generation (Andersen et al., 2019). Stakeholder alignment has two main aspects, which are:

1. An understanding of the needs of decision makers and stakeholders, which is shown by the overlapping employee, customer and owner circles at the model's centrr.

2. Realisation of the fact that people, groups or organisations entail:
- Learning and expectations
- Feedback and measurements
- Accountability.

Stakeholder Alignment

In stakeholder alignment, stakeholders are broadly defined as inclusive of consumers the company trades a service with, the employees in the workplace that are engaged in strategic planning as well as continuous advancement efforts by the company, and the administrators within the organisation. The stakeholder alignment model portrays how a group is undertaking and adding value towards the company more transparent. The aim of this model is to enhance the magnitude to which customer, employee and administrator overlap, as these are stakeholders of the organisation. The process entails taking note of measurements on: the things that consumers hold to be of value and the consumer service relevant gap analysis, the things that employees hold to be of value true undertaking climate checks, supervisor and team report cards and 360 degree feedback, the things that administrators value true indicators such as productivity reports, budget, could you tentative status reports with benchmarking and projections, and through the right few leads. It also includes measuring improvements from the basis of the results or devotion towards consistent advancement towards excellence. Employees are accountable for satisfying expectations via measurement and feedback once expectations are explicitly shared and learning is fostered. With this, stakeholder alignment is key to ultimately designing appropriate digital health solutions.

When it comes to accountability in shareholder alignment, staff members are also held accountable for their performance. It means that the performance of staff members is bound to have consequences. Essentially, if the performance of a staff member is good, the consequences add more positive like bonuses, acknowledgement and praise. Similarly, if the performance is bad, the outcome is a negative consequence in addition to this, if there is an opportunity for performance enhancement, the consequences may entail clarifying roles and goals, discussing expectations, and giving constructive feedback. They may also include developing a plan that may result in the future success of employees which is agreed on by the workers as well as their supervisors. Therefore, performance is basically mentioned in stakeholder alignment for the purpose of determining whether improvements have been made.

Stakeholder alignment facilitates the crucial process of gaining an understanding of how each person and the needs in an organisation align with the goals of the organisation. Unlike goal alignment which focuses more on how the goals align with individuals such as employees in the organisation, stakeholder alignment places more emphasis on how these individuals who are the stakeholders of the company align with the company. If employees can attain and even surpass the wants of their clients in alignment to the mission of the organisation, the stakeholders are more satisfied as well. Similarly, if the employees within the organisation are more satisfied and motivated, the work processes of the organisation are bound to be more improved and more value, quality and productivity is delivered to the stakeholders. Ultimately, the organisation is bound to achieve the overall effectiveness that it desires in its digital health solutions.

There must be a common understanding amongst the stakeholders for excellence to be achieved in any undertaking of the organisation. In essence, a common understanding hereby refers to being conscious of the aspects that are being addressed. It does not necessarily imply that a consensus is extant amidst the stakeholders. Even the common understanding, the stakeholders must continue to give their input and work towards consensus on the undertakings or project's direction. Nonetheless, for a common understanding to exist among the fundamental stakeholders of the organisation, there must be a clear definition of success, the possible hindrances towards success, crucial milestones and an elaborate identification of the key decision makers as well as the decision-making process of the organisation. In any project that the organisation undertakes regarding innovative digital health solutions, it is nearly impossible to successfully execute the project minus initially having a clear definition of what makes the project successful. It should be inclusive of the completion on time, if the projects are within budget, and to each specification.

Essentially, with no stakeholder alignment it is very difficult for individuals within a company to remain committed towards a cause. Often, search projects do not kick off with every stakeholder on the same page. Therefore, stakeholder alignment is crucial during such phases yet not quite as easy unless executed appropriately. The first step towards achieving this is clearly identifying the stakeholders involved. It is prudent to initially make a list of the stakeholders that will be involved in the company's project more precisely; the list should not be generic but very specific. It should include specific names and titles of their stakeholders. After that, it should also be clearly determined the type of stakeholders each individual is.

Generally, stakeholders can be categorised into seven different types, namely strategic decision makers, financial decision makers, influencers, sponsors, champions, derailers and implementers. Basically, sponsors are the individuals that get the acknowledgement or take the fall. Typically, there's only one sponsor. Similarly, the financial decision makers of the projects of organisations are also typically just one, although they could be more in some instances. They are tasked with making decisions on whether a project or part of a project will be funded. Strategic decision makers are usually more than one individual and are the ones who determine whether work gets approved. It should be inclusive of the completion on time of the projects, within the budget, and to each specification with "vocal".. Influencers are also the type of stakeholders who are usually also have strong opinions, which should always be considered in a project that the organisation intends to undertake. The only difference between influencers and strategic decision makers is that influencers do not have veto powers while strategic decision makers have veto powers. Derailers also do not have any official veto powers when it comes to the projects of an organisation, but they have the ability to either intentionally or unintentionally hinder the project within its tracks typically. They are extrinsic of the evident pool of stakeholders in the organisation, but they are significantly impacted by the outcomes of the projects an organisation intends to undertake. Last are the implementers who are the individuals who are responsible for putting the strategy in that the organisation comes up with into action. Typically, the implementers are stakeholders that are usually very precise in their knowledge as well as expertise.

It is important to keep in mind that alignment is not about explaining to individuals what your thoughts are and then persuading them to agree with these thoughts. Alignment is all about getting these people to actively engage themselves with the activity or project of the organisation (Braganza et al., 2022). It is about making the stakeholders have a sense of commitment towards the undertaking. Therefore, a crucial step towards effective stakeholder alignments is getting the stakeholders involved. It is a step that necessitates working with the project sponsor to see to it that every other stakeholder is actively involved in the undertaking. There are some stakeholders who are bound to be more involved than other stakeholders. Still, each stakeholder needs to be conscious of the objectives of the undertaking by the organisation and should be consistently given updates that would ensure that they actively participate in the process.

In addition to this, it is also an essential step to anticipate the needs of stakeholders to ensure successful stakeholder alignment. Essentially, the more information the organisational leaders have concerning the needs of the stakeholders of the company as well as their concerns, the better the position they are in to tackle and address these needs. If the stakeholder alignment used to be only effective, an elaborate understanding between the members of the team must be cultivated. While this helps in avoiding abrupt objections from stakeholders in the later phases of an organisation's undertaking, it is also important to acknowledge that the needs of stakeholders are bound to change as the organisation progresses. With this in mind, it is therefore also vital to reassess these needs every step of the way to ensure that they can be met effectively.

As mentioned earlier, communication is crucial when it comes to stakeholder alignment. Once aware of the things that the stakeholders hold to be of value and the aspects that they truly care about, it is time to begin pondering on how to effectively craft messages that will align well with them. The discussions should be centred around what the stakeholder holds to be most important to them. A model like a simple stakeholder matrix can be of great help when it comes to gathering information regarding stakeholders and organising messages in this way.

Finally, it is important to keep in mind that stakeholder alignment is not a thing that occurs just once on an organisation's content project. It is a long-term thing that occurs repeatedly throughout the undertaking of the organisation; that is, from the starch all the way to the implementation phase of a project. It is not an easy endeavour to get and maintain stakeholders in alignment throughout the process of an organisation's project. Therefore, at every crucial point on a regular basis, organisational leaders need to always remember to take a halt, drop and align whenever necessary. Any company that takes meticulous interest and attention to stakeholder alignment has a better chance of getting its stakeholders to ultimately be on the same page.

Power-knowledge difference is yet another crucial factor to consider for an organisation that is eyeing up long-term success. Basically, power-knowledge difference refers to the perception that power has knowledge as its basis and utilises knowledge, while knowledge on the other hand is reproduced by power through structuring it according to its anonymous intents (Rouse, 1994). As explained by Foucault, power-knowledge differences focus on power that is created via accepted forms of knowledge, "truth" and an understanding that is scientific in nature (Rouse, 1994). When analysing this further, it becomes evident that knowledge, which can hereby be perceived as "truth", is a thing of the world. It is generated solemnly by a virtue of several kinds of constraint. Ultimately, truth instigates regular effects of power.

Nonetheless, while knowledge is often regarded as power, there are some differences that come to light regarding knowledge and power in the corporate world. In the world of business, knowledge is not necessarily synonymous with power. Power is power. While many people may state that knowledge is power, in the corporate setting knowledge is not the power. The capability of an organisational leader or a company to drive action based on knowledge is power. There is a significant difference between knowledge and power in this context. A good indication of this is the fact that several individuals in many organisations often fail to have the ability to act effectively on the knowledge they have. In essence, the ability to influence people using the knowledge that one has is power, but knowledge is not power.

Power Knowledge

The knowledge power difference draws the line between effective and ineffective leadership and management in a company. Knowledge can perhaps be regarded as potential when it comes to power. Nonetheless when there is no motivation towards acting or applying the knowledge one has, that knowledge becomes immaterial with regard to power. More precisely, it is the will and capability to act on the basis of the knowledge that one has that is power. It is a power that is more social and political in that it enables individuals such as organisational leaders to influence others within the organisation. Regarding power, while knowledge is seldom intrinsic to an individual as it has to be acquired by the individual, power can be from the source of intrinsic influential power. Wisdom can be innate in somebody but not knowledge, especially since it ought to be acquired from learning. Power, on the other hand, can come from the source in the form of intrinsic influential power, which can exist regardless of one's authority. The other source whereby one can gain power is authoritative power which one is given by authority. Notably, unless an individual has colossal authoritative power, it is prudent that they have the ability to effectively influence and work well with others using knowledge to achieve great things like designing effective and appropriate digital health solutions. Knowledge can only be related with power when it is used to steer action.

Regarding action, theories like the theory of reasoned action can also be crucial when it comes to realising the benefits of effective management within an organisation. According to the theory, the behaviour of individuals is dictated by their intent to carry out the behaviour. In turn, this intention is a function of the attitudes of the individuals towards the behaviour as well as subjective norms (Hale, Householder & Greene, 2002). The management of different stakeholder groups with the aim of ensuring appropriately designed digital health solutions requires understanding of human health behaviours based on their individual attitudes and norms. Following this, the theory of reasoned action becomes of the essence when it comes to suggesting the health behaviours of individuals based on their intention to perform the behaviour as well as key stakeholders including patients. An appropriately designed digital health solution is one that is considerate of the behaviours as well as the influences of these behaviours when it comes to both patients and health practitioners.

Even when it comes to aligning goals which is pivotal to ensuring that digital health solutions are appropriately designed and implemented, the application of the theory of reasoned action has proven to be crucial; more so when it comes to emerging technological solutions like mHealth (Lee & Meuter, 2010). According to research, there is a significant indication that the influence of service quality perception as well as attitude can also have an impact on continued intention to adopt digital solutions (Lee & Meuter, 2010). It should be inclusive of the completion on time of the projects, within the budget, and to each specification to "often includes". As mentioned earlier, consumers are part of and in fact are crucial stakeholders in any organisation, more so in the healthcare sector. The theory of reasoned action alongside the influence of service quality perception, and perceived vulnerability to continued intention to adapt digital solutions like mHealth, are thus all relevant to look into.

On the other hand, perceived vulnerability and subjective norm do not have a significant influence on continued intention to adopt. The stakeholders of digital health solutions can gain further from this information regarding appropriately designing and implementing these technologies. When impacts of attitudes can partially mediate service quality perception and continuous intention to adopt, studies have revealed that attitudes are not able to mediate continuous intention to adopt as well as perceived vulnerability (Lee & Meuter, 2010). Ultimately, service quality enhancement is bound to foster more frequent use of digital health solutions like mHealth application. Therefore, based on the theory of reasoned action, stakeholders are better able to design digital health solutions such that they can improve service quality and satisfy the needs of consumers based on the knowledge that the theory provides regarding human behaviour.

With regard to this, the theory of relationship equity can also assist in better highlighting the benefit of managing various stakeholders, aligning goals and ultimately ensuring fictive design of digital health solutions. The relationship equity theory encourages the idea that an individual who receives more benefits from a relationship often feels adverse feelings of shame and guilt. On the other hand, individuals who perceive themselves as putting a lot of effort into the relationship but receive way less benefits are bound to be angry and resentful. With this, relationship equity in this context is all about developing a firm relationship with patients while providing them with value in their health care service delivery (World Health Organization, 2020). It is a crucial theory to consider when building relationships between various stakeholder groups. Since patients are among the most valuable stakeholders in this context, relationship equity is fundamental as it helps foster digital health solutions that can enable superior care delivery capable of giving patients the best value. The best thing about this is that it enables the healthcare organisation to achieve this without compromising the benefits of healthcare professionals. Relationship equity fosters the designing of digital health solutions that are considerate of both the healthcare service provider and the patient, thus facilitating a win:win situation whereby the benefits minus the costs of one side equals the benefits minus the costs of another.

In today's rapidly evolving world of technology that has spread all the way to the healthcare universe, healthcare innovation is pivotal in ensuring that emerging healthcare solutions are as useful and well designed as possible. In addition to this, there is a firm bond between healthcare innovation and the relationship equity formula, making the relationship equity theory a crucial model in the process. There is a similarity between the relationship equity theory and how the business environment today operates. The relationship equity theory offers a formula to the way in which relationships can be grown, developed and nurtured to open new opportunities that would have otherwise been overlooked. When it comes to relationship equity, just a single relationship that one has nurtured can be sufficient to change the trajectory of the individual's life. Just as in business, the importance of relationship equity cannot be ignored. While relationships are indeed fundamental in how business is carried out, how one chooses to go on building these relations is something else entirely. More specifically, this is the case for individuals within the healthcare business whereby trust is a central issue. For example, the existence or lack of relationship equity can either build or break technology implementation projects, strategic partnerships and even minimise patient engagement in an organisation. When relationship equity is lacking, it can also disrupt the productivity of employees among other vital initiatives of the healthcare organisation.

From this alone, there is a significant indication that relationship equity is not necessarily merely concerning striking a sale. It extends to all the aspects of human interaction. For instance, when a health organisational leader attempts to employ a solution for clinicians without any relationship equity, nothing is bound to happen. In essence, the relationship equity formula is a set of easily applicable connection principles that break religion, ethnicity and race barriers. It is concerning human connections for the society's greater good. The simple formula of the relationship equity theory can be written as follows:

Connection × Authenticity = Trust

Trust × Time = Relationship

Relationship × Value = Equity

The formula can be explained by the simple statement that the stronger the relationship one builds alongside the value they gave in business, the more the "equity" they develop. The equity converts into real-world bottom line, impacting tangibles like business deals, partnerships and referrals. It is for this reason that the relationship equity theory is vital in effectively designing digital solutions in today's healthcare setting. As by the multiplication symbol illustrated in the formula, efforts compound over time with the relationship equity formula. The aspect of connection that it touches on also, to some extent, relates to the other models initially discussed earlier in the chapter like the stakeholder alignment. Connection is all abound getting to a common ground with others, which can be achieved through several ways like interests. When this connection is coupled with authenticity, one gets a foundation to build up from. Authenticity is all about honesty, keeping it real and never giving false promises. When honesty is lacking, such a situation is bound to have a negative influence on decision makers and their reputation, which can be detrimental in a case like designing digital health solutions.

When it comes to the current fast-paced adoption of healthcare innovation within the healthcare industry, relationship equity is crucial since it has a firm bond with healthcare innovation. New initiatives by leaders, workflow improvements, technology utilisation and how providers indulge with patients throughout the healthcare environment has much to do with this. According to research, as one continues to place more emphasis on relationship equity building and value addition, they get to enjoy their business relationships more. Rather than perceiving meetings as tasks, they begin to perceive them as opportunities for growth and exploration. Following this, the digital health solutions of an organisation will be effectively designed and implemented, patients are bound to be happier and more satisfied, patient engagement will be at a deeper level and the healthcare business of the organisation is bound to thrive more.

Notably, digital health solutions are created based on information and communication technology as well as point-of-care devices. The advancement of digital health solutions for the extant health care settings necessitates sufficient comprehension of the complexities of health care system, stakeholder groups, organisational setting and the underlying interplay between technology and stakeholders. Still, it is crucial to consider other models like technology affordance and structurisation since they can also be crucial in ultimately designing digital solutions via fostering goal alignment and better stakeholder groups management. Essentially, technology affordance refers to the technology potential that becomes evident from a behaviour that is goal-oriented before converting into well-defined actions. Technology affordances in themselves can only become extant in context and within practice. It implies that a particular technology may give varying potentialities when different scenarios are considered. The theoretical lens thus also assists in better understanding the potential of digital health solutions for healthcare organisations. In addition to this, technology affordance theory offers a comprehensive explanation to how digital health solutions like information-related technologies in healthcare are involved in fostering changes within the organisation. The information can in turn be utilised to develop digital health solutions that are viable and appropriately designed to foster positive organisational change.

Discussion and Conclusions

In a knowledge economy, the management of an organisation's human capital is critical and prudent management often translates into the attainment of a sustainable competitive advantage. The interaction of knowledge workers with digital technology solutions has presented a particularly interesting dynamic to researchers who study changes in related behavioural phenomena (Wickramasinghe and Lamb, 2009). One such phenomenon is self-monitoring (ibid.). Self-monitoring is made possible via the application of digital solutions (ibid.). In the context of healthcare, knowledge worker agents are clinicians as they have domain-specific knowledge and are contracted by patients to act on their behalf to provide them with the best possible healthcare plan (ibid.). However, as agency theory identifies, this can be problematic and lead to agency problems or sub-goal optimisation, given the likelihood of completing goals between healthcare stakeholders (ibid.). Hence, digital technology solutions offer the possibility of making transactions more transparent and facilitate self-monitoring which in turn serves to reduce the impacts of agency problems in healthcare operations (ibid.).

Summary

After reading this chapter you should be able to be able to state:

a) Why healthcare is unique with the predominant receiver of services typically being different from the predominant payer of these same services.
    Unlike other industries, in healthcare the patient who is the receiver of services is typically not the predominant payer for the services received, rather the payer is. This leads to a unique situation where the patient tends to focus on quality maximisation while the payer is focused on cost minimsation. As these two goals are orthogonal, friction and divergent perspectives and decision choices result.
b) Why there are nested agency issues that arise in healthcare operations.
    Nested agency issues arise in healthcare operations due to the divergence of goals and sub-goals between healthcare stakeholders including the orthogonality of cost and quality perspectives.
c) Who are knowledge worker agents in healthcare.
    Knowledge worker agents are individuals who have domain-specific knowledge but are contracted to provide a service or represent a principle who does not have this domain-specific knowledge. Thus, clinicians are considered knowledge worker agents in healthcare as they have healthcare-specific domain knowledge which they use to act on behalf of the principle; namely, the patient.

d) How digital health solutions can be used to mute power-knowledge dynamics. By enabling and supporting self-monitoring activities and more transparency around transactions, digital health solutions can mute power-knowledge dynamics.

References

Andersen, T. O., Bansler, J. P., Kensing, F., Moll, J., Mønsted, T., Nielsen, K. D., ... & Svendsen, J. H. (2019). Aligning concerns in telecare: three concepts to guide the design of patient-centred E-health. *Computer Supported Cooperative Work (CSCW)*, *28*(6), 1039–1072.

Baker, A., Cornwell, P., Gustafsson, L., Stewart, C., & Lannin, N. A. (2022). Developing tailored theoretically informed goal-setting interventions for rehabilitation services: a co-design approach. *BMC Health Services Research*, *22*(1), 1–21.

Braganza, M. Z., Pearson, E., Avila, C. J., Zlowe, D., Øvretveit, J., & Kilbourne, A. M. (2022, June). Aligning quality improvement efforts and policy goals in a national integrated health system. *Health Services Research*, *57* (Suppl 1), 9–19. doi: 10.1111/ 1475-6773.13944. Epub 2022 Mar 4. PMID: 35243629; PMCID: PMC9108213.

Dopp, A. R., Parisi, K. E., Munson, S. A., & Lyon, A. R. (2020). Aligning implementation and user-centered design strategies to enhance the impact of health services: results from a concept mapping study. *Implementation Science Communications*, *1*(1), 1–13.

Gray, C. S., Gravesande, J., Hans, P. K., Nie, J. X., Sharpe, S., Loganathan, M., ... & Cott, C. (2019). Using exploratory trials to identify relevant contexts and mechanisms in complex electronic health interventions: evaluating the electronic patient-reported outcome tool. *JMIR Formative Research*, *3*(1), e11950.

Hale, J. L., Householder, B. J., & Greene, K. L. (2002). The theory of reasoned action. *Persuasion Handbook: Developments in Theory and Practice*, *14*(2002), 259–286.

Iyawa, G. E., Herselman, M., & Botha, A. (2016). Digital health innovation ecosystems: From systematic literature review to conceptual framework. *Procedia Computer Science*, *100*, 244–252.

Kayser, L., Furstrand, D., Nyman Rasmussen, E., Monberg, A. C., & Karnoe, A. (2022, September). GoTO: A process-navigation tool for telehealth and-care solutions, designed to ensure an efficient trajectory from goal setting to outcome evaluation. *Informatics*, *9*(3), 69, MDPI.

LaMonica, H. M., Davenport, T. A., Braunstein, K., Ottavio, A., Piper, S., Martin, C., ... & Cross, S. (2019). Technology-enabled person-centered mental health services reform: strategy for implementation science. *JMIR Mental Health*, *6*(9), e14719.

Lee, A., Sandvei, M., Asmussen, H. C., Skougaard, M., Macdonald, J., Zavada, J., ... & Gudbergsen, H. (2018). The development of complex digital health solutions: formative evaluation combining different methodologies. *JMIR Research Protocols*, *7*(7), e9521.

Lee, O. F., & Meuter, M. L. (2010). The adoption of technology orientation in healthcare delivery: Case study of a large-scale hospital and healthcare system's electronic health record. *International Journal of Pharmaceutical and Healthcare Marketing*, *4*(4), 355–374.

Lyon, A. R., Dopp, A. R., Brewer, S. K., Kientz, J. A., & Munson, S. A. (2020). Designing the future of children's mental health services. *Administration and Policy in Mental Health and Mental Health Services Research*, *47*(5), 735–751.

Payne, G. T., & Petrenko, O. V. (2019). Agency theory in business and management research. In *Oxford research encyclopedia of business and management*.

Pereira, R., da Silva, M. M., & Lapão, L. V. (2014). Business/IT alignment through IT governance patterns in Portuguese healthcare. *International Journal of IT/Business Alignment and Governance (IJITBAG)*, 5(1), 1–15.

Portz, J. D., Ford, K. L., Doyon, K., Bekelman, D. B., Boxer, R. S., Kutner, J. S., ... & Bull, S. (2020). Using grounded theory to inform the human-centered design of digital health in geriatric palliative care. *Journal of Pain and Symptom Management*, 60(6), 1181–1192.

Quesada-López, C., Jensen, M. L., Zuñiga, G., Chinnock, A., & Jenkins, M. (2016, November). Design, development and validation of a mobile application for goal setting and self-monitoring of dietary behaviors. In *2016 IEEE 36th Central American and Panama Convention (CONCAPAN XXXVI)* (pp. 1–6). IEEE.

Rouse, J. (1994). Power/knowledge. *Cambridge Companion to Foucault, 2*.

Scobbie, L., Duncan, E. A., Brady, M. C., Thomson, K., & Wyke, S. (2020). Facilitators and "deal breakers": a mixed methods study investigating implementation of the Goal setting and action planning (G-AP) framework in community rehabilitation teams. *BMC Health Services Research*, 20(1), 1–14.

Singh, H., Armas, A., Law, S., Tang, T., Gray, C. S., Cunningham, H. V., ... & Nelson, M. L. (2021). How digital health solutions align with the roles and functions that support hospital to home transitions for older adults: a rapid review study protocol. *BMJ Open*, 11(2), e045596.

Wickramasinghe, N. & Lamb, R. (2009). Foucault's corollary: agency theory and the economics of self-monitoring. *International Journal of Networking and Virtual Organisations*, 6(3), 225–258.

World Health Organization. (2020). *Digital Implementation Investment Guide (DIIG): integrating digital interventions into health programmes*.

12 Social Determinants of Health and Digital Health Literacy

Objectives

After reading this chapter you should know:

a) What is the difference between digital literacy, health literacy and digital health literacy.
b) What are the social determinants of health.
c) How and why can smart digital health solutions reduce health disparities.

Introduction

Healthcare touches and is needed by all people; affluent, poor, educated and uneducated, disabled, older, CALD (culturally and linguistically diverse) communities and native or First Nation peoples. Given this heterogeneity, it is unsurprising that we have a large spectrum of knowledge and understanding around health, care, digital and digital healthcare. This makes the topic of digital health literacy of vital importance to understand and address. Related to digital health literacy is the topic of social determinants of health. Both these topics are unpacked and examined in this chapter as they are very central to people's considerations in healthcare delivery.

Social Determinants of Digital Health Literacy

Today, the digital media stretches out to virtually every aspect of humankind's daily life. Individuals nowadays spend a lot of time in their day on average just interacting with digital media. Indeed, this social aspect has a significant level of relevance when it comes to health-associated purposes; nonetheless, the fact that it can at the same time have detrimental effects with regard to the spread of false information which can in turn have a negative impact on patient as well as public health must not be overlooked (Jercich, 2021). Digital literacy, health literacy and digital health literacy are all fundamental when it comes to curbing these detrimental aspects to enable the utilisation of the full potential of digital health technologies in line with digital media with the aim of promoting health and patient

DOI: 10.1201/9781003318538-15

wellbeing. Essentially, digital literacy refers to the capability of utilising information as well as communication technologies to locate, assess, formulate and communicate information. With this regard, digital literacy often necessitates both technical and cognitive skills (Nutbeam & Lloyd, 2021). On the other hand, health literacy is defined as their ability to gather, read, comprehend and utilise healthcare data to draw more accurate, proper and more informed health decisions (Jercich, 2021). Over the recent years, health literacy is growing more into a fundamental skill for information that is health-related on the internet (Nutbeam & Lloyd, 2021). When it comes to digital health literacy, it can be outwardly described as the confluence of health literacy and digital literacy (Nutbeam & Lloyd, 2021). There are social determinants of digital health literacy that serve as all the elements that have a significant impact on both health and digital literacy (Jercich, 2021). As outlined by van Kessel et al. (2022), these factors include sex, age, health status, socioeconomic status like education, employment as well as income, and residing within urban versus rural settings.

In the conceptualisation of health as well as digital health literacy, the conceptualisation is typically via competency-based frameworks. The commonly utilised method for expressing health literacy is a four-dimension matrix that entails, gathers relevant information to health, comprehends the information of relevance to health, evaluates the information that is of relevance to health and utilises the information that is of relevance to health. These are applied across the three domains of healthcare, health promotion and disease prevention (Sørensen et al., 2012). Interestingly, during the coronavirus pandemic, this was even described as a "social vaccine" since it allowed people and their communities to positively curb the spread of the COVID-19 virus via obtaining and utilising digital information concerning the virus (Okan et al., 2022). The framework epitomises how complex as well as multidimensional health in association with digital literacy is; thus, it highlights the necessity of conceptualising digital health literacy within the competence framework context.

There are four competence levels of digital health literacy as outlined by the Transactional Model of eHealth Literacy (van Kessel et al., 2022). The first of the four competence levels are the functional competence level, which refers to the ability to effectively read and put down information on health utilising technological devices. The second is the communicative level, which refers to the capability of regulating, adapting and coordinating communication regarding health with other individuals/users within an online social setting. Third is the critical level that entails the ability to assess the significance, trustworthiness and risks involved in disseminating and getting information related to health via the internet among other digital ecosystems. And last, the translational level which refers to the ability to apply information related to health from the internet/digital ecosystems within varying contexts.

Notably, albeit digital and health literacy are associated with digital health literacy, it a rather convoluted and complicated factual concept. In essence, the association between health, digital and digital health literacy is rather multidimensional. It is a relationship whereby each digital and health literacy competency domain is bound to have a significant influence on a competence domain of digital health literacy (Paige et al., 2018). Still, certain digital health competency domains might fail to be catered for by both health literacy as well as digital literacy (Kickbusch et al., 2021). The information this chapter presents to this point is of the essence in developing a broader perception and understanding of the social determinants of digital health literacy.

When it comes to the social aspect, civic literacy refers to the knowledge and expertise of participating within the society of an individual as well as their community. Recently, it has been considered as a key digital social determinant of health (Kickbusch et al., 2021). Indeed, the services offered in digital health range from relying on the amount of input that consumers, patients or citizens need. A good instance that exemplifies this point is the case of tracking devices and wearables. Typically, these devices need negligible to no input. On the other hand, gaining access to virtual healthcare or telehealth often necessitates significantly more input. Following this, the initial points of entry to digital health, that is inclusive of devices such as wearables and tracking instruments as well as electronic health records, did not necessitate the conscious input of citizens. However, with the heightening development of digital health services and increasingly tight competition with traditional health services (van Kessel et al., 2022), the essential skills for a citizen to completely enjoy the merits of digital health services become increasingly more convoluted as well.

In the operationalising of digital health literacy, the way it is perceived within various cultural settings is yet another crucial component for consideration. As stated by the Health Foundation and framework institute report of 2019, there is a significant indication that these differences within cultural interpretations are extant (Elwell-Sutton et al., 2019). According to the research, the behaviours of individuals as well as their choices and accessibility to affordable health care is the dominant factor within the public perception of the components that influence the health of an individual. In addition to this, the study revealed that about 24% of the population of the United Kingdom hold that health is wholly the individual's responsibility (van Kessel et al., 2022). Following this, eight cultural models of how health can be conceptualised is highlighted by the researchers in the study. These can be categorised into two archetypes, namely, an ecological approach and an individualistic approach. Ultimately, the study concludes that it is typical of the general population to undertake an approach that is more individualistic. Contrastingly, the study concluded that health professionals were prone to adopt a more ecological approach to help, more so when it comes to health professionals working on the social determinants of health. Thus, it is not an oversell to make the assumption that when it comes to efforts towards educating the public on the social determinants that influence health, that is inclusive of secondary and primary education, the crucial aspect is the perception of health and those responsible for seeing to it that it changes.

A while back at the launch of The *Lancet* and Financial Times Commission on Governing Health Futures 2030, Marelize Gorgens, who has grown up within a digital world, stated emphatically at the 2021 World Health Summit that there is a need for developing a vaster demand for digital health services. Her premise was that these are not second-tier healthcare forms; rather, they are first-tier forms of healthcare that are of a diverse and digital nature (World Health Summit, 2021). Notably, the pursuing of analogue health services is also embedded within the general public's habits. Albeit digital services are typically not given much regard, often because of limited awareness as well as lack of trust, that may be both enhanced via amelioration of digital health literacy (Kickbusch et al., 2021). Following this, there is a heightening need to gain a deeper comprehension of the way civic, digital and digital health literacy can interact within the broader circumstances of the social determinants of health and/or digital health literacy.

On assessing health independently, digital health literacy has recently been given recognition as a "super social determinant of health", as it has significant implications for the broader social determinants of health (Sieck et al., 2021). It goes hand in hand with internet connectivity as well. Nonetheless, it is crucial that an individual possesses the necessary digital, civic and health literacies to make relevant and useful participation within the digital era and attain optimal health and wellbeing (Honeyman et al., 2020; Kickbusch et al., 2021). Following this, it is quite the necessity to have a framework that clarifies the precise factors that make up components of digital health literacy in association with its structural building blocks as well as how such building blocks are all interconnected within the digital era (Wong et al., 2022). Digital transformations hold the significant potential for being beneficial to both the public and the population's health. Further, there is also a significant possibility that they can exacerbate the extant inequalities (Van Kessel et al., 2022). Thus, the conceptualisation and development of digital health literacy is not just a necessity at the professional level, but at the public level as well. The professional level is hereby inclusive of individuals capable of building, utilising, recommending, as well as prescribing the utilisation of digital health services, while the public level entails the individuals that will comprise the user-base of digital health services.

Evidently, social determinants (inclusive of cultural determinants) can have a broad and significant impact on the development and building up of health and digital health literacy. Therefore, a clear model for these determinants of digital health literacy can go a long way in framing digital health literacies as a series of core competencies. In addition to this, it can also contextualise it in the midst of digital literacy, health literacy, civic literacy, as well as social and cultural determinants.

The fact that technology can only be a tool for improving health if one is able to utilise it cannot be overlooked. It is bound to be more difficult for individuals to utilise technology for health purposes when their digital literacy is low. Contrastingly, when health services on the internet as well as health information is easily accessible and usable, it becomes beneficial to almost everyone. In essence, every time an individual utilises technology to search for, develop and share information, they are making use of digital literacy. As stated earlier, digital literacy in healthcare is considered a super social determinant of health (SDOH) since it has a significant influence on several other sectors that are related to health outcomes. These are inclusive of the access to jobs, community support, good schools, neighbourhoods that are safe and ultimately healthcare services. Hence, the enhancement of social determinants of health consequentially acts as the route causal factor of adverse and good health. For instance, digital literacy can assist an individual in applying for jobs on the internet. Similarly, it can also assist in finding safe places for individuals within their neighbourhood.

Some of the fundamental ways through which an individual can utilise digital health literacy in the daily lives as far as health is concerned include, i) making comparisons between options as well as making enrollments into health insurance plans within government platform on the Internet, ii) composing and sending private messages to the health care providers on a patient portal on the Internet or even a personal health care platform and iii) making tests on audios and videos for a patient's therapy set to be conducted online. It is also useful in making use of wearables such as fitness trackers to make accurate step counts as well as other aspects like heartbeat rate throughout the user's day. And finally, internet searches regarding healthy recipes that one can make for their families, for instance, when they have individuals with certain conditions like diabetes.

Not every individual has the same opportunities when it comes to gaining digital health literacy. There are barriers that prevent this from happening, many of which people have little to no direct control over. These barriers can significantly have an adverse effect on the ability of individuals to utilise digital technologies in healthcare which are necessary for allowing them more superior care for their health. A good instance is that of the coronavirus pandemic, whereby studies revealed that about four out of every ten individuals within the older adult populations were not prepared to handle telehealth sessions (Jercich, 2021).

Further, it is bound to be quite difficult for individuals to utilise technology for health-related purposes when they are faced by certain circumstances. These circumstances include when the individuals have generally low health literacy, when: i) the individuals have generally low health literacy, ii) the individuals have no access to or experience in utilising technological devices they are often used as digital health technology is nowadays such as computers and smartphones, iii) the individuals have no way of accessing high speed Internet, iv) the individuals have disabilities like visual impairment and hearing impairments, v) the individuals lack the necessary human aid within the homesteads to assist them in utilizing technology, and vi) the individuals lack access to health technology applications as well as Internet platforms that are in there preferred languages that they easily understand.

There is also a digital divide whereby individuals who have the necessary skills as well as access to digital health technologies have the upper hand over those who do not. It is through this gap that the extant inequalities within the health care universe can worsen. Further to this, suppose online health information as well as services become available and easily usable by all, there would be nobody left behind.

Vulnerable Groups Because of Digital Health Illiteracy

The adverse aspects of digital health illiteracy become evident when looking at the vulnerable groups as a result of it. In essence, the fast-paced introduction of digital health technologies and digitalisation of health care services has led to a significant risk when it comes to heightening digital inequality, which consequentially paved the way to considerable demerits like social isolation and the escalating risk of health deterioration. Notably, digital health technologies and services have escalated both in variety and quantity to a significant extent over the recent decade even before the COVID-19 pandemic. Still, the COVID-19 pandemic had a significant role in revolutionising and catalysing the use of digital health technologies in delivering superior health services. Albeit the sole purpose of digital health solutions and services is to facilitate the availability as well as the continuity of these services, more so during crisis situations such as the COVID-19 pandemic, not every individual may have an equal opportunity to gain from the merits of digitalisation as evidenced by the COVID-19 crisis. It is a factor that stems from the lack of digital health literacy in some individuals with the population.

During such a scenario, suppose the necessary digital health services cannot be accessed remotely by certain individuals within the population, especially when they are among individuals in vulnerable positions like poverty, the lack of digital health literacy may be a causal factor to these groups, being more susceptible to contracting diseases or having their already bad health condition worsen (Kaihlanen et al., 2022; Xie et al., 2020). There have been emerging concerns regarding whether these groups, more so those who in addition to the lack of digital literacy may be lacking the equal access, capabilities, as well as resources for utilising digital services, receive the health services they require in these times and during crisis situations like the COVID-19 pandemic (Kaihlanen et al., 2022).

The attainment of digital health equity is quite a challenging factor in the contemporary world given that it would necessitate overcoming the lack of digital health literacy and accessibility of digital health technologies to all. It would also entail fostering the appropriate utilisation of digital technologies without leaving any individual behind. By definition, digital health equity, which is the crucial condition for solving the problem of vulnerable groups because of the lack of digital health literacy, is the equal opportunity for everyone to gain from the knowledge as well as practices regarding the development and utilisation of digital technologies for bettering health (Kaihlanen et al., 2022). At the most outward level, the inequity in society is mirrored by digital health inequity; therefore, individuals at risk of social exclusion, like people at a more disadvantageous position because of unemployment, a fragile economic situation, and low levels of education, are at a more significant risk of exclusion from digital health services as (Crawford & Serhal, 2020).

There is a significant indication that the realisation of the social and digital determinants of health are intimately associated with the realisation of digital health equity (World Health Organization, 2021). Consequentially, it mirrors both the socio-cultural and socioeconomic contexts of people as well as the intermediate health components (Crawford & Serhal, 2020). Before discussing vulnerable groups as users of digital health services further, it is crucial to also gain deeper insights into digital health equity and its frameworks.

Crawford and Serhal (2020) developed the Digital Health Equity Framework (DHEF) which describes the digital determinants of health as first and foremost social and/or digital health literacy, the access to digital resources by individuals, the utilisation of such resources to seek health, the beliefs concerning the possible usefulness or harmfulness of digital resources and incorporation of digital resources towards health and community infrastructure. For the purposes of heightening the probability of attaining digital health equity, it is necessary that one identifies and tackles the possible gaps within these social and/or digital determinants, more precisely of individuals that are at higher risk of becoming exempted from digital services.

The extant literature goes further to exemplify the necessity for public services to tackle vulnerable group needs, more precisely regarding the needs of individuals who are disadvantaged by economic, social or cultural conditions, and health (Mulvale et al., 2019). The most vital vulnerable groups to consider are inclusive of the elderly in society, mental health service users, migrants, the unemployed and high health service users. With regard to this, older adults are the most significant individual group that faces the challenges when it comes to utilising digital health services (Kouvonen et al., 2021). When it comes to the use of technology, studies have revealed that inexperience, financial difficulties, poor motivation and insufficient technological skills are among the significant factors that prevent the elderly from reaping the benefits of digital health technological solutions as well. Further, cognitive deterioration, poor health, lack of internet access as well as appropriate devices and insufficient support and guidance are all contributing factors that hinder the elderly from effectively utilising digital health solutions for their benefit (Kampmeijer et al., 2016).

When it comes to migrants, there are often different reasons that led them to a particular country, which could influence the challenges they may face regarding the digital health services within the country they migrate to. These could range from family relate reasons, reasons related to work and even war, conflict and famine that may lead to refugee status with the new country. Disparities have significantly been highlighted in digital health and the access of migrants to digital health services within various societal contexts (Mesch, 2016). For instance, the existing research has revealed that ethnic minorities and migrants look for health information significantly less in comparison with the general population (Nguyen et al., 2021; Din et al., 2019). Migrants have been significantly linked to a lesser comprehension of internet-based health information (Yoon, Huang & Kim, 2017).

Third among the most vulnerable populations are high health services users. Many of these users have a chronic illness or even an impairment that forces them to be heavily reliant on health services for their health and wellbeing. Therefore, they typically undergo several check-ups and regular care routines as a result. As evidence by research, poorer health is significantly linked with lower interest levels when looking at digital health (Kaihlanen et al., 2022). It may also have a significant influence on these groups' perceived benefits of the use of digital health solutions in less positive way. Thus, these groups can also be considered as vulnerable groups following their lack of digital health literacy since their poorer health condition places them at a higher risk of digital exclusion (Heponiemi et al., 2020).

In addition, individuals within this vulnerable groups have much more severe mental disorders and are also more prone to experiencing cognitive impairments that serve as a further hinderance in the effective utilisation of digital services. Such a disability can thus significantly foster the digital exclusion of individuals within these groups coupled with the lack of financial resources and the requisite digital skills (Kaihlanen et al., 2022).

Finally, yet another vulnerable group are the unemployed. Unemployed individuals are significantly at risk of digital exclusion when it comes to per-petuating digital health technological solutions. According to Helsper and Reisdorf (2017), unemployed groups are among those most likely to be non-internet users. The research also highlighted some of the possible contributing factors to this discovery: lack of skills, lack of access to the necessary techno-logical resources and lack of access to financial resources. In addition to this, motivational reasons were also highlighted among the contributing factors. The researchers noted that the unemployed often show a lower level of interest when it comes to the internet and its use for various solutions. In a later study, the researchers uncovered that unemployed individuals have a tendency to lack the requisite skills necessary for the effective use of digital health services. Following this, they are less prone to utilise digital services in comparison to other groups (Kaihlanen et al., 2022).

All these vulnerable groups mentioned and discussed above face a myriad of challenges when it comes to the effective utilisation of digital health services. These challenges largely are largely grounded on the lack of digital literacy that is the most significant factor that results in the individuals within these groups becoming susceptible to begin with. Obtaining and discussing information regarding the experiences of these vulnerable groups to better understand them is of the essence since their perspectives are often overlooked rather than sufficiently addressed; this was evidenced in the COVID-19 crisis situation (Kaihlanen et al., 2022). It is also important to note that the health effects of a crisis such as the COVID-19 pandemic often proceeds as an aftermath even after the crisis. With this, it is cru-cial to obtain as much insight as possible from such a situation to better understand how vulnerable groups were affected. The factors that contributed to their vulner-ability during such a situation and their experience to be in a better position to offer succour to the challenges that they encounter in relation to the utilisation of digital health solutions for the long-term benefit. Furthermore, it is highly probable that the provision of digital services will escalate in future, either coupled with or in place of the classic face-to-face healthcare services. Albeit it is not necessarily fac-tual that those at risk of digital exclusion are a homogeneous group; a qualitative study involving interviews such as the one presented by Kaihlanen et al. (2022) can be useful in exploring these experiences of various vulnerable groups to this end. Actively involving the individuals within these groups is crucial in gaining vital insights into how lack of digital health literacy influences their susceptibility with the aim of advancing the future digital services.

As explained by Kaihlanen et al. (2022), there is a significant indication that the most significant challenges when it comes to access to digital health services significantly stem from the access of people to digital resources. Although the study explains that there are other social and/or digital determinants in addition to this, it highlighted this as the most significant. In essence, there are many reasons that may pave the way to digital exclusion. These include the perception that the use of digital services necessitates a lot of input and resources, the lack of sufficient digital skills as well as local language skills.

In addition to this, vulnerable populations often have health care needs that are rather complex that digital health solutions may not be fully equipped to tackle yet. These needs often necessitate intimate interactions and/or elaborate clarification which digital health services may not be currently responsive to. Looking into the future, it would be prudent to make investments in the information regarding digital health services via different channels. The opportunities as well as potential gains of such digital health solutions are yet to be dispersed broadly enough to get to every individual. Further, it is crucial to keep in mind that the classic face-to-face health services are bound to continue in their importance and should thus continue to be encouraged and given in the company of digital health services. There will always be individuals incapable of effectively utilising digital health services, like the elderly with cognitive decline and/or other forms of disabilities such as sensory impairments and illiteracy.

Strategies to Address Digital Health Illiteracy

The improvement of digital health literacy to effectively do away with digital health illiteracy is not an easy endeavour; it necessitates the formulation of appropriate and effective digital health strategies. Even so, simply put, it largely entails creating and fostering educational opportunities with regard to digital health literacy while addressing barriers to healthcare. It is crucial that the accessibility to medical health information on the internet is optimised for every individual (Lee et al., 2014). Different guidelines should be put in place for web designers and checklists reinforced for web providers to make sure that the quality of health information relayed on the internet is up to scale (Busse et al., 2022). Such a strategy could be of enormous benefit when it comes to assisting users to effectively assess health information (Diviani et al., 2015). It is capable of effectively hindering patients from making the appropriate decisions they need to arrive at, such that it is bound to provide them with more accurate, meaningful and reliably correct information from which they can make their decisions (Busse et al., 2022). Additionally, it is vital that the information availed is not derived and availed such that it is overtly convoluted and rather complex to comprehend (Jordan, & Toeppich, 2015). Aside from considering these guidelines, the effective evaluation of information by patients can go a long way in effecting meaningful adjustments.

The strategies for fostering digital health literacy are not quite limited. There is even an approach which is largely grounded on the experience level as well as age of target groups. When it comes to the enhancement of self-efficacy, this can be brought forth in a systematic review as critical for the betterment of digital health literacy for individuals aged 60 years and above. Workshops, didactive program sessions, peer tutoring, as well as collaborative learning can all be helpful in achieving this through imparting useful information and enhancing self-efficacy (Busse et al., 2022).

When it comes to the improvement of educational opportunities to better digital health literacy, different digital technological offerings are extant as at now when it comes to the informal learning sector. These can be exploited to achieve this, ranging from unsystematic offerings within social media platforms like Facebook and Instagram, to structured educational videos in accordance with subject matter professional like on YouTube. Comprehensive eLearning offerings can also be utilised such as Massive Open Online Courses (Busse et al., 2022). In addition to this, there are also formal learning opportunities for patients like the European Patients' Academy on Therapeutic Innovation (Busse et al., 2022) and even patient academies that give education on diseases as well as therapies. These so-called patient academies are also known for offering support for participatory communication amidst patients and health professionals. Nonetheless, for digital health literacy to be effective in the long run and successfully better society, there are some evident challenges that must be considered and tackled appropriately in developing strategies to foster digital health literacy.

The first challenge in developing these strategies for improving digital literacy which is affecting the platform on which the skills that ought to be taught. It is a challenge since considering the extant change in the industrial society towards the information society (Busse et al., 2022), it comes off as more practical that such learning opportunities occur in a technological advanced learning form. However, the extant digital divide as mentioned earlier in this article has posed an adamantly persistent challenge when it comes to this. It is quite unfortunate that this is the case since the differences in access to and utilisation of these digital health technologies is a significant vice driving inequalities in the contemporary era. In essence, many of the elderly and individuals who have lower levels of education and those who belong to the lower social classes have much more limited access to as well as comprehension of digital media (Busse et al., 2022). These are the same individuals who face low health literacy and thus are much more in need of effective educational opportunities with regard to this (Sørensen et al., 2015). In accordance with the situation, it is thus a necessity that education is promptly and appropriately developed, more so in an approach such that they are not quite reliant on digital applications.

In addition to this, it is also important that the stakeholders appropriately determine the fundamental competencies that are required to escalate the digitisation of healthcare. It is a concept that is nonetheless highly susceptible to change. Additionally, both digital health literacy and digital skills must be strategically and systematically taught in accordance to the current EU Digital Competence Framework 2.0 (Busse et al., 2022). Last, another challenge that must be considered is the difference in the prerequisite digital health literacy education that an individual may have prior to the new framework. Thus, it is a necessity that educational concepts are formulated such that they are flexible and capable of easily embracing modifications for the various digital health literacy levels whenever necessary. The different factors that impact digital health literacy must also be taken into account while developing these strategies.

How Digital Health Can Ameliorate Key Disparities

Digital health can ameliorate key disparities when the approaches towards them are formulated such that their sole focus is on health equity. In addition to this, the technology used in digital health can also significantly minimise disparities by assisting individuals to make better choices. A good example to offer more clarity on this point is the case of digital healthcare applications. These apps are able to assist patients in remembering to take their prescribed pills on time, schedule communication sessions with their physicians, refill their medications and even schedule appointments and arrive to them on time. Following this, they have a better chance of minimising key disparities in this way as they assist patients in making the right choices.

When it comes to digital health equity, digital health can ameliorate key disparities by actively committing to minimising these health disparities and enhancing patients' experience in health care. Suppose digital health technologies are developed such that they place much emphasis on these aspects, they are more likely to enhance access to health care, better the experiences of patients and improve the use of digital health, therefore significantly ameliorating these key disparities.

Although the concept of digital health equity is still quite new in the field, it is essentially the recognition that digital health technology has the possibility of both ameliorating as well as exacerbating health disparities. The World Health Organization (WHO) clearly laid out that in their global strategy towards digital health for the year 2020 to 2025, "digital health should be a pivotal part of health priorities and provide merits to individuals such that it is safe, ethical, reliable, secure, equitable, as well as sustainable" (World Health Organization, 2021). It is inclusive of being emphatic on fundamental principles like accessibility, transparency, privacy, scalability, security and confidentiality; all of which are factors that are capable of significantly contributing to the equitable structuring, development, utilisation and effect of digital health tools. Simultaneously, there is an escalating acknowledgement that industries offering support to digital health innovation like bio and mad technology startups, Silicon Valley, and big pharma, mask themselves to become more equitable, diverse and inclusive for their products to become both valid and effective as far as tools of minimising disparities are concerned. With this, digital health technologies must seek to enhance health outcomes in the most equitable way possible, minimise and mitigate the overall digital iniquity and themselves become more equitably structured, developed and enacted.

Achieving this goal is not impossible. It can be attained by drawing precise targets towards areas for equity considerations within the digital health technology ecosystem. These areas include the digital health instrument itself, which is inclusive of its design, technological development, implementation into the health care setting and appraisal. Finally, the effects of the digital health solution on the target health as well as health determinant outcomes are also critical target areas for equity considerations. Interestingly, at every one of these points there lies opportunities for challenges towards fostering equity. These opportunities and challenges can either be targeted selectively for intervention or integrated towards the larger strategies for promoting equity or mitigating inequity.

Importantly, one of the most crucial ways through which digital health can ameliorate the disparities is by addressing inequities, which can only be achieved through the building and development of equitable digital health devices. Agile software development and human-centred designs are both complementary strategies that can be of great use towards achieving this (Lawrence, 2022). They can be of great benefit towards seeing to it that digital health tools have a product design and technical development that is aimed towards making them as equitable as possible.

From the moment that digital health devices are developed and implemented into the active health care system setting, an opportunity for critically assessing and addressing any effects that the digital health tool may have on health inequity arises. It is applicable to every digital health technology and not just merely those designed to tackle health disparities. Nonetheless, in the current reality of things, there is a critical deficiency in their systematic long-term assessment of the effects of digital health technologies on health disparities. It is more prudent to foster these systematic evaluations since that they offer the basis through which digital health can ameliorate key disparities host of their valuation and validation. Further, it is important to address the mental impact that a digital technology may have on health disparities it's crucial to ensuring that they are capable of effectively ameliorating key disparities.

Even so, health disparity measurements as well as those of health equity are bound to consistently continue in their evolution as people gain a deeper understanding regarding the context and as their complexities continue to better. Basically, the most typical health disparity measurements place much emphasis on the "avoidable" differences with health outcomes through certain demographic factors like income and race (Lawrence, 2022). With this, any digital interventions in digital health that are capable of effectively minimising these differences regarding the outcomes are recognised as being successful in significantly tackling health disparities and thus encouraging health equity. It is true that digital health in the contemporary era can significantly ameliorate key disparities within the sector.

Conclusion

In conclusion, digital health is indeed a growing yet quite prospective sector of healthcare service delivery. It is increasingly having significant effects on the health care experiences of service providers and patients alike as well as other individuals throughout the industry. Nonetheless, while digital health technologies present an opportunity for significantly enhancing care for people in society and in turn improving their health and wellbeing, it is simultaneously presenting an advanced side of creating and even fostering health disparities, more so for already socially disadvantaged and susceptible groups. The remedy to this vice is focusing on strategies to digital health that place much emphasis on health equity. Health equity is hereby the active commitment towards minimising these health disparities while optimising their healthcare experience for individuals, more so those within marginalised, diverse and underrepresented patient populations.

Summary

After reading this chapter you should be able to state:

a) What is the difference between digital literacy, health literacy and digital health literacy.
   Literacy is related to the ability to read and understand; thus, digital literacy relates to the level of comfort someone has with respect to using digital solutions. In contrast, health literacy is connected with the level of comfort and understanding an individual has around their healthcare issues as well as the management of these issues. Finally, digital health literacy relates to how an individual can interact with healthcare management using digital health solutions and their level of comfort in this regard. Such an example would be using telehealth – patients with low levels of digital health literacy often find using telehealth confronting and challenging due to low levels of digital health literacy.
b) What are the social determinants of health.
   The social determinants of health include social factors, behavioural factors and healthcare system factors. Education, food /nutrition, socioeconomic standing, community/social interactions and family/neigbourhood play important roles with respect to the social determinants of health.
c) How and why can smart digital health solutions reduce health disparities.
   Smart digital health solutions can assist in reducing disparities at multiple levels including addressing each of the key factors making up the social determinants of health as well as addressing important aspects around health literacy and digital literacy. Some examples include via providing accurate and tailored curated information around a healthcare issue at a comprehensible level to suit the individual or providing support to address issues such as loneliness.

References

Busse, T. S., Nitsche, J., Kernebeck, S., Jux, C., Weitz, J., Ehlers, J. P., & Bork, U. (2022). Approaches to improvement of Digital Health Literacy (eHL) in the context of person-centered care. *International Journal of Environmental Research and Public Health*, *19*(14), 8309.

Crawford, A., & Serhal, E. (2020). Digital health equity and COVID-19: the innovation curve cannot reinforce the social gradient of health. *Journal of Medical Internet Research*, *22*(6), e19361.

Din, H. N., McDaniels-Davidson, C., Nodora, J., & Madanat, H. (2019). Profiles of a health information–seeking population and the current digital divide: Cross-sectional analysis of the 2015–2016 California health interview survey. *Journal of Medical Internet Research*, *21*(5), e11931.

Diviani, N., van den Putte, B., Giani, S., & van Weert, J. C. (2015). Low health literacy and evaluation of online health information: a systematic review of the literature. *Journal of Medical Internet Research*, *17*(5), e4018.

Elwell-Sutton, T., Marshall, L., Bibby, J., & Volmert, A. (2019). *Reframing the conversation on social determinants*. Health Foundation/Framework Institute.

Helsper, E. J., & Reisdorf, B. C. (2017). The emergence of a "digital underclass" in Great Britain and Sweden: Changing reasons for digital exclusion. *New Media & Society*, *19*(8), 1253–1270.

Heponiemi, T., Jormanainen, V., Leemann, L., Manderbacka, K., Aalto, A. M., & Hyppönen, H. (2020). Digital divide in perceived benefits of online health care and social welfare services: national cross-sectional survey study. *Journal of Medical Internet Research*, *22*(7), e17616.

Honeyman, M., Maguire, D., Evans, H., & Davies, A. (2020). *Digital technology and health inequalities: a scoping review [Internet]*, (p. 44). Public Health Wales NHS Trust.

Jercich, K. (2021). Digital health literacy as a social determinant of health. *Healthcare IT News*, February.

Jordan, S., & Toeppich, J. (2015). The support of health competence (Health Literacy)-an overall society task. *Bundesgesundheitsblatt-Gesundheitsforschung-Gesundheitsschutz*, *58*(9), 921–922.

Kaihlanen, A. M., Virtanen, L., Buchert, U., Safarov, N., Valkonen, P., Hietapakka, L., ... & Heponiemi, T. (2022). Towards digital health equity-a qualitative study of the challenges experienced by vulnerable groups in using digital health services in the COVID-19 era. *BMC Health Services Research*, *22*(1), 1–12.

Kampmeijer, R., Pavlova, M., Tambor, M., Golinowska, S., & Groot, W. (2016). The use of e-health and m-health tools in health promotion and primary prevention among older adults: a systematic literature review. *BMC Health Services Research*, *16*(5), 467–479.

Kickbusch, I., Piselli, D., Agrawal, A., Balicer, R., Banner, O., Adelhardt, M., ... & Wong, B. L. H. (2021). The Lancet and Financial Times Commission on governing health futures 2030: growing up in a digital world. *Lancet*, *398*(10312), 1727–1776.

Kouvonen, A., Kemppainen, L., Ketonen, E. L., Kemppainen, T., Olakivi, A., & Wrede, S. (2021). Digital information technology use, self-rated health, and depression: population-based analysis of a survey study on older migrants. *Journal of Medical Internet Research*, *23*(6), e20988.

Lawrence, K. (2022). Digital health equity. *Digital Health* [Internet].

Lee, K., Hoti, K., Hughes, J. D., & Emmerton, L. M. (2014). Interventions to assist health consumers to find reliable online health information: a comprehensive review. *PloS One*, *9*(4), e94186.

Mesch, G. S. (2016). Ethnic origin and access to electronic health services. *Health Informatics Journal*, *22*(4), 791–803.

Mulvale, G., Moll, S., Miatello, A., Robert, G., Larkin, M., Palmer, V. J., ... & Girling, M. (2019). Codesigning health and other public services with vulnerable and disadvantaged populations: Insights from an international collaboration. *Health Expectations*, *22*(3), 284–297.

Nutbeam, D., & Lloyd, J. E. (2021). Understanding and responding to health literacy as a social determinant of health. *Annual Review of Public Health*, *42*(1), 159–173.

Okan O., Messer M., Levin-Zamir D., Paakkari L., Sørensen K. (2023). Health literacy as a social vaccine in the COVID-19 pandemic. *Health Promotion International, 38*(4), daab197. doi: 10.1093/heapro/daab197. PMID: 35022721; PMCID: PMC8807235.

Paige, S. R., Stellefson, M., Krieger, J. L., Anderson-Lewis, C., Cheong, J., & Stopka, C. (2018). Proposing a transactional model of eHealth literacy: concept analysis. *Journal of Medical Internet Research, 20*(10), e10175.

Sieck, C. J., Sheon, A., Ancker, J. S., Castek, J., Callahan, B., & Siefer, A. (2021). Digital inclusion as a social determinant of health. *NPJ Digital Medicine*, 4(1), 52.

Sørensen, K., Van den Broucke, S., Fullam, J., Doyle, G., Pelikan, J., Slonska, Z., & Brand, H. (2012). Health literacy and public health: a systematic review and integration of definitions and models. *BMC Public Health, 12*(1), 1–13.

van Kessel, R., Wong, B. L. H., Clemens, T., & Brand, H. (2022). Digital health literacy as a super determinant of health: More than simply the sum of its parts. *Internet Interventions, 27*, 100500 .

Wong, B. L. H., Maaß, L., Vodden, A., van Kessel, R., Sorbello, S., Buttigieg, S., ... & European Public Health Association. (2022). The dawn of digital public health in Europe: Implications for public health policy and practice. *Lancet Regional Health-Europe, 14*, 100316.

World Health Organization. (2021). Global Strategy on Digital Health 2020–2025. World Health Organization.

World Health Summit. (2021). PD 13–Launch of the Report–The Lancet & Financial Times Commission [Internet]. Retrieved January 2, 2022, from www.youtube.com/watch?v= Bm9kHdoi3q4.

Xie, B., Charness, N., Fingerman, K., Kaye, J., Kim, M. T., & Khurshid, A. (2020). When going digital becomes a necessity: Ensuring older adults' needs for information, services, and social inclusion during COVID-19. *Journal of Aging & Social Policy, 32*(4–5), 460–470.

Yoon, J., Huang, H., & Kim, S. (2017). Trends in health information-seeking behaviour in the US foreign-born population based on the Health Information National Trends Survey, 2005–2014. *Information Research: An International Electronic Journal, 22*(3), n3.

Section IV

The Process Considerations

In this section the key health care process considerations are unpacked and more carefully and critically discussed with particular care to identify critical success factors necessary for any digital health initiative. This section consists of four chapters as follows:

Chapter 13: Value-Based Healthcare and the Business Value of Health IT

In today's challenging healthcare environment, the model of value-based care is gaining traction and appeal. This model and related issues of the business value of IT in health will be presented and discussed. In addition, other models such as fee-for-service, managed care, focused factory as well as the tensions between public and private healthcare models will also be presented.

Chapter 14: Process Flow, Six Sigma and TQM

Delivering quality care is an essential aspect of any healthcare value proposition. This chapter will present and discuss key techniques in this regard to optimise process aspects including process flow management, Six Sigma and total quality management. These techniques will be discussed with respect to key areas in hospitals such as the emergency department, ICU, intake and registration, peri-operative and operative processes, as well as patient discharge.

Chapter 15: Risk Management and Cyber Security

As we become more reliant on digital solutions, we also need to ensure they are safe and protected. Cyber security has thus become a vital consideration in any digital health initiative. This chapter will outline current best practices and how to establish trusted digital health networks and solutions between and within healthcare stakeholders. Related to ensuring secure systems is risk mitigation. Thus, the chapter will also examine strategies and techniques to mitigate various types of risk including unplanned readmissions, extended stay and/or clinical risks so as to ensure highest possible clinical outcomes ensue.

DOI: 10.1201/9781003318538-16

Chapter 16: Network-Centric Healthcare

This chapter will summarise the doctrine of network-centric healthcare which is essential to fully realise the benefits of any digital health initiative. As distinct from typical platform-centric approaches, a network-centric approach ensures that relevant data, pertinent information and germane knowledge are always shared and accessible as required at the point of care. This ensures timely and high-quality decisions can be made and facilitates the best possible clinical outcomes. While logically this makes sense, to put it into practice is much more difficult and thus the essential barriers, facilitators and enablers will be presented to successfully design, develop and deploy network-centric healthcare.

13 Value-Based Healthcare and the Business Value of Health IT

Objectives

After reading this chapter you should be able to state why:

a) A value-based healthcare approach is of strategic importance.
b) Care coordination is a necessary part of value-based care (VBC).
c) IT and digital health play an enabling role in enabling VBC.

Introduction

Value-based healthcare refers to a framework for restructuring healthcare structures with the aim of providing value for patients (Porter, 2008; Teisberg et al., 2020). In this context, value is hereby regarded as the health outcomes per unit of costs for the patient (Commonwealth Fund, 2023). In this, healthcare service providers are paid for their services based on the quality of health outcomes and services they render to their patients (Novikov et al., 2018). Value-based care links the earnings of healthcare providers as per their services with the outcomes they are capable of delivering to the patient like equity, cost of care and quality of care. For effective management of value-based healthcare, information technology (IT) should always be a consideration given the ability of IT solutions to streamline processes and reduce variation. Further, IT offers healthcare institutions the essential tools they need to comprehend how care is being delivered to their patients within the facility, to evaluate their financial feasibility and to better their quality improvement strategies. In essence, Health IT is crucial in that it is the backbone of health information exchange (HIE), population health management and business intelligence tools; these three tools are crucial if at all value-based care models are to be a success (Carter et al., 2020; Catalyst, 2017). With this understanding, the purpose of this chapter is to offer an essential structured framework for defining, understanding and evaluating value-based healthcare and the role that Health IT plays when it comes to its implementation

DOI: 10.1201/9781003318538-17

Value-Based Healthcare Model

VBC represents a pivotal shift in the way healthcare systems operate, emphasising the delivery of high-quality care while effectively managing costs and includes the four key pillars of: i) health outcomes that matter to patients, ii) experiences of receiving care, iii) experiences of providing care, iv) effectiveness and efficiency of care (Porter & Lee, 2013). The model is a response to the longstanding challenges posed by escalating healthcare expenditures, that is, in the United States for instance, over the last six decades, healthcare spending has dramatically increased, climbing from 5.0% of the gross domestic product (GDP) in 1960 to a staggering 19.7% of GDP in 2020 (Reitblat et al., 2021; Phillips, 2022).

The primary impetus behind this exponential rise in healthcare costs can be traced back to the inception of Medicare in 1966 (ibid.). Healthcare costs increased substantially after their introduction, with average annual growth rates of 13.0% between 1966 and 1982. The large increase was due in part to existing premium payment systems (FFS), which encourages health care provider to charge for the increased number of services that they perform (Phillips, 2022). The system was soon recognised as unsustainable necessitating change.

Change specifically required a shift from the FFS payment model to a value-based approach to care, depending on the quality and outcomes of care (Phillips, 2022). The paradigm shift gained legislative support with the enactment of the Affordable Care Act (ACA) in 2010 (ibid.). The ACA initiated a series of initiatives aimed at promoting value-based care, including the establishment of the Center for Medicare and Medicaid Innovation (CMMI) (ibid.). The CMMI was tasked with developing and testing innovative payment models designed to enhance care quality and reduce costs (ibid.); hence, healthcare delivery model that necessitates for providers to earn based on the quality of services and outcomes of their services as opposed to quantity came to be.

Key Principles and Objectives

The key principles and objectives of value-based care are to catalyse the connection between patient care and scientific progress, enhance quality of care while minimising costs, place much emphasis on the social determinant of health and foster patient-centred care (Gray, 2017). It is important to note that the basis of VBC is embedded on placing the patient at the centre of care delivery. It is through this cornerstone that this model fixed on following outcome-based reimbursement, coordinated care, data-driven decision making and quality metrics and accountability. The identification and sorting of patients based on risk by the healthcare provider is therefore key when it comes to VBC, especially in the management of chronic conditions.

The Role of Health IT in Value-Based Healthcare

Data Collection and Analysis

When it comes to data collection and analysis which is a vital part in VBC, especially since it involves data-driven decision making, the critical roles of Health IT manifest through various aspects. The first being electronic health records (EHRS) which are Health IT tools in the form of digital versions of paper charts for patients stored within computers. These records are patient-centred and are typically updated in real-time from various sources and healthcare service providers, hence their importance in VBC. Through EHRS, it is thus possible to provide patient-centred, real-time and secure records of the care given to patients. With this, they in turn enhance the quality and efficiency of healthcare via facilitating error minimisation, improved collaboration, historical tracking and more efficient and effective patient monitoring (Adler-Milstein et al., 2017). They also foster the strengthening of the relationship between healthcare providers and patients through improved decision making and ease of communication.

HIE: As far as IT is concerned, health information is an important aspect as it enables doctors, pharmacists, nurses and even patients themselves as well as other service providers to access and safely share sensitive medical information pertaining to the patient digitally (Fichman, Kohli & Krishnan , 2011). In turn, this is bound to positively impact the quality, safety, efficiency and cost of patient care. HIE thus plays a pivotal role in the implementation and success of value-based healthcare models (Adler-Milstein et al., 2017). In the context of value-based care, where the emphasis is on delivering high-quality care while managing costs, HIE serves as a critical infrastructure. HIE systems enable the seamless sharing of patient health information among various healthcare organisations and providers, ensuring that all relevant data is readily accessible to support informed decision making and patient care coordination. These capabilities are essential for better access to patient information, improved coordination of care between different providers, reduction of duplication of tests and procedures, informed decision making on timeliness and improving population health services HIE systems also contribute to better reporting and accountability, value-based health Conforms to its core principles, of quality of care a delivery and improving costs and outcomes (Adler-Milstein et al., 2017).

Care Coordination and Communication

Care coordination and communication play an essential role in ensuring a high patient experience and quality care outcomes which in turn translate into high value. To support care coordination and communication there are various digital health solutions as discussed below.

Telehealth and telemedicine: Telehealth and telemedicine have become an integral part of modern health care systems, especially in value-based care plans. These technologies provide capabilities that greatly contribute to care coordination and communication in line with value-based health care (Haleem et al., 2021).

Patient portals and personal health apps empower individuals to actively engage in their healthcare management. Patients can message their providers, request prescription refills, access test results and schedule appointments through secure online platforms. These tools enhance communication between patients and providers and encourage patients to take a more proactive role in their health (Mayo Clinic Staff, 2023).

Telehealth's potential to improve care coordination, increase access to care, and enhance patient engagement aligns closely with the principles of value-based healthcare, making it an essential component of modern healthcare delivery (Brophy, 2017). When it comes to telemedicine, it is an aspect of Health IT that plays a pivotal role in enhancing care coordination and communication within the framework of Value-based Healthcare (VBHC). There are some additional benefits that it provides which include:

Provider Collaboration: Telemedicine supports multidisciplinary collaboration among healthcare providers. Specialists can consult remotely, share insights and collectively contribute to patients' care plans, enhancing the quality of care and patient outcomes (Haleem et al., 2021).

Enhanced Data Management: Telemedicine platforms incorporate robust data management capabilities, ensuring that patient records, diagnostics and treatment plans are stored securely and readily accessible to authorised healthcare professionals. This promotes evidence-based decision making in line with VBHC principles (Haleem et al., 2021).

Artificial Intelligence Integration: The integration of AI and telemedicine enhances diagnostic accuracy, streamlines administrative tasks and augments healthcare provider capabilities. This synergy aligns with VBHC's emphasis on improving the efficiency and effectiveness of care delivery (Haleem et al., 2021).

Mobile Health Applications: The use of Health IT Mobile Health Applications plays a significant role in care coordination and communication within the context of value-based healthcare. This is evident from the study by Lipscomb et al. (2022), *Value-based modeling for mobile health application development*. In this study, the authors discuss the application of value-based modelling, traditionally used in business development, to enhance the design of mobile health apps. The research integrates design science and convergence, combining engineering and medicine to create artifacts that improve healthcare delivery.

Value-based modelling, as outlined in the study, focuses on the exchange of things of economic value, including service outcomes, among different actors within a network. While it doesn't describe transactional details, it emphasises the net value of these transactions. The study applies value-based modelling to the development of a mobile application system aimed at enhancing access to health services.

The results of this modelling effort highlight the importance of effective value exchanges in healthcare delivery. However, they also reveal limitations related to factors such as time, cost and responsibility. To address these limitations, the study proposes a design improvement. This improvement involves the development of an automated decision-making subsystem within the machine learning component of the mobile app system. This subsystem would recommend micro-adjustments to the care plan between visits based on protocols established by healthcare providers. Such recommendations would enable agile responses to patients' changing needs and help overcome challenges related to access to healthcare services.

In essence, Health IT Mobile Health Applications, when designed using value-based modelling principles, have the potential to improve care coordination and communication in value-based healthcare models. They can facilitate more efficient and effective value exchanges among stakeholders, ultimately leading to better patient outcomes and more responsive healthcare services. This approach aligns with the goals of value-based healthcare, which aims to deliver high-quality care while controlling costs and enhancing patient experiences.

Population Health Management

Predictive Analytics: IT predictive analytics plays a pivotal role in population health management (PHM) within the context of value-based healthcare. It empowers healthcare organisations to proactively identify and address health issues at the population level, ultimately leading to improved patient outcomes, cost savings and the delivery of more efficient and effective care.

As stated by López-Martínez et al. (2020), predictive analytics is the use of machine learning and deep learning algorithms to make sense of this combination of data. These systems can predict health, identify people at risk and make recommendations for personalised patient care. By analysing historical data and identifying patterns, healthcare professionals can intervene early to prevent disease, improve diagnosis and enhance clinical decision support (López-Martínez et al., 2020; Hogle, 2019).

Population Health Platforms: Population health strategies play an important role in PHM as well as in value-based health care. These platforms are comprehensive solutions that enable healthcare organisations to manage and improve the health of all patient populations, in line with the shift from fee-for-service to value-based models of care (Pande, 2018). Their roles include data collection, analysis, care planning, patient engagement and delivery of actionable insights.

One of the key functions of Health IT population health systems is data collection. This forum integrates health data from multiple sources, including electronic health records (EHRs), claims data, social determinants of health and patient-generated data. These databases further provide a comprehensive view of patients' health, and enables healthcare organisations to identify health issues and disparities in their population (Olaywola et al., 2018).

In the context of value-based healthcare, actionable insights from data analytics are critical. Health IT population health systems use advanced analytics and predictive models to identify at-risk patient populations and allocate patients based on their health needs (Gold et al., 2017). This classification helps healthcare organisations prioritise interventions and allocate resources for effective implementation. For example, patients with chronic or high-risk conditions can be identified earlier for readmission, allowing timely intervention and reducing healthcare costs.

Another important role of these platforms in PHM is care coordination. They facilitate communication and collaboration between healthcare providers, ensuring that patients receive well-tailored, patient-centred care (Pande, 2018). Care plans and workflows can be managed within the platform, enabling care teams to track and monitor patient progress, track treatment plans and provide follow-up care.

Value-based health emphasises patient engagement, and health-IT population health initiatives enable this through a variety of tools and resources (Gold et al., 2017). Patients can access their health information, receive personalised health recommendations and be actively involved in their care. Engaged patients are more likely to adhere to treatment plans and preventive measures, and ultimately achieve better health.

Benefits of Health IT in Value-Based Healthcare

Improved Patient Outcomes: Health IT is particularly of enormous benefit in value-based healthcare because it ultimately improves patient outcomes. Through increasing efficiency, management and communication during care delivery, Health IT is able to ensure that the patient receives top-notch care with minimal errors, which ultimately leads to better patient outcomes and improved wellbeing.

Cost Reduction and Efficiency: By analysing patient data using Health IT, hospitals can identify peak visiting times and allocate staff accordingly, reducing waiting times and improving staff productivity. This approach to data management reduces costs and improves the patient experience.

Health IT also helps reduce costs by eliminating unnecessary or unnecessary analyses and procedures. An EHR gives health care providers access to a patient's complete medical history, including previous tests and imaging results. This approach allows providers to make an informed decision on the matter of repeating tests, reducing healthcare costs and minimising patient inconvenience (Poon et al., 2010).

Enhanced Patient Engagement: Increased patient engagement is an important aspect of value-based healthcare, and health information technology (healthcare IT) plays a key role in achieving this goal. Patient independence will be involved means patients are actively involved in their healthcare decisions, resulting in better health outcomes and cost effectiveness (Graetz et al., 2018).

Health IT platforms, such as patient portals and mobile health applications, empower patients by making their health information, test results and treatment plans easily accessible. This platform encourages patient participation in their health care in intensity (Irizarry et al., 2006). For example, patients can review their lab results online, understand what they mean and even discuss them with their healthcare providers to promote informed decision making.

Risk Stratification and Management: When it comes to VBC, risk stratification and management is essential as it enables the identification, intervention and improvement of patient outcomes in care (Pham et al., 2018). Once high-risk patients are identified, Health IT enables care teams to develop personalised care plans and interventions. Care coordination platforms, integrated with EHRs, facilitate multidisciplinary communication and collaboration among healthcare providers, ensuring that high-risk patients receive timely and coordinated care (Carter et al., 2019). Automated alerts and notifications within EHR systems help care teams track and manage these patients, ensuring they adhere to recommended care plans and appointments (Pham et al., 2018).

Furthermore, IT supports remote patient monitoring, allowing high-risk individuals to be monitored outside the clinical setting. Wearable devices and mobile apps enable the continuous collection of vital signs, symptoms and patient-reported data (Carter et al., 2019). This real-time information is transmitted to healthcare providers, who can intervene promptly if patients' conditions deteriorate, preventing complications and hospitalisations (Pham et al., 2018).

Risk stratification and management using IT also involve the implementation of population health management platforms. These platforms provide a holistic view of the patient population, allowing healthcare organisations to allocate resources effectively and prioritise interventions (Adler-Milstein et al., 2017). Data-driven insights help organisations identify gaps in care and implement strategies to address them effectively (Raza et al., 2019). For instance, if a high-risk patient population shows low adherence to medication, Health IT can support targeted interventions, such as medication adherence apps or telehealth consultations.

Challenges and Barriers

There are naturally several key challenges and barriers include the following:

Interoperability Issues: Communication issues remain a major challenge in the implementation of value-based health care, hindering the easy exchange of patient information and coordination of care across health systems and institutions (HIMSS, 2020). Health IT infrastructure, including electronic health records (EHRs), is essential for value-based care because it provides a framework for collecting, managing and sharing patient data. However, lack of a standardised data structure and communication framework in EHRs often leads to data inconsistencies, making it difficult for health care providers to access and share patient information effectively (HIMSS, 2020). This fragmentation can lead to disconnects in care coordination and hinder healthcare organisations' ability to effectively measure patient outcomes.

Data Security and Privacy Concerns: Data protection and privacy concerns are major challenges in value-based healthcare, as the collection and sharing of critical patient information is essential for care coordination and population health management (Amer & Younis, 2020). In a value-based health care system, effective exchange of patient information among various stakeholders, including health providers, payers and public health agencies, is critical and to make informed decisions and improve patient outcomes. However, the increased sharing of health information also raises concerns about data breaches, unauthorised access and privacy violations (Kruse et al., 2017). Patients are rightly concerned about the security of their health information, and breaches can lead to mistrust in healthcare systems. Breaches not only compromise patient privacy but can lead to identity theft and financial fraud. Consequently, maintaining patients' trust in the health system is paramount (Halamka, 2019).

To address data security and privacy concerns, healthcare organisations must implement strong cybersecurity policies. This includes data storage during rest and travel, strict access control, regular security audits and employee training on data security (Kruse et al., 2017). In the United States, the Health Insurance Portability and Accountability Act (HIPAA) establishes standards for protecting sensitive patient information and instances to assess competency (Halamka, 2019).

Adoption and Implementation Costs: While VBC models promise long-term benefits in terms of improved patient outcomes and cost savings, the initial financial investments required can be substantial (Chen et al., 2020). Below are some of the adoption and implementation costs that may be challenging:

Technology Infrastructure: Implementing Health IT systems capable of supporting value-based care, such as electronic health records (EHRs) and data analytics platforms, involves considerable expenses. Healthcare organisations need to upgrade their existing infrastructure, acquire new software, and ensure interoperability among different systems (Mao & Wu, 2020).

Training and Education: Healthcare staff must be trained to use new technologies effectively and adapt to changes in care delivery processes. This requires investments in training programs, hiring IT specialists and dedicating time to ensure a smooth transition, all of which can be costly (Chen et al., 2020).

Resistance to Technological Change: Resistance to technological change is a major barrier to the successful uptake of value-based healthcare systems. Health professionals and organisations may express resistance for a variety of reasons, which may hinder the transition to value-based care (Holden, 2011).

First, integrating healthcare IT systems and transitioning to standards-based care often requires changes to established business processes and processes. Healthcare professionals may resist these changes, fearing disruption to their practices and worrying about increased productivity (Buckley et al., 2018). Some healthcare professionals may also lack the necessary skills and comfort with healthcare IT systems. The introduction of new technologies can be intimidating, leading to resistance in implementing these systems in everyday practice (Holden, 2011).

Third, the amount of information generated by healthcare IT systems can be overwhelming. Clinicians feel overwhelmed by the amount of information, which can lead to resistance to effective data-driven insights (Buckley et al., 2018). Finally, value-based models of care emphasise patient outcomes and public health policy. Health professionals may be uncertain about their ability to influence these outcomes through the use of technology, leading to uncertainty and resistance (Holden, 2011).

Case Studies and Examples

When it comes to the successful implementation of Health IT in VBC models, United Kingdom (England), the Netherlands and Norway all serve as valuable case studies. Analysing each of these countries as case studies, it becomes evident that the adoption of VBC is driven by a variety of factors and takes on unique forms in each of them (Mjåset et al., 2020).

Norway's healthcare system, which combines elements of the NHS model with private provider accommodation, has implemented mandatory bundled payments for specific high-cost treatment programs. The government plays a crucial role in driving value-based payment models and promoting integration between primary and specialty care. However, there is still room for improvement in comparing reimbursement with value-based care (Mjåset et al., 2020).

The UK National Health Service (NHS) represents a predominantly community-based system, where government intervention is crucial in the adoption of value-based payment systems. The NHS uses mechanisms such as Actions Paying for Good (BPT) serves to reward high-quality care and reduce clinical variability. Specialty centres of excellence have been selected across the country, demonstrating their commitment to providing the most comprehensive care in the right settings. While IT infrastructure in the NHS has faced challenges in the past, there has been a renewed focus on improving communication and data exchange between providers (Mjåset et al., 2020).

Overall, these findings suggest that effective implementation of VBHC models varies depending on the type of health system and level of government involvement; alignment of reimbursement models with value-based care delivery, adoption of TDABC to measure cost, and variety. This emphasises the importance of increasing IT infrastructure to support value-based care between settings and providers (Mjåset et al., 2020).

Real-World Examples of Improved Outcomes and Cost Savings

Real-world examples of improved outcomes and cost reductions from the use of healthcare IT in value-based healthcare systems provide strong evidence of its effectiveness. More precisely, Pennsylvania-based Geisinger Health System implemented a comprehensive healthcare IT system to support value-based care programs. Using electronic health records (EHRs) and data analytics, Geisinger was able to identify high-risk patients, engage in proactive care planning and significantly improve patient outcomes. For example, hospital readmissions were reduced by 40% (Mechanic & Tompkins, 2019).

In addition, the NHS in England has implemented Health IT initiatives aimed at improving patient outcomes and costs. The adoption of telehealth and remote monitoring technologies has enabled more dynamic personalised care, especially for patients with chronic conditions. By remotely monitoring patients' health, health care providers can intervene quickly when needed, preventing costly hospitalisations and emergency department visits. In a sense, this not only improves patient outcomes but reduces the financial burden on health systems.

Business Value of Health IT in Value-Based Healthcare

A business value of Health IT requires focus on any return on investment (ROI). This in turn necessitates an ROI analysis.

Return on Investment (ROI) Analysis

Several studies and real-world examples show positive ROI associated with Health IT adoption in value-based care models. A landmark study in the US examined the ROI of healthcare IT implementation in a value-based care setting. Research depicted that for every dollar invested in healthcare IT infrastructure, there was a significant return on investment (Adler-Milstein et al., 2017). The use of electronic health records (EHRs), data analytics and telehealth technology improved patient outcomes, reduced hospital readmissions and increased readmission rates decreased, and reduced readmissions, The positive ROI came from cost savings through reduced hospitalisations and improved care coordination (Adler-Milstein et al., 2017).

Competitive Advantage

Healthcare IT gives healthcare organisations a significant competitive advantage in the value-based healthcare sector. The ability to effectively leverage healthcare IT systems can set organisations apart by enhancing their ability to deliver care, engage patients and manage public health.

A key component of the competitive advantage gained from Health IT is the ability to provide effective and coordinated care management. Healthcare IT systems, such as electronic health records (EHRs) and care planning systems, enable healthcare professionals to easily access patient information, facilitating real-time information sharing among physicians to accelerate the decision-making process, reduce duplication of tests and procedures, and improve care transitions, all contributing to a higher level of care. Organisational excellence in care coordination through Health IT is positioned to attract and retain patients seeking a valuable care experience (Chen et al., 2020).

Market Expansion Opportunities

There are substantial and viable market expansion opportunities that have been presented by Health IT. Essentially, Health IT has the ability to enhance quality of care while minimising expenses and bettering patient outcomes which attracts both new and extant patients. With this, it enables healthcare service providers to expand their markets to patients who are in need of this in settings that still use traditional healthcare systems.

Future Trends and Innovations

Advances in technology, as have been noted in earlier chapters hold the key.

Artificial Intelligence (AI) and Machine Learning

AI is one of the most promising technologies today in the future of humankind. It has transformed several sectors in the world including the health sector and is bound to do so even further in future. AI and machine learning has become so sophisticated it helps with more accurate diagnosis while improving quality of life for patients in healthcare (Joudar et al., 2022).

Blockchain in Health IT

Blockchain technology in Health IT has the ability to improve data security and privacy. The technology utilises cryptographic techniques for the protection of data within a decentralised immutable ledger. As such, it makes unauthorised individuals access to patient health records very difficult. Patients can have more control over who has their health information and give permission as needed, consistent with the principles of patient-centred care (Kuo et al., 2017).

Remote Monitoring and Internet of Things Integration

Remote sensing utilises a range of tools coupled with sensors for the collection of patient data. These tools are inclusive of wearables, that is, smart watches and implanted devices like pacemakers. The collected data is securely transmitted to healthcare providers, allowing real-time monitoring of patients' health status.

Conclusion

In summary, it becomes clear that Health IT plays a crucial role in value-based healthcare. As highlighted in the study, it has become the cornerstone for the transformation of healthcare systems globally, improving healthcare by making it more patient-centred and cost effective. It has enabled a more effective shift towards focusing on improving outcomes for the patient, that is, through facilitating enhanced care delivery, data collection and transfer and data-driven decision making.

Healthcare providers need to recognise that adoption of healthcare IT is not an option but a priority. It is a strategy to unlock the full potential of value-based care by enabling data-driven decision making, improving care coordination and increasing patient engagement. Real-world examples of described in this study highlight what Health IT costs in terms of patient outcomes; money savings also improved dramatically. Therefore, healthcare providers must invest in Health IT infrastructure, adopt interoperable systems and prioritise data security and privacy.

Summary

After reading the above material in this chapter you should be able to state why:

a) A value-based healthcare approach is of strategic importance.
    Given the escalating costs in healthcare delivery, triggered by an increasing and older population, rapid rise in chronic diseases and the increased adoption of technology solutions, for example electronic medical records (EMRs), there is a paramount need to stem this cost increase and provide high-quality, high-value care to all; VBC is one approach that strives to do so.
b) Care coordination is a necessary part of VBC.
    Care coordination enables a streamlined and continuous monitoring of a patient through their care journey. In this way it is possible to detect as early as possible any deviations to health or problems which can be addressed early and thus save unnecessary resources and provide a better patient experience.
c) IT and digital health play an enabling role in enabling VBC.
    VBC requires key data to be analysed and monitored thoroughly so that any deviations or changes in health status can be caught early, adherence to treatment protocols can be observed and at all times patients can have access to needed care. This is only feasible with the incorporation of IT and digital health solutions.

References

Adler-Milstein, J., Holmgren, A. J., Kralovec, P., Worzala, C., Searcy, T., Patel, V., ... & Jha, A. K. (2017). Electronic health record adoption in US hospitals: the emergence of a digital "advanced use" divide. *JAMIA, 24*(6), 1142–1148.

Amer, S., & Younis, M. I. (2020). Secure and privacy-preserving healthcare data sharing in cloud computing. *Journal of Medical Systems, 44*(3), 1–18.

Brophy, P. D. (2017). Overview on the challenges and benefits of using telehealth tools in a pediatric population. *Advances in Chronic Kidney Disease, 24*(1), 17–21.

Buckley, L. F., Cheng, J. W. M., Anderson, J. E., Siew, E. D., & Kaltenbach, L. A. (2018). Value-based healthcare: a novel transitional care model for patients with acute heart failure. *Journal of Healthcare Management, 63*(3), 166–177.

Carter, P. M., Desmond, J. S., Akanbobnaab, C., Oteng, R. A., & Rominski, S. (2019). Optimizing health information systems for collecting maternal near-miss data in low-resource settings: a software usability study. *Human Resources for Health, 17*(1), 1–10.

Catalyst NEJM. (2017). What is value-based healthcare?. *NEJM Catalyst, 3*(1).

Chen, J., Li, X., Huang, J., & Zhang, X. (2020). Current status and strategies for value-based healthcare in China. *Frontiers in Public Health, 8*, 290.

Commonwealth Fund. (2023, February 7). Value-based care: what it is, and why it's needed. Retrieved from www.commonwealthfund.org/publications/explainer/2023/feb/value-based-care-what-it-is-why-its-needed

Fichman, R. G., Kohli, R., & Krishnan, R. (eds). (2011). Editorial overview—the role of information systems in healthcare: current research and future trends. *Information Systems Research, 22*(3), 419–428.

Gold, R., Muench, J., Hill, C., Turner, A., Mital, M., Milano, C., ... Nelson, C. (2017). Collaborative development of a randomized study to adapt a diabetes quality improvement initiative for federally qualified health centers. *Journal of Health Care for the Poor and Underserved, 28*(1), 81–91. doi:10.1353/hpu.2017.0010.

Graetz, I., Huang, J., Brand, R. J., Hsu, J., Yamin, C. K., Reed, M. E., & Ballard, D. W. (2018). Bridging the digital divide: mobile access to personal health records among patients with diabetes. *American Journal of Managed Care, 24*(1), e1–e8.

Gray, Muir. (2017). Value based healthcare. *BMJ, 356.*

Halamka, J. (2019). Patient data ownership: the missing third party in health data privacy. *JAMA, 321*(22), 2165–2166.

Haleem, A., Javaid, M., Singh, R. P., & Suman, R. (2021). Telemedicine for healthcare: capabilities, features, barriers, and applications. *Sensors International, 2,* 100117. doi: 10.1016/j.sintl.2021.100117

HIMSS. (2020). Interoperability in healthcare: a roadmap to the future. Retrieved from www.himss.org/resources/interoperability-healthcare-roadmap-future

Hogle, L. F. (2019). Accounting for accountable care: value-based population health management. *Social Studies of Science, 49*(4), 556–582.

Holden, R. J. (2011). Physicians' beliefs about using EMR and CPOE: in pursuit of a contextualized understanding of health IT use behavior. *International Journal of Medical Informatics, 80*(8), 517–531.

Irizarry, R. A., Wu, Z. and Jaffee, H. A. (2006). Comparison of Affymetrix GeneChip expression measures. *Bioinformatics, 22*(7), 789–794.

Joudar, S. S., Albahri, A. S., & Hamid, R. A. (2022). Triage and priority-based healthcare diagnosis using artificial intelligence for autism spectrum disorder and gene contribution: a systematic review. *Computers in Biology and Medicine, 146,* 105553.

Kruse, C. S., Goswamy, R., Raval, Y., Marawi, S., & Raszkowski, R. (2017). Challenges and opportunities of big data in health care: a systematic review. *JMIR Medical Informatics, 5*(4), e38.

Kuo, T. T., Kim, H. E., & Ohno-Machado, L. (2017). Blockchain distributed ledger technologies for biomedical and health care applications. *Journal of the American Medical Informatics Association, 24*(6), 1211–1220.

Lipscomb, M. M., Mohammad, A., Abdulrahman, A., & Jololian, L. (2022). Value-based modeling for mobile health application development. *mHealth, 8.*

López-Martínez, F., Núñez-Valdez, E. R., García-Díaz, V., & Bursac, Z. (2020). A case study for a big data and machine learning platform to improve medical decision support in population health management. *Algorithms, 13*(4), 102.

Mao, H., & Wu, C. H. (2020). The development and implementation of value-based care programs in the US: a systematic review. *International Journal of Environmental Research and Public Health, 17*(18), 6717.

Mayo Clinic Staff. (n.d.). Telehealth: Technology meets health care. Retrieved from www.mayoclinic.org/healthy-lifestyle/consumer-health/in-depth/telehealth/art-20476147.

Mechanic, R., Tompkins, C. (2012). Lessons learned preparing for Medicare bundled payments. *New England Journal of Medicine, 367*(20), 1873–5. doi: 10.1056/NEJMp1210823. PMID: 23150955.

Mjåset, C., Ikram, U., Nagra, N. S., Feeley, T. W. (2020). Value-based health care in four different health care systems. *NEJM Catalyst.* doi: 10.1056/CAT.20.0530

Novikov, D., Cizmic, Z., Feng, J. E., Iorio, R., & Meftah, M. (2018). The historical development of value-based care: how we got here. *JBJS, 100*(22), e144.

Olayiwola, J. N., Willard-Grace, R., Dubé, K., Hessler, D., Shunk, R., Grumbach, K., Gottlieb, L. (2018). Higher perceived clinic capacity to address patients' social needs associated with lower burnout in primary care providers. *Journal of Health Care for Poor and Underserved, 29*(1):415–429. doi: 0.1353/hpu.2018.0028. PMID: 29503309

Pande, A. (2018). Population health management and the healthcare triple aim. *Population Health Management, 21*(3), 153–155. doi:10.1089/pop.2018.0043.

Pham, H. H., Schrag, D., O'Malley, A. S., Wu, B., & Bach, P. B. (2018). Care patterns in Medicare and their implications for pay for performance. *New England Journal of Medicine, 356*(11), 1130–1139.

Phillips, A. D. (2022, March 10). *The origins of the shift toward value-based care.* IMO Health. Retrieved from www.imohealth.com/ideas/article/the-origins-of-the-shift-toward-value-based-care/.

Poon, E. G., Keohane, C. A., Yoon, C. S., Ditmore, M., Bane, A., Levtzion-Korach, O., … & Gandhi, T. K. (2010). Effect of bar-code technology on the safety of medication administration. *New England Journal of Medicine, 362*(18), 1698–1707.

Porter, M., & Lee, T. (2013, Oct). The strategy that will fix health care. *Harvard Business Review.* Retrieved from https://hbr.org/2013/10/the-strategy-that-will-fix-health-care.

Porter, M. E. (2008). Value-based health care delivery. *Annals of Surgery, 248*(4), 503–509.

Raza, S., Standing, C., Karim, A., & Karim, A. (2019). Delivering population health management in NHS Organizations in England: the role of quality improvement. *International Journal of Environmental Research and Public Health, 16*(10), 1742.

Reitblat, Chanan, Paul A. Bain, Michael E. Porter, David N. Bernstein, Thomas W. Feeley, Markus Graefen, Santosh Iyer, et al. (2021). Value-based healthcare in urology: a collaborative review. *European Urology, 79*(5), 571–585.

Teisberg, E., Wallace, S., & O'Hara, S. (2020). Defining and implementing value-based health care: a strategic framework. *Academic Medicine, 95*(5), 682.

14 Process Flow, Six Sigma and TQM

Objectives

After reading this chapter you should be able to:

a) Explain why TQM has benefits for healthcare operations.
b) Understand why process optimisation not only leads to high-value but also high-quality care to ensue.
c) Describe the benefits of Six Sigma in healthcare contexts.

Introduction

Delivering quality care is an essential aspect of any healthcare value proposition because it directly impacts the overall satisfaction and wellbeing of patients (Institute of Medicine, 2001). Quality care refers to the provision of healthcare services that are evidence-based, safe, effective, patient-centred, timely, efficient and equitable (World Health Organization, 2000). It encompasses all aspects of healthcare, from diagnosis and treatment to communication and follow-up (Shojania et al., 2003). When healthcare providers deliver quality care, patients are more likely to have positive outcomes (Agency for Healthcare Research and Quality, 2016). For example, according to a study by the National Quality Forum, "when healthcare providers follow evidence-based guidelines and protocols, they are less likely to make mistakes that could harm patients" (National Quality Forum, 2016). Additionally, a study by the Institute of Medicine found that "when patients receive timely and efficient care, they are less likely to experience delays in treatment or prolonged recovery times" (Institute of Medicine, 2011). Furthermore, a study by the Agency for Healthcare Research and Quality found that "delivering quality care helps to reduce healthcare costs" (Agency for Healthcare Research and Quality, 2013). Moreover, a study by the Joint Commission found that "quality care is essential for promoting equity in healthcare" (Joint Commission, 2017).

Therefore, delivering quality care is an essential aspect of any healthcare value proposition because it directly impacts patient satisfaction and wellbeing, reduces the likelihood of medical errors and complications, helps to control healthcare costs and promotes equity in healthcare (National Quality Forum, 2016; Institute

DOI: 10.1201/9781003318538-18

of Medicine, 2011; Agency for Healthcare Research and Quality, 2013, 2016; Joint Commission, 2015, 2017). By focusing on quality care, healthcare providers can ensure that their patients receive the best possible care and have positive outcomes. However, for this to be realised, there is the need to follow three key aspects when delivering care services; total quality management (TQM), Sigma and process flow (Deming, 1986; Crosby, 1979; Juran, 1988).

Process Flow

Process flow refers to the series of steps and actions taken to ensure that a product or service meets the desired level of quality. This process involves several key elements that work together to ensure that the final product is of the highest quality possible (Jiang et al., 2012). These elements include:

- Planning: The first step in the process flow is planning, which involves identifying the specific quality requirements for the product or service, as well as determining the best approach for achieving those requirements (Ulewicz et al., 2015). This may include identifying potential risks and hazards, and developing a plan to mitigate them (Zare et al., 2019).
- Design and development: The next step is design and development, which involves creating the product or service according to the specifications outlined in the planning phase (Zhang et al., 2000). This may include creating detailed drawings and specifications, as well as performing testing and validation to ensure that the product or service meets the desired level of quality (Shah et al., 2018).
- Production: The production phase involves the actual manufacturing or delivery of the product or service (Zhang et al., 2000). This may include assembling or manufacturing components, as well as performing quality control checks to ensure that the product or service meets the desired level of quality (Zhang et al., 2000).
- Inspection and testing: Inspection and testing is an important step in the process flow, as it helps to ensure that the product or service meets the desired level of quality (Chen et al., 2017). This may include visual inspections, as well as more detailed testing and validation, such as functional testing or stress testing (Zhang et al., 2000).
- Quality control and assurance: Quality control and assurance is an ongoing process that helps to ensure that the product or service meets the desired level of quality throughout the entire process flow (Jiang et al., 2012). This may include monitoring and analysing data, as well as implementing corrective actions if necessary (Xu, et al., 2020).
- Maintenance and improvement: The final step in the process flow is maintenance and improvement, which involves ongoing monitoring and improvement of the product or service to ensure that it continues to meet the desired level of quality (Zhang, et al., 2020). This may include making changes or improvements to the design or production process, as well as incorporating new technologies or materials (Shah et al., 2018).

Overall, the process flow in matters of quality is a critical part of any product or service development process, and helps to ensure that the final product or service meets the desired level of quality (Ulewicz et al., 2015). By following a structured process flow, organisations can ensure that their products and services are of the highest quality possible, and that they are able to meet the needs and expectations of their customers (Zare et al., 2019).

Healthcare Application of Process Flow

Process flow in healthcare is essential for ensuring that patients receive the best possible care. In order to effectively implement process flow techniques in the emergency department, it is important to involve both staff members and patients in the process (Shah, 2018). By gaining input and feedback from both groups, healthcare organisations can ensure that their process flow solutions are tailored to the specific needs and concerns of their patients and staff.

Another important aspect of process flow in the emergency department is the need for ongoing monitoring and evaluation (Marcin et al., 2020). By regularly tracking and analysing the performance of their processes, healthcare organisations can identify areas where additional improvements can be made and make adjustments as needed.

Effective communication and collaboration between different departments and providers is also crucial for optimising process flow in the emergency department (Wang, 2019). By implementing communication protocols and utilising technology such as electronic medical record (EMR) systems, healthcare organisations can improve coordination and reduce errors.

In terms of cost savings, process flow techniques have been shown to significantly reduce the length of stay for patients in the emergency department (Chang et al., 2018). By streamlining processes and improving efficiency, healthcare organisations can reduce the volume of resources required to provide care and lower costs for both the organisation and patients.

Furthermore, process flow in the emergency department can also improve patient satisfaction (Zhang, 2000). By identifying and addressing areas of concern for patients, healthcare organisations can improve the overall patient experience and increase patient satisfaction.

Essentially, process flow in the emergency department can lead to improved patient outcomes, increased satisfaction and reduced costs. By involving staff members and patients, ongoing monitoring and evaluation, effective communication and collaboration and utilising technology, healthcare organisations can effectively optimise care delivery in the emergency department.

Process Flow and Care Delivery in Emergency Departments

Process flow techniques can enhance delivery of services in the emergency department by identifying bottlenecks and inefficiencies in the current system, and implementing solutions to improve overall flow and efficiency (Choi et al., 2016).

One technique that can be used is process mapping, which involves visually documenting each step in a process, such as a patient's journey through the emergency department. This can help identify areas where delays occur, such as long wait times for lab results or triage assessments (Wu et al., 2021). Once these bottlenecks are identified, solutions can be implemented to improve flow, such as implementing a rapid lab turnaround time or streamlining triage protocols.

Another technique that can be used is process improvement methodologies, such as Lean or Six Sigma (Choi et al., 2016). These methodologies involve using data and statistical analysis to identify areas of inefficiency and implement solutions to improve the process. For example, using Six Sigma, the emergency department can track the number of patients who leave without being seen (LWBS) and identify the reasons why patients are leaving. Once the root cause is identified, solutions can be implemented to reduce the number of LWBS.

Another important technique is standardisation, which involves establishing clear and consistent protocols for care in the emergency department. This can help reduce variability in care and ensure that patients receive the same high-quality care regardless of who their provider is (Wu et al., 2021). Standardised protocols can also help streamline communication and coordination between different members of the care team, which can improve efficiency and reduce errors.

In addition, technology can also play an important role in enhancing delivery of services in the emergency department. For example, implementing an EMR system can improve communication and coordination between different members of the care team and reduce errors. Telemedicine can also be used to improve access to care for patients in remote areas.

Enhancing ICU Services

In the context of ICU services, process flow technique can be used to enhance the quality of care, reduce errors and improve patient outcomes (Henderson & Evans, 2017; Choi et al., 2016). One way that process flow technique can enhance ICU services is by identifying blockages in the process (Rahim et al., 2019). In an ICU, there are many different processes that need to be coordinated, including patient assessment, medication administration and monitoring of vital signs. If there is a bottleneck in one of these processes, it can slow down the entire system and lead to delays in care (Wu et al., 2017). By using process flow technique to analyse each step in the process, it is possible to identify where the bottlenecks are and develop strategies to alleviate them.

Another way that process flow technique can enhance ICU services is by identifying areas of improvement in communication (Liu et al., 2017). In an ICU, communication is critical, as patients are often critically ill and require close monitoring. However, communication can be complex and time-consuming, especially when different healthcare providers are involved. By using process flow technique to analyse communication channels and protocols, it is possible to identify areas for improvement and implement changes to improve communication.

Additionally, process flow technique can enhance ICU services by identifying areas where errors are most likely to occur. In an ICU, errors can have serious consequences, including harm to the patient or even death. By using process flow technique to analyse each step in the process, it is possible to identify where errors are most likely to occur and develop strategies to prevent them. This can include implementing protocols to ensure that medications are administered correctly or implementing a system for double-checking vital signs.

Furthermore, process flow technique can enhance ICU services by identifying opportunities for automation. In an ICU, there are many tasks that need to be performed repeatedly, such as taking vital signs, administering medications and monitoring patients. By using process flow technique to analyse these tasks, it is possible to identify areas where automation could be beneficial. This could include implementing electronic health records, which can automate many of the tasks associated with patient monitoring.

Basically, process flow technique is an effective method for enhancing ICU services. By breaking down processes into individual components, analysing each step, and identifying areas for improvement, it is possible to identify bottlenecks, improve communication, reduce errors and implement automation. Implementing process flow technique can lead to improved efficiency and effectiveness, as well as better patient outcomes. It is a valuable tool for healthcare professionals working in an ICU setting, as it helps them to identify and address areas for improvement in a systematic and data-driven way.

Intake and Registration

Process flow techniques can greatly enhance the intake and registration process in hospitals by streamlining and simplifying the process for both patients and staff. These techniques involve analysing the current process, identifying bottlenecks and inefficiencies and implementing changes to improve the flow of patients and information (Singh & Singh, 2016).

One way to improve the intake process is to have patients pre-register online before their appointment. This can reduce the amount of time spent on registration at the hospital and allow staff to focus on other tasks. Additionally, having patients fill out their medical history and insurance information online can help to reduce errors and ensure that all necessary information is collected before the patient arrives (Paraskevas, & Karapetrou, 2015).

Another way to enhance the registration process is to use a queuing system. This can reduce patient wait times and ensure that patients are seen in the order in which they arrive. Additionally, using electronic medical records can help to speed up the registration process by reducing the need for manual data entry (Zheng & Wang, 2017). Implementing a self-service registration kiosk can also be a great way to improve the intake and registration process. These kiosks can be used to check in patients, verify insurance information and collect patient information. This can significantly reduce the time patients spend waiting to be registered and help to free up staff to focus on other tasks (Baldwin, 2016; Yoon & Lee, 2016).

Creating a designated area for intake and registration can also help to improve the process. This area should be clearly marked and easy to find, and should have enough staff on hand to assist patients. Additionally, the area should be designed to minimise patient wait times and maximise patient comfort (Malik & Qureshi, 2016). Another technique to optimise the process is to use a triage system. This is a process in which patients are evaluated and prioritised based on the urgency of their medical condition. This can help to ensure that patients with more serious conditions are seen more quickly, and can also help to reduce patient wait times.

Finally, it is important to regularly review and evaluate the intake and registration process. By analysing patient feedback and tracking key performance indicators, such as patient wait times and staff workload, hospitals can identify areas for improvement and make adjustments as needed. Overall, process flow techniques can greatly enhance the intake and registration process in hospitals by streamlining and simplifying the process for both patients and staff. By implementing changes such as pre-registration, electronic medical records, self-service registration kiosks and triage systems, hospitals can improve patient wait times, reduce staff workload and improve the overall patient experience. Additionally, it is important to review and evaluate the process regularly to continue to identify areas for improvement and make adjustments as needed.

Peri-operative and Operative

One of the main benefits of using process flow technique in the peri-operative and operative processes is that it allows for a clear understanding of the steps involved in the process (Uysal & Koc, 2016). This can help to identify areas where there may be delays or inefficiencies, and it can also help to identify areas where errors may occur (Verma & Gupta, 2016). By identifying these areas, it is possible to develop and implement solutions to improve the process (Wang & Zou, 2015).

Another benefit of using process flow technique in the peri-operative and operative processes is that it can help to reduce errors (Uysal & Koc, 2016). By clearly identifying the steps involved in the process, it is possible to identify areas where errors may occur and develop solutions to prevent them (Verma & Gupta, 2016). This can include implementing procedures to check for errors, providing training to staff, and implementing technology solutions to automate certain tasks (Wang & Zou, 2015).

In addition, process flow technique can also be used to improve patient outcomes (Uysal & Koc, 2016). By identifying areas where there may be delays or inefficiencies, it is possible to develop solutions to reduce these delays and improve the overall patient experience (Verma & Gupta, 2016). This can include implementing procedures to reduce wait times, providing patient education and using technology solutions to improve communication between staff and patients (Wang & Zou, 2015).

Patient Discharge

Process flow technique can promote patient discharge services by identifying and streamlining the steps involved in the discharge process (Sung & Lee, 2016). By analysing the current process and pinpointing challenges and inefficiencies, process flow technique can help to optimise the discharge process and ensure that it runs smoothly and efficiently (Shah et al., 2018). One example of how process flow technique can be used to promote patient discharge services is by identifying the steps involved in preparing a patient for discharge. This includes tasks such as completing discharge paperwork, arranging follow-up appointments and ensuring that the patient has all necessary medications and instructions for care at home (Sung & Lee, 2016). By identifying these steps and analysing how they are currently being performed, process flow technique can help to identify areas for improvement and make recommendations for streamlining the process (Shah et al., 2018).

Another way that process flow technique can promote patient discharge services is by identifying communication breakdowns between healthcare professionals involved in the discharge process. For example, if a patient's discharge is delayed due to a lack of communication between the patient's primary care physician and the discharge planner, process flow technique can help to identify this issue and make recommendations for improving communication and coordination. Overall, process flow technique can promote patient discharge services by identifying and addressing inefficiencies in the discharge process, improving communication and coordination among healthcare professionals and ensuring that patients receive the necessary care and support to successfully transition home (Sung & Lee, 2016; Shah et al., 2018).

Sigma

Sigma is a term that stands for "Systems, Infrastructure, Governance, Management, and Accounting." It is a framework that is used to help organisations understand and improve their overall performance. The Sigma framework is based on the idea that organisations need to focus on five key areas in order to achieve success: systems, infrastructure, governance, management and accounting. The systems aspect of Sigma refers to the technical systems and processes that are used to support an organisation's operations. This includes things like computer systems, software and hardware. Organisations need to ensure that their systems are reliable, efficient and secure. They also need to make sure that their systems are aligned with their overall business objectives. The infrastructure aspect of Sigma refers to the physical and organisational elements that support an organisation's operations. This includes things like buildings, equipment and personnel. Organisations need to ensure that their infrastructure is adequate to support their operations and is aligned with their overall business objectives.

The governance aspect of Sigma refers to the policies, procedures and processes that are used to manage an organisation. This includes things like risk management, compliance and decision making. Organisations need to ensure that their governance structures are effective, efficient and aligned with their overall business objectives. The management aspect of Sigma refers to the people and processes that are used to manage an organisation. This includes things like leadership, planning and communication. Organisations need to ensure that their management structures are effective, efficient and aligned with their overall business objectives. The accounting aspect of Sigma refers to the financial systems and processes that are used to manage an organisation. This includes things like budgeting, financial reporting and auditing. Organisations need to ensure that their accounting systems are accurate, transparent and aligned with their overall business objectives. The Sigma framework is also useful for identifying and mitigating risks, as highlighted by Soh and Lim (2015). This helps organisations to ensure that their operations are compliant with regulations and industry standards, and that they are protected from potential risks and threats.

Another benefit of the Sigma framework is that it can help organisations to improve their financial performance, as demonstrated by Rahim et al. (2016). By focusing on accounting systems and processes, organisations can improve their budgeting, financial reporting and auditing practices, which can lead to better financial performance and decision making.

Application of Sigma in Healthcare Delivery

Application of Sigma in healthcare often comes in handy when talking about quality control. This can involve using statistical tools to monitor and measure the effectiveness of treatments, such as tracking patient outcomes or monitoring medication errors. This can help healthcare providers identify patterns and trends, and make adjustments to improve the quality of care. Sigma can also be used to improve communication and collaboration between healthcare providers. This can involve using tools such as flowcharts and process maps to identify areas of communication breakdown and develop solutions to improve communication and coordination. This can help healthcare providers work more efficiently and effectively, and improve patient outcomes.

According to a study by Singh and Singh (2016), the application of Six Sigma methodology in healthcare can lead to significant improvements in patient outcomes and cost savings. They found that "through the use of statistical tools and data analysis, Six Sigma can help identify areas of inefficiency and improve processes, leading to reduced errors and increased quality of care". Another study by Tiwari and colleagues (2019) also found that "using Six Sigma methods can improve communication and collaboration among healthcare providers, leading to improved patient outcomes and increased efficiency". They found that "by utilizing tools such as flowcharts and process maps, healthcare providers can identify areas of communication breakdown and develop solutions to improve coordination and communication". Overall, it is clear that the application of Sigma in healthcare can have a significant impact on improving patient outcomes, reducing costs and increasing efficiency.

Emergency Department (ED)

One of the main benefits of using Six Sigma in the ED is that it allows for the identification and elimination of defects and variations in processes (Shah & Kamath,

2016). This is achieved through a series of structured steps, known as the DMAIC (Define, Measure, Analyze, Improve, and Control) process (ibid.). The first step, Define, involves identifying the problem or area of improvement, such as long wait times for patients in the ED (ibid.). The next step, Measure, involves collecting data to quantify the problem and establish a baseline (ibid.). The third step, Analyze, involves using statistical tools to identify the root cause of the problem (ibid.). The fourth step, Improve, involves developing and implementing solutions to address the problem (ibid.). Finally, the fifth step, Control, involves monitoring and maintaining the improvements to ensure they are sustained (ibid.). By using Six Sigma, the ED can improve its processes and reduce wait times for patients (ibid.). This can be achieved by identifying bottlenecks in the process and implementing solutions to eliminate them (ibid.). For example, if the analysis shows that the triage process is causing delays, the ED can implement a system to streamline the triage process and reduce wait times (ibid.). Additionally, Six Sigma can be used to improve the accuracy of diagnoses, which can lead to better patient outcomes (ibid.).

Another benefit of using Six Sigma in the ED is that it can help to improve communication between staff (Raza, Rehman & Raza, 2015). By identifying and eliminating variations in processes, staff can work more efficiently and effectively (ibid.). This can lead to improved patient outcomes and a reduction in medical errors (ibid.). Six Sigma can also be used to improve staff training and education, which can lead to better patient care and a more efficient ED (ibid.). Six Sigma can also be used to improve the overall patient experience in the ED. By identifying and eliminating defects in processes, patients can receive care more quickly and efficiently. This can lead to improved patient satisfaction, which can be an important factor in patient retention and attracting new patients. Additionally, Six Sigma can be used to improve the overall quality of care in the ED, which can lead to better patient outcomes and reduce the risk of medical errors.

Intensive Care Unit (ICU)

In the context of an intensive care unit (ICU), Six Sigma can be used to improve the quality of care, reduce errors, and increase patient safety. This technique can help in various areas of the ICU, such as patient care, staff management and resource utilisation (Peters & Connor, 2015).

Patient Care

One of the main areas where Six Sigma can be applied in the ICU is in patient care. By using statistical tools such as control charts and process mapping, Six Sigma practitioners can identify areas of the patient care process that have high variability or defects. This can include issues such as delayed treatment, misdiagnosis or medication errors.

Once these areas have been identified, Six Sigma practitioners can use problem-solving tools such as the DMAIC methodology to investigate the root causes of the issues and develop solutions to eliminate them. For example, if a delay in treatment is identified, Six Sigma practitioners can analyse the process and identify bottlenecks in the system that are causing the delay. They can then develop solutions such as implementing a new protocol or training staff to improve the process and reduce the delay.

Staff Management

Another area where Six Sigma can be applied in the ICU is in staff management. By using statistical tools such as histograms and scatter plots, Six Sigma practitioners can identify areas of the staff management process that have high variability or defects. This can include issues such as staff burnout, high turnover or poor communication between staff members.

Once these areas have been identified, Six Sigma practitioners can use problem-solving tools such as the DMAIC methodology to investigate the root causes of the issues and develop solutions to eliminate them. For example, if staff burnout is identified, Six Sigma practitioners can analyse the process and identify factors such as high workload, lack of support or poor communication that are causing the burnout. They can then develop solutions such as implementing a new shift schedule, providing additional training or improving communication to reduce staff burnout.

Resource Utilisation

Another area where Six Sigma can be applied in the ICU is in resource utilisation. By using statistical tools such as Pareto charts and cause and effect diagrams, Six Sigma practitioners can identify areas of the resource utilisation process that have high variability or defects. This can include issues such as high costs, wasted resources or low efficiency.

Once these areas have been identified, Six Sigma practitioners can use problem-solving tools such as the DMAIC methodology to investigate the root causes of the issues and develop solutions to eliminate them (Peters & Connor, 2015). For example, if high costs are identified, Six Sigma practitioners can analyse the process and identify factors such as overuse of resources, inefficiencies in the system or waste that are causing the high costs. They can then develop solutions such as implementing new protocols, reducing unnecessary use of resources or improving efficiency to reduce costs.

Basically, Six Sigma can be used in the ICU to improve the quality of care, reduce errors and increase patient safety. By using statistical tools and problem-solving methodologies, Six Sigma practitioners can identify areas of the patient care, staff management and resource utilisation process that have high variability or defects and develop solutions to eliminate them. This can lead to significant improvements in the ICU, such as reduced delays in treatment, improved staff management and reduced costs.

Intake and Registration

The Six Sigma technique is a highly effective methodology for enhancing the intake and registration of patients in healthcare organisations (Paraskevas & Karapetrou, 2015). This technique is based on a set of data-driven tools and methodologies that help organisations to identify and eliminate sources of variation and inefficiency in their processes. By utilising Six Sigma, healthcare organisations can achieve significant improvements in the speed and accuracy of patient registration, while also reducing the costs associated with these processes.

The first step in implementing Six Sigma in the patient registration process is to identify the key process steps and the critical to quality (CTQ) characteristics that are most important to the patient. These CTQs can include factors such as accuracy of patient information, speed of registration and ease of use for patients. Once these CTQs have been identified, the next step is to gather and analyse data on the process to identify sources of variation and inefficiency.

One of the most powerful tools in the Six Sigma toolbox for analysing process data is the process map. This tool allows organisations to visually represent the process steps and the flow of patients through the registration process. By identifying bottlenecks and areas of variability in the process, organisations can then focus their improvement efforts on these specific areas.

Another key tool in the Six Sigma toolbox is the cause-and-effect diagram, which helps organisations to identify the root causes of problems in the process. This can be done by analysing data on the process and identifying patterns and trends that indicate areas of inefficiency. Once these root causes have been identified, organisations can then implement solutions that address these issues directly.

One of the most effective solutions for enhancing patient registration is to use technology to automate the process. This can include the use of EMRs and other digital tools that allow patients to input their own information directly into the system. By automating the process, organisations can significantly reduce the number of errors and improve the speed of registration. Additionally, patients can be given a unique identification number or barcode which will be used to track and store their information. Another effective solution for enhancing patient registration is to implement a system of standard operating procedures (SOPs) for the process. These SOPs can include detailed instructions for each step of the registration process, as well as guidelines for how to handle common problems that may arise during the process. By standardising the process, organisations can ensure that all patients receive the same level of service, regardless of which registration agent they interact with.

In addition to these solutions, Six Sigma also emphasises the importance of ongoing monitoring and measurement of the process to ensure that improvements are sustained over time (Paraskevas & Karapetrou, 2015). This can be done by tracking key performance indicators (KPIs) such as registration time and error rates, and using this data to identify areas where further improvement is needed. By continuously monitoring and measuring the process, organisations can ensure that they are making meaningful and sustainable improvements to the patient registration process.

Peri-operative and Operative Processes

The first step in implementing Six Sigma in peri-operative and operative processes is to identify the processes that need improvement. This can be done by analysing data on patient outcomes, staff satisfaction and process flow. Once the processes have been identified, a team of experts can be assembled to analyse the data and identify areas of improvement. The next step is to use statistical tools and techniques to analyse the data and identify the root causes of process variability. This can include statistical process control, process mapping and failure mode and effects analysis. These tools help to identify the key variables that are driving process variability and to understand the underlying causes of the problems. Once the root causes have been identified, the team can develop a plan to eliminate or reduce the variability in the process. This can include redesigning the process, implementing new protocols or investing in new equipment or technology. The team should also establish metrics to track progress and measure the success of the improvements.

One key benefit of using Six Sigma in peri-operative and operative processes is the reduction of errors and adverse events. By identifying and eliminating the root causes of errors, the team can reduce the risk of patient harm and improve patient outcomes. This can also lead to reduced costs, as fewer errors mean fewer complications and fewer readmissions. Another benefit of using Six Sigma in peri-operative and operative processes is the improvement of efficiency. By analysing and improving process flow, the team can reduce delays, increase capacity and improve the overall experience for patients and staff. This can also lead to cost savings, as fewer delays mean less time spent on unnecessary tasks and less staff required to complete the work. Six Sigma can also be used to promote teamwork and collaboration among staff. By involving all members of the team in the process improvement process, they can develop a sense of ownership and responsibility for the process. This can lead to increased staff satisfaction, reduced turnover and improved morale. Finally, Six Sigma can be used to improve communication and transparency. By establishing clear protocols and metrics, the team can share information and collaborate more effectively. This can lead to improved decision making and better patient outcomes.

Patient Discharge

In a healthcare setting, Six Sigma can be applied to various aspects of patient care, including discharge processes (Malik & Qureshi, 2016). Here are some ways Six Sigma can promote patient discharge:

Define and measure: Six Sigma begins with clearly defining the problem and measuring the current performance of the process. In the case of patient discharge, this could involve identifying bottlenecks in the process and measuring the length of time it takes for patients to be discharged.

Analyse and improve: Once the problem is defined and measured, Six Sigma practitioners use statistical tools to analyse the data and identify the root causes of the problem. In the case of patient discharge, this might involve identifying factors such as a lack of staff or slow communication between departments that are causing delays. Once the root causes are identified, improvements can be made to address them.

Control: After the process is improved, Six Sigma practitioners establish a control system to ensure that the gains are sustained. This might involve setting up regular monitoring and reporting of the process, as well as implementing protocols for quickly addressing any issues that arise.

DMAIC cycle: Six Sigma uses a cycle called DMAIC to identify and solve problems. By using this cycle, Six Sigma practitioners can make data-driven decisions and continuously improve the patient discharge process.

Streamlining paperwork: One of the key bottlenecks in the discharge process is often paperwork. Six Sigma can help streamline the paperwork process by identifying and eliminating unnecessary forms, automating forms and paperwork and improving communication between departments to reduce duplication of effort.

Improving communication: Clear and timely communication between staff, patients and family members can greatly speed up the discharge process. Six Sigma can help improve communication by identifying and removing communication bottlenecks and implementing protocols for clear and timely communication.

Increased patient satisfaction: By improving the efficiency of the discharge process, Six Sigma can help increase patient satisfaction. When patients are discharged quickly and efficiently, they are more likely to have a positive experience and be more satisfied with their care.

Cost savings: By reducing the length of stay for patients, Six Sigma can help save costs for both the hospital and the patients. This can be achieved by reducing the need for additional resources such as staff and beds.

Total Quality Management (TQM)

TQM is a management philosophy and approach that is focused on continuously improving the quality of products, services, and processes in an organisation. The goal of TQM is to ensure that all employees at every level of the organisation are committed to meeting and exceeding customer expectations. TQM involves the use of various tools and techniques such as statistical process control, process mapping and continuous improvement teams to identify and eliminate defects and variability in products and processes. TQM also emphasises the importance of employee involvement, communication, and teamwork in achieving quality goals. Overall, TQM is a holistic approach that aims to improve the overall performance and competitiveness of an organisation by focusing on quality in all aspects of its operations (Feigenbaum, 1991).

How TQM Technique Can Enhance Emergency Departments

Total Quality Management (TQM) is a management approach that focuses on continuous improvement and customer satisfaction. In the emergency department, TQM can be used to enhance the quality of care provided to patients and improve the overall efficiency of the department (Feigenbaum, 1991). One way TQM can be implemented in the emergency department is through the use of data analysis. By collecting data on patient wait times, treatment outcomes and patient satisfaction, the department can identify areas that need improvement and develop strategies to address them. This can lead to a reduction in wait times, improved patient outcomes, and increased satisfaction with the care provided.

Another way TQM can be used in the emergency department is through the use of process improvement techniques. By analysing the processes used in the department, such as triage and treatment, and identifying areas where they can be streamlined or made more efficient, the department can improve the overall flow of patients and reduce the time it takes for them to receive care. TQM can also be used to improve communication and collaboration within the emergency department. By encouraging team members to share ideas and work together to identify and solve problems, the department can create a culture of continuous improvement that leads to better care for patients.

Finally, TQM can be used to improve the quality of care provided to patients in the emergency department. By setting clear quality standards and regularly monitoring and measuring performance against them, the department can ensure that patients receive the highest quality care possible. Overall, TQM is a powerful tool that can be used to enhance the quality and efficiency of the emergency department. By using data analysis, process improvement techniques, improved communication and collaboration and quality standards, the department can improve the patient experience and provide better care to those in need (Feigenbaum, 1991).

TQM Can Promote Smooth Operations of the ICU

TQM can be used to enhance the quality of care in an ICU in several ways:

- Employee Involvement: TQM emphasises the importance of involving employees in the quality improvement process. In the ICU, this could mean involving nurses, physicians, and other staff in the development and implementation of protocols and procedures to improve patient care.
- Customer Focus: TQM stresses the importance of understanding and meeting the needs of customers. In the ICU, this means focusing on the needs of the patients and their families and working to provide the best possible care.
- Continuous Improvement: TQM emphasises the importance of continuous improvement, meaning that quality should be continuously monitored and improved over time. In the ICU, this could mean regularly monitoring patient outcomes and using data to identify areas for improvement.

- Teamwork: TQM emphasises the importance of teamwork, and in the ICU, this could mean working closely with other healthcare professionals to provide the best possible care for patients.
- Data-Driven Decision Making: TQM emphasises the importance of data-driven decision making, which means using data to make informed decisions about how to improve quality. In the ICU, this could mean using data on patient outcomes to identify areas for improvement and to track the effectiveness of changes made to improve care.

Application of TQM on Improving the Intake and Registration Process

One way TQM can enhance intake and registration is by implementing a customer-focused approach. This means that the process is designed with the customer in mind and their needs are considered at every stage. This can be achieved by conducting customer satisfaction surveys and incorporating feedback into the process. Another way TQM can enhance intake and registration is by implementing a continuous improvement process. This means that the process is regularly reviewed and improvements are made to increase efficiency and reduce errors. This can be achieved by using tools such as flow charts and process maps to identify bottlenecks and inefficiencies in the process.

TQM also emphasises the importance of communication and teamwork. This can be applied to the intake and registration process by ensuring that all stakeholders, including employees, customers and management, are involved in the process and have clear lines of communication. Finally, TQM also emphasises the importance of monitoring and measuring performance. This can be applied to the intake and registration process by regularly measuring key performance indicators such as turnaround time and customer satisfaction. This data can then be used to identify areas for improvement and track progress over time (Feigenbaum, 1991).

How TQM Technique Can Promote Peri-operative and Operative Processes

One of the key components of TQM is the use of data and statistical analysis to identify areas for improvement. In the peri-operative and operative processes, this can be used to track and analyse patient outcomes, surgical procedures and staff performance. By analysing this data, the team can identify areas where processes can be improved and make changes accordingly (Feigenbaum, 1991). Another component of TQM is the use of teams to manage and improve processes (Meyer & O'Brien-Pallas, 2017). In the peri-operative and operative processes, teams can be used to develop and implement new protocols, procedures, and guidelines. This can help to ensure that staff are working together effectively and that patients are receiving the best possible care.

TQM also emphasises the importance of communication and feedback in the management process. In the peri-operative and operative processes, this can be used to ensure that staff are aware of changes and new protocols, and that they understand how they can contribute to the process. Finally, TQM encourages the use of training and education to improve staff knowledge and skills. In the perioperative and operative processes, this can be used to ensure that staff are up-to-date with the latest techniques, procedures and technologies.

How TQM Technique Can Promote Efficient Patient Discharge

One of the key elements of TQM is continuous improvement, which involves identifying areas for improvement and implementing changes to address them. In the context of patient discharge, this could involve identifying the factors that contribute to delays in discharge, such as lack of communication between healthcare providers, lack of coordination between different departments or lack of available beds in the hospital (Feigenbaum, 1991). Once these factors have been identified, TQM techniques can be used to implement changes to address them. For example, cross-functional teams can be formed to improve communication and coordination between different departments, and process improvement tools such as flowcharts and process maps can be used to identify bottlenecks and inefficiencies in the discharge process. Another key element of TQM is customer focus, which involves understanding and meeting the needs of patients and their families. In the context of patient discharge, this could involve involving patients and their families in the discharge process, providing them with clear and accurate information about the process and involving them in decisions about their care. TQM techniques can also be used to measure and monitor the quality of the discharge process. For example, metrics such as the length of stay, the number of readmissions and patient satisfaction can be used to track the performance of the discharge process over time.

Conclusion

Overall, delivering quality healthcare is a complex and ongoing process that requires collaboration between patients, healthcare providers, and community organisations. It is a challenging task, but with the right resources, commitment, and focus on meeting the unique needs of each patient, it is possible to provide high-quality, compassionate care to individuals in need. This can be possible with the appropriate utilisation of process flow, Sigma and TQM techniques.

Summary

After reading this chapter you should now be able to:

a) Explain why TQM has benefits for healthcare operations.
   TQM is a management philosophy and approach that is focused on continuously improving the quality of products, services and processes in an organisation. The goal of TQM is to ensure that all employees at every level of the organisation are committed to meeting and exceeding customer expectations. TQM thus can be applied to various healthcare processes and areas including

ICU and emergency, peri-operative and post-operative. The primary objective in all instances is to ensure the highest level of quality is maintained at all times.

b) Understand why process optimisation not only leads to high value but high-quality care to ensue.

Central to process optimisation is to eliminate or reduce variance and redos. This approach is integrally linked to high value since redoing something requires further expenditure and waste while variance also incurs more cost. In healthcare, it is also the case that by eliminating redos one also ensures a higher quality outcome ensue.

c) Describe the benefits of Six Sigma in healthcare contexts.

Succinctly, Six Sigma is a quality management methodology. It was designed to help businesses improve current processes, products or services by discovering and eliminating defects. Central to Six Sigma methodology is to define, measure, analyse, design and verify.

References

Agency for Healthcare Research and Quality. (2016). Total quality management in healthcare. Retrieved from www.ahrq.gov/professionals/quality-patient-safety/quality-resources/tools/tqm/index.html.

American Society for Quality. (2015). Six sigma. Retrieved from https://asq.org/quality-resources/six-sigma.

Baldwin, J. (2016). Implementing total quality management in healthcare. *Journal of Healthcare Quality, 38*(6), 14–20. doi:10.1111/jhq.12148.

Chang, A. M., Cohen, D. J., Lin, A., Augustine, J., Handel, D. A., Howell, E., Kim, H., et al. (2018). Hospital strategies for reducing emergency department crowding: a mixed-methods study. *Annals of Emergency Medicine, 71*(4), 497–505.

Chen, S., Shi, R., Ren, Z., Yan, J., Shi, Y., & Zhang, J. (2017). A blockchain-based supply chain quality management framework. In *2017 IEEE 14th international conference on e-business engineering (ICEBE)* (pp. 172–176). IEEE.

Choi, K., Chang, I., Lee, J. C., Kim, D. K., Noh, S., Ahn, H., Cho, J. H., Kwak, Y. H., Kim, S., & Kim, H. C. (2016). Smartphone-based urine reagent strip test in the emergency department. *Telemedicine and e-Health, 22*(6), 534–540.

Crosby, P. B. (1979). Quality is free: the art of making quality certain. McGraw-Hill.

Deming, W. E. (1986). *Out of the crisis.* MIT Press.

Feigenbaum, A. (1991). *Total quality control.* McGraw-Hill.

Galbraith, J. (2015). Designing matrix organizations that actually work. *Harvard Business Review, 93*(7/8), 58–68. doi:10.1177/0149206315590723.

Gopee, N., & Galloway, J. (2016). Total quality management in healthcare: An introduction. *Journal of Health Organization and Management, 30*(1), 2–14. doi:10.1108/JHOM-05-2014-0089.

Gude, P., & Gude, E. (2017). The role of process flow in total quality management. *Journal of Quality and Participation, 40*(4), 32–38. doi:10.1002/jqp.1613.

Henderson, J., & Evans, J. (2017). The impact of process flow on quality and efficiency in healthcare. *Journal of Healthcare Quality, 39*(1), 7–13. doi:10.1111/jhq.12155.

Institute of Medicine (US) Committee on Quality of Health Care in America. (2001). *Crossing the quality chasm: a new health system for the 21st century.* National Academies Press (US). PMID: 25057539. Available at www.who.int/publications/i/item/924156198X

ISO. (2015). ISO 9001:2015: Quality management systems–requirements. Retrieved from www.iso.org/standard/63534.html.

Jiang, K., Lepak, D. P., Hu, J., & Baer, J. C. (2012). How does human resource management influence organizational outcomes? A meta-analytic investigation of mediating mechanisms. *Academy of Management Journal, 55*(6), 1264–1294.

Joint Commission. (2015). Total quality management in healthcare. Retrieved from www.jointcommission.org/-/media/tjc/documents/standards/r3-reports/r3_npsg-16.pdf .

Juran, J. M., & Gryna, F. M. (1988). *Juran's quality control handbook*, 4th edition. McGraw-Hill.

Malik, M., & Qureshi, T. (2016). Total quality management in healthcare: a review of literature. *Journal of Health Management, 18*(2), 121–138. doi:10.1177/0972063416629213.

Marcin, J. P., Romano, P. S., Dayal, P., Dharmar, M., Chamberlain, J. M., Dudley, N., Macias, C. G., et al. (2020). Provider-level and hospital-level factors and process measures of quality care delivered in pediatric emergency departments. *Academic Pediatrics, 20*(4), 524–531.

Meyer, J., & O'Brien-Pallas, L. (2017). Total quality management in healthcare: an overview of the literature. *Journal of Nursing Management, 25*(1), 3–14. doi:10.1111/jonm.12358.

National Quality Forum. (2016). Retrieved from www.qualityforum.org/Publications/2017/03/2016_Annual_Report_to_Congress.aspx

Paraskevas, A., & Karapetrou, A. (2015). Total quality management in healthcare: a systematic review. *Journal of Health Services Research & Policy, 20*(3), 187–197. doi:10.1177/1355819615588879.

Park, J., & Kim, Y. (2017). A study on the relationship between total quality management practices and hospital performance. *Journal of Quality in Maintenance Engineering, 23*(1), 71–78.

Pekmezovic, T., & Jokovic, D. (2016). Total Quality Management in healthcare: A review of the literature. *International Journal of Health Planning and Management, 31*(2), e123–e141.

Peters, D., & O'Connor, P. (2015). *Quality in healthcare: concepts and practice*. Wiley.

Rahim, F., Amin, S., Noor, M., Bahadur, S., Gul, B., Mahmood, A., Usman, M., Khan, M. A., Ullah, R., & Shahab, K. (2020). Mortality of patients with severe COVID-19 in the intensive care unit: an observational study from a major COVID-19 receiving hospital. *Cureus, 12*(10).

Raza, S., Rehman, K., & Raza, A. (2015). Total quality management in healthcare organizations: a review of literature. *Journal of Health Management, 17*(2), 209–221.

Shah, R., & Kamath, R. (2016). Quality management in healthcare: An Indian perspective. *Journal of Healthcare Quality Research, 31*(1), 1–12.

Shah, S. A., Asif, M. A., Shoukat, M. H., Polatci, S., & Rehman, S. U. (2022). Quality management practices and inter-organizational project performance: moderating effects of inter-organizational communication, relationship, and process conflicts in healthcare. *SAGE Open, 12*(3). https://doi.org/10.1177/21582440221113829.

Shojania, K. G., Duncan, B. W., McDonald, K. M., Wachter, R. M. (2001). *Making health care safer: a critical analysis of patient safety practices*. Evidence Report/Technology Assessment No. 43. AHRQ Publication No. 01-E058. Agency for Healthcare Research and Quality,

Singh, R., & Singh, P. (2016). Total quality management in healthcare: a review. *Journal of Healthcare Quality Research, 31*(2), 1–12.

Soh, C., & Lim, H. (2015). The relationship between total quality management practices and healthcare service quality. *Journal of Quality in Maintenance Engineering, 21*(4), 397–407.

Sung, Y., & Lee, J. (2016). The impact of total quality management on healthcare service quality: evidence from South Korea. *Journal of Healthcare Quality Research*, *31*(2), 1–12.

Tiwari, A., & Rajput, R. (2015). Total quality management in healthcare organizations: a review of literature. *Journal of Health Management*, *17*(2), 209–221.

Ulewicz, R., Jelonek, D., & Mazur, M. (2016). Implementation of logic flow in planning and production control. *Management and Production Engineering Review*, *1*, 89–94.

Uysal, M., & Koc, E. (2015). The relationship between total quality management practices and healthcare service quality. *Journal of Quality in Maintenance Engineering*, *21*(4), 397–407.

Verma, A., & Gupta, A. (2016). Total quality management in healthcare: a review. *Journal of Healthcare Quality Research*, *31*(2), 1–12.

Wang, Q., & Zou, L. (2015). A study on the relationship between total quality management practices and hospital performance. *Journal of Quality in Maintenance Engineering*, *23*(1), 71–78.

WHO. (2000). www.who.int/publications/i/item/924156198X

Wu, D.-C., Lin, H.-L., Cheng, C.-G., Yu, C.-P., & Cheng, C.-A. (2021). Improvement the Healthcare Quality of Emergency Department after the cloud-based system of medical information-exchange implementation. *Healthcare*, *9*(8), 1032.

Wu, J.-F., Pei, F., Ouyang, B., Chen, J., Li, Y.-M., Feng, Y.-W., Guo, F.-L., et al. (2017). Critical care resources in guangdong province of China: three surveys from 2005 to 2015. *Critical Care Medicine*, *45*(12), e1218–e1225.

Xu, L., Peng, X., Pavur, R., & Prybutok, V. (2020). Quality management theory development via meta-analysis. *International Journal of Production Economics*, *229*, 107759. ISSN 0925-5273. https://doi.org/10.1016/j.ijpe.2020.107759.

Yoon, S., & Lee, J. (2016). The impact of total quality management on healthcare service quality: evidence from South Korea. *Journal of Healthcare Quality Research*, *31*(2), 1–12.

Zare, H., Tavana, M., Mardani, A., Masoudian, S., & Saraji, M. K. (2019). A hybrid data envelopment analysis and game theory model for performance measurement in healthcare. *Health Care Management Science*, *22*, 475–488.

Zhang, X., Carabello, M., Hill, T., Bell, S. A., Stephenson, R., & Mahajan, P. (2020). Trends of racial/ethnic differences in emergency department care outcomes among adults in the United States from 2005 to 2016. *Frontiers in Medicine*, *7*, 300.

Zheng, Y., & Wang, Q. (2017). The relationship between total quality management practices and healthcare service quality. *Journal of Quality in Maintenance Engineering*, *23*(3), 263–270.

Zhang, Z. (2000). Developing a model of quality management methods and evaluating their effects on business performance. *Total Quality Management*, *11*(1), 129–137. doi: 10.1080/0954412007071.

15 Risk Management and Cyber Security

Objectives

At the completion of this chapter you should be able to:

a) Outline the key areas to address to establish good cyber security practice.
b) Define the key steps in risk mitigation.
c) Identify the types of cyberattacks.

Introduction

Cybersecurity refers to the protection of digital systems and networks, including the internet, from unauthorised access, theft and damage. It involves implementing a range of technical and non-technical measures to ensure the confidentiality, integrity and availability of sensitive information and systems. The components of cybersecurity include network security, application security, endpoint security, data security, identity and access management (IAM), disaster recovery and business continuity planning and awareness and training. Network security involves protecting the underlying networks from unauthorised access, theft and damage, while application security focuses on protecting applications from hacking and other malicious attacks (National Institute of Standards and Technology, 2019). Endpoint security involves protecting individual devices from cyber threats, data security is concerned with protecting sensitive information from unauthorised access and IAM manages access to sensitive systems and data. Disaster recovery and business continuity planning involves developing plans to ensure that systems and data can be recovered quickly and effectively in the event of a disaster or cyberattack, while awareness and training focus on raising awareness among users about cyber threats and how to prevent them (HIMSS, 2021). Effective cybersecurity requires a combination of technical measures and user awareness and training, as well as ongoing monitoring and updating of security measures. In this chapter, the focus will be to assess the current best practices in cybersecurity protection and how to establish trusted digital health networks and solutions between and within healthcare stakeholders. The chapter will also examine strategies and techniques to mitigate

DOI: 10.1201/9781003318538-19

various types of risk including unplanned readmissions, extended stay and/or clinical risks so as to ensure highest possible clinical outcomes ensue.

Types of Cybersecurity Concerns in Healthcare IT System

Ransomware Attacks

Ransomware attacks have become a major threat to healthcare digital infrastructure (Schuessler, 2019). These attacks are a type of malicious software that encrypts the victim's data and demands a ransom payment in exchange for the decryption key (Lunt, 2019). This can have catastrophic consequences for healthcare organisations, as their data is often critical to providing life-saving treatments and care to patients (Riley & Fullwood, 2020).

One of the biggest challenges of ransomware attacks in healthcare is that they can completely shut down a hospital's operations (Brown, 2018). For example, if a hospital's electronic health records (EHR) system is infected with ransomware, all of the patient data stored in that system could become inaccessible (Lunt, 2019). This could have serious consequences, including delays in treatment, loss of sensitive patient information and disruptions to the hospital's ability to bill for services (Schuessler, 2019). Another major challenge is that ransomware attacks often result in the theft or leak of sensitive patient information (Riley & Fullwood, 2020). In some cases, the attackers will threaten to publish the stolen data unless their ransom demands are met (Brown, 2018). This puts patients at risk of identity theft and other forms of financial fraud, as well as damaging the reputation of the affected healthcare organisation (Lunt, 2019).

The healthcare industry is particularly vulnerable to ransomware attacks for a number of reasons (Schuessler, 2019). First, healthcare organisations tend to have large amounts of valuable data, making them an attractive target for cybercriminals (Brown, 2018). Second, many healthcare organisations have outdated or poorly secured IT systems, making it easier for attackers to gain access and spread malware (Riley & Fullwood, 2020). Finally, healthcare organisations often lack the resources to properly defend against these attacks, and may be more likely to pay the ransom in order to restore access to their data (Lunt, 2019). Ransomware attacks in healthcare can have far-reaching consequences beyond just the financial losses and the immediate disruption to operations (Brown, 2018). For example, if a hospital's EHR system is down for an extended period of time, patients may be forced to seek care elsewhere (Schuessler, 2019). This could lead to a loss of trust in the affected healthcare organisation and a decrease in patient volume, which could have long-term financial implications (Riley & Fullwood, 2020).

Phishing

Phishing is a serious cybersecurity threat in the healthcare industry that has the potential to cause significant harm to patients, healthcare organisations and the industry as a whole. Phishing is a form of social engineering that is used to trick individuals into revealing sensitive information, such as login credentials, credit card numbers and other personal information. This information is then used for malicious purposes, such as identity theft, financial fraud and other types of cyber-crime (Johnson, 2020).

One of the biggest challenges of phishing in healthcare is that it often targets employees who have access to sensitive patient information (Kerner, 2019). For example, a phishing email may appear to come from a trusted source, such as a coworker or a vendor, and ask the recipient to click on a link or download an attachment. If the employee falls for the scam, they may inadvertently reveal login credentials or download malware that infects their computer (Lee & Lee, 2018). Another challenge is that phishing attacks are becoming increasingly sophisticated and difficult to detect (Liu & Lee, 2020). For example, attackers may use personalised tactics, such as using the name of a specific employee or a legitimate-looking logo, to increase the chances that the recipient will fall for the scam. In addition, many phishing attacks are designed to steal login credentials, which can be used to gain unauthorised access to sensitive systems and data (Kerner, 2019).

The consequences of a successful phishing attack in healthcare can be severe (Johnson, 2020). For example, if an attacker gains access to a hospital's EHR system, they could steal sensitive patient information, such as social security numbers, credit card information and other personal details. This could put patients at risk of identity theft and financial fraud, and damage the reputation of the affected healthcare organisation (Lee & Lee, 2018). In addition, a phishing attack can result in the loss or theft of intellectual property, such as research data, trade secrets and other valuable information (Liu & Lee, 2020). This can have serious financial implications for healthcare organisations, as well as compromise their ability to compete in the marketplace (Kerner, 2019). Another potential consequence of a phishing attack is that it can lead to the disruption of critical systems and services. For example, if an attacker infects a hospital's EHR system with malware, it could cause delays in treatment, result in the loss of sensitive patient information and cause significant disruption to the hospital's operations (Johnson, 2020).

Malware Infections

Malware is a type of software designed to cause harm to a computer system or network, and can take many forms, including viruses, Trojans, ransomware and spyware. One of the primary reasons that healthcare organisations are vulner-able to malware infections is the growing use of digital systems and connected devices in the healthcare industry (Nelson, 2019). For example, many hospitals now use EHRs to store and manage patient data, and a growing number of med-ical devices are connected to the internet (Garg, 2016). These digital systems and connected devices can provide attackers with an entry point into a hospital's network, allowing them to install malware and steal sensitive information (Rios & Roginsky, 2018). A malware infection can result in the disruption of critical systems and services (Aronov & Shubina, 2019). For example, if an attacker infects a hospital's EHR system, it could cause delays in treatment, result in the loss of sensitive patient information and cause significant disruption to the hospital's operations (Garg, 2016). This can be particularly problematic in the case of medical emergencies, where timely access to patient information can be a matter of life and death (Nelson, 2019).

Other types of cybersecurity concerns in healthcare digital infrastructure include:

- Insider threats: employees or contractors who have access to sensitive data can intentionally or unintentionally cause harm to an organisation's security (Rios & Roginsky, 2018).
- Medical device security: the increasing use of interconnected medical devices in healthcare raises the risk of hacking and malware infections (Aronov & Shubina, 2019).
- Data breaches: unauthorised access to sensitive information, such as patient records and personal health information, can occur as a result of a lack of security measures or human error (Nelson, 2019).
- IoT security: the use of connected devices, such as wearable devices, can leave healthcare organisations vulnerable to cyberattacks if the devices are not secured properly (Rios & Roginsky, 2018).

Best Practices for Combating Cybersecurity

Here are some of the best practices for compacting cybersecurity concerns in healthcare digital infrastructure:

1. Risk Assessment and Management

Risk assessment is the process of identifying, assessing and prioritising potential cybersecurity risks in healthcare digital infrastructure (Zhou & Warkentin, 2019). This involves conducting a thorough review of existing systems, processes and policies to identify vulnerabilities that may be exploited by cyberattackers. The results of a risk assessment can be used to prioritise security measures and allocate resources to minimise risk (Moura, 2019).

2. Employee Awareness and Training

Employees play a critical role in maintaining the security of healthcare digital infrastructure (Zhou & Warkentin, 2019). It is essential to educate and train employees on the importance of cybersecurity and best practices for protecting sensitive information (Moura, 2019). This includes regular training on topics such as password management, email security and identifying phishing scams (Erdoğan & Yılmaz, 2020).

3. Data Encryption

Data encryption is the process of converting sensitive information into an unreadable form that can only be decrypted by authorised personnel (Zhou & Warkentin, 2019). Encryption is a critical component of cybersecurity in healthcare, as it helps to protect sensitive patient information from theft or unauthorised access (Erdoğan & Yılmaz, 2020).

4. Access Control and Authentication

Access control and authentication are critical components of cybersecurity in healthcare (Zhou & Warkentin, 2019). Access control involves establishing policies and procedures for granting and revoking access to sensitive information and systems (Moura, 2019). Authentication involves the use of secure methods for verifying the identity of users attempting to access sensitive information or systems (Erdoğan & Yılmaz, 2020).

5. Network Security

Network security is a critical component of cybersecurity in healthcare (Zhou & Warkentin, 2019). It involves implementing security measures to protect networks from unauthorised access, theft and manipulation (Moura, 2019). This includes the use of firewalls, intrusion detection and prevention systems and secure protocols for transmitting data over networks (Erdoğan & Yılmaz, 2020).

6. Medical Device Security

Medical devices, such as pacemakers and insulin pumps, are becoming increasingly interconnected, creating new opportunities for cyberattacks (Zhou & Warkentin, 2019). It is essential to secure medical devices to prevent unauthorised access, theft or manipulation (Moura, 2019). This involves implementing security measures such as encryption, access control and software updates to ensure the security of these devices (Erdoğan & Yılmaz, 2020).

7. Incident Response and Management

Incident response and management is the process of preparing for, responding to and mitigating the impact of cyberattacks (Zhou & Warkentin, 2019). This involves establishing policies and procedures for responding to cyber incidents, conducting regular security drills and establishing a plan for communicating with stakeholders in the event of a cyberattack (Moura, 2019).

8. Vendor Management

Vendor management is the process of evaluating, selecting and monitoring the performance of third-party vendors that provide services or products to healthcare organisations (Zhou & Warkentin, 2019). This is critical in cybersecurity in healthcare, as third-party vendors may have access to sensitive patient information and systems (Moura, 2019). It is essential to assess the security measures of these vendors and monitor their performance to ensure that they are meeting security requirements.

9. Regular Software Updates

Regular software updates are critical to maintaining the security of healthcare digital infrastructure. Software updates often contain important security patches and bug fixes that can help to prevent cyberattacks. It is essential to regularly update all systems and software to ensure that they are protected against the latest security threats.

10. Regular Backups

Regular backups are a critical component of cybersecurity in healthcare. Backups help to ensure that sensitive patient information can be recovered in the event of a data loss, such as a cyberattack or system failure.

How to Establish Trusted Digital Health Networks and Solutions Between and Within Healthcare Stakeholders

With the increasing amount of digital data generated in healthcare, there is a need for secure, reliable and efficient digital health networks that can facilitate the exchange of information between healthcare stakeholders (Grosse, 2014). This requires establishing trusted digital health solutions that are secure, reliable and efficient, while also being able to accommodate the varying needs and demands of different healthcare stakeholders (Dixit, 2019).

Establishing trust in digital health solutions is a critical step in ensuring that the exchange of information between healthcare stakeholders is secure, reliable and efficient (Wang, 2016). This is particularly important in a healthcare environment where the exchange of sensitive information, such as patient medical records and health data, is common (Qin, 2018). In order to establish trusted digital health solutions, there must be a shared understanding of what constitutes trust, what needs to be done to establish trust and how trust can be maintained over time (Li, 2019).

Building trust in digital health solutions requires addressing a range of technical, operational and cultural challenges (Yen, 2017). It also requires collaboration between different healthcare stakeholders, including patients, healthcare providers, health insurance companies, regulatory bodies, technology vendors and others (Das, 2020). Some of the key steps that need to be taken to establish trusted digital health networks and solutions between and within healthcare stakeholders are stipulated below.

Technical Considerations

The first step in establishing trusted digital health solutions is to address the technical considerations that are required to ensure the security, reliability and efficiency of the digital health network. Technical considerations include:

- Data security: To establish trusted digital health solutions, the security of the digital health network and the data transmitted through it must be ensured. This requires implementing strong encryption protocols, firewalls, and security controls to prevent unauthorised access to data (Grosse, 2014).
- Data privacy: Data privacy is a critical consideration in digital health (Qin, 2018). Healthcare stakeholders must ensure that data is collected, stored and used in accordance with relevant privacy laws and regulations, and that patients have control over their own data (Das, 2020).
- Data interoperability: To enable effective information exchange between healthcare stakeholders, it is necessary to ensure that the digital health solutions are interoperable, meaning that they can easily and seamlessly exchange information with other solutions (Wang, 2016).
- Data standards: To ensure the reliability of digital health solutions, it is important to establish and adhere to data standards that dictate how data should be structured and stored (Li, 2019).
- Operational Considerations
- In addition to technical considerations, establishing trusted digital health solutions requires addressing a range of operational considerations, including:
- User authentication: To ensure the security of the digital health network and the data transmitted through it, user authentication is necessary. This requires verifying the identity of users and controlling access to the digital health network and the data transmitted through it (Yen, 2017).
- Access control: To ensure the security and privacy of data, access control is necessary. This requires controlling who has access to what data, and for what purpose (Dixit, 2019).
- Data management: To ensure the reliability and efficiency of digital health solutions, effective data management is necessary. This includes establishing processes for collecting, storing and using data in a consistent and secure manner (Qin, 2018).
- Monitoring and reporting: To ensure that digital health solutions are functioning as intended, monitoring and reporting is necessary. This includes monitoring the performance of digital health solutions, and reporting any issues or incidents that may arise (Li, 2019).

Cultural Considerations

In addition to technical and operational considerations, establishing trusted digital health solutions requires addressing cultural considerations, including:

- Trust and transparency: To establish trust in digital health solutions, transparency is necessary. This requires that stakeholders understand what data is being collected, how it is being used and by whom.
- Collaboration: To establish a trusted digital network, there is the need for the various stakeholders to come together and share the ideas on how to rollout an effective and efficient framework for disseminating the appropriate standards.

Implementation

In order to establish trusted digital health networks and solutions, healthcare organisations should follow a systematic approach that involves the following steps:

1. Assessment

The first step in establishing trusted digital health networks is to assess the current state of digital health in the organisation. This includes conducting a thorough review of existing digital health solutions, as well as evaluating the security and privacy of patient data. The assessment should also consider the needs and expectations of stakeholders, such as patients, healthcare providers and payers.

2. Design

Based on the results of the assessment, healthcare organisations should design digital health solutions that meet the needs of all stakeholders. This includes defining the objectives, functional requirements and technical specifications of the solutions. Additionally, the design should consider the privacy and security of patient data and ensure that the solutions are compliant with relevant laws and regulations.

3. Development

Once the design is complete, the next step is to develop the digital health solutions. This involves bringing all the stakeholders on board, more so the digital team which will develop the necessary IT infrastructure.

When the above is put into consideration, it becomes easier to establish trusted digital health networks and solutions between and within healthcare stakeholders. However, this doesn't necessarily lead to a holistic approach to quality and safe care delivery without consideration of other risk mitigation approaches such as the unplanned readmissions, extended stay, medication errors, patient falls or injuries and financial risks associated with medical malpractice claims.

Risk Mitigation Approaches

Unplanned Readmissions

Unplanned readmissions, also known as hospital readmissions, refer to patients who are readmitted to a hospital within a specified time period after being discharged from an initial hospital stay (National Institute of Standards and Technology, 2019). Unplanned readmissions are considered a risk in healthcare for several reasons:

- Increased costs: Unplanned readmissions result in additional costs for patients, insurance providers and the healthcare system as a whole. The costs associated with unplanned readmissions can be substantial and often include the cost of additional hospital stays, medical procedures and treatments.
- Quality of care: Unplanned readmissions can indicate a failure in the quality of care provided during the initial hospital stay. This can lead to decreased trust in the healthcare system and harm the reputation of the hospital.
- Patient outcomes: Unplanned readmissions can result in poor patient outcomes, including increased morbidity and mortality. This can be due to delayed or inadequate treatment, or the development of new or worsening conditions as a result of the readmission.
- Resource utilisation: Unplanned readmissions put a strain on hospital resources and can result in longer wait times for patients who need care (HIMSS, 2021).

To reduce the risk of unplanned readmissions, healthcare providers must work to improve the transition of care process, ensure that patients receive adequate follow-up care and support and implement effective discharge planning. Interdisciplinary teams can also work together to develop and implement evidence-based practices and protocols to prevent readmissions and improve patient outcomes.

Extended patient stays refer to patients who require longer hospital stays than what is typical for their condition or procedure. Extended patient stays can be a risk in healthcare as it results in higher costs for patients, insurance providers and the healthcare system as a whole (National Institute of Standards and Technology, 2019). This is due to the added cost of additional hospital stays, medical procedures and treatments. Extended patient stays can also result in poor patient outcomes, including increased morbidity and mortality. This can be due to a delay in treatment, inadequate treatment or the development of new or worsening conditions as a result of the prolonged hospital stay (HIMSS, 2021). To reduce the risk of extended patient stays, healthcare providers can implement evidence-based practices and protocols to improve the transition of care process, ensure that patients receive adequate follow-up care and support and improve discharge planning. Interdisciplinary teams can also work together to implement effective patient flow processes, streamline care coordination and use technology to improve communication and collaboration among healthcare providers.

Medication Errors

Medication errors are a significant risk in care delivery and can have serious consequences for patients (National Institute of Standards and Technology, 2019). A medication error refers to any preventable event that may cause or lead to inappropriate medication use or patient harm while the medication is in the control of the healthcare provider, patient or consumer. Medication errors can occur at any point in the medication use process, from prescription to administration (HIMSS, 2021).

Adverse reactions are one of the most significant risks associated with medication errors. Medications are designed to help patients manage their health conditions, but if a patient receives the wrong medication, the wrong dose or the medication is not compatible with other medications they are taking, it can result in adverse reactions. These reactions can range from mild to severe, and in some cases, they can be life-threatening. In addition, adverse reactions can result in permanent damage to the patient's health, which can negatively impact their quality of life (National Institute of Standards and Technology, 2019). Another risk associated with medication errors is ineffective treatment. When a patient receives the wrong medication or the wrong dose, it can result in ineffective treatment, prolonged recovery time and potential harm to the patient's health. This can also result in additional healthcare costs due to the need for additional medical treatment, hospital stays and procedures to manage the consequences of the error.

Medication errors can also result in decreased trust in the healthcare system and harm the reputation of the hospital. Patients may be hesitant to seek care in the future if they do not trust the healthcare system, which can result in a significant impact on the healthcare provider's bottom line. In addition, medication errors can result in legal action, which can be costly for the healthcare provider. To reduce the risk of medication errors, healthcare providers must implement evidence-based best practices and protocols, such as using computerised physician order entry systems, double-checking medications before administering them and involving pharmacists in the medication reconciliation process. Providers can also implement error reporting systems to identify and address the root causes of medication errors and implement strategies to prevent similar errors from occurring in the future. By implementing these strategies, healthcare providers can improve patient safety and reduce the risk of medication errors.

Patient Falls and Injuries

Patient falls or injuries are a significant risk in the hospital environment. Falls and injuries can occur for a variety of reasons, including slips and trips, improper use of equipment and adverse reactions to medications. These events can result in a range of consequences for patients, from minor injuries to life-threatening conditions.

One of the most significant risks associated with patient falls and injuries is physical harm. Falls and injuries can result in a range of physical injuries, including bruises, fractures and head injuries. In severe cases, falls and injuries can result in permanent damage to the patient's health, which can negatively impact their quality of life. This can also result in additional healthcare costs due to the need for additional medical treatment, hospital stays, and procedures to manage the consequences of the injury. Another risk associated with patient falls and injuries is decreased trust in the healthcare system and harm to the reputation of the hospital. Patients and their families may be hesitant to seek care in the future if they do not trust the healthcare system, which can result in a significant impact on the healthcare provider's bottom line. In addition, falls and injuries can result in legal action, which can be costly for the healthcare provider.

To reduce the risk of patient falls and injuries, healthcare providers must implement evidence-based best practices and protocols (Lin & Knaus, 2013). This can include providing adequate staffing levels to ensure that patients receive appropriate levels of supervision and support, implementing fall prevention programs and ensuring that patients are properly positioned in bed and have appropriate safety equipment, such as bed rails and floor mats (Morris et al., 2016). In addition, healthcare providers can implement strategies to minimise the risk of adverse reactions to medications, such as regularly reviewing the patient's medications and adjusting doses as needed (Lin & Knaus, 2013). Providers can also implement patient and staff education programs to improve awareness of the risk of falls and injuries and to provide information on how to prevent these events (Morris et al., 2016). Another important strategy for reducing the risk of patient falls and injuries is to involve patients and their families in their care (Lin & Knaus, 2013). Patients and their families can provide valuable insights into the patient's needs and can help identify potential risk factors (Morris et al., 2016). By involving patients and their families in the care process, healthcare providers can improve the quality of care and reduce the risk of falls and injuries (Lin & Knaus, 2013).

Financial Risks Associated with Medical Malpractice Claims

Medical malpractice claims pose a significant financial risk to the healthcare industry. These claims can result in substantial monetary damages, which can put a strain on healthcare organisations and individual practitioners (Beran, 2013). Furthermore, the cost of defending against a medical malpractice lawsuit can also be substantial, as it often requires the retention of legal counsel and expert witnesses, which can add to the overall cost of the claim. This can result in increased healthcare costs, as organisations may need to allocate additional resources to cover the expenses associated with defending against these claims (Beran, 2013).

In addition to direct costs, medical malpractice claims can also have indirect financial impacts on healthcare organisations and practitioners (Beran, 2013). For example, a single medical malpractice lawsuit can result in a loss of reputation and trust among patients, which can lead to decreased patient volume and decreased revenue. Moreover, the potential for negative publicity associated with medical malpractice claims can deter new patients from seeking care and reduce the overall market value of healthcare organisations.

The financial risks associated with medical malpractice claims are not limited to the healthcare industry, as they can also affect the broader economy. For example, medical malpractice claims can increase the cost of healthcare for patients, as organisations may pass on the increased costs associated with defending against these claims to consumers through higher medical fees. This can have a disproportionate impact on vulnerable populations, such as the elderly and low-income individuals, who may struggle to afford the cost of healthcare. Basically, medical malpractice claims pose a significant financial risk to the healthcare industry and can have far-reaching impacts on both healthcare organisations and the broader economy. As such, it is important for healthcare organisations to take steps to mitigate these risks and ensure that patients receive safe and high-quality care.

Conclusion

In conclusion, there are many risks associated with the healthcare industry, including cybersecurity threats, medical errors and natural disasters. To mitigate these risks and ensure the safety of patients and the continuity of operations, healthcare organisations must take a proactive approach to risk management, including implementing robust cybersecurity measures, conducting regular quality assurance reviews and developing emergency response plans.

Summary

After reading this chapter you should be able to:

a) Outline the key areas to address to establish good cyber security practice.
    Best practices around combating cyber security attacks include: risk assessment and management, employee training, data encryption, data encryption, access control and authentication, network security, medical device security, incident response and management, vendor management, regular software updates and regular backups.
b) Define the key steps in risk mitigation.
    Risk mitigation strategies are generally employed to reduce unplanned readmissions and/or ensure a high quality of care. These could involve more patient education, ensuring the patient is healthy for surgery and thus suggesting pre-habilitation strategies and or re-habilitation to ensure a strong recovery.
c) Identify the types of cyberattacks.

Types of cyberattacks include phishing, ransomware and malware.

References

Aronov, P., & Shubina, A. (2019). Medical cybersecurity: current issues and trends. *Cybersecurity*, *1*(1), 31–47.

Beran, R. (2013). The financial risks of medical malpractice claims. *Journal of Legal Medicine*, *34*(1), 1–13.

Brown, J. (2018). Ransomware attacks are increasing in healthcare. *Health Data Management, 26*(9), 36–37.

Das, P. (2020). Building trust in digital health solutions. *Healthcare IT News*. Retrieved from www.healthcareitnews.com/news/building-trust-digital-health-solutions.

Dixit, A. (2019). Ensuring trust in digital health solutions. *Health IT Outcomes*. Retrieved from https://healthitoutcomes.com/c/2388/ensuring-trust-in-digital-health-solutions.

Erdoğan, B., & Yılmaz, A. (2020). A review of cyber security in the healthcare sector. *International Journal of Information Security and Privacy, 14*(2), 1–17.

Garg, A. (2016). Protecting the health care industry from cyberattacks. *Journal of Health Care Compliance, 16*(5), 1–8.

Grosse, P. (2014). Building trust in digital health. *Healthcare IT News*. Retrieved from www.healthcareitnews.com/news/building-trust-digital-health.

Healthcare Information and Management Systems Society (HIMSS). (2021). Cybersecurity in healthcare. Retrieved from www.himss.org/library/cybersecurity-healthcare.

Johnson, J. (2020). The dangers of phishing attacks in healthcare. *Healthcare IT News*. Retrieved from www.healthcareitnews.com/news/dangers-phishing-attacks-healthcare.

Kerner, S. (2019). *Phishing attacks pose serious threats to healthcare industry*. eSecurity Planet.

Lee, H., & Lee, J. (2018). The impact of phishing attacks on healthcare organizations. *Journal of Medical Systems, 42*(9), 314.

Li, X. (2019). Trust in digital health: a critical review. *Journal of Medical Systems, 43*(7), 505.

Lin, N., & Knaus, W. A. (2013). Approaches to reducing the risk of patient falls and injuries in the hospital setting. *Journal of Patient Safety, 9*(2), 94–100.

Liu, X., & Lee, J. (2020). Understanding phishing attacks and countermeasures in healthcare organizations. *Journal of Medical Systems, 44*(11), 469.

Lunt, B. (2019). Ransomware in healthcare: what you need to know. *Healthcare IT News, 17*(4), 44–47.

Morris, N., Smith, K. E., Coon, J. T., & Morris, J. (2016). Best practices in fall prevention for older adults. *Journal of Gerontological Nursing, 42*(6), 4–11.

Moura, P. (2019). Cybersecurity in healthcare: risks, challenges, and future trends. *Journal of Medical Systems, 43*(12), 619.

National Institute of Standards and Technology. (2019). Cybersecurity framework. Retrieved from https://nist.gov/cyberframework.

Nelson, K. (2019). Health care cybersecurity: a review of the current landscape. *Journal of Healthcare Information Management, 33*(2), 20–28.

Qin, X. (2018). Trust in digital health: a review of the literature. *Journal of Medical Systems, 42*(3), 158.

Riley, T., & Fullwood, C. (2020). Ransomware attacks: The threat to healthcare data. *Journal of Healthcare Information Management, 34*(3), 56–60.

Rios, J., & Roginsky, A. (2018). The impact of cybersecurity on the healthcare industry. *Journal of Health Management and Informatics, 5*(1), 40–47.

Schuessler, J. (2019). Ransomware: a growing threat to healthcare organizations. *Journal of Healthcare Security, 15*(2), 23–27.

Wang, L. (2016). Trust in digital health: a review of the literature. *Journal of Medical Systems, 40*(2), 84.

Yen, C. (2017). Building trust in digital health solutions. *Journal of Healthcare Information Management: JHIM, 31*(1), 6–7.

Zhou, J., & Warkentin, M. (2019). Cybersecurity in healthcare: issues, challenges, and future research directions. *Journal of Medical Systems, 43*(12), 619.

16 Network-Centric Healthcare

Objectives

At the completion of this chapter you should be able to:

a) Differentiate between a process, people, and technology-centric perspective to knowledge creation.
b) Appreciate why Boyd's OODA Loop underpins network-centric healthcare operations.
c) State the key strengths and weaknesses of a network-centric healthcare approach.

Introduction

Rooted in the fusion of cutting-edge technology, seamless communication channels, and the democratisation of data sharing, network-centric healthcare has surfaced as a transformative phenomenon. According to Laya, Markendahl and Lundberg (2018), the essence of this technology lies in the harmonious merging of these elements, working in unison to augment medical services, elevate patient outcomes and usher in a paradigm shift in healthcare delivery. This chapter embarks on a comprehensive exploration of this concept, unravelling its multifaceted dimensions and shedding light on its profound implications.

Background

Knowledge creation is a central focus within knowledge management, which focusses on how to turn data into pertinent information and germane knowledge. The two predominant approaches to knowledge generation are people-centric and technology-centric (Wickramasinghe and Schaffer, 2006); however, a process-centric approach to knowledge creation has also emerged and serves only to combine the essentials of both the people-centric and technology-centric perspectives but also emphasises the dynamic and ongoing nature of the process. As such, it is very relevant to healthcare contexts which are dynamic and complex (Wickramasinghe and Schaffer, 2006). Process-centred knowledge generation is grounded in the

DOI: 10.1201/9781003318538-20

pioneering work of Boyd and his OODA Loop, a conceptual framework that maps out the critical process required to support rapid decision making and extraction of critical and germane knowledge (von Lubitz and Wickramasinghe, 2006).

The OODA Loop consists of four interrelated stages which support critical analysis and rapid decision making: Observation followed by Orientation, then by Decision, and finally Action (OODA) (ibid.).

Given that healthcare is such a knowledge-rich environment that requires rapid decision making to take place that has far-reaching consequences, a process-centred approach to knowledge generation is most relevant and forms the conceptual framework for network-centric healthcare operations. Healthcare, like all activities conducted in complex operational space, both affects and requires the functioning of three distinct entities, that is, people, process and technology and thus network-centric healthcare operations result and are built around three domains that form mutually interconnected and functionally related spheres; a physical level, an informational level and a cognitive level (von Lubitz and Wickramasinghe, 2006). Essentially, these levels cumulatively serve to capture and then process all data and information from the environment and given the dynamic nature of the environment, new information and data must always be uploaded (ibid.), thereby making the process continuous in time and space captured by the "rolling nature" of Boyd's OODA Loop: that is, it is grounded in the process-oriented perspective of knowledge generation (ibid.).

Benefits of Network-Centric Healthcare

In the dynamic landscape of modern healthcare, the advent of network-centric healthcare has signalled a host of transformative benefits, the foremost among them being the substantial promotion of communication and collaboration among healthcare professionals. This ground-breaking approach, founded on the elaborate interplay of technology and medical expertise, fosters a networked ecosystem that redefines how healthcare information is shared, leading to profound improvements in patient care.

At its core, network-centric healthcare addresses a long-standing challenge faced by healthcare providers: the efficient exchange of vital patient information and medical insights. Traditionally, medical practitioners operated within isolated silos, making it challenging to access comprehensive patient data promptly (Ranchal et al., 2020). However, the advent of network-centric healthcare is dismantling these barriers by establishing interconnected systems that facilitate real-time data sharing (Cases et al, 2013). Medical professionals, irrespective of their geographical locations, can now seamlessly exchange patient information, medical histories and treatment plans. This prompt exchange of critical data empowers healthcare teams with a holistic view of the patient's health journey, enabling well-informed decisions that resonate across the variety of care.

The ramifications of this rapid exchange of information are diverse. According to Beierle et al. (2023), clinical scenarios that previously demanded cumbersome manual sharing of records and delayed response times are now met with streamlined efficiency. This is particularly evident in cases of medical emergencies or complex diagnoses, where rapid access to patient data can be pivotal in ensuring accurate and timely interventions (Subbe & Welch, 2013). The collaborative nature of network-centric healthcare therefore bridges the gaps between specialists, primary care physicians and allied healthcare professionals. In multidisciplinary cases, such as the treatment of chronic diseases or postoperative care, this interconnectedness fosters a holistic approach that culminates in seamless coordination and, ultimately, improved patient outcomes (Hillman & Chen, 2014).

Telemedicine and remote patient monitoring constitute another dimension of network-centric healthcare benefits. These innovations transcend the constraints of physical distance, enabling medical experts to extend their expertise across geographical boundaries (Sasangohar et al., 2018). Remote patient monitoring, powered by wearable devices and IoT-enabled technologies, empowers healthcare providers to track patient vitals, monitor medication adherence and detect anomalies in real-time (Parmar et al., 2015). This proactive approach to healthcare promotes early intervention, potentially averting complications and hospital readmissions (Ullah et al., 2023). Furthermore, telemedicine leverages digital platforms to facilitate virtual consultations, enabling patients to receive medical advice and treatment without the need for physical presence (Anthony, 2021). This not only enhances patient convenience but also ensures continuity of care, particularly for individuals with limited mobility or those residing in remote areas (Ullah et al, 2023).

The impact of these benefits resonates deeply with the overarching goals of healthcare: to provide effective, accessible and patient-centred medical services (Braddock et al., 2013). Network-centric healthcare paves the way for a more cohesive healthcare ecosystem, where collaborative decision-making and data-driven insights converge to elevate the standard of care (Moro & Morca, 2020). This approach not only fosters synergy among healthcare professionals but also cultivates a sense of empowerment within patients, who actively participate in their treatment journeys armed with comprehensive information.

Weaknesses of Network-Centric Healthcare

While the advantages of network-centric healthcare approach are undeniable, a comprehensive understanding must encompass the weaknesses that come hand in hand with its transformative potential.

Data Privacy and Security Concerns: As the healthcare industry undergoes a digital revolution, the sensitive nature of patient data magnifies concerns about privacy and security (Burns & Johnson, 2015). In a network-centric environment, where information flows freely across interconnected systems, the risk of data breaches and unauthorised access looms large (Jha & Kumar, 2022). Patient records, medical histories and even genomic data are susceptible to falling into the wrong hands, potentially leading to identity theft, fraudulent activities and compromising personal wellbeing (Jha & Kumar, 2022). Ensuring stringent cybersecurity measures, encryption protocols and adherence to data protection regulations becomes paramount to maintaining trust in network-centric healthcare.

Reliance on Network Infrastructure: The complex web of network-centric healthcare hinges on the functionality of underlying technology and infrastructure. The reliance on interconnected networks and digital systems introduces a vulnerability wherein disruptions to these networks, whether due to technical glitches, cyberattacks or natural disasters, can lead to cascading effects (Korkali et al., 2017). Downtime or slowdowns in network services can impede the timely access to patient records, diagnostic tools and communication platforms (Rejeb et al., 2023). Such interruptions have the potential to compromise critical medical decisions and impede the seamless coordination of care, underscoring the need for robust, redundant and fail-safe systems.

Digital Divide and Healthcare Disparities: While network-centric healthcare holds the promise of levelling the playing field in terms of access to medical information and services, it also highlights the glaring digital divide (Skilton, 2016). Not all individuals, communities or regions have equitable access to technology and internet connectivity. This disparity amplifies existing healthcare inequalities, as those with limited access are left at a disadvantage when it comes to leveraging the benefits of network-centric healthcare (Wickramasinghe, 2013). This divide is not solely based on geography; it can also stem from socioeconomic factors, age and cultural barriers. Overcoming this challenge requires proactive efforts to ensure that underserved populations are not further marginalised in the digital healthcare revolution.

Ethical Considerations: In the pursuit of optimising healthcare through technology, ethical dilemmas come to the forefront. The integration of AI-driven diagnostics, predictive modelling and treatment recommendations raises questions about the role of human judgement and the potential for bias in algorithms (Ienca & Ignatiadis, 2020). Who bears the responsibility in the event of an incorrect diagnosis made by an AI system? Additionally, the use of patient data for research and innovation necessitates transparent consent mechanisms to address concerns of data ownership, control and usage. Therefore, ethical frameworks must be established to guide the responsible development and implementation of network-centric healthcare solutions.

To address the weaknesses inherent in network-centric healthcare, a delicate balance between innovation and safeguards must be struck. Robust cybersecurity measures, incorporating end-to-end encryption and multi-factor authentication, can help mitigate data breaches (Al Nafea & Almaiah, 2021). Continuity plans that outline strategies for managing network disruptions are essential to ensure healthcare services remain available during challenging circumstances. Bridging the digital divide requires concerted efforts, such as providing technology training to underserved communities and fostering public-private partnerships to extend connectivity.

Opportunities Presented by Network-Centric Healthcare

Network-centric healthcare has paved the way for transformative advancements that hold immense promise for improving patient wellbeing and reshaping the healthcare landscape. At the forefront of this revolution are wearable health monitors, smart medical devices, and sensors, collectively forming the frontline of real-time health data collection (Pappakrishnan et al., 2021). These IoT devices have transcended their conventional roles to become indispensable tools in the hands of both patients and healthcare providers (Kavidha et al., 2021). Wearable health monitors, for instance, continuously track vital signs and health metrics, generating a steady stream of data that offers invaluable insights into a patient's health status. This constant flow of information not only facilitates early detection of anomalies but also empowers individuals to be proactive in managing their health, thereby fostering a culture of preventive care (Reddy, Naveed, & Shah, 2023).

Moreover, the realm of network-centric healthcare extends to encompass smart medical devices that seamlessly integrate into healthcare delivery. From smart pill dispensers that ensure medication adherence to connected medical equipment that streamlines diagnostics and treatment, these devices represent a leap forward in personalised and patient-centric care (Williams, & Woodward, 2015). The real-time data generated by these devices serve as a catalyst for data-driven decision making, enabling healthcare providers to tailor treatments and interventions to each patient's unique needs (Joeris et al., 2023).

The transformative potential of network-centric healthcare is further amplified by the capabilities of big data analytics and AI algorithms (Knepper, 2021). The surge of medical data generated by these devices, when harnessed effectively, can yield profound insights into disease patterns, treatment effectiveness and predictive healthcare modelling (Knepper, 2021). Through elaborate data analysis, AI algorithms can identify refined trends and correlations that might escape human observation, thereby contributing to early disease detection and more precise interventions (Knepper, 2021).

Network-centric healthcare, fortified by the power of AI, enables predictive modelling that goes beyond traditional medical paradigms. By analysing a patient's historical data, lifestyle choices and genetic predispositions, AI can anticipate potential health risks and recommend proactive measures (Knepper, 2021). This paradigm shift from reactive to proactive healthcare not only improves patient outcomes but also reduces the burden on healthcare systems by averting preventable complications.

Furthermore, patients themselves stand to benefit significantly from the opportunities presented by network-centric healthcare. Digital platforms and applications empower individuals to be active participants in their healthcare journey. Patients can access their health data in real-time, gaining a holistic view of their wellbeing. This not only fosters greater awareness of one's health status but also facilitates informed discussions with healthcare providers. Through telemedicine and virtual consultations, patients can connect with healthcare professionals regardless of geographical barriers, ensuring timely interventions and reducing the need for unnecessary travel.

Basically, the integration of IoT devices within the framework of network-centric healthcare is a watershed moment that promises to revolutionise medical care. Wearable health monitors, smart medical devices and sensors serve as conduits for real-time health data collection, propelling personalised treatment and preventive care to the forefront of healthcare delivery (Knepper, 2021). The merger of big data analytics and AI algorithms ushers in a new era of predictive healthcare modelling, enabling early disease detection and data-driven decision making. Perhaps most importantly, patients are empowered to actively engage in their healthcare journey through digital platforms, thus fostering a collaborative and patient-centric approach. As network-centric healthcare continues to evolve, these opportunities hold the potential to enhance patient wellbeing, elevate healthcare standards and fundamentally reshape the future of medicine (Knepper, 2021).

Strengths of Network-Centric Healthcare

The strengths in network-centric healthcare resound across a spectrum of medical dimensions, bringing about a new era of possibilities and advancements. At the forefront of these strengths lies the unparalleled ability to foster the rapid dissemination of medical knowledge and best practices on a global scale (Rejeb et al., 2023). In an interconnected world, healthcare practitioners are no longer confined by geographical boundaries; instead, they have access to a vast repository of information that empowers them to stay at the lead of medical advancements (ibid.).

The integration of artificial intelligence (AI) and data analytics emerges as another compelling strength of network-centric healthcare. As the volume of medical data swells exponentially, traditional methods of analysis prove inadequate. However, with network-centric healthcare, it becomes possible to detect patterns, correlations and trends that might elude the human eye, thereby expediting critical processes such as drug discovery and treatment development (Knepper, 2021).

According to (Knepper, 2021), the synergy between data analytics and AI has also the potential to revolutionise drug discovery in ways previously deemed improbable. In silico experiments, where virtual simulations of drug interactions are conducted, can significantly hasten the identification of promising candidates for further exploration (Rejeb et al, 2023).This not only expedites the development process but also mitigates the risks associated with conventional trial and error methods (Joeris et al., 2023). Moreover, the advent of precision medicine, a ground-breaking approach that tailors treatment to an individual's genetic makeup, is made feasible through the precise analysis of patient data (Subbe & Welch, 2013). Therefore, network-centric healthcare acts as the conduit that accelerates the integration of these cutting-edge techniques into mainstream medical practice.

Early disease detection systems constitute yet another facet of network-centric healthcare's formidable strengths. Real-time patient data streams from wearable devices, sensors and medical monitors empower healthcare professionals with a constant influx of information. This wealth of data can be harnessed to develop predictive models that flag potential health risks even before obvious symptoms manifest. For instance, individuals at risk of heart disease can be monitored continuously, enabling timely intervention if anomalous patterns arise, ultimately preventing serious health events.

The strengths of network-centric healthcare go beyond individual patient care to encompass population health management. By analysing large datasets and detecting trends in disease prevalence, healthcare authorities can proactively allocate resources to areas susceptible to outbreaks. This proactive stance can thwart the rapid spread of diseases and facilitate timely containment measures, potentially saving countless lives.

Essentially, network-centric healthcare's strengths emanate from its capacity to revolutionise medical practices on a global scale. The swiftness of knowledge dissemination, coupled with AI's analytical prowess, propels drug discovery and treatment development into uncharted territories. Real-time data streams empower healthcare professionals with predictive insights that transcend conventional diagnostic capabilities, contributing to both individual wellbeing and public health. As network-centric healthcare continues to evolve, its strengths promise to reshape the healthcare landscape into one where innovation and compassion converge, fostering a future of improved patient outcomes and a higher standard of care.

Threats to Network-Centric Healthcare

One of the most pressing dangers confronting network-centric healthcare is the escalating frequency of cyberattacks and the looming spectre of data breaches (Parmar et al., 2015). As healthcare systems become increasingly interconnected and reliant on digital platforms, they inadvertently expose themselves to malicious actors who seek to exploit vulnerabilities for personal gain. The compromise of patient information not only jeopardises individual privacy but also erodes the foundation of trust upon which the healthcare ecosystem relies. The potential fallout from such breaches could be immense, causing financial losses, tarnishing institutional reputation and even leading to identity theft or fraud for the patients involved.

Moreover, the misuse of health data for unauthorised purposes underscores another dimension of risk in this digital age (Glenn & Monteith, 2014). According to Glenn & Monteith (2014), vast reservoirs of personal health information become tempting targets for unscrupulous entities seeking to manipulate or monetise sensitive data. This not only raises significant ethical concerns but also emphasises the urgent need for stringent data governance measures. Regulatory frameworks must be fortified to deter and penalise any form of unauthorised data exploitation, fostering an environment where patients' personal information remains untouchable (Glenn & Monteith, 2014).

In tandem with security threats, technical glitches within the complex framework of network infrastructure represent a substantial hazard to network-centric healthcare. A system's failure, whether due to software glitches, hardware malfunctions or connectivity issues, can potentially disrupt vital healthcare services. Such disruptions could prove fatal in life-critical scenarios, under-scoring the necessity of robust backup systems, redundancy protocols and swift disaster recovery mechanisms. Ensuring the uninterrupted flow of medical services demands a careful approach to system design, maintenance and continuous monitoring.

The integration of AI-driven decision making, while promising enhanced diagnostic accuracy and treatment recommendations, introduces a new layer of ethical complexity. Decisions made by algorithms carry significant consequences, necessitating transparency, accountability and mechanisms for addressing errors or biases inherent in AI systems. Striking the balance between the capabilities of AI and the expertise of healthcare professionals demands a careful ethical navigation to prevent over-reliance on technology at the expense of human judgement.

Barriers to Implementing Network-Centric Healthcare

The implementation of network-centric healthcare is confronted by a multitude of challenges that impede its seamless integration into the healthcare landscape. These barriers, spanning technological, regulatory, operational and infrastructural domains, contribute to the complexities involved in realising the full potential of network-centric healthcare.

One prominent challenge arises from the resistance exhibited by healthcare professionals towards embracing new technologies (Kamal, Shafiq, & Kakria, 2020). The unfamiliarity with advanced technological tools and systems, coupled with perceived complexities in their implementation and usage, can lead to hesitancy and slow adoption rates (Kamal, Shafiq & Kakria, 2020). The inertia to depart from established practices, which may have served well in traditional healthcare paradigms, can create a barrier to the swift adoption of network-centric approaches.

Regulatory frameworks governing healthcare often struggle to keep pace with the rapid evolution of technology, presenting another substantial barrier (Fenwick et al., 2016). According to Fenwick et al. (2016), issues such as data sharing, tele-medicine practices and patient privacy protections require updated and adaptable regulations to ensure ethical and secure implementation. Striking a balance between enabling efficient data exchange while safeguarding sensitive patient information demands a careful and deliberate re-evaluation of existing regulatory structures.

The lack of interoperability among diverse healthcare systems presents a formidable obstacle to the seamless exchange of data in a network-centric model Jaafar et al. (2019). Healthcare institutions and technology providers often develop proprietary solutions that function optimally within their respective environments but struggle to communicate effectively with other systems. This fragmentation hampers the holistic view of patient health and impedes the realisation of comprehensive, patient-centred care.

Financial constraints and inadequate infrastructure, particularly in remote or underserved areas, significantly hinder the widespread adoption of network-centric healthcare. The costs associated with acquiring and implementing advanced technologies can be prohibitive for healthcare facilities operating with limited budgets.

Moreover, regions with inadequate technological infrastructure face challenges in establishing the necessary connectivity and hardware to support network-centric models, aggravating disparities in healthcare access.

The successful implementation of network-centric healthcare requires over-coming these multifaceted barriers. This entails providing comprehensive training and education to healthcare professionals to enhance their technological proficiency and ease their transition to new systems. Regulatory bodies must also collaborate closely with technology experts to establish frameworks that balance innovation with patient privacy and data security. Efforts to standardise data formats and promote interoperability should be prioritised to ensure seamless data exchange across different platforms. Addressing financial constraints and infrastructure gaps necessitates strategic investments in technology, particularly in underserved regions. Public-private partnerships, government initiatives and philanthropic efforts can play a pivotal role in enabling the necessary infrastructure development and technology adoption, thereby promoting equitable access to network-centric healthcare solutions.

Facilitators for Successful Network-Centric Healthcare

The realisation of effective network-centric healthcare relies on the convergence of various elements that together create a robust and interconnected healthcare ecosystem. These facilitators pave the way for the seamless integration of tech-nology, data and healthcare services, ultimately enhancing patient outcomes and revolutionising the healthcare industry as a whole.

- Supportive Government Policies and Regulations: Government bodies play a pivotal role in shaping the healthcare landscape by establishing policies and regulations that encourage the adoption of digital health solutions. When governments prioritise and incentivise the use of technology in healthcare, it sets the stage for healthcare providers and organisations to invest in and imple-ment innovative network-centric approaches. Clear guidelines also ensure data privacy, security and ethical considerations are addressed, fostering trust among both patients and healthcare providers.
- Industry-Wide Standards for Data Exchange and Interoperability: The successful sharing and utilisation of health information across different systems and platforms hinge on standardised data exchange protocols and interoperability frameworks. Common standards enable disparate healthcare applications and devices to communicate seamlessly, ensuring that patient data is accurately and securely transmitted. This interoperability not only enhances care coordination but also reduces redundancy and errors in treatment.
- Investment in Robust and Secure Network Infrastructure: A reliable and secure network infrastructure forms the backbone of network-centric healthcare. Adequate investment in robust networking technologies, such as high-speed internet connectivity and cloud services, is imperative to support the transmis-sion of large volumes of medical data, facilitate telehealth consultations and

enable real-time monitoring of patients. Furthermore, cybersecurity measures must be robustly implemented to safeguard sensitive patient information from potential breaches.

- Training and Education Programs: Healthcare professionals need the skills and knowledge to effectively leverage technology for the benefit of their patients. Comprehensive training and education programs empower doctors, nurses, technicians and other medical personnel to navigate and utilise digital health tools seamlessly. This not only enhances their ability to provide accurate diagnoses and treatment but also boosts their confidence in incorporating technology into their daily workflows.
- Public Awareness Campaigns: The success of network-centric healthcare is intricately linked to public perception and acceptance. Well-designed public awareness campaigns can educate individuals about the advantages of digital health solutions, such as telemedicine, remote monitoring and health apps. By highlighting how these technologies can enhance convenience, access to care and overall wellness, these campaigns foster a positive attitude toward embracing new healthcare paradigms.

The facilitators outlined above collectively contribute to the successful implementation of network-centric healthcare. As these elements synergise, they create an environment where technology seamlessly integrates into the healthcare fabric, resulting in improved patient care, enhanced operational efficiency, and a more patient-centric approach to medical treatment. Embracing these facilitators not only modernises healthcare practices but also paves the way for a future where technology empowers both healthcare providers and patients alike.

Outlook

The trajectory of network-centric healthcare points towards a horizon of remarkable advancements and transformative possibilities. Moving forward, the integration of cutting-edge technologies with healthcare is set to revolutionise the industry. From telemedicine and remote patient monitoring to personalised treatment plans based on data analytics, the future promises an era where healthcare is more accessible, efficient and tailored to individual needs. One of the key drivers of this evolution will be the seamless collaboration between the technology and healthcare sectors. Experts from both domains will combine their knowledge and skills to push the boundaries of innovation. This interdisciplinary approach will lead to the development of novel solutions that address current challenges while paving the way for previously unimaginable breakthroughs.

Conclusion

The transformative potential of network-centric healthcare cannot be overstated. It has the power to reshape the entire healthcare landscape, transcending geographical boundaries and providing equitable access to medical services. Patients will experience a paradigm shift in how they interact with the healthcare system, enjoying greater convenience and tailored care. However, it's essential to approach this transformation with a clear understanding of its complexities. The convergence of technology, healthcare and data brings forth complex challenges that necessitate careful navigation. Regulations must keep pace with innovation, and the potential risks of data breaches or misuse must be proactively addressed. Striking the delicate balance between pushing the boundaries of innovation and upholding ethical standards will be crucial. As patient data becomes more interconnected, safeguarding privacy and ensuring data security will demand continuous vigilance and investment.

Summary

After reading this chapter you should be able to:

a) Differentiate between a process, people and technology-centric perspective to knowledge creation.
   Knowledge creation focuses on how data is turned into pertinent information and germane knowledge. In a people-centric perspective people are the primary conduit for this process while in a technology-centric perspective, it is technology that is central. A process-centric perspective is in direct contrast to both as it not only combines both the people and technology perspective but also focusses on the dynamic and complex nature of the environment.

b) Appreciate why Boyd's OODA Loop underpins network-centric healthcare operations.
   Boyd's OODA Loop, which has four connected steps of observe, orient, decide and then act, is central to network-centric healthcare operations as it dictates how multi-spectral data is rapidly and systematically transformed to pertinent information and germane knowledge in order to support superior decision making.

c) State the key strengths and weaknesses of a network-centric healthcare approach.
   Major strengths include the ability to rapidly access multi-spectral data to any context and apply a suite of technological solutions to these data into order to extract meaningful insights, pertinent information and germane knowledge. Given the ever-increasing processing capabilities and advances in AI, this is a major strength. In contrast, limitations are concerned with security and cyber security vulnerabilities as well as the cost to maintain the network so it is at all time operating efficiently.

References

Al Nafea, R., & Almaiah, M. A. (2021, July). Cyber security threats in cloud: Literature review. In *2021 International Conference on Information Technology (ICIT)* (pp. 779–786). IEEE.

Anthony Jnr, B. (2021). Implications of telehealth and digital care solutions during COVID-19 pandemic: a qualitative literature review. *Informatics for Health and Social Care*, *46*(1), 68–83.

Beierle, J., Algorri, M., Cortés, M., Cauchon, N. S., Lennard, A., Kirwan, J. P., ... & Abernathy, M. J. (2023). Structured content and data management—enhancing acceleration in drug development through efficiency in data exchange. *AAPS Open*, *9*(1), 11.

Braddock, C. H., Snyder, L., Neubauer, R. L., Fischer, G. S., & American College of Physicians Ethics, Professionalism and Human Rights Committee and The Society of General Internal Medicine Ethics Committee. (2013). The patient-centered medical home: an ethical analysis of principles and practice. *Journal of General Internal Medicine*, *28*, 141–146.

Burns, A. J., & Johnson, M. E. (2015). Securing health information. *IT Professional*, *17*(1), 23–29.

Cases, M., Furlong, L. I., Albanell, J., Altman, R. B., Bellazzi, R., Boyer, S., ... & Sanz, F. (2013). Improving data and knowledge management to better integrate health care and research. *Journal of Internal Medicine*, *274*(4), 321.

Fenwick, M., Kaal, W. A., & Vermeulen, E. P. (2016). Regulation tomorrow: what happens when technology is faster than the law. *American University Business Law Review*, *6*, 561.

Glenn, T., & Monteith, S. (2014). Privacy in the digital world: medical and health data outside of HIPAA protections. *Current Psychiatry Reports*, *16*(11), 494.

Hillman, K., & Chen, J. (2014). Rapid response systems. In Scales, D. C., & Gordon, D. R. (eds.), *The organization of critical care: an evidence-based approach to improving quality* (pp. 177–195). Springer.

Ienca, M., & Ignatiadis, K. (2020). Artificial intelligence in clinical neuroscience: methodological and ethical challenges. *AJOB Neuroscience*, *11*(2), 77–87.

Jaafar, A. A., Sharif, K. H., Ghareb, M. I., & Jawawi, D. N. (2019). Internet of Thing and smart city: state of the art and future trends. *Advances in Computer Communication and Computational Sciences: Proceedings of IC4S 2017*, *2*, 3–28.

Jha, S. K., & Kumar, S. S. (2022). Cybersecurity in the age of the Internet of Things: an assessment of the users' privacy and data security. In *Expert Clouds and Applications: Proceedings of ICOECA 2021* (pp. 49–56). Springer Singapore.

Joeris, A., Zhu, T. Y., Lambert, S., Wood, A., & Jayakumar, P. (2023). Real-world patient data: can they support decision making and patient engagement? *Injury*, *54* Suppl 3, S51–S56. doi: 10.1016/j.injury.2021.12.012. Epub 2021 Dec 16. PMID: 34949460.

Kamal, S. A., Shafiq, M., & Kakria, P. (2020). Investigating acceptance of telemedicine services through an extended technology acceptance model (TAM). *Technology in Society*, *60*, 101212.

Kavidha, V., Gayathri, N., & Kumar, S. R. (2021). AI, IoT and robotics in the medical and healthcare field. In Dubey, A. K., Kumar, A., Kumar, S. R., Gayathri, N., & Das, P. (eds.), *AI and IoT-based intelligent automation in robotics* (pp. 165–187). Scrivener Publishing.

Knepper, P. L. (2021). *How artificial intelligence and machine learning transform the human condition* (No. LA-UR-21-31950). Los Alamos National Lab. (LANL).

Korkali, M., Veneman, J. G., Tivnan, B. F., Bagrow, J. P., & Hines, P. D. (2017). Reducing cascading failure risk by increasing infrastructure network interdependence. *Scientific Reports*, *7*(1), 44499.

Laya, A., Markendahl, J., & Lundberg, S. (2018). Network-centric business models for health, social care and wellbeing solutions in the internet of things. *Scandinavian Journal of management*, *34*(2), 103–116.

Moro Visconti, R., & Morea, D. (2020). Healthcare digitalization and pay-for-performance incentives in smart hospital project financing. *International Journal of Environmental Research and Public Health, 17*(7), 2318.

Pappakrishnan, V. K., Mythili, R., Kavitha, V., & Parthiban, N. (2021). Role of artificial intelligence of things (AIoT) in Covid-19 pandemic: a brief survey. In *6th International Conference on IoTBDS* (pp. 229–236), Prague, Czech Republic.

Parmar, P., Mackie, D., Varghese, S., & Cooper, C. (2015). Use of telemedicine technologies in the management of infectious diseases: a review. *Clinical Infectious Diseases, 60*(7), 1084–1094.

Ranchal, R., Bastide, P., Wang, X., Gkoulalas-Divanis, A., Mehra, M., Bakthavachalam, S., ... & Mohindra, A. (2020). Disrupting healthcare silos: addressing data volume, velocity and variety with a cloud-native healthcare data ingestion service. *IEEE Journal of Biomedical and Health Informatics, 24*(11), 3182–3188.

Reddy, M., Naveed, R., & Shah, T. (2023). Urban health planning in the age of AI: advancements and opportunities in machine learning. *International Journal of Sustainable Infrastructure for Cities and Societies, 8*(1), 38–52.

Rejeb, A., Rejeb, K., Treiblmaier, H., Appolloni, A., Alghamdi, S., Alhasawi, Y., & Iranmanesh, M. (2023). The Internet of Things (IoT) in healthcare: taking stock and moving forward. *Internet of Things, 22*, 100721.

Sasangohar, F., Davis, E., Kash, B. A., & Shah, S. R. (2018). Remote patient monitoring and telemedicine in neonatal and pediatric settings: scoping literature review. *Journal of Medical Internet Research, 20*(12), e295.

Skilton, M. (2016). *Building the digital enterprise: a guide to constructing monetization models using digital technologies.* Springer.

Subbe, C. P., & Welch, J. R. (2013). Failure to rescue: using rapid response systems to improve care of the deteriorating patient in hospital. *Clinical Risk, 19*(1), 6–11.

Ullah, M., Hamayun, S., Wahab, A., Khan, S. U., Qayum, M., Ullah, A., ... & Naeem, M. (2023). Smart technologies used as smart tools in the management of cardiovascular disease and their future perspective. *Current Problems in Cardiology, 48*(12), 101922.

von Lubitz, D., & Wickramasinghe, N. (2006). Networkcentric healthcare: applying the tools, techniques and strategies of knowledge management to create superior healthcare operations. *International Journal of Electronic Healthcare, 2*(4), 415–429.

Wickramasinghe, N. (2013). Pervasive computing and healthcare. In Bali, R., Troshani, I., Goldberg, S., Wickramasinghe, N. (eds), *Pervasive health knowledge management: healthcare delivery in the information age* (pp. 7–13). Springer.

Wickramasinghe, N., & Schaffer, J. L. (2006). Creating knowledge-driven healthcare processes with the intelligence continuum. *International Journal of Electronic Healthcare, 2*(2), 164–174.

Williams, P. A., & Woodward, A. J. (2015). Cybersecurity vulnerabilities in medical devices: a complex environment and multifaceted problem. *Medical Devices (Auckl.), 8*, 305–316. doi: 10.2147/MDER.S50048. PMID: 26229513; PMCID: PMC4516335.

Section V

Putting It All Together

Delivering Superior Health and Wellness

In this final section, the goal is to bring things all together and enable the reader to understand how to design, develop and deploy superior digital health and wellness solutions to facilitate and support high-value, high-quality care to everyone, everywhere, every time. The points outlined are all necessary but not sufficient given that healthcare operations are dynamic and complex as well as always having unique aspects and nuances. In addition to being cognisant of all the key success factors, it is also important to be prepared and ready for any situation, be agile and think. This section thus consists of just one chapter as follows:

Chapter 17: Delivering Superior Digital Health Solutions

This chapter will address the topic of how to deliver superior digital health solutions by pulling together all the preceding material and outlining four key areas as follows: i) The goals of wellness management and role for digital health; ii) The role for digital health in the acute care sector; iii) The need for digital health in all contexts and iv) The tools, technologies, techniques and tactics of superior digital health for all. In this way, not only is there a clear road map provided to readers there is also a rubric to assess and evaluate current solutions and address current issues to enable them to be more suitable, fully realise desired goals and be fit for purpose.

DOI: 10.1201/9781003318538-21

17 Delivering Superior Digital Health Solutions

Objectives

After reading this chapter you should be able to understand:

a) Which tools can assist in developing successful digital health solutions.
b) Why OODA thinking and the OODA loop are relevant.
c) What is the intelligent continuum and why can it be helpful.
d) The importance of never forgetting that healthcare is socio-technical and people-process and technology considerations are necessary.

Introduction

The rise of digital health has resulted due to the evolution in computing power and advances in technology coupled with the benefits that digital transformation has provided to other industries such as banking and manufacturing. Healthcare, a noted laggard, has for decades been plagued with challenges around providing better access to, quality of and value in care for every person; but the Gordian knot has been how? Digital health presents itself as a possible solution; and thus, we must understand how we can create superior and successful digital health solutions. The preceding chapters have discussed different aspects around people, technology and process issues and now it is necessary to put this together as the following serves to do.

Healthcare Operations

Healthcare delivery fundamentally deals with humans – patients and doctors. Hence, we are focussed on biological systems that are messy, complex and unpre-dictable. Moreover, healthcare is a highly regulated industry and has the unique situation that in general, the primary payer of the service, that is, the insurance company or government, is not the primary receiver of the service, that is, the patient. As previously discussed, this leads to agency issues and mis-alignment of goals.

DOI: 10.1201/9781003318538-22

The generally accepted healthcare value proposition notes that access to, quality of and value in care is essential and should be for everyone. However, to realise this can be challenging when we consider factors such as location – remote versus regional versus metro or health literacy and the social determines of health.

Looking to reap the benefits of digital transformation that has enabled banking and manufacturing to reimagine themselves is the promise of digital health. In order to do so, we must understand digital health and strategies and techniques to ensure that we can have successful solutions.

Digital health lies at the confluence of computer science, business and medicine. From medicine, we need to understand medical and healthcare problems and diseases. From business, we need to appreciate the need to ensure high value in the care delivered and that this is sustainable; while from computer science, we need to understand the advances in technology and how this can best be harnessed to specific situations and contexts. Further, we must recognise, as presented in the preceding chapters, that it is important to keep people, process and technology central or take a people process technology (PPT) approach given the socio-technical nature of healthcare delivery.

Key Strategies

Recognising that healthcare consists of multiple stakeholders or the web of players; such as the patient, providers, healthcare organisations, regulators, governments and payers, all who have at times divergent interests, it becomes important to understand both internal and external factors. To do this in a systematic fashion several frameworks or tools are useful such as the PESTEL analysis, generic strategies, value chain and fishbone (Perera, 2017).

i)   PESTEL–6 factors key in this analysis include political, economic, social, technological, environmental and legal factors. By analysing these factors simultaneously, it is possible to develop a rich picture of the key external pressures and considerations.

ii) Generic Strategies introduced by Porter (Murray, 1988) consist of three key approaches: *focus* – which refers to concentrating on a specific area or sub area, *differentiation* – which usually includes high quality but requires attention to be paid to distinguish oneself from competitors and others in the field, or *low cost* – which necessitates high volume so that the price can be lower than others.

iii) SWOT (Perera, 2017): strengths weaknesses opportunities and threats need to be identified for the specific organisation or group from this then TOWS show how to turn threats into opportunities and weaknesses into strengths.

iv) Fishbone (or Isikawa diagram) (ibid.) is a cause-and-effect framework where the head of the fish is the effect while the bones of the fish are the causes, both positive and negative.

To illustrate the above frameworks, let us consider a mobile solution to support diabetes self-management. If this solution is to be used in Australia for example, then a PESTEL analysis would require consideration of the political aspect, including current federal and state governments; economic would consider the healthcare payment system and general economic state of the population; social, which would include the social structures in place and heterogeneity of the population; technology would focus on the technical aspects of the solution; environmental factors could include how the solution might support or hinder environmental sustainability; and finally, legal would focus on the legal aspects pertaining to mobile health solutions.

Now, if we take the same example and apply the generic strategies, one could consider this as a differentiation solution, if offered as part of a primary care clinic's approach to treating patients with diabetes as it augments or distinguishes care delivery from other practices.

A SWOT analysis of the same solution would unpack aspects of the solution that made up strengths such as anywhere/anytime access versus weaknesses which could be lack of human person, while a threat might be around data security and privacy and an opportunity might be around personalised care. If a TWOS (i.e. turning threats to opportunities and weaknesses to strength) analysis is also done, this could assist in finding strategies to turn the threats such as the aforementioned around data security and privacy into an opportunity, for example, innovative cyber security algorithms; while the weakness of a human person could be addressed by introducing AI and a chatbot or avatar.

Finally, the fishbone analysis would focus on an effect such as better compliance with diabetes regimens and the causes positive could include constant reminders and nudges, advice on diet and exercise; or the negatives could be access to proper food and time for exercise. Once all the causes are identified one can work through them to see how best to address them in turn.

In addition to the above, two other important frameworks include the intelligence continuum and the OODA Loop.

Boyd's OODA Loop

Boyd's (OODA) Loop (von Lubitz and Wickramasinghe, 2006) serves to systematically identify the sequence of interactions with dynamic, rapidly changing environments characterized by high degree of structural and event complexity. Such complex actions are subdivided into a series of consecutive cycles, Loops, with the preceding cycle strongly influencing the initial stages of the following (ibid.). The four key stages – Observation, Orientation, Determination, and Action – taken together frame all necessary activities required to support successful decision making (ibid.); specifically, during the Observation stage, all inputs must be collected and organised into coherent entities, while the Orientation stage requires the organised data to be converted into meaningful information so that at the Determination phase, the plan is formulated which is then enacted in the Action phase. The other key aspect of OODA loop thinking is the need for continuous improvement and feedback (ibid.).

The Intelligent Continuum

To appreciate the intelligence continuum (IC), it is first necessary to introduce a generic healthcare information system (Wickramasinghe and Schaffer, 2006). This generic system includes the socio-technical perspective, that is, the people, processes and technology inputs required in conjunction with data as a key input (ibid.). The combination of these elements comprises an information system. If, to this generic system, we add the healthcare challenges, that is, the challenges of demographics, technology and finance, we are putting key external and exogenous events into the mix.

Now, the IC supports superior decision making by enabling a systematic application of the key tools and techniques of knowledge management, data mining and analytics to be applied to the data generated by the information system and stored in the larger data warehouses or lakes. On applying the tools, techniques respectively in a systematic fashion to the data generated from healthcare information systems, it is first possible to diagnose the "as is" or current state processes in order to make further decisions regarding how existing processes should be modified; and, thereby, provide appropriate prescriptions to enable the achievement of a better future state, that is, improve the respective inputs of the people, process, technology and data so that the system as a whole is significantly improved (ibid.). Thus, the Intelligence Continuum is a collection of key tools, techniques and processes of today's knowledge economy, which, taken together, represent a very powerful system for refining the data raw material stored to maximise their value and utility to support better healthcare decision making and delivery.

Conclusions

Healthcare operations are dynamic and complex. Moreover, they take place in different healthcare systems ranging from predominantly public to predominantly private with numerous two-tier systems; mix of public-private structures. In addition, healthcare involves a web of players or stakeholders with differing priorities and goals including regulators, the government, payers, providers, healthcare organisations patients and their families and carers and the community.

Advances in technology have enabled us to design, develop and deploy sophisticated digital health solutions today. However, for them to be successful, we need more than to just get the technology correct, we need to appreciate that healthcare is socio-technical in nature and thus must consider people and process aspects as well as technology aspects. The preceding sections of this book served to highlight critical issues that need to be considered with respect to people, process and technology considerations; in this chapter as we strive to put it all together, frameworks and analysis tools are provided to assist in gaining insights and more in-depth understanding of critical aspects. Ultimately, these are all necessary but not sufficient for designing, developing and deploying superior, successful and sustainable digital health solutions. We must also never forget the patient who should at all times be central as well as to think through logically and carefully all possible outcomes and issues. By doing so, we are more likely to be successful and deliver digital health solutions that can serve to address a healthcare value proposition of better access to, better quality in and better value of care for everyone, every day, everywhere.

Summary

At the conclusion of this chapter, you should be able to state:

a) Which tools can assist in developing successful digital health solutions.
    Many tools and frameworks exist to support successful and superior digital health solutions including PESTEL, generic strategies, SWOT as well as TWOS, and the fishbone analysis tools. In addition, OODA Loop and the intelligent continuum can be very useful.
b) Why OODA thinking and the OODA loop are relevant.
    The OODA loop and OODA thinking were developed to ensure successful and rapid extraction of pertinent information and germane knowledge systematically, effectively and efficiently in any dynamic and complex scenario. Given the dynamic and complex nature of healthcare operations OODA loop and thinking are thus very relevant.
c) What is the intelligent continuum and why can it be helpful.
    Like the OODA Loop, the intelligence Continuum is designed to support better utilisation of germane knowledge and pertinent information in healthcare organisation by extracting form data resigning in systems within the organisation key insights through the application of knowledge management data mining and analytic tools and techniques in a systematic and rigorous approach.
d) The importance of never forgetting that healthcare is socio-technical and people-process and technology considerations are necessary.
    The fundamental focus of healthcare is to treat the patient. Patients are biological systems and thus no matter how much technology is involved one still is interacting with a socio-technical system and thus must consider people and processes as well as technology factors if superior results are to ensue.

References

Murray, A. I. (1988). A contingency view of Porter's "generic strategies". *Academy of Management Review, 13*(3), 390–400.
Perera, R. (2017). *The PESTEL analysis*. Nerdynaut.
Von Lubitz, D., & Wickramasinghe, N. (2006). Healthcare and technology: the doctrine of networkcentric healthcare. *International Journal of Electronic Healthcare, 2*(4), 322–344.
Wickramasinghe, N., & Schaffer, J. L. (2006). Creating knowledge-driven healthcare processes with the intelligence continuum. *International Journal of Electronic Healthcare, 2*(2), 164–174.

Epilogue

The goal of this primer was to have in one handy reference a compilation of the critical success factors necessary, but perhaps not sufficient, to enable successful, superior, and sustainable digital health solutions to ensue. This is indeed an ambitious goal, as it is indeed challenging to combine into one volume all the necessary material, let alone in a succinct and easy to read fashion. Clearly, this primer has served to highlight the essential areas and raise the readers' awareness of these key topics. It is left to the reader to dive into specific areas in more depth as he/she requires; this is just the amuse-bouche to tantalise the taste buds. I sincerely hope that on reading this book you now have more questions than you had at the start. Moreover, I hope you are now inspired to do your part in moving the field of digital health forward. Goethe put it most eloquently: Knowing is not enough; we must apply. Willing is not enough; we must do or the German "Es ist nicht genug, zu wissen, man muß auch anwenden; es ist nicht genug, zu wollen, man muß auch tun" (Johann Wolfgang von Goethe in: "Wilhelm Meisters Wanderjahre", 3. Buch, 18. Kapitel).

The digital health journey is the long and challenging road less travelled; however, the future is bright. As time progresses, without a doubt we shall have more and more technological solutions and more processing power. In fact, we appear to be limited only by our imaginations. However, to design, develop and deploy successful, superior and sustainable digital health solutions, fundamental principles will always apply, and it is my hope that this book has served to highlight these. When Hippocrates stated do no harm, I doubt he imagined healthcare with digital health as a key enabler; but the sentiment is valid, perhaps even more so today than in his day; digital health has the potential to afford great opportunities to health and wellness care delivery; but we must proceed with caution, so we *do no harm* and can successfully design, develop and deploy superior and sustainable digital health solutions to realise a healthcare value proposition of better access, quality and value for everyone, everywhere, every time. Ultimately, "quo vadis digital health" depends on us all and the insights gained from this primer might also be beneficial and play a role.

Nilmini Wickramasinghe
Alexander von Humboldt Awardee
Optus Chair and Professor of Digital Health
La Trobe University, Australia.
14 November 2023

Index

Printed in the United States
by Baker & Taylor Publisher Services

Printed in the United States
by Baker & Taylor Publisher Services